THE MALINES CONVERSATIONS REVISITED

† D. J. Card. Mercier, Arch. de Malines.
21 Juillet 1918.

M. PIRON

BIBLIOTHECA EPHEMERIDUM THEOLOGICARUM LOVANIENSIUM

LXXXV

THE MALINES CONVERSATIONS REVISITED (1921- 1926)

BY

JOHN A. DICK

LEUVEN
UNIVERSITY PRESS

UITGEVERIJ PEETERS
LEUVEN

1989

CIP KONINKLIJKE BIBLIOTHEEK ALBERT I, BRUSSEL

ISBN 90 6186 317 1 (Leuven University Press)
D/1989/1869/20
ISBN 90 6831 174 3 (Uitgeverij Peeters)
D/1989/0602/26

© Leuven University Press/Presses Universitaires de Louvain
Universitaire Pers Leuven
Krakenstraat 3, B-3000 Leuven-Louvain (Belgium)

Uitgeverij Peeters, Bondgenotenlaan 153, B-3000 Leuven (Belgium)

TABLE OF CONTENTS

APPENDICES

FRONTISPIECE:
Portrait of Cardinal Mercier by Maria Van Humbeeck-Piron (Leuven 1918).

INTRODUCTION

> To be discouraged is a cowardice. And
> in my heart of hearts I know that the
> object for which in different ways we
> are struggling will one day in God's
> good time be accomplished.
>
> Halifax to Janssens
> 9 January 1932

The Malines Conversations — held consecutively December 6-8, 1921; March 14-15, 1923; November 7-8, 1923; May 19-20, 1925; and October 11-12, 1926 — were a series of ecumenical discussions between English representatives of the Anglican Church and Continental European representatives of the Roman Catholic Church. Except for the last Conversation, they were held under the presidency of the Belgian Cardinal Mercier.

Today, sixty-three years after the Malines Conversations, we can credit them with two accomplishments: one in the area of Roman Catholic/Anglican ecumenical relations; and the other in the evolution of post-Modernist Roman Catholic theology.

Pope Paul VI called attention to the ecumenical significance of the Malines Conversations in October 1966, when he sent greetings to Cardinal Suenens on the occasion of the fortieth anniversary of the Conversations. "The Conversations", said Pope Paul, "mark an epoch in this looking and preparing for the perfect unity of those who believe in Christ. The spirit of openness and Christian brotherhood which characterised them made it possible to approach the delicate, and at times difficult questions which separate the two Communions, in a common effort towards the establishment of unity in truth and love"[1]. The Conversations marked the first time since the sixteenth century that Anglican and Roman Catholic theologians had gathered around the same table. They proved that such ecumenical dialogue was possible, stimulated Roman Catholic interest in ecumenism; and were a direct inspiration to Roman Catholic ecumenical pioneers at Vatican II. In 1966 when Pope Paul VI placed his episcopal ring on the finger of the Archbishop of Canterbury, Dr. Arthur Michael Ramsey, he was repeating a similar gesture performed by Cardinal Mercier, on his deathbed, when he gave his ring to Lord Halifax.

The questions raised and discussed at Malines have been the same

1. *The Commemoration of the Malines Conversations*, in *Collectanea Mechliniensia* 52 (1967), p. 14.

questions raised and explored in recent years by the Anglican/Roman Catholic International Commission: ARCIC. And the answers flowing from ARCIC echo the answers which flowed from Malines.

In terms of the development of twentieth century Roman Catholic theology, the Conversations were a significant step forward, because they again raised the possibility of theological pluralism within the Roman Catholic Church. They marked therefore a positive move towards the unfettering of Roman Catholic theology from the shackles of anti-Modernist rigidity and frenzy.

In an effort to provide a comprehensive understanding of the Malines Conversations, this book begins with a survey of the Roman Catholic/ Anglican situation in England prior to the Conversations; and then analyses the events and personalities behind each of the five Conversations. In seven appendices, episcopal letters and other documents have been reproduced to provide the reader with important background material. For this same reason, the reader will also find a listing of brief biographical sketches of people who played significant roles in the story of the Malines conversations. *The Malines Conversations Revisited* is a development of a doctoral dissertation, *English Roman Catholic Reactions to the Malines Conversations* defended at the Catholic University of Louvain (Katholieke Universiteit Leuven) on 30 April 1986. The work of earlier scholars is acknowledged and appreciated, and has helped establish the focus for the present book.

Twenty years after the Malines Conversations, Robert Kothen wrote a little commemorative book[2] which pointed out that Cardinal Bourne and most English Roman Catholics had been opposed to the Malines Conversations. He based much of his interpretation on Ernest Oldmeadow's biography of Cardinal Bourne[3]. Oldmeadow clearly portrayed Bourne as another incarnation of his predecessor Cardinal Vaughan. A few years later, the English Dominican, Henry St. John, repeated and praised the position of Kothen[4].

Forty years after the Malines Conversations, Louvain's Professor Roger Aubert was able to examine the archives at Malines; and he brought new insight and important clarifications to the history of the Conversations. Aubert pointed out that Oldmeadow had not been an accurate biographer and that he had also presented a very biased interpretation of Bourne's reactions towards the Conversations. In fact, Aubert raised the suspicion that Oldmeadow's Bourne was more Oldmeadow than Bourne! Other historians, such as R.J. Lahey, J.D. Holmes, and B. Pawley and M. Pawley, have followed and reinforced the original insight of Aubert.

2. R. KOTHEN, *Catholiques et Anglicans – Vingt ans après les Conversations de Malines*, Lille, 1946.

3. E. OLDMEADOW, *Francis Cardinal Bourne*, 2 vols., London, 1944.

4. H. ST. JOHN, *Essays in Christian Unity*, Westminster, 1955.

From 1983 to 1986, in preparation for the doctoral dissertation defended in April 1986, a detailed study was made of Lord Halifax's papers at the Borthwick Institute, York; Cardinal Bourne's in the Archbishop's House, Westminster; those of Lord Halifax's confidant Aloïs Janssens at the Scheutist house in Louvain; those of Francis Woodlock, S.J., among the archives of the English Province of the Society of Jesus in London; and those of Archbishop Davidson and Archbishop Lang at Lambeth Palace, London. The papers of Cardinal Mercier in the Archdiocesan Archives at Malines were also re-examined as well as some unclassified documents belonging to Mercier's successor Cardinal Van Roey. The results of this research reveal some significant developments beyond Aubert's original findings.

Certainly many people have given me support and encouragement and have helped make this book a reality.

Thanks are due to Joske 't Hart, my wife, and to Brian, our son, for their patient love, support, and encouragement. Similar thanks go to the Dick and 't Hart families.

I am grateful to many Louvain professors who have enlightened and motivated me over the years. In oftentimes uncanny fashion the spirit of Louvain has beguiled and inspired me from our first encounter in 1965 to the present day. My parents, in fact, have often commented: "Something happened to Jack when he went to Louvain!"

Professor Robrecht Boudens took a chance with me. "Just who are you?", he asked me at our first meeting. I am proud to say that I am one of his students. I am grateful for his guidance, friendly support, and his meticulous criticism of my manuscript. For me it was also a special honor to be able to defend my dissertation on the anniversary of his own doctoral defense.

For special help with the technical aspects of preparing the final manuscript, I thank especially Karel D'huyvetters, Vince Sansone, Dan Frett, and Michael McKiernan.

To Pastor Peter Gregory, Marie MacCarthy, and the people of Our Lady of Mercy Parish in Waterloo and to Rector John Costanzo and the staff and students of The American College, the Dick 't Hart family remains grateful for moral support, lasting friendship, and financial backing.

"By wisdom a house is built. By discernment the foundation is laid. By knowledge its storerooms filled with riches of every kind, rare, and desirable". [Proverbs 24:3-4]

To my family, colleagues, and friends I say thank you for sharing your wisdom, discernment, and knowlege.

January 19, 1989   John A. Dick
Fifty-fifth anniversary of the death of Lord Halifax

CHAPTER ONE

ROMAN CATHOLIC/ANGLICAN RELATIONS
FROM THE DU PIN - WAKE CORRESPONDENCE (1717-1719)
TO THE DEATH OF CARDINAL VAUGHAN (1903)

English Roman Catholic reactions to the Malines Conversations (1921-1926) cannot be appreciated apart from an understanding of the pre-Malines evolution of English Roman Catholicism and of Roman Catholic/Anglican relations. In this first chapter, we achieve such an understanding by sketching major events and personalities from the sixteenth century separation of Canterbury from Rome to the death of the third Archbishop of Westminster in the early twentieth century — a death which would mark a significant turning point in Anglican/Roman relations.

We begin by surveying three early attempts at bridging the gap between Canterbury and Rome: the Du Pin - Wake Correspondence (1717-1719); the Oxford Movement (1833-1845); and the Phillipps-Bloxam Correspondence (1841). We then examine more closely the development of English Roman Catholicism under the first three Archbishops of Westminster: Wiseman, Manning, and Vaughan.

Nicholas Wiseman's tenure as Archbishop of Westminster (1850-1865) began with the restoration of the Roman Catholic hierarchy and was characterized by factional in-fighting among power groups within the English Roman Church. It was also a time of ecumenical overtures by Frederick George Lee and Ambrose Phillipps de Lisle and ecumenical attacks by, especially, Henry Manning. Wiseman also witnessed and contributed to the rise and the fall of English Liberal Catholicism.

The success of Ultramontanism underscored all the events of Henry Manning's tenure at Westminster (1865-1892). On the ecumenical plane, it was also the era of Edward Pusey's Eirenicon and of the fortuitous meeting of Lord Halifax and Etienne Fernand Portal in Madeira. Halifax and Portal also planted the seeds of a trend which would flower during the Malines Conversations: in ecumenical relations deal directly with Rome or Continental Catholics since there is no point conversing with English Roman Catholics.

During Herbert Vaughan's administration (1892-1903) we will see the hardening of relations between Canterbury and Westminster and the appearance of Leo XIII's *Ad Anglos* and *Apostolicae Curae*.

1. *The Du Pin - Wake Correspondence 1717-1719*

From the time of King Henry VIII's Act of Supremacy (1534) separating the *ecclesia anglicana* from the See of Rome to the start of the Oxford Movement (1833), there had been one significant attempt by individual churchmen to bring about some sort of communion between Canterbury and Rome. The project began in France in February 1717, when the well-known Gallican theologian and patristic scholar from the Sorbonne, Louis Ellies Du Pin (1657-1719)[1] wrote to the Archbishop of Canterbury, William Wake (1657-1737), expressing his desire for a corporate union of the Church of England with the Church of France. "I wish most earnestly", wrote Du Pin, "some way might be found for the English and French Churches, to enter into union. We are not so entirely different from each other in most matters that we could not be mutually reconciled. And I would that all Christians might be one fold under one supreme shepherd, even the Lord Jesus Christ our Saviour"[2]. Du Pin, with the support of his colleague at the Sorbonne, Patrick Piers de Girardin, had been able to contact the Archbishop of Canterbury through William Beauvoir who was at that time chaplain to the British Ambassador in Paris, a position which William Wake had held from 1682 to 1685. Beauvoir had written to Wake that Du Pin was working on a draft-scheme for union, Du Pin's *Commonitorium*.

For two years Du Pin and Wake corresponded. Wake maintained strict privacy about his side of the correspondence, writing in his own hand because "I dare not trust my secretary with it"[3]. Du Pin shared his side of the dialogue with de Girardin, who went public and gave a lecture at the Sorbonne about the Gallican-Anglican "negotiations for ecclesiastical union"[4]. The Archbishop of Paris, Cardinal Louis Antoine de Noailles (1651-1729)[5] was aware of the correspondence and

---

1. Between 1686 and 1691, Du Pin published his six volume *Nouvelle bibliothèque des auteurs ecclésiastiques* which was attacked by J.B. Bossuet and censured by the Archbishop of Paris in 1691. Between 1694 and 1698, he published his nine volume *Histoire des controverses et des matières ecclésiastiques*; between 1701 and 1703 the five volume *Histoire de l'Église et des auteurs ecclésiastiques du XVI siècle*; in 1708 the seven volume *Bibliothèque des auteurs ecclésiastiques du XVII et du XVIII siecle* (two volumes of the later appearing in 1711); and his *L'Histoire ecclésiastique du XVII siècle*; all of which, along with his *Traité de la puissance ecclésiastique et temporelle* were put on the Index in 1757.
2. N. SYKES, *William Wake, Archbishop of Canterbury*, vol. 1, Cambridge, 1957, p. 258.
3. *Ibid.*, p. 284.
4. *Ibid.*, p. 261.
5. Louis Antoine De Noailles was created a cardinal in 1700 by Pope Innocent XII and made head of the Sorbonne in 1710. He was a strong supporter of Gallican ideals. His commendation of *Réflexions morales* by P. Quesnel made him suspect (especially among the Jesuits) of Jansenism. He opposed the bull *Unigenitus* and formally appealed against it in September 1718. Although he accepted it in 1728, he privately recanted before his death in 1729.

approved of it but refused to make any public comment about it — to the great annoyance of the Archbishop of Canterbury, as expressed by Wake in a letter to Beauvoir: "My task is pretty hard, and I scarce know how to manage myself in this matter. To go any further than I have done, even as a divine only of the Church of England, may meet with censure. And as Archbishop of Canterbury I cannot treat with those gentlemen. I do not think my character at all inferior to that of an Archbishop of Paris; on the contrary, without lessening the authority and dignity of the Church of England, I must say it is in some respects superior. If the Cardinal were in earnest for such a union, it would not be below him to treat with me himself about it. I should then have a sufficient ground to consult with my brethren, and to ask His Majesty's leave to correspond with him concerning it"[6].

The Du Pin-Wake correspondence did not involve English Roman Catholics. And the focus of the exchanges was the Sorbonne theologians' wish, very much in the spirit of Jean Baptiste Bossuet's 1682 *Declarations of the Gallican Clergy*, for "union with the Church of England as the most effectual means to unite all the Western Churches" against papal intransigence and interference[7]. The project achieved some significant agreement on at least twenty-three of the *Thirty-nine Articles*. But civil and religious opposition to the correspondence on both sides of the channel grew so strong that by the time of Du Pin's death on June 6, 1719 there was little hope for immediate reunion. Du Pin, in fact, never saw William Wake's final letter to him which marked the end of these negotiations: "May it suffice to have designed something in so great a task; and perhaps to have cast some seeds in the ground which at length will bear manifold fruit. Meanwhile let us (for this none can deny us), embrace each other as brethren and members of the same mystical body"[8].

In view of later ecumenical discussions between representatives of the Churches of Canterbury and Rome, and in particular the Malines Conversations, to say nothing of the aftermath of Vatican I's Constitution *Pastor Aeternus!* (1870) it is interesting to note the 1718 exchange of ideas between Louis Du Pin and Archbishop Wake about the papal office:

Du Pin to Wake: "In regard to the jurisdiction of the Roman Pontiff, as regards the State, it is restricted within narrow bounds, so that it can be of no prejudice to us. For as to temporals he has no power; and in spirituals he is held within the rules of the ancient Canons. He can do nothing in those things which relate to the government of the Bishop in his own Diocese; he cannot ordain or enact anything pertaining to

---

6. *Ibid.*, p. 266.
7. G.K.A. BELL, *Christian Unity: The Anglican Position*, London, 1949, p. 61.
8. SYKES, *op. cit.*, p. 295.

discipline; he cannot excommunicate anyone, or claim anything else to himself. His primacy (namely, that he holds the first place among Bishops, as all antiquity affirms, and the Greeks themselves, although rent from the Roman Church, confess) we acknowledge. But the Primacy does not give him a higher grade among Bishops: he is only their fellow-bishop, though first among Bishops"[9].

Wake replying to Du Pin: "The honour which you give to the Roman Pontiff differs so little, I deem, from that which our sounder theologians readily grant him, that, on this point, I think, it will not be difficult, on either side, either to agree altogether in the same opinion, or mutually to bear with a dissent of no moment"[10].

For a decade, de Girardin and Wake stayed in touch with each other, through correspondence and visits. In 1721 Pierre François Le Courrayer (1681-1776), professor of theology and librarian at St. Geneviève in Paris also joined the remaining correspondents, in what had now become a sharing of theological opinions. Le Courrayer's interest was Anglican orders. His correspondence with Wake was extensive; and his two books, the *Dissertation sur la Validité des Ordinations des Anglais et la Succession des Évêques de l'Église Anglicane, avec les preuves justificatives des faits avancés* completed in 1721 but publication delayed due to censorship until 1723 (when it was published in Nancy, France, with the name of a Brussels bookseller on the title-page!) and the *Défense de la Dissertation* (1726) were important, well-known, and controversial. Le Courayer had the support of Cardinal de Noailles but was censured by twenty-two other French bishops. Excommunicated in 1728 he sought refuge in England, where he remained until his death. Though he never joined the Anglican Church, he was buried in the cloister of Westminster Abbey[11].

After the Du Pin-Wake Correspondence it would be one hundred and fourteen years before the next major Anglican/Roman Catholic event: the Oxford Movement.

2. *The Oxford Movement 1833-1845*

A detailed analysis of the personalities and events of the Oxford Movement is not the concern of this book. Literature about the Movement is extensive and readily available[12]. It is appropriate,

9. BELL, *op. cit.*, p. 67.

10. *Ibid.*, p. 67.

11. H.R. McADOO, *Anglican/Roman Catholic Relations, 1717-1980*, in J.C.H. AVELING, D.M. LOADES, and H.R. McADOO (eds.), *Rome and the Anglicans*, Berlin/New York, 1982, p. 157.

12. For detailed information about the Oxford Movement, see for instance: O. CHAD-WICK, *The Mind of the Oxford Movement*, London, 1963; R.W. CHURCH, *The Oxford Movement: Twelve Years*, London, 1891; C. DAWSON, *The Spirit of the Oxford Movement*,

however, to examine the manner in which the Oxford Movement contributed to setting the stage for future relations between the English Roman Catholic Church and the Anglican Church.

The Oxford Movement was a wave of theological and spiritual renewal within the High Church element of the Anglican Church. Its promoters sought to defend the Church against the aggressions of the civil government and to retrieve doctrines and patterns of Christian living which were part of the Church's heritage but had become corrupted or neglected. It came at a time when that Church "seemed to have lost all sense of its divine origin, mission, and authority"[13]. The message of the Movement was communicated through "Tracts for the Times" — thus the Movement was known as "Tractarianism" and its promoters as "Tractarians". And as Alec Vidler observes, there was "magic of one kind or another"[14] about the Movement's principal personalities. They were: Richard Hurrell Froude (1803-1836), John Keble (1792-1866), John Henry Newman (1801-1890) and Edward Pusey (1800-1882). The Tractarians concentrated on a key passage of the Nicene Creed: "I believe in One, Holy, Catholic, and Apostolic Church". They stressed a return to Catholic as opposed to Protestant values, insisting that the Church holds divine authority as part of God's visible kingdom; that sacraments are necessary channels of grace; and that the bishops are successors of the apostles in their ministry and teaching. The Movement began on July 14, 1833[15] when John Keble, reacting against passage by the British Parliament of the "Irish Church Temporalities Bill" which suppressed ten Irish Anglican sees, preached his "Sermon on National Apostasy" in the church of St. Mary the Virgin, Oxford. And though the story of Ritualism and of the influence of Edward Pusey[16] extend well into the 1860's, most historians date the end of the Oxford Movement with John Henry Newman's profession of Roman Catholic faith to Father Dominic Barberi on October 9, 1845[17].

New York, 1933; L.E. ELLIOTT-BINNS, *Religion in the Victorian Era*, London, 1953 (first published in 1936); G. FABER, *Oxford Apostles*, London, 1954; E.R. FAIRWEATHER (ed.), *The Oxford Movement*, New York, 1964; E. JAY (ed.), *The Evangelical and Oxford Movements*, Cambridge, 1983; M.R. O'CONNEL, *Oxford Conspiration*, New York, 1953.

13. A.R. VIDLER, *The Church in an Age of Revolution*, Harmondsworth, New York, 1961 (reprint, 1981), p. 49.

14. *Ibid.*, p. 49.

15. See Newman's remark in B. MARTIN, *John Henry Newman His Life and Work*, London, 1982, p. 56. "I have ever considered and kept the day as the start of the religious movement of 1833".

16. After Newman's conversion, the focus of the movement shifted from Oxford and Tractarianism to Ritualism. In popular language, the movement was now called "Puseyism" (as different from the earlier "Newmanism", and "Newmania") by the movements cynical opponents. See: H.P. LIDDON, *Life of Edward Bouverie Pusey*, vol. II, 2d ed., London, 1894-1898, p. 139.

17. "His (Newman's) secession in 1845, of which there had been many premonitions, marked the end of the Oxford movement proper". VIDLER, *op. cit.*, p. 54.

After Newman's conversion, Keble and Pusey took over leadership of an already faltering Movement. They moved its headquarters away from Oxford; and they focused more attention on pastoral and liturgical matters than doctrinal. The Oxford Movement marked such a major change in English Christianity that its impact on Anglican/Roman Catholic ecumenical relations would last well into the twentieth century.

In one sense the Oxford Movement was conservative, academic, and clerical. It appealed to upper class, educated, High Church people. Pusey's comment that "The Tracts found an echo everywhere. Friends started up like armed men from the ground. I only dreaded our becoming too popular"[18], was more optimistic rhetoric than a reflection of reality. The Tractarians reached very few people in the factories, workshops, mills, and mines of England. The Evangelicals appealed more to these people. And the Oxford Movement, especially after *Tract 90*, had the effect of alienating the Evangelicals and driving them into the arms of the Low Church.

The history of the Oxford Movement is also a story of religious paradox. The Movement gave many Anglicans a better understanding of Roman Catholicism; yet it also increased their fears that an aggressive Catholicism, stirred up by the Anglican return to "Catholic" ideals and by the energy and fervor of new converts from Anglicanism, would swallow the Church of England. Their fears were re-inforced by people like Ambrose Phillips de Lisle and Nicholas Wiseman, whom we will consider later in this chapter, and by the musings of continental Roman Catholics like Ignatius von Döllinger (1799-1890) who viewed the Movement as a nursery for converts and wrote to Edward Pusey in September of 1842 that the eyes of all Germany, "of Protestants as well as of Roman Catholics, are turned in fear or hope towards Oxford"[19]. As John Henry Newman observed, "the Anglo-Catholic party suddenly became a power in the National Church and an object of alarm to her rulers and friends"[20]. From the beginning, the Oxford Movement did not have the sympathy of most Anglican bishops. After Newman wrote *Tract 90*, they became openly hostile.

In *Tract 90* Newman had attempted to show that the *Thirty-Nine Articles*, a form of "confession of faith" for the Anglican Church going back to 1563, implied a distinction between Catholic teaching and the dogmas of Rome. He asserted further that the *Articles* did not condemn Catholic teaching nor did they condemn entirely Roman dogma. In effect Newman was denying the Protestant character of the Articles. Reactions from Anglican Church leaders were quick, negative, and angry. Four Oxford tutors immediately censured *Tract 90*. Newman's

18. *Ibid.*, p. 52.
19. LIDDON, *op. cit.*, p. 295.
20. J. H. NEWMAN, *Apologia Pro Vita Sua* (1865), London, 1902, p. 76.

bishop, Bagot, ordered him not to publish any more tracts. Bishop Phillpotts of Exeter condemned *Tract 90* as "offensive and indecent and absurd ... as well as incongruous and unjust"[21]. From *Tract 90* on, the Tractarians "came under an official ban and stigma"[22].

Converts from the Oxford Movement certainly increased the numbers, prestige, and influence of English Roman Catholics. But these Anglican converts were also attracted to and supported the Ultramontane theories of Roman and papal supremacy and the introduction of Italian devotions and Roman rituals. They would prove to be most unwelcome among the "Old" English Roman Catholics and be a source of much division and conflict. A few of them would eventually play a major role in the Romanizing of English Catholicism. William George Ward (1812-1882), Frederick Oakley (1802-1880), Frederick William Faber (1814-1863), and John Dobree Dalgairns (1818-1876) left Anglicanism after Newman's conversion. Another wave of converts "went over" after the 1851 Gorham case[23] which had convinced them that official Anglicanism was too much under state control and incapable of meeting their ideals. Among these converts we find: Henry Manning (1808-1892) who wrote to Hope-Scott just before his conversion: "It is either Rome or licence of thought and will"[24]; William Maskell (1814-1890) who had conducted the examination of Gorham for Bishop Phillpotts, and Robert Isaac Wilberforce (1802-1857).

Perhaps the greatest paradox of the Oxford Movement is that it did much to prepare the Anglican Communion for the modern ecumenical movement. "Insular though the Movement was in its original concern and conception, its inner logic has compelled its sons to open their eyes to Christendom. It may be that the alienation of the Tractarians from Protestantism as they knew it has kept Anglo-Catholics, as a body, from doing full justice to the Churches of the Reformation. But the serious questioning of the separate existence of the Anglican Church, which inevitably arose out of the Tractarians' growing sense of kinship with traditional Catholicism, has led not only to a persistent quest for reunion with Rome and with the Orthodox East, but also in due course to a vital concern for the reunion of all believers in one visible fellowship. Furthermore, the Oxford Movement's effective demonstration of the Anglican Church's freedom from 'confessional' ties and of

21. L.E. ELLIOTT-BINNS, *Religion in the Victorian Era*, p. 99.

22. D. CHURCH, *The Oxford Movement*, p. 296.

23. Henry Phillpotts (1778-1869) the Bishop of Exeter had refused a parish to Rev. George C. Gorham in 1847 because Gorham had questionable views on baptismal regeneration. The Court of Arches in Canterbury backed the bishop's decision; however, the Judicial Committee of The Privy Council reversed the Phillpotts' decision in 1851. For many Tractarians and others, this unwarranted and unprecedented intervention in doctrinal matters was the final outrage.

24. A.W. HUTTON, *Cardinal Manning*, London, 1892, p. 77.

its sole dependence on the Bible and the historic standards of faith and order common to East and West has shed more than a little light on the true 'ecumenical' vocation of Anglicanism"[25].

And years later, Lord Halifax would look back to his youthful involvement with the Tractarians as the life-changing event which took him to Malines.

3. *The Phillipps - Bloxam Correspondence 1840*

In the autumn of 1840, at about the same time that John Henry Newman sat down to study the *Thirty-Nine Articles* in preparation for *Tract 90*, Ambrose Phillipps de Lisle (1809-1878)[26], an enthusiastic but somewhat naive Roman Catholic convert, and John Rouse Bloxam (1807-1891), an Anglican priest who had been Newman's curate at Littlemore from 1837 to 1840, met briefly and by chance at St. Bernard's Monastery in Leicester. The meeting would lead to an active ecumenical correspondence between the two men lasting throughout 1841. The Phillipps-Bloxam Correspondence[27] is noteworthy not because of any positive and lasting accomplishments but because it focused attention on the key questions which would surface in later ecumenical dialogues and especially at Malines: Should the Roman Catholic Church unite with the whole Anglican Church or just with the Anglo-Catholics? Does unity between the two Churches require the break-up of the Anglican Church? Does it require the break-up of the English Roman Catholic Church?

The correspondence began with Phillipps' 1841 letter of January 25

---

25. E.R. FAIRWEATHER, *The Oxford Movement*, New York, 1984, p. 13.

26. Ambrose Lisle March Phillipps was born of Anglican parents and converted to Roman Catholicism when he was sixteen. In 1835 he donated 250 acres of Charnwood Forest for the building of the Cistercian monastery of Mount St. Bernard. In 1838 he helped found the Association of Universal Prayer for the Conversion of England; and in 1857, the Association for Promoting the Unity of Christendom. After 1862 when he inherited the family property, he signed himself Ambrose Phillipps de Lisle.

27. "It was Dr. Bloxam's intention at one time to publish entire this correspondence. The title he had intended for this collection of letters was: 'A Chapter in the History of the Oxford Movement', to which was added a sub-title 'A Correspondence in A.D. 1841 between Ambrose Lisle Phillipps (de Lisle) of Grace Dieu Mannor, Leicestershire and the Rev. John Rouse Bloxam, M.A., St. Mary Magdalen College Oxford, on the subject of a Reunion between the Church of England and of Rome to which are added Letters on the same subject by the Rev. John Henry Newman, B.D., Fellow of Oriel, the Rev. Frederick William Faber, M.A., Fellow of University, the Rev. George William Ward, M.A., Fellow of Balliol'. On November 18, 1877 he wrote to the Reverend Dr. F.L. Lee, Vicar of All Saints' Lambeth: 'For certain reasons I have given up all intention of printing the correspondence between Ambrose Phillipps, myself, and many other persons in 1841 on the subject of "Reunion"'. MS. Letters Rev. Dr. Bloxam, Rev. Dr. Lee, p. 90, given to Magdalen College by Colonel Reginald Lee". R.D. MIDDLETON, *Newman and Bloxam*, Westport, 1971 (originally published 1947), p. 101, note.

(Feast of the Conversion of St. Paul) in which he detailed his proposal for corporate union between the two Churches.

Phillipps envisioned the Anglicans expelling from their Church all Protestants, leaving a Uniate Church in communion with Rome. "You shall lay aside your modern Common Prayer, we our Roman Rite, and let the ancient rites of Sarum and of York resume their place... The Service of God according to the holy Sarum rite might be celebrated in all Cathedral, Collegiate, and Conventual Churches in the Latin tongue"[28]. Some English would be allowed in liturgies of parish Churches. The English clergy would be able to keep their wives. Future clergy would be allowed to marry. Invocation of saints would be dropped from the liturgy. The English Church would be free to make its own decisions about use of holy images. There were no problems with transubstantiation or any other main doctrines. And finally, "No man can dispute the fact that the acquisition of nine millions of new members numbering amongst them many peers and noble gentlemen (and I cannot lay the English, Irish, and Scottish Catholics at a lower number than 9 millions) would greatly strengthen the Anglican Church; it would totally paralyse the dissenters, it would heal all the political disputes between England and Ireland, it would render the Church property perfectly impregnable... Many even of the Calvinistic clergy would be converted, the rest might then be ejected for heresy, and pensioned off for their lives, so that no one could complain"[29].

Phillipps also sent a copy of his letter to *The Tablet* which reacted, in Phillipps' words, with "an explosion of vulgarity and bitterness of ignorance and shallow reasoning"[30]. The editor of *The Tablet* also observed that "a distinguished divine", who was certainly Wiseman[31], also sided against Phillipps.

Bloxam showed Phillipps' letter to John Henry Newman and to other friends. Some of the readers reacted positively. Newman reacted cautiously, with an anonymous letter to Phillipps, which he asked Bloxam to pass along to him[32].

Newman's entire letter is given here. It is particularly interesting in view of his later conversion and because it so accurately reflects what would be the spirit behind the Malines Conversations, when men of learning and ability would gather in charity to make peace not war.

Phillipps was upset by Newman's letter. Bloxam showed Newman the correspondence. Newman too became disturbed and wrote on March 2, 1841 to Bloxam that he could anticipate nothing fruitful

28. *Ibid.*, pp. 105-106.
29. *Ibid.*, p. 107.
30. *Ibid.*, p. 113.
31. *Ibid.*, p. 114.
32. *Ibid.*, pp. 118-120.

coming from Phillipps' proposals for unity: "I do not suppose there is a single member of our communion, of any religious feeling, but would, *abstractly*, wish a reunion between them and us; but what we are all deeply impressed with, for one reason or other, is its hopelessness. This the Archbishop of Canterbury has expressed in his late Charge: 'The dissenters' he says 'which separated the Churches of the East and the West, and the corruptions and intolerance which drove the Protestants from communion with Rome, have been most injurious to the Catholic Church. A reconciliation *would indeed be desirable*; but reunion with Rome has been rendered *impossible* by the sinister policy of the Council of Trent'. I quote this for the single purpose of showing by it what is at once the wish and the despair of the Church of England...

"We are all agreed, if Mr. Phillipps will excuse me in saying it, in *distrusting* Rome, as hollow, insincere, political, ambitious, and unscrupulous. I am not saying whether or not we exaggerate, but this would be our common impression; and I think it is founded on this undeniable truth, that Rome has not upon her at this day, at least to our view, the Note of Sanctity. We see much of her gaining power by political party, intrigue, and tumult; we hear much of disputations; much of societies, publications and tracts; but very little of inward religion"[33].

In effect, Newman wished to wash his hands of Phillipps because he was already in the center of the storms arising from *Tract 90*. Bloxam tells us that Newman did correspond again with Phillipps, but apparently nothing of this correspondence has survived[34].

On June 27, 1841, Newman wrote to Bloxam about his annoyance at Phillipps and his alarm that some of Phillipps' Anglican friends, among them "Mr. Wackerbarth", were threatening to desert the Anglican Church: "As to Mr. Phillipps letter, of course one cannot but admire and respect his zeal but he certainly is going too fast. From the first I have said that I did not expect a union in *one* day. I remain in that opinion. The idea of our agitating in our Church for one, is preposterous. I will have recourse to no such means. The sentiment must be left to *grow up* in our body, not forced upon it. As to Mr. W. etc — his friends *may* succeed in gaining from us one or two men; I shall be deeply sorry for it, but *he and his* will have *more cause* to be sorry. If *anything* is calculated more than another to throw back the tendencies to union among us, it will be proselytism from us to the Church of Rome".

"It is impossible to read Mr P's letter without the deepest interest. Where our sympathies are so much the same, why should we be separated, except

33. *Ibid.*, pp. 122-123.
34. *Ibid.*, p. 137.

that there is a strong body in both Churches whose antipathies are more powerful still, and because this body has the governing authorities on its side. I cannot wonder that our authorities should feel as they do, considering what the Church of Rome practically is, nor can I wonder that the Church of Rome should feel as it does considering what we are, and have been, at least the majority of us.

This I feel most strongly and cannot conceal it, viz. that, while Rome is what she is, union is impossible — that we too must change I do not deny.

Rome must change first of all in her spirit. I must see more sanctity in her than I do at present. Alas! I see no marks of sanctity or if any, they are chiefly confined to converts from us. 'By their fruits ye shall know them', is the main canon Our Lord gives us, to know true pastors from false. I do verily think that, with all our sins, there is more sanctity in the Church of England and Ireland, than in the Roman Catholic bodies in the same countries.

I say not all this in reproach, but in great sorrow. Indeed I am ever making the best of things before others, when the R.Cs are attacked but I cannot deny this great lack. What Hildebrand did by faith and holiness, they do by political intrigue. Their great object is to pull down the English Church. They join with those who are *further* from them in creed to oppose those who are nearer to them. They have to do with such a man as O'Connell. Never can I think such ways the footsteps of Christ. If they want to convert England, let them go barefooted into our manufacturing towns, let them preach to the people, like St. Francis Xavier, let them be pelted and trampled on, and I will own that they can do what we cannot; I will confess that they are our betters far. I will (though I could not on that ground join them). I would gladly incur their reproach. This is to be Catholics; this is to secure a triumph. Let them use the proper arms of the Church, and they will prove that they are the Church by using them.

I can feel nothing but distrust and aversion towards those who offer peace yet carry on war: this I have felt and expressed before this, but what gives me an interest in Mr. P and makes me feel grateful to him is that he has taken the opposite course, and in taking it has exposed himself to obloquy (sic) from those whom he is opposing. He is doing as much as one man can do; but nothing is really done till much more is done. What a day it will be, if God ever again raises up holy men, Bernards or Boromeos, in their communion. But even if this were done, difficulties would not be at an end, though I think, sanctity being secured, everything would ultimately follow. This is not the place to go into controversial matters nor is it necessary since the previous difficulty of the sadly degenerate state of Rome, is first to be removed. But when it is removed, they still would have to explain authoritatively many portions of their formularies, which they at present interpret in a sense which seems to us very uncatholic.

And then after all, I see nothing to make me think it would be other than a sin for any of us to *leave* our Church. We must make our Church move. If indeed, so far from moving, she rushed (which God forbid and which is profane even to suppose) into open heresy instead, and the Church of Rome on the other hand had cleansed herself of her present faults, in such a state of things I can conceive its being a duty to leave our Church and join the Roman. I do not feel it a duty on any other hypothesis.

Now these contingencies being so remote, or rather impossible at least in our day, it would seem that nothing is left for pious Roman Catholics and ourselves to do in the way of *direct* union. Our duty seems rather to lie in trying to be one with each other in heart, and in doing what we can to improve our own bodies respectively. No one can say that much has not been done on the part of many of our members to improve the state of the English Communion let Roman Catholics do as much. I hail Mr. P's late conduct as a proof that they will do much, but they have much to do before they will have done as much as some of us have done. I long to see them begin the work of Christian charity. I wish I could see a movement on the part of their *clergy*. I earnestly wait for the time when men of learning and ability will come forward, not to advocate any recognition of our Church I am not asking for that but to speak and act kindly towards a body which has done much to repress many heresies (as they must confess) and is nearer them than any other Christian communion. I would call upon them to break their connections with those who agree with them in no one principle; to influence the tone of their periodical publications; to give up the uncatholic proceedings which disgrace their worship so commonly (such as music meetings in Chapels); to be preachers of sanctity and to raise a feeling of the necessity of a moral reformation. Their success rests with themselves. The English never will be favourably inclined to a plotting intriguing party but faith and holiness are irresistible"[35].

The Phillipps-Bloxam Correspondence ended when Bloxam's Anglican friend Richard Waldo Sibthorp converted to Rome[36]. Bloxam was deeply shaken, as we read in his letter to Phillipps, written from Magdalen on the Vigil of All Saints. It marked the end of their ecumenical correspondence:

"I was afraid that you would not altogether like my last letter, but as it appeared to me that your expectations were raised to see a number of members of our Church leave it, and that *in a short time*, and betake themselves to your communion, I thought it would be but honest in me, to tell you wherein I differed in opinion from Ward in this respect... When I spoke of one or two joining your Church immediately I alluded to the report respecting Mr. Wackerbarth, and also to the case of our friend Sibthorp, of whom you would learn from Dr. Gentili... My head is now throbbing with the agitation caused by recent events, and I must for a time seek calm and quiet. I speak candidly when I tell you that however desirous I may be of re-union I have never yet felt the slightest conviction that it is my own *individual* duty to leave the Church of England; and my repugnance to the notion is so great that I must decline any discussion of it. It is too fearful a thing to be trifled with...

35. *Ibid.*, pp. 147-148.
36. Sibthorp eventually returned to Anglicanism, a move which greatly upset Wiseman. He attributed Sibthorp's "defection" to mental illness resulting from an accident which had changed his ideas "in the most extraordinary manner". J. FOWLER, *Richard Waldo Sibthorp*, London, 1880, pp. 72-78.

Pray do not be offended at anything I write, for I am in a wretched state..."[37].

Among his personal papers Bloxam also left a note, which even more powerfully expressed his feelings and stressed the issue of corporate reunion vs. individual conversions: "The fact was that the secession of Sibthorp, and the evident eagerness of Dr. Wiseman and Mr. Phillipps to receive deserters from our camp, whilst these negotiations were carried on, at once dispelled the notion of a Reunion of the Churches which vanished like a dream; and I no longer took any part in the correspondence with Mr. Ambrose Phillipps..."[38].

4. Nicholas Wiseman
Archbishop of Westminster 1850-1865

By the middle of the nineteenth century, the English Roman Catholic population was expanding and changing the character of English Catholicism. The wave of conversions flowing from the Oxford Movement brought people of "superior cultural background and dauntless enthusiasm"[39] into the Roman community. And the influx of Irish workers due to the great famine of 1845-1848 led to the development of an aggressive Roman Catholic middle class. The English stage was being set for a Roman Catholic revival. Nicholas Wiseman would be a central figure in that drama.

The career of Nicholas Patrick Wiseman (1802-1865) can be divided into two phases: the Roman and the English.

He was born in Seville, grew up in Waterford, educated at Ushaw. In 1818 he left for Rome to become one of the first to study at the reopened English College. There he would develop a deep devotion to the See of Peter: "It was something above earthly to see an Emperor and Empress, a queen, dukes and princes of the highest blood kneeling before the sovereign vicar of Christ"[40]. He remained in Rome for twenty-two years. He received a doctorate in 1824 and was ordained in 1825. In 1827 he published three dissertations about a Syrian version of the Old Testament, *Horae Syriacae*, which gained him international acclaim as a scholar and helped him, in his direct appeal to the Pope, to become appointed Professor of Oriental Languages in the Roman University. In 1828 he became Rector of the English College and in that position he became the Roman representative of the English bishops. And there he would also become acquainted with John Joseph Ignatius von Döllinger (1799-1890), Vincenzo Gioberti (1801-1852),

37. *Ibid.*, pp. 160-161.
38. *Ibid.*, p. 161.
39. R. AUBERT, P. E. CRUNCIAN, J.T. ELLIS, F.B. PIKE, J. BRULS, and J. HAJJAR, *The Church in a Secularized Society*, New York/London, 1978, p. 210.
40. B. FOTHERGILL, *Nicholas Wiseman*, London, 1963, p. 25.

Johan Joseph von Görres (1776-1848), Henri Dominique Lacordaire (1802-1861), Felicité Robert de Lamennais (1782-1854), Charles René Forbes de Montalembert (1810-1870), and Antonio Rosmini (1797-1855). When the convert George Spencer arrived at the English College, Wiseman came in touch with the Oxford Movement, which convinced him that the time was ripe for a Roman Catholic revival in England. His beliefs were further strengthened in 1832 when John Henry Newman and Richard Hurrell Froude visited him. In 1835 Wiseman visited London and gave a series of lectures on Catholic beliefs. "I have two lectures every week. The effect has been a thousand times beyond my expectations... Everyone agrees that a most successful experiment has been made..."[41]. They were published in London in 1836 as: *Lectures on the Principal Doctrines and Practices of the Catholic Church*. This was Wiseman's first real experience of the English Church. He found that his sensitivities were more in line with Roman ways of doing things than with the formal, timid, and austere ways of the 'Old Catholics'. Before returning to Rome, Wiseman helped found the *Dublin Review*. From this time on, Wiseman would devote the rest of his life to the Catholic revival in England and the restoration of the English Roman Catholic hierarchy.

In 1840 Wiseman returned to England as coadjutor to Bishop Walsh in the central district. He also became President of Oscott College in Birmingham, where he befriended a distinguished group of Oxford Movement converts. Before leaving Rome for England, Wiseman had written an article for the *Dublin Review*, "Catholic and Anglican Churches", drawing a parallel between Donatism and Anglicanism. The essay, with its key phrase *securus judicat orbis terrarum*, had a profound impact on Newman.

In 1848 Wiseman was appointed Vicar Apostolic for London. And on September 29, 1850 Pius IX restored the English hierarchy, replacing the eight vicariates apostolic with an archbishopric based at Westminster. Nicholas Wiseman was named Archbishop of Westminster and created cardinal on the following day. On October 7, Wiseman published his triumphalist pastoral letter *From Out of the Flaminian Gate*. "The great work, then, is complete", he wrote. "What you have long desired and prayed for is granted. Your beloved country has received a place among the fair Churches, which, normally constituted, form the splendid aggregate of Catholic Communion; Catholic England has been restored to its orbit in the ecclesiastical firmament, from which its light had long vanished, and begins now anew its course of regularly adjusted action round the centre of unity, the source of jurisdiction, of light, and of

41. *Ibid.*, p. 289.

vigor. How wonderful all this has been brought about, how clearly the hand of God has been shown in every step..."[42].

Reaction to Wiseman's tactless exuberance was strong and bitter not only from segments of the British press and groups of Anglicans but also from the Old Catholics who resented his pompous way of arousing the public. In the *Times* of October 14, we read that Wiseman's appointment to Westminster was "one of the grossest acts of folly and impertinence which the Court of Rome has ventured to commit since the Crown and people of England threw off its yoke"[43]. "The Archbishop of York spoke of the 'indecent aggression', the Bishop of Chichester of this 'audacious aggression' and the Bishop of London, who asked his clergy to preach controversial sermons, of a 'subtle aggression'. All but two of the Anglican bishops considered it necessary to protest to the Queen..."[44]. An *Ecclesiastical Titles* bill was rushed through Parliament, making it unlawful for Catholic bishops to take their titles from places in the United Kingdom. (The bill was never enforced and was repealed in 1871.) And on Guy Fawkes Day (November 5) anti-Catholic mobs pelted priests, broke windows of Catholic churches, and burned the Pope and the Cardinal in effigy. And the diplomatic Roman Catholic bishop of Birmingham, William Bernard Ullathorne (1806-1889), muttered about the restoration "if it could have been quietly promulgated amongst ourselves at that period, we should have settled down in peace"[45].

In fact things did settle down a bit more peacefully after the publication of Wiseman's somewhat irenic *Appeal to the English People* on November 20, 1850.

Wiseman was indeed the first resident English cardinal since Reginald Pole (1500-1558) and he tried to act with supreme and autocratic control over the English Catholic Church. But that was a difficult task, because the English Roman Catholic Church over which he presided was a divided house, composed of Old Catholics, Liberal Catholics, and Ultramontanes.

After the Reformation, the English Roman Catholic Church had been reduced to a missionary regime directed by a small landed aristocracy and domestic chaplains, often operating in isolation of each other. The descendents of these Catholics were the 'Old Catholics'. "Hereditary Catholics, steeped in tradition and profoundly distrustful of new ideas or practices", who in the Wiseman era "found fault with many of their co-religionists as being either too liberal or too

42. *Ibid.*, pp. 293-297 for entire pastoral.
43. J.D. HOLMES, *More Roman Than Rome: English Catholicism in the Nineteenth Century,* London, 1978, p. 75.
44. *Ibid.*, p. 76.
45. B. WARD, *The Sequel to Catholic Emancipation*, vol. 2, London, 1915, p. 285.

Romanising"[46]. Many of the Old Catholics greeted the restored hierarchy with mixed reactions, hardly considering it a "Second Spring", as Newman had done at the 1853 First Provincial Synod of Westminster. For them it was clearly the symbol of Roman control over their Church and marked the end of their long hegemony. More an autumn than a spring.

The Old Catholics were clearly a thorn in Wiseman's side. "The lack of co-operation and even opposition from the Old Catholics threw him into fits of depression when he felt completely isolated"[47]. They resented his Roman ways of doing things, such as trying to centralize authority in his hands and introducing Italian devotions, Roman vestments, and continental — especially Italian — missionaries. He resented their "Gallican" independence and the fact that most of the bishops had come from the Old Catholic stock. In 1862 for instance, most of the bishops stayed away from the annual Low Week meeting of the English bishops. In particular Wiseman had struggles with Thomas Joseph Brown, Bishop of Newport and Menevia from 1850 to 1880; Thomas Grant[48], Bishop of Southwark from 1851 to 1870; Alexander Goss, Bishop of Liverpool from 1856 to 1872; and William Bernard Ullathorne, Bishop of Birmingham from 1850 to 1888.

Wiseman's most serious episcopal difficulties, however, involved his friend of earlier English College days Bishop George Errington (1804-1886). Wiseman gradually came to realize that he had made a mistake when in 1855 he had him appointed coadjutor at Westminster with right of succession. Errington's Old Catholic loyalties came to the surface in his independent episcopal decisions and especially in his removal of William George Ward (1812-1882) and other Ultramontanes from the diocesan seminary. Frederick William Faber (1814-1863), the Oratorian convert and hymn writer, expressed Wiseman's growing sentiments when he said that if Errington became Archbishop of Westminster: "it will take fifty if not a hundred years to restore England to the pitch of Ultramontanism which she now has reached"[49]. The view was widely shared by Wiseman's friends, especially Henry

46. AUBERT, op. cit., p. 210.

47. HOLMES, op. cit., p. 68.

48. "The Bishop of Southwark from his long residence in Rome has learnt all the trickiness, and underhand intrigue practised by some persons here, but he has not imbibed the generous, noble Spirit, which I look upon as the great characteristic of the Holy See. I have reason to suppose that by means of his letters he has been doing an immense deal of mischief at Propaganda, and especially lately when he has been the great supporter of the Archbishop of Trebizond against Cardinal Wiseman. Besides he is the sworn enemy of all the converts who are active and zealous, although he professes friendship towards them. He is the great supporter of the Old high and dry school". Monsignor George Talbot about Bishop Grant, with reference to Bishop Errington, in HOLMES, op. cit., p. 100.

49. W. WARD, The Life and Times of Cardinal Wiseman. Vol. 2, London, 1900, p. 370.

Manning and Monsignor George Talbot[50], Pius IX's special advisor on English affairs, who unjustly accused Errington of "anti-Romanism, Anglo-Gallicanism"[51] and eventually got Pius IX to remove him from his coadjutorship at Westminster. We will see later that Cardinal Merry del Val will play a role similar to that of Talbot: becoming special papal advisor about matters English and accusing his opponents at Malines of anti-Romanism and Anglo-Gallicanism. Errington's removal marked the turning point in the battle between the traditional "Old" English Catholicism and the new Roman Ultramontanism. It was also this antagonism between Ultramontanes and Old Catholics which led to the undoing of further attempts at church unity, during Cardinal Wiseman's administration, promoted by Ambrose Phillipps de Lisle and his friend Frederick George Lee.

In 1856 Frederick George Lee (1832-1902) an Anglican priest[52] and theological writer with an acerbic pen founded *The Union* newspaper. A few months later Phillipps de Lisle published his brief pamphlet *On the Future Unity of Christendom*, which asserted that "the difference between Catholics and Church of England men is far more verbal than real"[53]. Both publication events led their authors to co-found in September 1857 the Association for Promoting the Unity of Christendom, or A.P.U.C. as it was commonly known. In its early history, Wiseman backed the A.P.U.C. and Pius IX had high hopes for it[54] until Manning and Talbot convinced both men that the movement was undermining the Roman position. Most of the Tractarians refused to support it, from the start, because of Lee's outspokenness. By 1864 the A.P.U.C. counted seven thousand members, one thousand of whom

50. "Talbot effectively influenced the Pope for almost twenty years in his attitude towards English Catholics. He became an inflexible supporter of Wiseman and Manning, and an opponent of the other bishops who deeply resented what one of them called, the 'backstairs influence' which was used unfairly against them. Ullathorne bluntly described Talbot as 'the pest of the English Bishops'". HOLMES, *op. cit.*, pp. 73-74.

51. Discussing Errington in a letter he wrote to Wiseman, Talbot revealed his true Machiavellian nature: "As for your Coadjutor, I have thought it more straightforward and open on my part to tell him what my opinion of him is. I told him plainly that I thought him radically Anti-Roman in Spirit and Anglo-Gallican, although I did not for a moment suppose that he would maintain any Gallican proposition or even Gallican theory. Therefore I said that he could not ever agree with your Eminence whom I looked upon as my beau ideal of a Roman Bishop". HOLMES, *op. cit.*, p. 95.

52. It appears that Lee was secretly consecrated "Bishop of Dorchester" at or near Venice in 1877 by a "bishop in communion with the See of Rome". See H.R.T. BRANDRETH, *Dr. Lee of Lambeth*, London, 1951. In 1901, a year before his death, Lee became a Roman Catholic.

53. Quoted in O. CHADWICK, "The Church of England and the Church of Rome from the beginning of the nineteenth century to the present day", in E.G.W. BILL (ed.), *Anglican Initiatives in Christian Unity*, London, 1967, p. 80.

54. C. BUTLER, *The Life and Times of Bishop Ullathorne 1806-1889*, vol. 1, London, 1926, p. 345.

were Roman Catholic, three hundred Eastern Orthodox, and the remainder Anglican.

The *Union* became *The Union Review* in 1863. It soon became apparent that the paper had not changed its tune or its tone. Lee and Phillipps were offending the one group of Roman Catholics whom they could least afford offending: the Ultramontanes. *The Union Review* published articles in which Old Catholics attacked, almost by name, leading Ultramontanes such as Henry Manning, Frederick Faber, and R.A. Coffin, calling them "rhapsodical Anglican parsons" who had been turned into "sentimental unmanly priests"[55].

The Association for Promoting the Unity of Christendom was condemned by Rome on September 16, 1864; and Roman Catholics were no longer allowed to be members. And before the year was out, Manning's *The Holy Spirit in the Church of England* would provide yet another set-back for relations between Roman Catholics and Anglicans and hint at things to come during his tenure at Westminster.

Before taking a closer look at Henry Manning, however, a few observations about English Liberal Catholics are in order.

If the woes of Old Catholics under Cardinal Wiseman pointed to the rise of English Ultramontanism, the struggles of English Liberal Catholics during his Westminster administration pointed to a nearly complete Ultramontane victory over the English Roman Catholic Church. A victory which would also bring a hardening of English Roman Catholic attitudes which would persist up to the Malines Conversations.

In general Liberal Catholicism contained a variety of not always easily delineated movements trying to bridge the religious, intellectual, social, and political divisions between the Church and nineteenth century society.

In England John Henry Newman, with his stresses on intellectual freedom and on the role of the laity, was perceived by Liberal Catholics as their ideal. "I want a laity, not arrogant, not rash in speech, not disputatious, but men who know their religion, who enter into it, who know just where they stand, who know what they hold, and what they do not, who know their creed so well, that they can give an account of it, who know so much of history that they can defend it. I want an intelligent, well-instructed laity... In all times the laity have been the measure of the Catholic spirit"[56].

After 1857, when Richard Simpson (1820-1876) and John Acton (1834-1902) assumed editorial responsibility for the *Rambler* (called *The Home and Foreign Review* after 1862), that paper became the organ of the English Liberal Catholic movement. From the start, English Liberal

55. CHADWICK, *op. cit.*, p. 81.
56. J.H. NEWMAN, *The Present Position of Catholics in England*, London, 1903, pp. 390-391.

Catholics had a difficult time. They had already alienated the Old Catholics by looking down on them and writing critically about their low intellectual standards. And the Ultramontanes were suspicious about the Liberal Catholic disregard for Rome as the locus of all truth. For a while in 1859, Newman was editor; and his article "On Consulting the Faithful in Matters of Doctrine", published in his second and last issue as editor, brought immediate calls for the author's condemnation. "Full of inaccuracies" and "certainly detestable" wrote George Talbot[57]. And "totally subversive of the essential authority of the Church in matters of faith", complained Bishop Brown of Newport in a letter to the Vatican[58]. In 1863 at the Congress of Malines, Montalembert gave two speeches: "A Free Church in a Free State", urging separation of Church and State; and "Liberty of Conscience", rejecting religious intolerance and persecution. Acton, writing in the *Home and Foreign Review*, found Montalembert's speeches cause for rejoicing. Cardinal Wiseman, who had been present at Malines and, according to Professor Lamy of Louvain, gave "a complete fiasco"[59] of a speech about the state of Catholicism in England, avoided criticizing Montalembert and even prevailed upon William George Ward not to attack Montalembert in the *Dublin Review*. Other Ultramontanes were less guarded. Pius IX sent Montalembert a private letter of rebuke.

In September 1863 another congress was held, this time a congress of Catholic scholars at Munich. The theme of the congress was academic freedom in relation to the teaching of the Church. Döllinger's presidential address on "The Past and Present of Catholic Theology" was hailed by Acton in the *Home and Foreign Review* as "the dawn of a new era"[60] in Catholic theology. Döllinger drew distinctions between dogma and theological elaboration, between an infallible Church and fallible Church authorities, and he called for a transformation of Catholic theology consistent with "the idea that Christianity is history, and that in order to be understood it must be studied in its development"[61]. Rome was quick to react.

A Papal Brief to the Archbishop of Munich dated December 21, 1863, but not published until March 5, 1864, condemned the notion of the independence of scholarly research from ecclesiastical authority. This "Munich Brief" stunned Acton and convinced him that he was conscience-bound to cease publication of the *Home and Foreign Review*. As Acton saw it, the Munich Brief was "an elaborate statement of

57. HOLMES, *op. cit.*, p. 114.
58. *Ibid.*, p. 114.
59. "The Diaries of L.C. Casartelli", Ushaw, March 7, 1900, in *Ushaw Magazine* 85 (1974) 36-7.
60. J. ACTON, "The Munich Congress", in D. WOODRUFF (ed.), *Essays on Church and State*, London, 1952, p. 199.
61. *Ibid.*, p. 181.

opinions and intentions on a point practically fundamental which are
incompatible with our own. I, at least, entirely reject the view here
stated. If it is accepted by the *Home and Foreign Review*, the *Review*
loses its identity and the very breath of its nostrils. If it is rejected, and
the proclamation of the Holy See defied, the *Review* cannot long escape
condemnation, and cannot any longer efficiently profess to represent
the true, authoritative Catholic opinion. In either case I think the
Review forfeits the reason of its existence. It cannot sacrifice its
traditions or surrender its representative character. There is nothing
new in the sentiments of the rescript; but the open aggressive declaration and the will to enforce obedience are in reality new. This is what
places us in flagrant contradiction with the government of the Church"[62].

In April 1864, Acton announced the end of the *Home and Foreign
Review* in an article in the *Review* titled "Conflicts with Rome". It was
indeed the swan song of English Liberal Catholicism. All that remained
was an obituary and burial. The obituary, of sorts, came in the last
chapter of Newman's *Apologia Pro Vita Sua* in which he lamented
the course of events since the Munich Brief. He criticized the Ultramontanism of William George Ward by referring to "a violent party, which
exalts opinions into dogmas, and has it principally at heart to destroy
every school of thought but its own"[63]. And he expressed his disappointment with Roman authority. "It is so ordered on high that in our
day Holy Church should present just that aspect to my countrymen
which is most consonant with their ingrained prejudices against her,
most unpromising for their conversion"[64]. Shortly thereafter, on
December 8, 1864, Pius IX began the burial of Liberal Catholicism with
his Encyclical *Quanta Cura* and the attached *Syllabus Errorum*, which
unmistakably condemned a major position of Liberal Catholicism: that
"the Roman Pontiff can and ought to reconcile himself to and come to
terms with progress, liberalism, and modern civilization"[65].

By 1870 with Vatican Council I's constitution *Pastor Aeternus*
English Liberal Catholicism was finished. There would be only one last
and brief outburst from Acton, writing in the *Times* in 1874 on the
occasion of William Gladstone's denunciation of the Vatican decrees:

"It would be well if men had never fallen into the error of suppressing truth and encouraging error for the better security of religion. Our
Church stands, and our faith should stand, not on the virtues of men,
but on the surer ground of an institution and a guidance that are

---

62. From a letter Acton wrote to Simpson on March 8, 1864, quoted in F.A. GASQUET,
Lord Acton and His Circle, London, 1906, pp. 317-318.

63. J.H. NEWMAN (ed. Wilfred Ward), *Apologia Pro Vita Sua*, London, 1931, p. 351.

64. WARD, *Life of Newman*, vol. 1, p. 14.

65. "*Romanus Pontifex potest ac debet cum progressu, cum liberalismo et cum recenti
civilitate sese reconciliare et componere*", paragraph LXXX, *Syllabus Errorum* attached to
Quanta Cura, found in *Acta Apud Sanctam Sedem*. Vol. III, Rome, 1867, p. 176.

divine. Therefore I rest unshaken in the belief that nothing which the inmost depths of history shall disclose in time can ever bring to Catholics just cause of shame or fear"[66].

5. Henry Manning
Archbishop of Westminster 1865-1892

Henry Edward Manning (1808-1892) descended from a family of merchant-bankers. As an Oxford educated Anglican priest he was a champion against rationalism and contemporary social evils. He had little direct contact with the Oxford Movement, although he did stay in touch with its leading figures. On April 6, 1851, as a reaction to the Gorham Judgment, he left Anglicanism and was received into the Roman Catholic Church at the Jesuit church on London's Farm Street. Ten months after his conversion, Cardinal Wiseman ordained him to the priesthood and Manning immediately set off for Rome's *Accademia dei Nobili Ecclesiastici*, where he remained for three years under the favorable eye of Pius IX. By 1854 Manning had received the D.D. degree from the Pope. In 1856 Wiseman appointed him inspector of schools for the Archdiocese of Westminster. In 1857 at Wiseman's instigation he founded the Oblates of St. Charles in Bayswater. And the Old Catholic families were growing uneasy about his advancement in the Roman Church, his strong support for papal temporal power, and later about the role he would play in the removal of Bishop Errington as coadjutor to Wiseman.

In April 1865, two months after Cardinal Wiseman's death, Pius IX appointed Henry Manning Archbishop of Westminster[67]. (When he heard the news, W.G. Ward had his family sing the *Te Deum*!) At Vatican I Manning would prove to be a staunch defender of papal primacy and infallibility. And at home he would be a hard worker for his three goals: a Catholic education for the young (NOT at Oxford or Cambridge as Wiseman had wanted!); rescuing Catholics from intemperance (from 1867 on he supported the great temperance movement: the United Kingdom Alliance); and improving the diocesan clergy, along lines indicated in his popular devotional book *The Eternal Priesthood* published in 1833. In 1875 he was raised to the cardinalate.

"Manning's theological views were simple and direct. Any church or communion which did not claim to be infallible automatically forfeited any authority over the consciences of its members... Catholicism was

66. Letter of Lord Acton to the Times, quoted in J.L. ALTHOLZ, *The Liberal Catholic Movement in England*, London, 1962, p. 243.
67. The names of Bishops Clifford, Errington, and Grant had been sent to Rome. Clifford and Grant later withdrew their names. Errington was obviously unacceptable to the Pope and for a few days Pius IX debated about appointing Manning, Ullathorne, or even George Talbot. See HOLMES, *op. cit.*, p. 155.

identical with 'perfect Christianity' and Ultramontanism was identical with Catholicism"[68]. During Manning's administration at Westminster, Ultramontanism came to full bloom in the English Roman Catholic Church and a new trend developed in Anglican/Roman Catholic ecumenical relations: *ignore English Roman Catholics in all such endeavors and deal directly with Rome.*

Before becoming Archbishop of Westminster, Henry Manning had already shown his lack of ecumenical sensitivity in an inflammatory attack on the Anglican Church: *The Workings of the Holy Spirit in the Church of England,* written a few months after the spring 1864 appearance of Newman's *Apologia Pro Vita Sua.* Manning declared that the Anglican Church was "the mother of all the intellectual and spiritual aberrations which now cover the face of England"[69].

Edward Pusey, about whom Pius IX had said "I compare him to a bell, which always sounds to invite the faithful to the Church, and itself always remains outside"[70], was quick to respond. In 1865 he published his *Eirenicon* which was a defense of the Anglican Church and a sincere and genuine appeal for Christian unity. "Our highest union with one another", Pusey wrote, "is an organic union with one another through union with Christ"[71]. Pusey was critical of some elements in the Roman tradition which he found unacceptable and unnecessary for Anglicans who might unite with the Roman Church: e.g. exaggerated Marian devotion, the declaration of the Immaculate Conception, and papal infallibility. He saw papal primacy as no problem; and he thought that each side could explain its fundamental dogmas to the satisfaction of the other. But he made two tactical errors: one, he attacked the *Syllabus Errorum*; the other, he misread the contemporary Roman Catholic Church.

Pusey had not taken time to read the *Syllabus Errorum* until his *Eirenicon* was in type. Then, just before publication, he attached a postscript to the *Eirenicon* in which he attacked the *Syllabus*, the influence of the Jesuits on Rome, and papal infallibility. And he asked Roman Catholics to unite with the Anglican Church against Roman distortions of the Catholic Faith[72].

---

68. HOLMES, *op. cit.,* p. 157.

69. H.E. MANNING, *The Workings of the Holy Spirit in the Church of England,* London, 1864, p. 30.

70. A comment made to Dean Stanley on a visit to Rome in 1863, quoted in VIDLER, *op. cit.,* p. 157.

71. E.B. PUSEY, *Eirenicon,* 1865, p. 46.

72. As to his misreading of the signs of the times: "Pusey was not quite able to see the contemporary Roman Catholic Church, and therefore suffered from an illusion. He was a man of books and documents and manuscripts, not a man of contemporary society. The Roman Church to which he appealed was not the Roman Church of Pius IX or of Manning, or of the looming Vatican Council. It was the Roman Church of 150 years

Pusey's first *Eirenicon* therefore was not well received by English church leaders in either tradition. (It had been well received in France by the independent-minded Archbishop of Paris, Georges Darboy (1813-1871) and other French bishops)[73]. He wrote a second *Eirenicon* in 1869 and a third in 1870. Pusey tried to submit doctrinal propositions for consideration at Vatican I but when his third *Eirenicon*, titled *Is Healthful Reunion Possible?*, reached the Rome post office it was refused and sent back to him. All later editions of the book would be re-titled *Healthful Reunion, as Conceived Possible Before the Vatican Council*. "I have done all I could", Pusey wrote to Newman on August 26, 1870, "and now have done with controversy and *Eirenica*[74].

A second major deterioration in Roman Catholic/Anglican relations during Manning's Westminster years involved unfinished business from the Wiseman tenure concerning the condemned Association for Promoting the Unity of Christendom. In April 1864, the English bishops had sent a letter to the Holy Office expressing their concerns about the Association for Promoting the Unity of Christendom. In September 1864 the Holy Office answered them in a letter, signed by Cardinal Patrizi, prohibiting Catholics from participating in what the Holy Office considered the heretical activities of the Association. Shortly after the letter was made public in England, a delegation of one hundred and ninety-eight Anglican clergy supporters of the A.P.U.C. drafted a letter to Patrizi complaining that the Holy Office had unfairly judged them. Before sending their letter to Rome, they appealed in writing to Cardinal Wiseman. He assured them that he would send their letter, with a friendly cover letter, to Cardinal Patrizi. Wiseman died before he could keep his promise. The matter ended up in the hands of Monsignor Talbot and Archbishop Manning, who had "no belief in the movement, no great trust in its advocates, no hope of its success"[75].

Talbot, after consulting with the Pope, forwarded the Anglicans' letter to Patrizi. He then asked Manning to advise him about the most

before; the Church of Bossuet and of Du Pin. Pusey appealed to a Gallican Catholicism to unite with an Anglicanism revived in its Catholic heritage. If Rome had stood still while Canterbury changed, the appeal would have met a response. But Rome had changed as much, if not more, than Canterbury. Pusey appealed in 1865 to a Gallicanism which hardly existed any longer. And therefore, to most of its recipients, the *Eirenicon* looked not like an irenicon but like a Protestant pamphlet. In appealing to them it simultaneously required them to repudiate the most powerful religious movement within their Church". CHADWICK, *op. cit.*, pp. 83-84.

73. For more detailed information about Pusey's connections with the French and with the Belgian Jesuit, Victor de Buck, see S.T.L. paper of J.P. JURICH, *The Ecumenical Relations of Victor de Buck, S.J., with Anglo-Catholic Leaders on the Eve of Vatican I*, Université Catholique de Louvain, 1970.

74. LIDDON, *op. cit.* vol. IV, p. 193.

75. E.S. PURCELL, *Life of Cardinal Manning*, vol. II, London, 1895, p. 277.

appropriate response from the Holy Office. Manning offered suggestions: *"They have been in no sense misunderstood. The Holy Office most
truly appreciated* their position and their statements. Their present
answer is proof enough. They say that they do not believe that there are
three churches *de jure*, but only *de facto*. But this denies (1) the
exclusive unity of the Catholic and Roman Church, and (2) its exclusive
infallibility, and (3) the universal duty and necessity of submission to
it"[76]. On November 8, 1865 the Holy Office sent its reply to the one
hundred and ninety-eight Anglican clergymen. And on Epiphany 1866,
Manning issued his pastoral letter on the *Reunion of Christendom*. In an
appendix to his pastoral letter, Manning included the two letters from
the Holy Office — the September 16, 1864 letter to the English bishops
and the November 8, 1865 letter to the Anglican supporters of
A.P.U.C. In the text of his pastoral, Manning summarized the letter of
November 8:
1. That the unity of the Church is absolute and indivisible, and that the
Church has never lost its unity, nor for so much as a moment of time
ever can.
2. That the Church of Christ is indefectible, not only in duration, but
in doctrine; or, in other words, that it is infallible, which is a Divine
endowment bestowed upon it by its Head, and that the infallibility of
the Church is a dogma of the faith.
3. That the primacy of the Visible Head is of Divine institution, and
was ordained to generate and to preserve the unity both of faith and of
communion, that is, both internal and external, of which the See of
Peter is the centre and the bond.
4. That therefore the Catholic and Roman Church alone has received
the name Catholic.
5. That no one can give to any other body the name of Catholic
without incurring manifest heresy.
6. That whosoever is separated from the one and only Catholic
Church, howsoever well he may believe himself to live, by the one sin of
separation from the Unity of Christ is in the state of wrath.
7. That every soul, under pain of losing eternal life, is bound to enter
the only Church of Christ, out of which is neither absolution nor
entrance into the kingdom of heaven"[77].

In 1868 Charles Lindley Wood (1893-1934) — "Lord Halifax" of the
Malines Conversations — became the second president of the English
Church Union, "the agency and theological clearing-house of the
Anglo-Catholic wing of the State Church"[78]. And in the winter of

---

76. Manning in a letter to Talbot on July 18, 1865, quoted in PURCELL, *op. cit.*, p. 281.
77. H.E. MANNING, "The Reunion of Christendom. A Pastoral Letter to the Clergy",
1866, quoted in PURCELL, *op. cit.*, p. 286.
78. NORMAN, *op. cit.*, p. 369.

1889-1890, the ecumenically-inclined Anglican Halifax met the liberal Catholic Etienne Fernand Portal (1855-1926) in Madeira. There they became friends and laid the foundations for the debates, during Cardinal Vaughan's Westminster tenure, about the validity of Anglican Orders. Halifax and Portal, reacting to an English Roman Catholic climate largely created by Cardinal Manning and re-inforced by Cardinal Vaughan "were at least partly responsible for a trend which persisted until very recent times. It may be put crudely thus: negotiate with Rome or with the Catholics of the Continent; for it is no use conversing with the English Roman Catholics"[79].

When Manning died in January of 1892, Pope Leo XIII said "a great light of the Church has gone out"[80]. Manning had established a hard line with the Anglicans and pulled the English Catholic Church into a more united Ultramontane house. "Nevertheless, by his administrative ability and social concern, through his personal relations with public figures and his sympathy for the poor, Manning gained public recognition for the Catholic Church in the life of the English nation, contributed towards reducing the 'leakage' and gave the poverty-stricken Irish immigrants greater confidence in the English hierarchy. This social concern coupled with a radical sympathy for Ireland and a romantic view of the medieval church won for Manning the respect and affection of the working classes and the left wing which was manifested so clearly at his funeral. Yet Manning was never as successful in winning the masses to the Church as he had hoped, while his successor was more concerned with ending the 'leakage' than with attracting the working classes and made no attempt to continue his policy"[81].

6. Herbert Vaughan
Archbishop of Westminster 1892-1903

Herbert Alfred Vaughan (1832-1903) descended from an Old Catholic family but was as decidedly Ultramontane as Cardinal Manning, his friend from common student days at Rome's *Accademia dei Nobili Ecclesiastici*. All of his five sisters became nuns. Five of his seven brothers became priests, among them: Roger William Vaughan (1834-1883), second Archbishop of Sydney, Australia, and Bernard John Vaughan, S.J. (1847-1922) the internationally known preacher.

Vaughan was ordained in 1854, the same year the Immaculate Conception was proclaimed, and sent by Cardinal Wiseman to be (at the age of twenty-three) Vice-President of St. Edmunds seminary in Ware. There he became entangled in the Ultramontane struggles which

79. CHADWICK, *op. cit.*, p. 88.
80. E. NORMAN, *Roman Catholicism in England*, Oxford/New York, 1985, p. 92.
81. HOLMES, *op. cit.*, p. 192.

would result in Bishop Errington's removal as coadjutor to Wiseman. In 1857 he joined the community founded by Manning, the Oblates of St. Charles. He went on a North and South American fund-raising trip in 1863 so that in 1866 he could found and establish the St. Joseph's Missionary Society at Mill Hill. As he expressed in a letter to his friend Lady Herbert of Lea, he hoped the Mill Hill Society would plant a truly *papal* and *Roman* Catholicism throughout the world. "Next our oath contains a special clause obliging each student who takes it in a particular manner to maintain the authority and to defend the rights of the Holy See wherever he may be sent. Our missionaries will go out as Roman as any Roman and as specially devoted to the Pope. It seems to me that the times and the character of England, and her position in the world make it clear that the woof must be laid upon papal warp"[82].

In 1868 Vaughan bought *The Tablet* to promote his Ultramontane views, and in 1878 he bought the *Dublin Review* for the same reason.

In 1872 through the influence of Cardinal Manning he became the second bishop of Salford. And in 1892, Archbishop of Westminster — choosing to receive the *pallium* in London rather than Rome because it was "too good a trump-card against the Anglican to throw away"[83]. Dom Francis Aidan Gasquet (1846-1929), who would play an important role representing Vaughan in the Anglican Orders controversies, preached at Vaughan's Westminster installation. Vaughan became cardinal in 1893.

Between 1894 and 1897 Cardinal Vaughan became officially involved in the debates and controversies leading to Pope Leo XIII's rather mild *Ad Anglos* (1895) and his traumatic *Apostolicae Curae* (1896). Vaughan's major concern would be Anglican Orders "which he originally regarded with amusement, then with impatience and finally with obvious dislike"[84].

The story of the Anglican Orders controversy began with the chance meeting of two men in the winter of 1889: Lord Halifax[85] (1839-1934), an English aristocrat who had become attracted to Tractarianism when a student at Oxford; and Etienne Fernand Portal (1855-1926), a young French Vincentian priest. Halifax and his wife had journeyed to Madeira with their seriously ill son, Charles, hoping that the warm climate would aid the boy's convalescence. There they met Portal, a disciple of the French reforming bishop Felix Antoine Philibert Dupan-

82. S. LESLIE (ed.), *Letters of Herbert Cardinal Vaughan to Lady Herbert of Lea*, London, 1942, p. 89.

83. *Ibid.*, p. 405.

84. HOLMES, *op. cit.*, p. 218.

85. Charles Lindley Wood (1839-1934), Second Viscount Halifax, was educated at Eton and Christ Church, Oxford where he came under the influence of E.B. Pusey, J.M. Neale, H.P. Liddon, and R.I. Wilberforce. He was a strong High Churchman, who gave up a career in politics to dedicate his life to Anglo-Catholic and ecumenical concerns. Hereafter in the dissertation he will be referred to as Lord Halifax.

loup (1802-1878), who had also come to Madeira with lung problems. Halifax and Portal were kindred spirits who became friends almost instantly. They often took long walks along Madeira's coastal *caminho novo*, enlightening each other about their respective Christian traditions and inspiring each other to work for church unity. For them Madeira was not only like a meeting on Sinai but also a "university" where the historical and theological foundations for restoration of Christian unity were examined[86]. Portal, especially, emerged from the Madeira encounter greatly transformed. He had gone to the Portuguese island convinced that reunion meant "return" and "submission" to Rome. In fact he had asked Halifax to make his submission to Rome[87] — in somewhat the same way that Cardinal Mercier would, at a turning point in the Malines Conversations, ask Halifax to make his submission. Halifax firmly refused. Gradually Portal came to realize that reunion meant not submission to Rome, as Newman had done, but *union by convergence*. Portal became convinced that although divided the churches were essentially one. A year after their meeting, Portal would write to Halifax on March 16, 1891 that Halifax had displaced his center of gravity[88]. Portal and Halifax had embarked on a "new road" leading to the nineteenth century Roman examination of Anglican Orders.

It is not our purpose here to give a detailed analysis of all the factors and events connected with *Ad Anglos* and *Apostolicae Curae*. Many eminent researchers have more than adequately explored this topic. Among them we find especially noteworthy: John Jay Hughes in *Absolutely Null and Utterly Void*, Washington, 1968; Lord Halifax in *Leo XIII and Anglican Orders*, London, 1912; Regis Ladous in *L'Abbé Portal et la campagne anglo-romaine*, Lyon, 1973; and Bruno Neveu in *Mgr Duchesne et son Mémoire sur les ordinations anglicanes* in *The Journal of Theological Studies*, October 1978, pp. 443-482. We are concerned, however, about the roles and reactions of key personalities in the debates — people whom we will again observe during the Malines Conversations — and especially the involvement of English Roman Catholics.

The original desire to focus on Anglican Orders as a way of advancing ecumenical discussions between the churches of Rome and Canterbury came from Portal. Halifax saw no need to establish the validity of Anglican Orders but was in agreement that an examination of Anglican

---

86. *"Madère ne fut pas seulement un 'Sinaï', mais une université où furent examinés les fondements historiques et théologiques d'une restauration de l'unité visible".* R. LADOUS, *L'Abbé Portal et la campagne anglo-romaine 1890-1912*, Lyon, 1973, p. 57.

87. *"Portal ne s'est pas dégagé tout de suite de ce schéma classique, et c'est bien le rôle d'un nouveau Newman qu'il a d'abord voulu faire jouer à Lord Halifax".* LADOUS, *ibid.*, p. 58.

88. *"Oui, vous avez déplacé mon centre de gravité et je penche décidément beaucoup du côté des choses anglaises".* *Ibid.*, p. 63.

Orders could be a helpful way of getting representatives of the two churches to sit down together.

As Roger Aubert points out: "There was no initial intention of keeping the English Catholics out of the discussion"[89]. Cardinal Vaughan had been approached by Halifax in July of 1893. He agreed to support requests to the Vatican to examine the archives; but felt a discussion of papal authority should precede any discussion about Anglican Orders. Halifax and Portal ignored Cardinal Vaughan's advice. "With the benefit of hindsight, a case can be made for maintaining that the reunion campaign went wrong at the start by a too early introduction of the theme of Orders"[90]. Halifax and Portal saw the Orders discussion as a means to setting up a formal dialogue aimed at corporate reunion. The Orders matter however, soon became a question and an end in itself.

In December 1893, Portal, using the pseudonym of Fernand Dalbus, wrote an article in *La Science Catholique*, titled *Les Ordinations Anglicanes*. Portal hoped his readers would read between the lines of his argument and conclude in favor of the validity of Anglican Orders and of Apostolic Succession. For him the Orders matter was *"une question de fait et non de foi"*[91]. His article, and articles to follow, certainly got people talking on both sides of the English Channel. As J.G. Lockhart observed: "The hunt was now fairly up on both sides of the Channel. Cardinal Bourret, Bishop of Rodez and Vabres, wrote to Portal criticising such of his conclusions as favored Orders, and Dr. Wordsworth, Bishop of Salisbury, such as disputed them; and both *The Guardian* in London and the *Univers* in Paris opened their columns to a learned but lively controversy"[92].

In 1894 Halifax broached the topic with Edward White Benson (1829-1896), Archbishop of Canterbury and William Dalrymple Maclagen, Archbishop of York. In August of the same year, Portal traveled to England to confer with them and to gain firsthand knowledge about the Anglican Church. Benson's son describes his father's reactions: "One of those present said the Archbishop's whole attitude was one of the greatest caution, and that he kept the conversation as general as possible, avoiding any dangerous or compromising statements... The Archbishop's view from the first seems to have been that an attempt was being made from Rome, working through the sincere and genuine enthusiasm of Lord Halifax and the Abbé Portal, to compromise the official chief of the Anglican Church"[93]. The Archbishop of York was

---

89. AUBERT, *op. cit.*, p. 216.

90. J.C.H. AVELING, D.M. LOADES, H.R. McADOO (eds.), *Rome and the Anglicans*, Berlin/New York, 1982, p. 183.

91. LADOUS, *op. cit.*, p. 80.

92. J.G. LOCKHART, *Viscount Halifax*, vol. 2, London, 1935-1936, p. 46.

93. A.C. BENSON, *The Life of Edward White Benson*, vol. 2, London, 1899, p. 593.

less reserved. "Let us hope and trust", he said "that we are at the beginning of some thing really great in the interests of the Church"[94].

Portal had also been invited to a luncheon with Cardinal Vaughan at Westminster; but failed to attend because the invitation apparently got lost in the mail. Vaughan was upset about Portal's absence and doubted that it was accidental. And twelve years after the event, Edmund Bishop (1846-1917), who had also been at the luncheon would reveal his own opinion about Portal's absence: "Lord Halifax and Portal were asked to lunch by Cardinal Vaughan; I was there, delighted with the prospect of talking to the Abbé, and perfectly ignorant of the intrigue that was afoot. Lord Halifax came; we had lunch, conversation — most friendly and interesting, but from the Abbé Portal nothing but excuses for his absence. That's how the thing is done — with all such clerics, including Mgr Duchesne"[95]. Later, Halifax would try to keep Vaughan informed, but would finally admit that it was pointless: "I say it with regret: the whole of Cardinal Vaughan's conduct, as I think the correspondence makes sufficiently clear, was unworthy of him; and it is no less painful to have to admit that what is true of Cardinal Vaughan is true in its degree of Archbishop Benson... Few men have ever had so great an opportunity offered them as the Archbishop; no man, I think, ever so completely threw it away. On Cardinal Vaughan's shoulders rests the chief responsibility for the failure of all that was attempted"[96]. And as John Jay Hughes observes: "Vaughan did not hesitate to use the information thus supplied to him to frustrate what Halifax was trying to accomplish. Both in private and in public he consistently misrepresented the motives of Halifax and Portal"[97].

Meanwhile at the Vatican in 1894, an ecumenically-inclined Leo XIII (1810-1903)[98] encouraged by Cardinal Mariano Rampolla del Tindaro (1843-1913) his Secretary of State, who had worked for an end to the Armenian schism, was entertaining hopes of an Anglican return to Rome. "I hear they are on the point of coming over", he would tell Cardinal Vaughan[99]. At Leo XIII's request, Rampolla invited Portal to Rome to confer with the Pope. Portal met with the Pope on September 12 and suggested that the Pope write a letter to the Archbishops of Canterbury and York, inviting them to work for church unity and to set up ecumenical conferences. "I shall write that letter...", Leo XIII

94. HUGHES, op. cit., p. 50.
95. Ibid., p. 51-52.
96. Viscount HALIFAX, Leo XIII and Anglican Orders, London, 1912, p. 386.
97. HUGHES, op. cit., p. 38.
98. Leo XIII had especially high hopes for the reunion of the Oriental and Slavic Churches, reflected in his encyclical Grande Munus (September 30, 1880), the Eucharistic Congress in Jerusalem (1893), and his apostolic letter Orientalium Dignitas (November 30, 1894).
99. J.G. SNEAD-COX, Life of Cardinal Vaughan, vol. 2, London, 1910, p. 177.

said, "if only reunion with the Anglicans were possible ... then I could sing my *Nunc Dimittis*"[100]. Rampolla suggested that Portal draft a letter and even suggested Belgium as a place for church reunion conferences.

On September 15, the Pope changed his mind about writing a letter to the Archbishops of Canterbury and York. Rampolla was to write a letter to Portal which Portal was to show to Halifax and discuss with the two Anglican archbishops. After a favorable response from the Archbishops of Canterbury and York, the Pope would consider writing a personal letter to them.

Portal returned to England later in September to meet with Halifax and with the Archbishop of Canterbury, who was in bad spirits and distrusting of Roman Catholics since Cardinal Vaughan, a few days earlier, had launched a major attack against the Anglican Church during a meeting of the Catholic Truth Society at Preston. There Vaughan had insisted that the only possible road to reunion was submission of individual Anglicans to the infallible Holy See. He also suggested that the Catholic revival in the Anglican Church might have been the work of Satan[101].

Archbishop Benson could not believe that Vaughan would make such statements independently of the Pope and suspected "that a plot was afoot to induce him to make the first advances to Rome and to submit the validity of Anglican Orders to the judgment of the Pope" at the very same time that "the head and representative of the Roman Catholic Church in England, Cardinal Vaughan, is officially declaring in a series of public utterances the absolute and uncompromising repudiation by the Papal See of the Orders of the Anglican Church"[102].

Early in 1895, two Anglican scholars, Thomas Alexander Lacey (1853-1931) and E. Denny published a defense of Anglican Orders *De Hierarchia Anglicana Dissertatio Apologetica*. Louis Duchesne, who had been asked by the Pope to draw up a memorandum about Anglican Orders, sent his compliments to Lacey: "The position you defend seems to me to be indisputable. I have already expressed this opinion in the *Bulletin Critique*... I can tell you that my colleague, Mgr Gasparri, has completely abandoned the opinion he expressed in his treatise on Holy Orders... Since then he has made himself acquainted with the documents as well as with your proofs. In consequence he has made it known in a useful quarter that he shared your opinion, and has given the reasons for his change of mind.

"May it please God, amid all these studies and controversies, to

100. AVELING, *op. cit.*, p. 187.
101. For the complete text see H. VAUGHAN, *The Reunion of Christendom*, London, 1894. Excerpts can be found in HALIFAX, *Leo XIII and Anglican Orders*, p. 107ff.
102. G.K.A. BELL, *Christian Unity, the Anglican Position*, London, 1948, p. 69.

point out a path which will lead us to unity, or at least bring us as close to it as possible"[103]. Gasparri, by the way, would also be an early and strong supporter for the Malines Conversations.

At the same time Portal was busy in France founding an association to promote unity by convergence and establishing the ecumenical publication *La Revue Anglo-Romaine*.

In January 1895, an alarmed Cardinal Vaughan went to Rome. He told the Pope that Portal and Halifax had misrepresented the actual situation in England; that Portal and the Pope had very different views about the nature of reunion, i.e. convergence vs. submission; and that there was no possibility of corporate reunion. He further asserted that the Pope's involvement in the Anglican question could stop the flow of individual conversions to the Roman Church. Vaughan was backed in Rome by the English historian[104] from Downside Abbey, Francis Aidan Gasquet (1846-1929), and the English/Spanish Vatican diplomat Rafael Merry del Val (1865-1930)[105]. Gasquet had little interest in Anglican affairs but was thoroughly loyal to the Pope and to Vaughan. Merry del Val's attitude toward Anglicans and their Catholic friends was hostile. He accused Portal of "poisoning of men's minds ... by preaching Liberalism in religion". And he found Gasparri "simply an emissary of Portal's, full of Portal's ideas and ... at times hardly orthodox"[106].

103. HUGHES, *op. cit.*, pp. 63-64.

104. Gasquet was neither a good theologian nor a good historian, as many commentators have pointed out. See for instance John Jay Hughes: "It is not easy to place Gasquet on the theological map. He was no theologian, and made no pretence of being one... Like his great friend and mentor Edmund Bishop, who was vastly superior to Gasquet in intellectual power and learning, Gasquet frankly despised theology". He was on friendly terms with the Anglican historian James Gairdner, "until Gairdner could no longer swallow the historical errors and falsehood with which Gasquet's books were filled, and began to point them out in print". *Absolutely Null and Utterly Void*, pp. 217 and 222.

105. When he was twenty years old, Merry del Val caught the attention of Leo XIII who made him a monsignor while still a sub-deacon and sent him on diplomatic missions around the world. He was ordained when twenty-three. At thirty-five he was an archbishop and at thirty-eight Cardinal Secretary of State. He was Machiavellian in his loyalty to the Holy See. As J.J. Hughes points out in *Absolutely Null and Utterly Void*, p. 227 "The lack of a scholarly, critical biography of Merry del Val is greatly to be deplored".

In a letter to the author of this book, dated January 20, 1985, Professor Gary Lease from the University of California, who is working on a biography of Merry del Val, explained some of the difficulties: "As you may know, there was a mysterious fire in the study of Merry del Val's private secretary, who was the executor of his papers, and all collections were destroyed... The most likely source of information, the correspondence with MdV's childhood and adult intimate Denis Sheil, has disappeared. I traced it from the Oratory in Birmingham to Father de Zulueta in London, who said he briefly passed over it before sending it on to Rome for inclusion in MdV's process for beatification (early '50's). No one in Rome seems to have heard of it, much less to have seen it. This would be a very dangerous exchange, since Merry del Val told 'all' to Sheil".

106. HOLMES, *op. cit.*, p. 221.

On April 14, 1895, Leo XIII issued a letter not to the Archbishops of
Canterbury and York but to the English people. *Ad Anglos* was in fact
written by Vaughan with a bit of rewording here and there by Gasquet,
Edmund Bishop, and Merry del Val.

In *Ad Anglos* the Pope did not as such either recognize nor address
the Anglicans and he said nothing about Anglican Orders. He did grant
an indulgence to Catholics who prayed the rosary for the conversion of
England.

In the summer of 1895 at the Diocesan Conference, Archbishop
Benson, a bit puzzled and dismayed, made reference to the papal letter.
He said that once the Roman Communion had contained the whole of
Western Christendom but proved incapable of such a responsibility.
"And now the representative of the Roman Communion had, in his
desire for reunion, spoken to the English people as if they possessed no
Church at all, apparently in total ignorance of the existence of any
Church with any history or claims"[107]. He did not question the Pope's
kindness or sincerity but found his plea for unity terribly inadequate.
Another prominent Anglican's reactions were more positive.

In May 1896, former British Prime Minister William Ewart Gladstone (1809-1897) stirred up a bit of controversy by offering his
personal reactions: He found it "improbable" that a wise Pope would
set something in motion which would only widen the breach between
Canterbury and Rome and that certainly "wisdom and charity" would
prevent any investigations of the Curia from becoming "an occasion
and a means of embittering religious controversy"[108].

Gladstone truly felt optimistic about the Pope, but had no such
feelings about Cardinal Vaughan. He wrote Halifax that he was convinced
that Vaughan and "his band" would adopt "any means of defeating the
Pope in his present purpose"[109].

Unknown to Gladstone, and even to Halifax, Merry del Val was
winning over Leo XIII to his side and thwarting the influence of
Cardinal Rampolla. From now on Merry del Val, not Rampolla, would
be the Pope's advisor on matters English. On July 29, 1895, Merry del
Val wrote to Gasquet: that he hoped "the plan of action" would work
out but that he had anxious moments due to "the misleading actions of
those who are quite strangers to the whole question and to the situation
in England"[110]. Nearly a month later, on August 20, 1895, Merry del
Val could send an optimistic note to Gasquet: he was leaving for
England and wanted to see Gasquet because things had taken "a more

107. BENSON, *op. cit.*, pp. 618-619.
108. B. PAWLEY and M. PAWLEY, *Rome and Canterbury Through Four Centuries*,
London, 1974, p. 248.
109. HALIFAX, *Leo XIII and Anglican Orders*, p. 305.
110. Downside Abbey, Gasquet Papers, 942, Merry del Val to Gasquet, July 29, 1895.

favorable turn". Merry del Val's most recent meeting with the Pope had been very satisfactory. The Pope was in complete agreement with Gasquet and though there were still some dangers Merry del Val was convinced that he and Gasquet were "pretty sure now by hook or by crook of getting the questions properly sifted"[111].

On June 29, 1896, Leo XIII issued *Satis Cognitum*, an encyclical on Christian unity, which insisted that the only basis for the reunion of Christendom was recognition of the Pope as the sole source of jurisdiction in the Church and the necessary center of unity.

On September 13, 1896, Leo issued *Apostolicae Curae*, the bull which declared Anglican Orders "null and void"[112]. Aubert summarizes what had happened: "Anxious to sabotage the conversations between Catholic and Anglican experts envisaged by Halifax and Portal — conversations in which French experts would presumably have played a leading part — Vaughan prevailed on Leo XIII to revoke the question to Rome"[113]. Under the ultra conservative Cardinal Camillo Mazzella (1833-1900) a commission of inquiry was set up to investigate the historical, legal, and theological aspects of Anglican Orders. On Cardinal Rampolla's advice, the commission was given a balanced membership: four members in favor of validity or at least doubtful validity — A.M. de Augustinis, L. Duchesne, P. Gasparri, and T.B. Scannell; and four members opposed to validity D. Fleming, A. Gasquet, C. Llevaneras, and J. Moyes. (The president of the commission, Mazzella, and the secretary of the commission, Merry del Val, were also opposed to validity.) At Cardinal Vaughan's insistence, all eight were Catholic. Gasparri was allowed to confer in private with two Anglican theologians, T.A. Lacey and F.W. Puller, who had gone to Rome with official backing but no official mandate from the Archbishop of Canterbury.

Between March 24, 1896 and May 7, 1896, the commission met twelve times, spending a lot of time on a submission drawn up by Vaughan's three delegates (Fleming, Gasquet, and Moyes). The omissions and errors of this document have been carefully exposed by J.J. Hughes in *Absolutely Null and Utterly Void*. Needless to say, the document did not convert the members favoring validity. Merry del Val reported only four votes favoring nullity and the remaining four divided equally between validity and doubtful validity[114]. The commis-

---

111. *Ibid.*

112. *"Itaque omnibus Pontificum Decessorum in hac ipsa causa decretis usgueguague assentientes, eaque plenissime confirmantes ac veluti renovantes auctoritate Nostra, motu proprio certia scientia; pronunciamus et declaramus, Ordinationes ritu anglicano actas, irritas prorsus fuisse et esse, omniquoque nullas".* Apostolicae Curae, published by *The American Ecclesiastical Review*, New York, 1897, pp. 32-33.

113. AUBERT, *op. cit.*, pp. 218.

114. See B. NEVEU, "Mgr Duchesne et son Mémoire sur les ordinations anglicanes", in *Journal of Theological Studies* 29 (October 1978) pp. 443-482.

sion of course was only consultative and the final decision rested with
the Holy Office, but "Dom Gasquet and Canon Moyes, whose attitude
throughout the affair had been polemical rather than scholarly, were
preparing the ground for a condemnation, ably abbetted by ... R. Merry
del Val"[115]. The final decision of the Holy Office came in July, during a
two hour meeting in the presence of the Pope — and in Rampolla's
absence! The cardinals unanimously agreed that the question of Anglican
Orders had long since been settled in the negative sense. They could not
reverse an earlier decision. Portal was ordered to stop meddling in
English affairs. A few weeks later, September 13, 1896, came the bull
Apostolicae Curae, drafted by an exultant Merry del Val in consultation
with Gasquet. Later in this book, we will see, based on evidence in
various English archives, that Merry del Val and Gasquet would also
play major roles in stopping the Malines Conversations and closing the
Vatican damper on ecumenism.

Archbishop Benson was in Ireland when *Apostolicae Curae* came out
and he made brief reference to it in a speech in Dublin, commemorating
the restoration of the Cathedral of Kildare: "This very day the papers
tell us of another new defiance of history on the part of that great
Church, a new defiance of history which is perfectly in accord with all
we knew of Rome before ... a lesson of the greatest possible value to
those who have been led in quiet years to believe that the Church of
Rome has become other than it was"[116]. In October he returned from
Ireland and began working on an official reply but died before it was
completed.

The Lambeth Conference of 1897, meeting a few months later under
the presidency of Archbishop Frederick Temple (1821-1902) issued a
statement of regret that under present conditions it was impossible to
consider reunion with the Church of Rome. How different things would
be in 1920 when the Lambeth Conference would invite Rome to the
discussion table!

Cardinal Vaughan's official reaction to *Apostolicae Curae* came in an
address at the Catholic Conference of Hanley on September 28, 1896. It
clearly summed up his ecumenical career: "Reunion", he said, "means
submission to the Divine Teacher. When men have found the Divine
Teacher and determined, at whatever cost, to submit to Him, there will
be Reunion... The question of Anglican Orders, therefore, was never in
it... How can they any longer trust in a sacramental system which is
condemned as null and void by the Catholic Church? How shocking to
adore as Very God elements that are but bread and wine, and to bend
down after auricular Confession in order to receive a mere human and
useless Absolution...! Tarry not for Corporate Reunion; it is a dream,

---

115. AUBERT, *op. cit.*, p. 219.
116. BENSON, *op. cit.*, pp. 622-623.

and a snare of the evil one... The individual may no more wait for Corporate Reunion with the true Church than he may wait for Corporate Conversion from a grievous sin"[117].

Cardinal Vaughan's *Tablet* had shared his triumph shortly before the publication of the bull by proclaiming that the Anglican Church "a sect in manifest heresy and schism and as such as hateful as the contradictions of Korah, Dathan, and Abiram"[118].

In this chapter we have intentionally focused on Cardinal Vaughan's Roman Catholic/Anglican relations. In this sense, our look at Cardinal Vaughan has been a bit one-sided. Out of fairness, one must also acknowledge that in many other respects, Vaughan brought growth and vitality to his Church. He was a skilled administrator, "whose stamp upon the English Catholic Church could be discerned for more than half a century"[119]. Even his funeral would be a sign of his triumphant energy.

When he had become Archbishop of Westminster in 1892, Vaughan announced that one of his major projects would be the building of Westminster Cathedral. He laid the foundation stone in 1895. Westminster Cathedral opened in 1903 for his *requiem*.

117. H. VAUGHAN, *Leo XIII and the Reunion of Christendom*, London, 1897, pp. 15, 16, and 22.
118. PAWLEY, *op. cit.*, pp. 251-252.
119. NORMAN, *op. cit.*, p. 92.

THE FIRST MALINES CONVERSATION
AND EARLY TWENTIETH CENTURY DEVELOPMENTS
PRIOR TO IT

In the first chapter, we called attention to the growth and development of the English Roman Catholic Church under the first three
Archbishops of Westminster. For the remainder of the book, we focus
on events occurring during the tenure of the fourth Archbishop of
Westminster: Francis Bourne (1861-1935).

For nearly thirty-two years (September 11, 1903 - January 1, 1935)
Bourne was Archbishop of Westminster. During that time he witnessed
and experienced: the policies of three very different papal administra-
tions [Pius X (1903-1914), Benedict XV (1914-1922), and Pius XI (1922-
1939)]; the condemnation of Modernism (1907); the condemnation of
Abbé Portal (1908); the publication of Lord Halifax's *Leo XIII And
Anglican Orders* (1912); World War I (1914-1918) and Désiré Joseph
Mercier's rise to international fame as a hero of the Belgian resistance;
the expansion of the ecumenical spirit within the Anglican Church,
given concrete expression in the Lambeth Conference of 1920; the
Malines Conversations; and the Vatican warning about Roman Catholic
participation in ecumenical conferences — *Mortalium Animos* (1928).

In this second chapter, our particular concerns are Cardinal Bourne's
theological stance, the condemnation of Modernism and its implications for the Malines Conversations, the pre-Malines activities of
Halifax and Portal, the Lambeth Conference of 1920, and the First
Malines Conversation.

1. *Cardinal Bourne's Theological Stance*

Francis Bourne, the son of a convert post office clerk, was born in
1861 — the same year *l'Osservatore Romano* was founded. He was
educated in England at Ushaw; St. Edmunds, Ware; and Hammer-
smith; and on the continent at Saint-Sulpice, Paris; and Louvain[1].

---

1. Bourne spent about six months in Louvain. He wrote briefly about his time there in
his autobiographical notes of 1917: "My mother had returned to London in 1883, and I
spent that year's vacation there and in visits to friends. In October, by desire of Bishop
Coffin, I went to Louvain (*Collège du St. Esprit*) and there I met Mgr Mercier. My health
was not very good at Louvain and I suffered much from neuralgia. I therefore had to
return to England at Easter 1884". E. OLDMEADOW, *Francis Cardinal Bourne*. vol 1,
London, 1940, p. 98.

Before becoming Archbishop of Westminster, Bourne had been rector of the house of studies at Henfield Place, Sussex; rector of the diocesan seminary at Wonersh; and Bishop of Southwark.

In September 1903, a month after the new Pope's election, Pius X appointed Francis Bourne Archbishop of Westminster. He had been a dark horse candidate, and there was more than a little controversy about his appointment[2]. Vaughan's successor at Westminster was more of an administrator than a scholar. He greatly venerated the English Martyrs, but was "neither especially conservative nor especially progressive"[3]. For the Catholic Church in England he sought a strengthening and expansion of structures (he was a great builder of churches and schools), greater recognition of Catholics in English national life, and increased Roman Catholic membership through conversions from Anglicanism. He was known for his "marmoreal shyness"[4] though Evelyn Waugh's comment that he was "singularly disqualified from normal social intercourse"[5] was a bit too harsh. Francis Bourne's broad education, his fondness for French theology, and his practical temperament gave him a more open theological outlook than that of Vaughan or Manning. A careful examination of Bourne's papers, as we shall see, also reveals that he was much more positive about Anglican relations than either Lord Halifax or l'Abbé Portal believed or Ernest Oldmeadow, editor of the The Tablet and Bourne's chief biographer, lead people to believe[6]. Assessments of Bourne, similar to those of Gordon Wheeler in The English Catholics, 1850 to 1950: "With regard to Anglicanism, his attitude was much the same as that of his predecessors, and later on, in the 'Malines Conversations', he found himself in almost the identical position of Cardinal Vaughan at the time of Apostolicae Curae", or of Edward Norman in Roman Catholicism in England: "Bourne was basically hostile"[7], are distortions of the truth. In some respects Ernest Oldmeadow may have been, but Cardinal Bourne certainly was not a re-incarnation of Cardinal Vaughan.

Appointed to the same titular see as Wiseman, St. Pudenziana, Bourne was created a cardinal on November 27, 1911. Rumor had it that the delay in getting his red hat had been due to the involvement of the Papal Secretary of State, Cardinal Merry del Val, who criticized

2. For background about Bourne's election as Archbishop of Westminster see: S.LESLIE, Cardinal Gasquet. A Memoir, London, 1953, p. 80.

3. E. NORMAN, Roman Catholicism in England, Oxford, New York, 1985, p. 80.

4. D. MATHEW, Catholicism in England, London, 1938, p. 241.

5. NORMAN, op. cit., p. 109.

6. See for instance: R. AUBERT, "Cardinal Mercier, Cardinal Bourne, and the Malines Conversations", in One In Christ, 4 (1968) 372 379; and R. LAHEY, "Cardinal Bourne and the Malines Conversations", in A. HASTINGS, ed. Bishops and Writers, Wheathampstead, 1977, pp. 81-106.

7. G.A. BECK (ed.), The English Catholics 1850 to 1950, London, 1950, p. 175, and NORMAN, op. cit., p. 127.

Bourne's lack of firmness in dealing with Modernism at Wonersh Seminary and elsewhere[8]. Bourne, for instance, had refused to bow to requests that he silence Wilfrid Ward when Ward supported Modernistic ideas in the pages of his *Dublin Review*. And apparently as late as 1909, Bishop Peter Amigo (1864-1949) from Southwark had written a letter to Rome complaining about Bourne's dallying with Modernism[9].

Bourne was hardly a Modernist. He had simply, though temporarily, been caught in the web of fear, anxiety, and suspicion which characterized the era of Modernism in the Roman Catholic Church — "a campaign of denunciation which grew in volume as it proceeded and poisoned the whole atmosphere during the last years of Pius X's pontificate"[10].

2. *The Rise and Fall of Modernism and Its Implications for the Malines Conversations*

Modernism generally refers to a list of sixty-five errors condemned by Pius X in 1907 in his decree *Lamentabili Sane Exitu* and his encyclical *Pascendi Dominici Gregis*. These condemnations were enforced by practical follow-up measures: the appointment of vigilance committees in every diocese and, in 1910, the imposition of an anti-modernist oath on clerics and professors. These led to an anti-Modernism reign of terror, what Meriol Trevor has called "the Vatican's Stalinist era"[11]. It ended with the outbreak of the First World War and the election of Benedict XV.

The Modernists were not part of an organized body but were "a number of individual Roman Catholics, who in one way or another came to realize that the received teaching was out of harmony with contemporary thought, and who decided to do what they could to promote a reform of the Church's teaching"[12].

The most important Modernists were George Tyrrell (1861-1909),

---

8. "Merry del Val ... always criticized the 'spirit of liberalism and revolt' which he considered to be prevalent in England. As a result, Merry del Val made further unhappy interventions in English affairs, especially in the case of what later came to be known as the Modernist crisis. Thus, Father Denis Sheil of the Birmingham Oratory, found it necessary to deny any responsibility for the report that Archbishop Francis Bourne would never be made a cardinal while Pius X was alive; a report which apparently resulted from the fact that Vaughan's successor at Wetsminster was suspected of having been associated with 'Modernists'". J.D. HOLMES, "Cardinal Merry del Val An Uncompromising Ultramontane: Gleanings from his Correspondence with England", in *The Catholic Historical Review* 60 (1974) 58-59.

9. See G. LEASE, "Merry del Val and Tyrrell: A Modernist Struggle", in *The Downside Review*, n° 347 (April 1984) 133-156, esp. 150-152.

10. R. AUBERT, *The Church In A Secularized Society*, New York, Toronto, London, 1978, p. 200.

11. *Ibid.*, p. 202.

12. A.R. VIDLER, *The Modernist Movement in the Roman Church*, Cambridge, 1934, p. 8.

Baron Friedrich von Hügel (1852-1925), and Maude Petre (1863-1942) in England; Alfred Loisy (1857-1940) and Edouard Le Roy (1870-1954) in France; and Antonio Fogazzaro (1842-1911) and Ernesto Buonaiuti (1881-1946) in Italy.

In some respects the goals of the Modernists were similar to the goals of nineteenth century Liberal Catholics, especially those of Döllinger in Germany and Acton and Simpson in England. The Modernists, however, tended to be more philosophical and speculative. "They had first been struck by the incompatibility between many traditional tenets of Catholicism and the findings of modern scholarship, and they had felt bound to use scientific and historico-critical methods of study and to follow the argument wherever it led"[13].

Between 1890 and 1900, Alfred Loisy, inspired by the critical historical method of Louis Duchesne his instructor at the *Institut Catholique* in Paris, began to take a critical historical look at the Old and New Testaments. In 1900 he published an article critical of Leo XIII's 1893 encyclical *Providentissimus Deus*. Shortly thereafter he published two books which stirred up considerable controversy: *L'Évangile et l'Église* in 1902 and *Autour d'un petit livre* in 1903. *L'Évangile et l'Église* "more than any single event precipitated the Modernist Crisis"[14].

In the late summer of 1903, the newly elected Pius X appointed Raphael Merry del Val, "*il mio* Merry"[15], his Secretary of State. It soon became obvious that "Merry del Val was conducting the new pontificate with a new broom. The broom was turned on Modernists..."[16].

In 1904 George Tyrrell, Jesuit, convert from Anglicanism, and popular London preacher, publicly defended Alfred Loisy and condemned "the current theological conception of ecclesiastical jurisdiction as a criterion of historical and philosophical truth" and "the present theological domination which parasitically grips and strangles the Church, as ivy does the oak"[17].

Over the next three years, Tyrrell continued his assaults on the institutional Church. In February 1906 he was dismissed from the Jesuits. At this point, Mercier wrote to Rome. "We know that he sent a letter to Cardinal Merry del Val, Secretary of State on 11th of June 1906, asking him to speak to the Pope about Tyrrell's case and to insist for a quick regularization. However, since the secularization of religious

13. A.R. VIDLER, *The Church in an Age of Revolution*, Harmondsworth, 1981 (first published 1961), p. 180.

14. *Ibid.*, p. 184.

15. F.A. FORBES, *Rafael, Cardinal Merry del Val*, London, New York, Toronto, 1932, p. 92.

16. LESLIE, *op. cit.*, p. 90.

17. G. LEASE, "Merry del Val and Tyrrell", p. 138.

pertains to the Congregation of Bishops and Religious, the letter was forwarded to Cardinal Ferrata. Ferrata answered on the 18th of June. He empowered Mercier to receive Fr. Tyrrell into his diocese and to grant him permission to celebrate Mass 'on the condition however that the same (Tyrrell) pledge himself formally neither to publish anything on religious questions nor to hold epistolary correspondence without the previous approbation of a competent person appointed by Your Eminence'"[18]. Tyrrell, "who essentially was not very keen on Mercier's intervention"[19], would not agree to these conditions and therefore never went to Malines. After the condemnation of Modernism, relations between Tyrrell and Mercier were strained; and in 1908 in his lenten pastoral, Mercier warned about the dangers of Modernism and mentioned Tyrrell by name as a man profoundly imbued with the spirit of Modernism[20].

It was also in 1906 that Pius X issued a letter, *Piene l'animo*, warning of insubordination among the Italian clergy, and Fogazzaro's *Il Santo* and Lucien Laberthonnière's (1860-1932) *Essais de philosophie religieuse* and *Réalisme chrétien et l'idéalisme grec* were put on the Index. Later that same year, Tyrrell published a more systematic development of the ideas he had introduced in his original essay on Loisy, calling for a clear distinction between God's revelation and the Church as an authoritative (and not always reliable) institution. An angry Pius X reacted strongly during a consistory in April 1907. "He breathed fire and brimstone against those individuals who challenged his authority"[21]. On July 4, he issued *Lamentabili* and on September 8, *Pascendi*.

On September 30 and October 1, 1907, Tyrrell reacted by publicly attacking *Pascendi* in the *Times*. On October 10, an article he had written in 1904 — *Beati Excommunicati* — appeared in a major French journal, *La Grande Revue*, titled "*L'excommunication salutaire*"[22]. In this article Tyrrell asserted that "If every injury borne for conscience's sake is in the highest degree spiritually fruitful to the sufferer, this, the extremist of injuries, must, if rightly endured, bring with it an abundance of graces beyond all that in ordinary course would have

18. R. BOUDENS, "George Tyrrell and Cardinal Mercier. A Contribution to the History of Modernism", in *Église et Théologie* 1 (1970), p. 319.

19. R. BOUDENS, "Tyrrell's *Beati Excommunicati*", in *Bijdragen* 34 (1973), p. 295.

20. "*L'observateur le plus pénétrant du mouvement moderniste contemporain, le plus attentif à ses tendances, celui qui en a le mieux dégagé l'esprit et qui en est, peut-être, le plus profondément imbu, est le prêtre anglais Tyrrell*". G. TYRRELL, *Medievalism A Reply to Cardinal Mercier*, London, 1908, p. 197. (Tyrrell wrote this book as his reply to Mercier's mentioning his name in the cardinal's lenten pastoral of 1908. The book also contains French and English versions of the pastoral.)

21. LEASE, *op. cit.*, p. 141.

22. R. Boudens has published, for the first time, the original English manuscript of *Beati Excommunicati*. See R. BOUDENS, "Tyrrell's *Beati Excommunicati*", in *Bijdragen* 34 (1973) 293-305.

derived to him from the sacraments and ministrations of the Church"[23]. A furious Merry del Val wrote to Bourne on October 17 asking him if he had seen this "shocking and heretical"[24] article. Canon James Moyes, whom we saw earlier in the Anglican Orders controversies, wrote a long article in *The Tablet* attacking Tyrrell's condemnation of *Pascendi* in the *Times*. Finally on October 22, 1907, Tyrrell received a letter from Bishop Peter Amigo informing him of his excommunication and of the reservation to Rome of the lifting of the ban[25]. His excommunication, as Gary Lease found in his examination of "rediscovered" letters in the Southwark Archdiocesan Archives, was clearly the work of Merry del Val, who "could be appealed to almost limitlessly on such matters which affected loyalty to the Pope ... and which could be linked to the cause of Modernism"[26]. We will see that in coming years Merry del Val's "lynx-eyed"[27] surveillance for signs of Modernism would also play a significant role in undermining the Malines Conversations. He would always suspect Portal and Mercier of Modernistic tendencies; and he would fear that any union with the Anglican Church would bring Anglican Modernists into the Church of Rome.

Archbishop Bourne was not as alarmed about English Modernism as the papal Secretary of State. On December 7, 1907, Bourne could write to Merry del Val that the Modernist movement was a very small thing in England and that with Tyrrell's excommunication it had been destroyed[28]. Tyrrell's friend, Maude Petre[29], was denied the sacraments in her diocese but never excommunicated by name. Tyrrell died in 1909. Loisy was excommunicated in 1908. Buonaiuti was excommunicated in 1926. Le Roy and Von Hügel were never excommunicated. Le Roy's *Dogme et Critique*, however, was put on the Index in 1907.

Though Modernism was officially condemned in 1907 and the oath against Modernism imposed in 1910, the peak of anti-Modernist frenzy did not arrive until the years 1912-1913, due to the secretive tactics of the Integrists[30] and the *Sodalitium Pianum*.

---

23. *Ibid.*, p. 299.
24. AAW, Cardinal Bourne's papers, Tyrrell, Merry del Val to Bourne, October 17, 1907.
25. For a detailed treatment of Cardinal Merry del Val's involvement in the condemnation of George Tyrrell, see G. LEASE, "Merry del Val and Tyrrell", p. 146.
26. *Ibid.*, pp. 152-153.
27. LESLIE, *op. cit.*, p. 58.
28. AAW, Cardinal Bourne's papers, Tyrrell, Bourne to Merry del Val, December 7, 1907.
29. "Miss Petre had been for ten years the Provincial of the Daughters of Mary. She left with honour ... J.J. Heaney quotes a judgment on her by von Hügel that seems to sum her up best: 'A loving woman's heart appears there with much of a man's head, and the combination is as rare as it is beautiful'". R. BOUDENS, "George Tyrrell and Cardinal Mercier" (cf. *supra*, n. 18), p. 315.
30. Throughout this dissertation the term used will be "Integrists", the term favored

Inspired by Pius X's call in 1907 for diocesan vigilance committees, an Italian priest and publicist attached to the Vatican Secretariat of State, Umberto Benigni (1862-1934)[31] founded in 1909 a secret international anti-Modernist network: *Sodalitium Pianum* — the Sodality of St. Pius V, or *Sapinière* as it was also known — to implement condemnations against Modernism. It was indeed a kind of Vatican secrete police. And — thanks to the meticulous historical research of Emile Poulat in his *Intégrisme et catholicisme intégral* (Paris, 1969) — we now know for certain that *Sapinière* was subsidized by Pius X and that he knew about and approved of the activities of Benigni who gave him daily reports. *Sapinière*'s members were known as the Integrists.

"Devout and loyal Catholics in several countries were forced to endure an integrist witch hunt which was at least tolerated by the highest Roman authorities including the Pope and the Secretary of State... Members used codes and aliases — the Pope was 'Lady Micheline' or 'Michel' and Merry del Val 'Miss Romey' or 'George' — as they passed information and established contacts"[32]. Among those denounced by *Sapinière* and whose names would appear again in connection with the Malines Conversations were: Batiffol, Beauduin, Gasparri, Mercier, Rampolla, Portal, and della Chiesa. As R. Boudens observes, Mercier was indeed considered untrustworthy by the Integrists. On a list of cardinals drawn up by Integrists, one finds next to his name

---

by E. Poulat, R. Aubert, A.R. Vidler, and others. Some historians, however, use the term "Integralists", e.g., J.D. Holmes, J.J. Heaney, and G.J. O'Brien.

31. From 1906 to 1911 Benigni worked as an undersecretary in the press office of the papal Secretariat of State. There he collaborated with Cardinal Merry del Val, although the two men were not always in complete agreement. After leaving the Secretariat of State in 1911, he devoted himself completely to the Sodalitium Pianum until its dissolution by Benedict XV in 1921. After 1921, he worked on behalf of the Action Française. See AUBERT, *op. cit.*, p. 201.

See also A. HASLER, *How the Pope Became Infallible*, New York, 1981, pp. 252-253: "Thus Pius X not only helped pay for a system of informers and accusers, he also gave his blessing to covert methods, including espionage. Since the faith of the Church was threatened, all such means seemed justified. 'Pius X', Cardinal Pietro Gasparri noted for the record at the pope's canonization proceedings, 'approved, blessed, and encouraged a secret organization of spies inside and outside the hierarchy. This organization', Gasparri continued, 'spied on members of the hierarchy, even cardinals. In so doing, the pope was, in essence, approving, blessing, and encouraging a sort of Freemason lodge in the Church, something unheard of in the history of the Church. I am not the only one who felt that this was a grave matter. Cardinal Mercier (he was on the list of suspected persons who were to be kept under surveillance) thought so too'. ... During World War I, papers carried by an important member of the Benigni organization, the Belgian lawyer Alphonse Jonckx, were seized by the Germans and later made public. They incriminated Benigni so badly that his group could no longer justify its existence".

32. J.D. HOLMES and B.W. BICKERS, *A Short History of the Catholic Church*, New York, 1984, p. 256.

the phrase: "suspicious, known to be connected with all the traitors of the Church"[33].

Pius X died on August 20, 1914. Giacomo della Chiesa (1854-1922) was elected Benedict XV on September 3, 1914. One of his first acts — a bit of papal revenge — was to order Merry del Val to move out of his Vatican apartment[34]. Later that month he found an unopened letter to his predecessor, Pius X, which was a denunciation of himself as a Modernist, and he at once dispensed with Benigni's services[35]. Cardinal Domenico Ferrata (1847-1914) — who had also been denounced by the Integrists — became the new Secretary of State. Within two weeks, he had died and was replaced by Pietro Gasparri (1852-1934). On November 1, 1914, Benedict XV issued his first encyclical *Ad Beatissimi Apostolorum* which pleaded for an end to the witch hunts which had characterized the Integrists. The *Sodalitium Pianum* disbanded for a while but then renewed its activities. It was suppressed by the Holy See in 1921. Some of the Integrists, like Benigni, joined the ultra conservative political and religious league the *Action Française*. Others went underground. Some would resurface in the mid 1920's to plague the Malines Conversations. And in 1928, *Mortalium Animos* would be seen, at least in part, as a concession to Vatican Integrists.

3. *Abbé Portal and Lord Halifax:*
Between Apostolicae Curae *and the Malines Conversations*

"The unfortunate Abbé has at last been shut up...", proclaimed Merry del Val on September 10, 1896 at a "happy and exciting" dinner party at Gasquet's house in London celebrating the Anglican Orders decision that would be made public in a few days[36].

Merry del Val was mistaken. Immediately after *Apostolicae Curae*, l'Abbé Portal went through a series of quick disciplinary ups and

33. "*Mercier werd door de integristen trouwens als onbetrouwbaar beschouwd. Op een uit integristische bron stammende lijst van kardinalen staat naast zijn naam: 'louche, connu comme lié avec tous les traitres de l'Église*'". BOUDENS, *op. cit.*, p. 268.

34. "When Merry del Val became Pius X's Secretary of State in 1903 he fired della Chiesa from his post at the Secretariat of State, and ordered him to vacate his apartment at the Vatican. The Pope named him Archbishop of Bologna in 1907, but Merry del Val steadfastly refused to place della Chiesa's name on the list of candidates for cardinal's hats. Only three months before his death Pius X personally added della Chiesa's name to the list of creations at the consistory of May 1914... By the end of the summer Pius X was dead and della Chiesa had the satisfaction of murmuring that the stone which the builders had rejected had been made the headstone of the corner: and more practically asked Merry to vacate his rooms in the Vatican in the same terms which Merry had once served on him. 'We forgive but we cannot forget', said Benedict XV". J.J. HUGHES, *Absolutely Null and Utterly Void*, Washington, 1968, p. 224, note 50.

35. HOLMES and BICKERS, *op. cit.*, p. 256.

36. LESLIE, *op. cit.*, p. 70.

downs — all came from Rome. There were condemnations (via Merry del Val) and removal of condemnations (via Rampolla)[37]. Throughout, he showed tremendous stamina. He could keep silent for a while but he would never "shut up". On December 29, 1896, for instance, Portal wrote to Halifax: "More and more I believe that the movement has not been strangled. It has suffered a shock; but the stone has been thrown. The situation demands silence for the moment; but before long we will begin again more strongly"[38].

In the middle of June 1897, he learned that the Vatican was lifting disciplinary measures against him and that he had been nominated Superior of the *Grand Séminaire* in Nice. He had some concerns about accepting the position. On July 19 a letter from Rampolla would help him make up his mind. Rampolla assured him that the pope deplored the difficulties and hoped Portal would accept the position[39].

In August a joyful Portal headed for Nice, hoping that it would be another Madeira. "You will see my dear friend", he wrote Halifax on August 12, "and I am convinced that God will give us the grace to start again and, very simply, we will start again"[40].

Between 1897 and 1899, Nice became a gathering point for ecumeni-cally-inclined people from England and the Continent and Portal sent regular reports to Rampolla to keep him abreast of developments within Anglicanism, within the French Church, and within the English Roman Catholic Church. In August 1899 a new appointment for Portal. He returned to Paris to take charge of the new *Séminaire Universitaire Saint-Vincent-de-Paul*. Rampolla sent the Pope's blessings and his *"félicitations personnelles"*[41].

Portal was burning again with the ecumenical fire. He now focused attention on the Orthodox Church, as he wrote to Halifax: "It is still my conviction that I will only be able to get into England by way of Russia"[42]. He also began thinking in terms of world Christian unity.

At the end of August 1900, Portal went to Rome with the idea of

37. R. LADOUS, *L'Abbé Portal et la campagne anglo-romaine 1890-1912*, Lyon, 1973, pp. 393ff.

38. *"Je crois de plus en plus que le mouvement n'est pas étranglé. Il a subi un rude choc, mais la pierre est lancée… Le silence pour le moment, la situation le demande, mais un peu plus tard, nous commencerons de nouveau et de plus fort"*. *Ibid.*, p. 375.

39. *"Sa Sainteté déplore les difficultés qui ont surgi pour vous à cause d'une publicité qui n'était pas dans ses intentions. C'est pourquoi il vous encourage et ne voit pas d'inconvénient à ce que vous acceptiez la charge à laquelle la confiance de vos Supérieurs vous destine. Heureux de vous transmettre aussi la bénédiction de l'Auguste Pontife…"* *Ibid.*, p. 407.

40. *"Vous y viendrez, mon cher ami, et je suis convaincu que le Bon Dieu nous fera la grâce de nous permettre de recommencer, et nous recommencerons tout simplement"*. *Ibid.*, p. 408

41. *Ibid.*, p. 415.

42. *"Ma conviction est toujours que je ne puis rentrer en Angleterre que par la Russie"*. *Ibid.*, p. 416.

proposing to the Pope that the Vincentians be charged to found and promote throughout the whole world an association to work for the unity of all Churches. Rampolla was sympathetic but uneasy. The climate at the Vatican was not good for such a proposal[43]. The last thing the ninety year old Pope wanted to hear was another grand idea. Modernism was brewing, e.g. Loisy at the *Institut Catholique*. Across the Atlantic, Americanism "the phantom heresy"[44] was supposedly still rampant. Lord Halifax was trying to get John Ireland (1838-1918), Archbishop of St. Paul, and other American bishops involved in the Anglican/Roman Catholic dialogue[45]. Rampolla and Ferrata were pulling the Pope in one direction; Merry del Val and Gasquet in the opposite. When Portal asked for an audience, Leo XIII refused to see him.

Portal went into depression. He remained silent until December when he shared his sorrow with his community. It was a sad narration. His sufferings penetrated to the marrow of his bones. Rome lived in an artificial world... There was good will and faith; but nothing had been learned from history[46].

Leo XIII had refused to meet with Portal in 1900 yet he did not want to cut his ties with England. In 1902 he received King Edward VII in audience. And it was during this royal visit that, much to the delight of Merry del Val, Rampolla showed his lack of understanding of some things English: Rampolla and Merry del Val had gotten into an argument about a point of protocol and an angry Rampolla stayed away from the papal audience, inviting the King to meet with him at the Irish College[47]! On June 5, 1903 Halifax went to Rome to meet with Leo XIII. He was warmly received; and when Halifax asked the Pope about reunion, he replied that it was his dream – something he very much wanted[48]. On July 20, Leo XIII died.

43. *Ibid.*, p. 419.

44. A.R. VIDLER, *The Church In An Age of Revolution*, Harmondworth, 1981 (first published 1961), p. 244.

45. The Vatican reacted with alarm at Ireland's sermon to a Catholic Congress in 1889: "We should live in our age, know it, be in touch with it... It will not do to understand the thirteenth better than the nineteenth century... We should speak to our age, — of things it feels and in a language it understands... The Church of America must be, of course, as Catholic as even in Jerusalem or Rome; but as far as her garments assume color from local atmosphere, she must be American. Let no one dare paint her brow with a foreign tint or pin to her mantle foreign linings". Later in 1899, Leo XIII issued (what Merry del Val wrote) *Testem Benevolentiae* which condemned certain opinions "which some comprise under the head of Americanism". VIDLER, *op. cit.*, pp. 244 and 245.

46. "*Ma souffrance d'aujourd'hui est la continuation d'une souffrance intime, pénétrante jusqu'à la moelle... C'est nous (catholiques) qui ne sommes pas prêts pour l'union. Rome vit dans un monde factice. Il y a de la bonne volonté, il y a de la foi, malgré toutes les intrigues; mais l'histoire ne leur a rien appris. Ils ne savent pas l'histoire*". LADOUS, *op. cit.*, p. 422.

47. LEASE, *op. cit.*, p. 254.

48. "*C'est mon rêve, ce que je désire le plus*". LADOUS, *op. cit.*, p. 423.

In the meantime, Portal had decided to forget the present and direct his energies toward the formation of "*les apôtres de demain*"[49] at his *Séminaire Universitaire* by motivating them to realize that Christian unity could only be based on a general reform of the Church. His beliefs took concrete expression in 1904 — the same year that the Anglican convert, George Tyrrell, was pointing out abuses of ecclesiastical authority — when he announced the birth of a new publication: the *Revue Catholique des Églises*. The first issue appeared in January and in it Portal explained that the journal would provide information about the history, doctrine, organization, and activities of diverse Christian Churches[50]. But Portal was still thinking about his earlier idea for an association.

In the spring of 1905, along with Édouard Le Roy and Lucien Laberthonnière, he established *La Société d'Études Religieuses* to reflect on current philosophical and theological problems and work for Church unity. Portal insisted that the Society was Catholic and orthodox. Nevertheless his connections with Le Roy and Laberthonnière made it impossible for him to escape accusations of Modernism. In 1907 Benigni accused Portal of assisting with the publication of Le Roy's *Dogme et Critique*.

In May 1908, Papal Secretary of State Merry del Val had meetings about Portal with l'Abbé Guibert the Superior of he *Séminaire des Carmes* and with the vice rector of the *Institut Catholique*. In July Portal was ordered by his superior general to resign as director of the *Séminaire Universitaire,* to leave Paris until the end of the year, and to cease publication of *Revue Catholique des Églises* with the December issue.

To put it very simply, as Regis Ladous has observed, Merry del Val had a good memory and could carry a grudge for a long time. If a man had been too naive to direct an Anglo/Roman Catholic campaign in 1894-1896, he could not be expected to direct an important seminary. Simply put: "In 1908 Cardinal Merry del Val imposed a punishment (on Portal) which Bishop Merry del Val could not obtain in 1896"[51].

Portal tried to wrap himself in silence and obscurity. He was allowed to return to a small house in Paris and to meet with his young students.

49. *Ibid.*, p. 439.
50. *Ibid.*, p. 461.
51. "*Tout simplement, Merry del Val n'avait rien oublié. Quelqu'un d'assez naïf pour avoir dirigé la campagne anglo-romaine de 1894-1896 ne pouvait pas diriger un séminaire universitaire. C'était tout. Avec beaucoup de franchise, le Secrétaire d'État ne dissimulait pas l'aspect personnel de cette condamnation dont les conséquences étaient autrement graves que celles de 1896... Le Cardinal Merry del Val imposait en 1908 la punition que Monsignore Merry del Val n'avait pu obtenir en 1896. En un sens, la condamnation de 1908 est la sanction — longuement retardée — des événements de 1894-1896... Elle témoigne avant tout de la bonne mémoire et de la rancune tenace du Secrétaire d'État*". *Ibid.*, p. 471.

His hopes were still for Church unity but his thoughts went back to earlier and better times[52].

Halifax too had been reflecting on the past. In March 1912 he published his papers and recollections about Anglican Orders in *Leo XIII and Anglican Orders*. And he sent a copy to Portal.

In his April 4, 1912 thank you note to Halifax, a pessimistic Portal summed up what had been. For him and Halifax, it was now winter – and perhaps they would never see a new spring. He did hope that maybe they were only seeing the end of a first stage in the unity movement[53].

Indeed — eight years later, an upbeat Portal would meet with his old friend and lay the foundations for a new stage: the Malines Conversations.

Before concluding this "interim" look at Portal and Halifax, we have to take note of another meeting of ecumenical minds in 1915 — Lord Halifax's befriending of a Louvain professor of theology.

Shortly after the German military occupation of Louvain at the beginning of the First World War, Aloïs Janssens, a young professor of theology at the Scheut Theologicum in Louvain, went to London with his students. A providential event. Janssens would become acquainted with Anglicanism, meet Halifax on August 10, 1915, and become — after Abbé Portal — Halifax's chief advisor for the Malines Conversations about matters Roman Catholic[54].

4. *The Modern Ecumenical Movement and the Lambeth Conference of 1920*

In the years immediately preceding the First World War, there had been one major Protestant ecumenical gathering: the World Missionary

---

52. *"Je vous suis redevable de ce qu'il y a eu de meilleur dans ma vie"*. He wrote to Halifax on April 16. 1911. *Ibid.*, p. 475.

53. *"Pour nos idées, c'est l'hiver; pour nous, il est probable que nous ne verrons pas de nouveau printemps. Il n'y a donc qu'à travailler chez nous comme le font les paysans... Votre livre clot la série des actes commencés par ma brochure. C'est une fin. Espérons que ce n'est que la fin d'une première étape"*. *Ibid.*, pp. 476-477.

54. Professor Joseph Coppens first called attention to Janssens' behind the scenes role in the Malines Conversations: *"Zal ik overdrijven als ik beweer dat er in ons land niemand was die zoo persoonlijk als hij, zoo juist en zoo zeker, de Engelsche religieuse toestanden kende en zoo vanzelfsprekend was aangewezen om bij het heraanknoopen van onderhandelingen of samenspraken over kerkelijke hereeniging een leidende rol te spelen?"* J. COPPENS, *Een groot theoloog Pater Aloïs Janssens*, in *Boekengids* 23 (1945), p. 2; and *"On peut s'étonner de ce que personne ne fit appel à la compétence du Père Janssens dans les Conversations de Malines"*. J. COPPENS, *Une lettre inédite de Lord Halifax*, in *Union et désunion des chrétiens, Recherches œcuméniques*, Paris, 1963, p. 139. We are also grateful to Daniël Verhelst for his publication of Janssens correspondence with Lord Halifax and his diary. D. VERHELST, "Lord Halifax and the Scheut Father Aloïs Janssens", in *Ephemerides Theologicae Lovanienses* 43 (1967) 222-258.

Conference at Edinburgh in 1910, which many ecumenists now regard as the birth of the modern ecumenical movement[55]. No Roman Catholics had participated at this meeting. It is noteworthy however that a long and supportive letter from Geremia Bonomelli (1861-1914) Archbishop of Cremona was read at Edinburgh by his American friend Silas McBee[56].

The years following World War I saw a flowering of non-Roman Catholic ecumenical meetings and conferences, e.g.: the World Alliance Meeting at Oud Wassenaar in 1919, at which Nathan Söderblom (1866-1931), Lutheran Archbishop of Uppsala, tested the ground for his idea of an ecumenical council[57], Archbishop Davidson of Canterbury was cool about the idea. He sent a message to Söderblom that any such ecumenical council would have to include Roman Catholics and the Orthodox churches of the East. If Rome would not participate, Canterbury would not either. "If this can be as big as the Nicaean Council and do as much for the Church as that Council did for faith and order, I can be interested in it", Davidson wrote to him[58]. Söderblom had also tried without success to enlist the involvement of Cardinals Bourne and Mercier[59]. There was also a series of preparatory sessions — with invitations sent to the Vatican which were politely received and politely rejected[60]. These preparatory sessions resulted in three important

55. See for example: W.R. HOGG, Ecumenical Foundations, New York, 1952, p. 98; R. ROUSE, and S.C. NEILL, A History of The Ecumenical Movement 1517-1948, London, 1954, p. 355.

56. Given the fears of Modernism at the Time, Bonomelli's letter is especially noteworthy. An excerpt captures his outlook: "the most desirable and precious of human liberties, religious liberty, may now be said to be a grand conquest of contemporary humanity, and it enables men of various faiths to meet together, not for the purpose of hating and combating each other, for the supposed greater glory of God, but in order to consecrate themselves in Christian love to the pursuit of that religious truth which unites all believers in Christ... It is therefore legitimate to aspire to a unit of faith and of religious practice, and to work for its realization by the consecration of all energies of mind and heart. This is a work in which we in our day may well cooperate". G.H. TAVARD, Two Centuries of Ecumenism: The Search for Unity, New York, 1960, p. 91.

57. "Christendom calls for a common channel of utterance. From the throne of St. Peter, as well as from other parts of the Christian world, words have again and again gone forth which find echo in every truly Christian heart, and are spoken on its behalf. But a common platform is lacking. What I propose is an ecumenical council, representing the whole of Christendom, guiding, warning, strengthening, praying in the common religious, moral and social matters of mankind". B. SUNDKLER, Nathan Söderblom, His Life and Work, London, 1968, p. 231. Söderblom was not hopeful about Rome breaking from its "exclusive sectarian isolation" to participate.

58. Ibid., p. 235.

59. SUNDKLER, op. cit., pp. 192 and 195.

60. On May 16, 1919, for instance, Benedict XV received a deputation inviting him to a Faith and Order conference. The official reply declining the invitation said it would not be possible for the Catholic Church to participate in such a conference but that "His

ecumenical gatherings at Geneva during August 1920: Life and Work, Faith and Order, and the World Alliance. These Geneva meetings in turn laid the foundations for later world conferences: On Life and Work (Stockholm, 1925) and On Faith and Order (Lausanne, 1927).

The post-World War I conference with which we are especially concerned, because of its ecumenical overtones, was the 1920 sixth Lambeth Conference[61].

The Anglican Bishops met at Lambeth Palace from July 5 to August 7, 1920. They issued an encyclical letter — *An Appeal to All Christian People* — now commonly called the Lambeth Appeal; passed eighty resolutions; and received a number of reports from committees.

The report of the sub-committee "On Relation to and Reunion with Episcopal Churches", spoke about the "Latin Communion" by repeating a statement from the 1908 Lambeth Conference — that no scheme of reunion could ignore "the great Latin Church of the West" but "any advance in this direction is at present barred by difficulties which we have not ourselves created, and which we cannot of ourselves remove". Significantly the 1920 sub-committee than added: "Should, however, the Church of Rome at any time desire to discuss conditions of reunion we shall be ready to welcome such discussions"[62].

It was the *Appeal* however which had the greatest impact on Anglican/ Roman Catholic relations. "The time has come", said the bishops "for all the separated groups of Christians to agree in forgetting the things which are behind and reaching out towards the goal of a reunited Catholic Church"[63]. And then especially because it touched on the Orders question: "We believe that for all the truly equitable approach to union is by the way of mutual deference to one another's consciences. To this end, we who send forth this appeal would say that if the authorities of other Communions should so desire, we are persuaded that, terms of union having been otherwise satisfactorily adjusted, Bishops and clergy of our Communion would willingly accept from these authorities a form of commission or recognition which would

Holiness, however, by no means wishes to disapprove of the congress in question for those who are not in union with the chair of Peter". TAVARD, *op. cit.*, p. 93. On July 4, 1919, a decree from the Holy Office forbade Roman Catholic participation in Church unity congresses held by non-Roman Catholic Christians unless they had express permission from the Holy See.

61. The Lambeth Conference is a meeting of the bishops of the Anglican Church summoned every ten years by the Archbishop of Canterbury to discuss what is happening within the Anglican Communion. Decisions of the Lambeth Conference are not binding on individual bishops.

62. CONFERENCE OF BISHOPS OF THE ANGLICAN COMMUNION, *Encyclical Letter from the Bishops with the Resolutions and Reports*, London, 1922, p. 144. See Appendix A.

63. *Ibid.*, p. 134.

commend our ministry to their congregations, as having its place in the one family life"[64].

In fact, when writing about Orders, the Anglican bishops at Lambeth had not been thinking about the condemnation of their Orders by Leo XIII. They had the English Free Churches in mind, with whom they were currently involved in ecumenical conversations. In the case of a merger, the Lambeth bishops were saying, the Anglicans would call for a regularization of Presbyterian and Congregationalist ministry by their bishops and they would be willing to submit Anglican ministry to a similar regularization by the Free Churches.

The Lambeth Conference had had a particular situation in mind. "But once having admitted the principle of regularization of the ministry, there was no reason to refuse extending it to Rome"[65]. Furthermore Randall Davidson (1848-1930) the Archbishop of Canterbury did not object to such an interpretation and seemed to support it by his sending copies of the Appeal to Catholic leaders. And as we shall see, this interpretation was also supported by the Anglican participants in the first Conversation at Malines.

The Lambeth Conference had concluded on August 7, 1920. On August 13 that same year, Davidson sent a copy of the conference proceedings to Cardinal Bourne: "It is my duty and privilege", wrote Davidson "to send to Your Eminence for your information a copy of the Report of the Lambeth Conference of Bishops which has just closed... At least I have done my part in placing the outcome of our labours in Your Eminence's hands"[66].

On May 6, 1921, Bourne wrote to Davidson thanking him for the report and affirmed "the days are indeed anxious, but I feel with you that they may be the beginnings of much greater things"[67]. Three days before receiving Bourne's reply, Davidson had also sent copies of the Lambeth Conference report to Cardinal Mercier because of "the interest which Your Eminence has taken in all that concerns the Christian well-being of Western Europe"[68]; and to Cardinal Gasparri, Papal Secretary of State.

Mercier telegrammed his prayerful support to Davidson on May 21, 1921, asking God to crown with success the Archbishop's efforts[69]. On October 27, 1921, John Hervey Boudier (1860-1924) an Anglican priest

64. *Ibid.*, p. 135.

65. TAVARD, *op. cit.*, p. 100.

66. ALPL, Archbishop Davidson's papers, Correspondence with Roman Catholics, Davidson to Bourne, August 13, 1920.

67. ALPL, Archbishop Davidson's papers, Correspondence with Roman Catholics, Bourne to Davidson, May 6, 1921.

68. ALPL, Archbishop Davidson's papers, Correspondence with Roman Catholics, Davidson to Mercier, May 3, 1921.

69. AAM, *The Malines Conversations*, 1921, B I, Mercier to Davidson, May 21, 1921.

who had participated in the papal audience when Benedict XV had been given the Lambeth Conference document, made a personal report to Davidson about the Vatican's reactions.

Davidson's memo about his meeting with Boudier, found among his papers at Lambeth Palace Library, reveals that: (1) The Pope's reactions to the Lambeth Conference report were positive and Gasparri's absolutely ecstatic — "When he (Boudier) suggested that efforts should be made towards reunion the Pope said *proficiscere in nomine Domini* ... he had afterwards further talk with Gasparri and others. Gasparri threw his arms around his neck and said the words which Mr. Boudier several times repeated 'tell the Bishops the Holy See will welcome communications from them with open arms'". (2) Merry del Val was concerned about liberalism in the Anglican Church — Davidson mentions that Boudier had also seen Merry del Val and that they and others discussed "the difficulties which Rome felt in consequence of Liberalism in the Church of England". (3) The Vatican suggested that Anglican/Roman Catholic conversations not involve the English Roman Catholic bishops! — "Mr. Boudier pressed upon me that everyone had told him that the proper course would be for Anglican Bishops to approach Rome direct and not through the Roman Hierarchy in England"[70]. This last bit of information is especially intriguing in view of Cardinal Mercier's question, on October 19, 1921, to Halifax when he and Portal had approached him with their proposal: "Why do you not address yourselves first to the English Catholic authorities?" Halifax had replied: "Because their disposition is against it"[71]. Mercier accepted that simple response and acted on it — perhaps because he had heard the same thing as Boudier when he had been in Rome and met with Benedict XV and Gasparri in December 1920? As we shall see, an examination of Mercier's pre-Malines Conversations activities makes such a conclusion plausible.

5. *The First Malines Conversation, December 6-8, 1921*

For years the most common explanation for the genesis of the Malines Conversations has been that they were directly stimulated by the 1920 *Lambeth Appeal*[72]. But this explanation is only half correct.

---

70. ALPL, Archbishop Davidson's papers, unclassified memorandum of Davidson's meeting with John Hervey Boudier, October 27, 1921.

71. G.K.A. BELL, *Randall Davidson Archbishop of Canterbury*, London, New York, Toronto, 1952 (first published 1935), vol. 2, p. 1255.

72. See for example: TAVARD, *op. cit.*, p. 100: "Anglicans initiated the Malines Conversations"; ROUSE and NEILL, *op. cit.*, p. 298: "In 1920 the Lambeth Conference issued its Appeal to All Christian People, to which Cardinal Mercier, Archbishop of Malines, sent a cordial reply. The way was open for Halifax's second major ecumenical adventure"; W.H. VAN DE POL, *Anglicanism in Ecumenical Perspective*, Pittsburgh, 1965,

The *Lambeth Appeal* prompted Portal and Halifax to meet Mercier; but Mercier had already thought about organizing Anglican/Roman Catholic discussions, and had discussed them with Benedict XV, before receiving the *Lambeth Appeal* and before either Portal or Halifax had approached him.

Cardinal Mercier "had long nourished some fairly strong prejudices about the world of the Reformation"[73]; but his triumphal trip to the United States in the autumn of 1919 — honoring him as a World War I hero — somewhat like Portal's trip to Madeira, would enlighten and transform him. In the United States he found a sense of brotherhood with fellow Christians and *"un vif désir d'unit"*[74]. On October 20, 1919, in Detroit, Mercier addressed the General Convention of the Episcopal Church, which had greeted him enthusiastically "amidst tremendous applause"[75]. Toward the end of his speech, Mercier added: "I have greeted you as brothers in the service of common ideals, brothers in love of liberty and — let me add — as brothers in the Christian Faith"[76]. Mercier's words warmed the hearts of Anglicans in Detroit and heated the tempers of ecclesiastics in Boston and in Rome. William O'Connell (1859-1944) the Cardinal Archbishop of Boston read about Mercier's talk in the newspaper and denounced his fellow cardinal to the Holy Office[77].

On February 9, 1920, Cardinal Merry del Val wrote Mercier and asked him for an explanation of his Detroit remarks. The explanation did not please the Vatican. In April 1920, on the day before Easter, Benedict XV, in a hand-written letter, wrote to Mercier that his explanations were not *"jugées satisfaisantes"* and he reprimanded the Cardinal of Malines for his *"regrettable"* meeting with *"les pseudo-*

p. 71: "In a certain sense we can consider these (Malines) conversations as the fruit of the Lambeth Appeal"; and G.L. PRESTIGE, *The Life of Charles Gore*, London, Toronto, 1935, pp. 478-479: "The idea of these conversations had originated with the veteran Lord Halifax. Conceiving that the issue of the Lambeth Appeal for Christian reunion, in 1920, afforded a suitable opportunity for giving a practical turn to relations between Rome and Canterbury". Here of course Prestige completely ignores the influence of Abbé Portal on Halifax.

73. R. AUBERT, *Cardinal Mercier. A Churchman Ahead of his Time*, (s.l., s.d.), p. 21.

Ironically during negotiations leading to the Treaty of Versailles (1919) Mercier "took the initiative of approaching Clémenceau with a view to obtaining for Belgium, a Roman Catholic country, the Palestinian mandate, in a desire to preserve the Holy Places from Protestant England and especially from Zionism which was beginning to make itself felt". *Ibid.*, p. 14.

74. As he explained in his letter to Benedict XV on December 21, 1920. R. AUBERT, "L'histoire des Conversations de Malines", in *Collectanea Mechliniensia* 52 (1967) 43-54.

75. B. PAWLEY and M. PAWLEY, *Rome and Canterbury Through Four Centuries*, London, Oxford, 1981, p. 262.

76. R. AUBERT, *Cardinal Mercier. A Churchman Ahead of his Time*, p. 21.

77. BOUDENS, *Kardinaal Mercier en de Vlaamse Beweging*, pp. 270-271.

évêques épiscopaliens" and told him that it had been "*inadmissible*" that
he had used the expression "brothers in the Christian Faith"[78].

In December 1920, Mercier went to Rome to meet with the Pope.
There he not only explained himself but also surprised Benedict by
affirming that it was time the Catholic Church began participating in
ecumenical conferences! Mercier mentioned the earlier invitation from
Nathan Söderblom, but suggested to the Pope that it might be better to
begin with confidential talks. Benedict asked Mercier to put his
thoughts on paper. The next day, he sent his written proposal to the
Pope. He would like to invite one or two Anglican and Orthodox
theologians to Malines for a few days to meet with a sound and kindly-
disposed Catholic theologian for frank doctrinal discussions. The date
and form for such meetings, he would leave to the Holy Father[79].

Mercier never received an official reply to his December 21 letter[80].
On January 25, 1921, he wrote to his friend, Bishop Bonaventura
Cerretti (1872-1933) who was deputy Secretary of State for Benedict
XV. He had hoped that Cerretti would be able to get some positive
response from the Pope. On the same day that he was writing to
Cerretti (and as Mercier would explain in his letter to Cerretti) some-
thing unexpected and providential happened — he received a letter
from Abbé Portal, dated January 24, 1921.

Portal had not known Mercier personally but had admired him from
accounts of his activities. Mercier was not only the theologically
progressive[81] founder of the *Institut Supérieur de Philosophie* at Louvain

---

78. *Ibid.*, p. 271, note 14.
79. "*Je m'offre à faire une tentative. Après avoir demandé autour de moi des prières pour
une intention secrète de votre Sainteté, j'essayerais d'inviter à Malines successivement un ou
deux théologiens de chacune de ces principales églises dissidentes, anglicane et orthodoxe
surtout. Je les retiendrais pendant quelques jours et les mettrais en rapport avec un
théologien catholique d'une doctrine sûre et d'un cœur aimant. Dans l'intimité d'un tête à tête
avec la grâce de Dieu, la pénétration des âmes peut être beaucoup plus profonde. Mon unique
préoccupation serait de préparer les âmes loyales aux solutions que le Saint Siège se
réservait de donner à l'heure et dans la forme de son choix*". AAM, Cardinal Mercier's
papers, Journey to Rome, Mercier to Benedict XV, December 21, 1920.
80. "*Non seulement aucune trace n'en a été retrouvée jusqu'à présent dans les archives de
Malines, mais argument plus décisif le P. d'Herbigny, dans sa lettre du 11 mars 1922 parle
explicitement de 'l'absence de réponse'*". R. AUBERT, "Les Conversations de Malines. Le
Cardinal Mercier et le Saint-Siège", in *Bulletin de l'Académie Royale de Belgique, Classe
des Lettres*, 5th series, 53 (1967), p. 93, note 2.
81. "*Een bewijs van Merciers openheid in doctrinaire kwesties kan men nog vinden in zijn
sympatie voor de zeer ruimdenkende Italiaanse kardinaal Capecelatro, aartsbisschop van
Capua, die ervoor bekend stond de verdediging van vooruitstrevende figuren uit de Italiaanse
religieuze denkwereld op zich te nemen. Ook nog Merciers afkerigheid van de integristische
drijverijen, extreme reakties tegen het modernisme... Mercier was op doctrinair gebied niet
konservatief. Tot op het einde van zijn leven heeft hij, doorgaans voorzichtig, soms moedig,
gereageerd tegen alles wat een stagnatie van kennis en wetenschap zou kunnen betekenen*".
BOUDENS, *Kardinaal Mercier en de Vlaamse Beweging*, pp. 268-269.

and of the *Revue néoscholastique,* he was also the internationally acclaimed Belgian hero who had shown himself favorably disposed toward his "brother bishops" in the Episcopal Church.

Portal had written a brochure about the Sisters of Charity and had dedicated it to Mercier. Mercier had thanked him for the gesture. Portal then took the opportunity to send him a longer letter, recalling his involvement in the Anglican Orders discussions under Leo XIII. He explained to Mercier that Leo had considered conferences between Roman Catholics and Anglicans but that the English Roman Catholics had blocked them. But now Portal could see that the *Lambeth Appeal* had cleared the air because it seemed to imply discussions between the two churches as well as conditional re-ordination. Portal wondered if it wasn't time to set up discussions and also reminded Mercier that when Leo XIII had mentioned such discussions, the pope had spoken favorably about having them held in Brussels. He also sent Mercier a copy of an old letter from Rampolla in which Roman/Anglican discussions had been positively mentioned[82].

Mercier reacted with reserve, in a letter to Portal on February 3, 1921. He obviously wanted to wait to hear what Rome would say[83]. It is at this point that Portal and Halifax went to work on their own.

Portal knew that Halifax would be coming to the continent and he suggested that the two of them pay a personal visit to Mercier.

Halifax had planned an autumn trip across the channel. He wanted to see Portal again — their last meeting had been in 1914. They would tour the battle fields. And then they would stop by Malines and visit Mercier. Halifax was burning with new energy and enthusiasm[84]. "This

---

82. "*Cette proposition implique des conférences et une réordination sous condition. Il me semble que la presse catholique ne l'a pas assez remarqué et j'ignore s'il en est de même pour nos autorités. Mais ce dont on ne se souvient pas, c'est que l'initiative des conférences a été prise par Léon XIII. Je me demande s'il ne serait pas opportun de le rappeler aujourd'hui. J'ajouterai que comme lieu des conférences, Léon XIII nomma Bruxelles avec prédilection. Je ne sais si Votre Éminence jugera qu'il y aurait quelques conclusions pratiques à tirer de ces documents* (Portal had also enclosed a copy of an old letter from Rampolla) *et de ces considérations. Je les soumets à Votre Éminence, persuadé que, mieux que personne, elle peut en apprécier la valeur*". AAM, The Malines Conversations, II, Portal to Mercier, January 24, 1921.

83. AUBERT, *op. cit.,* p. 93, note 3.

84. Shortly before Portal's "inspiration" transformed him, Halifax had given up. On February 12, 1919 he had asked not to be nominated again for president of the English Church Union after holding that position for fifty years. On June 7, 1919 he celebrated his eightieth birthday. A little less than a month later, on July 3, his wife died. On March 25, 1920 he wrote to Mrs. Bellamy Longworth Storer: "Now at nearly eighty-one life is ended and I only want to be gone too". (Scheut Fathers Louvain, Aloïs Janssens papers, unclassified letter).

In June 1920, Halifax made what he thought would be his last speech in the House of Lords. With an at times unsteady voice, he told his peers: The sands of my life are very nearly run-out (J.G. LOCKHART, *Viscount Halifax,* vol. 2, London, 1936, p. 264). Little did he realize then that for him his ecumenical life had begun "at eighty".

visit to the Cardinal seems to me a complete inspiration", Halifax wrote to Portal on October 7, 1921[85]. Halifax would also ask the Archbishops of Canterbury and York to write letters which he could present to Mercier.

William Cosmo Gordon Lang (1864-1945) the Archbishop of York (and later from 1928 to 1942 the Archbishop of Canterbury) felt that a single letter and that from Archbishop Davidson to Mercier would be appropriate.

Davidson's letter to Mercier was polite but guarded. He recommended Halifax: "you would find a conversation with him consonant with the thought expressed in Your Eminence's letter to me of May 21st and of the visions set forth in the *Lambeth Conference Appeal*". But Davidson stressed that "Lord Halifax does not go in any sense as ambassador or formal representative of the Church of England"[86].

On October 17, 1921 Archbishop Lang from York sent Halifax his wishes and blessings for the visit to Malines: "I agree with you that formal conferences are almost useless unless they have been preceded by informal and private conferences to pave the way"[87].

Halifax met Portal at Calais on October 17. That same day they visited Poperinge, Ieper, and the Kemmelberg. They spent the next day in Brussels. On October 19, they had a long and pleasant meeting with Mercier at Malines. It was at this meeting that Mercier had asked them why they hadn't approached the English Roman Catholic leaders about their proposal and Halifax had replied that they were not well disposed toward such conferences. No doubt Halifax was still thinking about his experiences prior to *Apostolicae Curae*. Mercier then agreed to host another discussion between Anglicans and Roman Catholics to discuss points which separated the two Churches and said he would even go to Rome if necessary to discuss the matter with the Pope.

We find a note in Halifax's diary that Mercier thought he should try to find two dependable Anglicans who might come back to Malines and continue the conversation he, Portal, and Mercier had begun. The first Malines Conversation was on the horizon and Halifax was at the start of "perhaps the most astonishing adventure of his long life"[88]. "Everything seemed hopeful"[89].

After meeting with Mercier, Portal and Halifax continued their tour of battlefields, visiting Verdun and Rheims, and then going to Paris where they met with some old friends. After that Halifax left for England where he would report back to Archbishops Davidson and

85. LOCKHART, *op. cit.*, p. 268.
86. *Ibid.*, p. 269.
87. *Ibid.*, p. 270.
88. LOCKART, *op. cit.*, p. 265.
89. *Ibid.*, p. 271.

Lang, make contacts — on his own initiative — with Walter Howard Frere and Joseph Armitage Robinson[90], and have a meeting with Archbishop Bourne.

On November 4, 1921 an enthusiastic Portal wrote to him that they were indeed "beginning again"[91]. This time around Halifax hoped for better relations with the English Roman Catholic Church. He had gone to see Cardinal Vaughan in July 1893. Now on November 28, 1921 he went to see Cardinal Bourne, hoping that Bourne would be better disposed than Vaughan had been. He told Bourne he had been to see Cardinal Mercier. Bourne seemed pleased. "Ah! Cardinal Mercier", he said, "I know him well and have a great regard for him; we were at Louvain together. He is a great man, a most distinguished personality with strong influence. I am *very glad* you have seen him"[92]. Halifax explained that he would be returning to Malines, that he would report back to Bourne, and he hoped to be able "to ask for his good services to help in every possible way to bring about such conferences as Leo XIII discussed in 1894"[93]. He wrote to Portal the day after his visit that Cardinal Bourne was "completely sympathetic"[94]. And he also mentioned that Bourne had called his attention to the fact that he thought some steps were being taken at Rome on behalf of the Russian Orthodox Church[95]. Portal replied on December 1 that it was a great joy to hear the good news, and he wondered if they weren't on the threshold of a new era[96].

That new era was inaugurated on December 6, 1921 when three

90. Halifax and Portal had conferred about the qualifications of a number of Anglicans who could join them at Malines. On one point they were in agreement — "the impossibility of Gore"! (LOCKART, *op. cit.*, p. 273.) Charles Gore would be appointed by the Archbishop of Canterbury to attend the Third Malines Conversation as a break on Halifax.

91. *Ibid.*

92. BIY, The Malines Papers of Lord Halifax, Box 1, n° 35, Halifax to Portal, November 29, 1921.

93. *Ibid.*

94. *Ibid.*

95. Benedict had a special interest in the Eastern Church and the Orthodox Churches. On May 1, 1917 he had announced the establishment of the Sacred Congregation for the Oriental Church. On October 15 of the same year his proclamation *Orientis Catholici* established the Pontifical Oriental Institute in Rome. On March 12, 1919 he had asked Cardinal Gasparri to send a letter to Nicolai Lenin asking him to show respect toward the Russian Orthodox clergy. His encyclical *Principi Apostolorum* of October 5, 1920 which raised St. Ephrem, the Syrian monk and deacon of Edessa, to the rank of Doctor of the Church had greatly pleased Eastern Rite Catholics as well as Eastern schismatics because it had spoken kindly of them. On August 5, 1921, with the urging of Mercier, he wrote a letter on behalf of the victims of the Russian famine of 1921. Benedict also took a personal interest in the fate of Basil Tikhon (1865-1925) the Patriarch of Moscow who was the victim of bolshevik persecution.

96. BIY, The Malines Papers of Lord Halifax, Box 1, n° 39, Portal to Halifax, December 1, 1921.

Roman Catholics and three Anglicans sat down at a round table in the episcopal palace at Malines to begin a three day discussion which we now call the First Malines Conversation[97].

The Roman Catholic participants were Désiré Joseph Mercier (1851-1926), Archbishop of Malines and host; Fernand Etienne Portal (1855-1926); Joseph-Ernest van Roey (1874-1961), doctor of theology from Louvain, Mercier's Vicar General (from 1907), and (from 1926) Mercier's successor as Archbishop of Malines. The Anglican participants were Charles Lindley Wood, "Lord Halifax", (1839-1934); Walter Howard Frere (1863-1938), liturgist with Anglo-Catholic sympathies, Superior of the Community of the Resurrection at Mirfield, and (from 1923) Bishop of Truro; and Joseph Armitage Robinson (1858-1933) professor at Cambridge (1893-1899), Dean of Wells (from 1906), and a close personal friend of Archbishop Lang of York.

Their First Malines Conversation was a friendly exploratory session with ample time for free and informal discussion[98]. The general basis for discussion was a memorandum prepared by Halifax which dealt with the constitution of the Church, the nature of the sacraments, and the *Lambeth Appeal*. The question of Anglican Orders came up and created hardly a negative ripple because Frere and Robinson explained that the *Lambeth Appeal* could be interpreted as applying to Anglican/Roman relations. There was unanimous agreement on the necessity of visible Catholic unity. There was some discussion about the differences between fundamental and non-fundamental dogmas.

The group also considered the variety of theological positions and religious practice in the Anglican Church. Halifax had stressed the importance of this type of clarification before going to Malines. At the end of November 1921, he had written to Portal: "One cannot deny that the formulations can be explained in a different way and that many members of the Church of England would not explain the position and teaching of their church as I do. Cardinal Mercier must keep this point in mind... We have to admit that on our side we maintain a great tolerance for opinions which as such are heretical. One can give the

97. One should remember that the Malines Conversations simply evolved from one meeting to another. In fact during the meeting at Malines from December 6-8, 1921, the participants had considered the possibility of meeting again either at Halifax's Hickelton or Robinson's Wells. See J. LOCKART, *Charles Lindley Viscount Halifax*, vol. 2, London, 1936, p. 278.

98. For specific information about the contents of the Malines Conversations, the reader is advised to consult: the "official report" — Halifax's *The Conversations at Malines: 1921-1925*, London, 1928; the "unauthorized report" which stirred up a hornet's nest — Halifax's *The Malines Conversations: 1921-1925: Original Documents*, London, 1930; and Frere's *Recollections of Malines*, London, 1935. (Frere's book, by the way, is the only account of the proceedings at Malines which contains the authentic version of the memorandum which Halifax presented at the First Malines Conversation. See LOCKHART, *op. cit.*, p. 272.)

excuse of ignorance, but the fact cannot be contested"[99]. This point is significant. We will see that years later Halifax will be accused of intentionally mis-representing to Mercier the varied make-up of the Anglican Church.

The First Conversation was clearly a successful and hopeful beginning. There were no signs of fundamental disagreement, although main differences between the Churches were touched upon. Even when the Anglicans were confronted with the papacy as the only possible center of Church unity, "the Anglicans did not decline to recognize that, if the obstacles which obstruct such unity could be removed, recognition could rightly be given to the historical primacy or precedence belonging to the See of Rome"[100].

The conversation ended *"dans un sentiment de profonde émotion religieuse"*[101]. The Anglicans returned to London and immediately reported their pleasure. Robinson wrote Halifax that it had been "one of the most remarkable experiences of his life"[102]. Frere thought "there are great hopes of peace" provided news of the conversations was not made public[103]. And the Archbishop of Canterbury was "much impressed and confident" that the meeting "was both of importance and true service"[104].

Reactions from English Roman Catholics would come after Halifax's — much to Frere's and Robinson's dismay — surprising publication of news about "Discussions with Cardinal Mercier" in his book *A Call to Reunion* published in September 1922.

99. Halifax to Portal, November 30, 1921, quoted in J. DE BIVORT DE LA SAUDEE, *Anglicans et catholiques*, Paris, 1948, p. 51.

100. Viscount HALIFAX, ed. *The Conversations at Malines: 1921-1925*, London, 1928, p. 10.

101. Viscount HALIFAX, *The Conversations at Malines 1921-1925: Original Documents*, London, 1930, p. 26.

102. BIY, The Malines Papers of Lord Halifax, Box 1, n° 44, Robinson of Halifax, December 12, 1921.

103. LOCKART, *op. cit.*, p. 278.

104. BIY, The Malines Papers of Lord Halifax, Box 1, n° 44, Robinson to Halifax, December 12, 1921.

CHAPTER THREE

THE SECOND CONVERSATION

Immediately after the First Malines Conversation, the participants were enthusiastic and optimistic. It appeared that, without much difficulty, the two Churches were well on their way to achieving the expectations of the eighteenth century Du Pin-Wake correspondence, expressed here in a letter from Archbishop Wake: "To frame a common confession of faith, or liturgie (sic), or discipline, for both Churches, is a project never to be accomplished. But to settle each so that the other shall declare it to be a sound part of the Catholic Church, and communicate with one another as such; this may easily be done without much difficulty by them abroad, and I make no doubt but the best and wisest of our Church would be ready to give all due encouragement to it"[1].

The situation, however, soon became complex and uncertain. A papal death, a pastoral letter from Mercier extolling the papacy, curious interventions by two Jesuits with close ties to the Vatican, an unexpected publication and revelation by Lord Halifax, rumblings on both sides of the channel in response to that publication, and negotiations to secure authoritative backing from Canterbury and from Rome for any future conferences provided fifteen months of creative ferment which led to the Second Conversation on March 14 and 15, 1923.

1. Laying the Foundations for Formal Talks:
The Events of 1922

The events of 1922 are a bit of a puzzling maze — a crisscrossing of high level exchanges, by letter and by personal interview, among churchmen at Rome, Malines, London, Oxford, Paris, and Hickleton. The people involved in these exchanges (G.K.A. Bell[2], Archbishop

---

1. Archbishop Wake to W. Beauvoir, quoted in: G.K.A. BELL, *Randall Davidson*, London, 1952, p. 1255.

2. George Kennedy Allen Bell (1881-1958) was Archbishop Davidson's secretary from 1914 to 1929 and later became Davidson's chief biographer. He had a special interest in ecumenical affairs, became a leader in the Life and Work movement and played a prominent role in the Stockholm Conference of 1925. He became Bishop of Chichester in 1929. From 1948 to 1954 he was chairman of the central committee of the World Council of Churches, and from 1954 until his death honorary president of the World Council of Churches.

Davidson, Cardinal Gasparri[3], Lord Halifax, Michel d'Herbigny[4], Cardinal Mercier, l'Abbé Portal, Leslie Walker[5], and Pius XI[6]) were clearly communicating about the same desire: reunion conferences between Anglicans and Roman Catholics. They did not, however, always clarify for each other their individual beliefs about the implications of such reunion. It is not clear that they always knew (or wanted other parties to know) what they were individually saying in their confidential meetings and correspondence. Nor was there a consensus about who should participate in such conferences.

The events of 1922, therefore, still leave us with some baffling questions.

3. We recall that Gasparri had been a contributor to Abbé Portal's *Revue Anglo-Romaine*, a member of the papal commission on Anglican Orders, and an enthusiastic supporter of the Lambeth Appeal and the opening of discussions with the Anglicans.

4. Michel d'Herbigny (1880-1957) was professor of Sacred Scripture and theology at the Jesuit scholasticate in Enghien, Belgium from 1912 to 1921. Cardinal Mercier wrote the preface to his *Théologie du révélé* in 1921. He was director of graduate studies at the Gregorian University in Rome from 1921 to 1923. From 1923 to 1926 he was president and then from 1926 to 1931 rector of the Pontifical Oriental Institute. Pius XI had sent him on a secret mission to strengthen the Catholic Church in Soviet Russia by secretly consecrating Russian bishops. (D'Herbigny himself had been secretely consecrated by Eugenio Pacelli (later known as Pius XII) in the chapel of the papal nunciature in Berlin on March 29, 1926). The effort miscarried. D'Herbigny was expelled from Russia and the bishops were sent to the penal camps. He played an important role in the foundation of the Pontifical Russian College in Rome in 1929. He was also, from 1923 to 1937, special consultor for the Congregation of the Oriental Church. His principal work was *Theologica de Ecclesia*, a two volume work written in 1920-1921.

5. Leslie Ignatius Walker (1877-1958), member of the English Province of the Society of Jesus, attached to Campion Hall, Oxford, author of numerous articles about Church unity. Unfortunately his papers were not available to us, as we learned from Francis Edwards, S.J., archivist for the English Province of the Society of Jesus, in a letter of May 8, 1985: "Since we have a 40-year rule of access limitation to the papers of individual Jesuits, Leslie Walker's papers will not be available until 1998 and C.C. Martindale's until 2003".

6. Pius XI approved of the Malines Conversations but took a negative attitude toward the Protestant ecumenical movement as it came increasingly under the influence of Nathan Söderblom the Lutheran Archbishop of Uppsala. This negative attitude led to *Mortalium Animos* of January 6, 1928.

Throughout his papal reign (1922-1939) he maintained, however, a strong interest in the Eastern Catholic Churches, as indicated by a brief sampling of his activities on their behalf: His encyclical *Ecclesiam Dei* (November 12, 1923) honored the memory of the martyred Archbishop Josaphat of Polozk. He had a Jesuit novitiate for the Greek-Slavic Rite established in Albertyn, Poland. He promoted the Oriental Institute which had been founded by his predecessor Benedict XV. He had the Ethiopian and Ruthenian Colleges in Rome rebuilt. His encyclical *Rerum Orientalium* (September 8, 1928) promoted greater understanding of the Eastern Churches. In 1929 he authorized the start of the codification of Eastern Church Law under Cardinal Gasparri. And in 1935 he elevated the Syrian Rite Patriarch Tappouni to the cardinalate.

Pius XI had great respect for Michel d'Herbigny and considered him his special advisor on Eastern Church affairs.

Why, for instance, did the Jesuits Michel d'Herbigny and Leslie Walker work so energetically to become officially involved in any future Roman Catholic discussions with the Anglicans? Why did their efforts ignore Portal and Halifax? Why was there a five month delay between Mercier's reception of authoritative backing from the Holy See, for what would be the Second Conversation, and his announcing of such important news to Halifax? Was there support from the Vatican and from Lambeth Palace for excluding Portal and Halifax from any future reunion conference? And were d'Herbigny and Walker — wittingly or unwittingly — representing the interests of Cardinals Gasquet and Merry del Val? R. Aubert[7] and the Pawleys[8] scratch the surface of these questions in their detailed explorations of documents found in the archives at Malines.

It now appears to us that the archives of Archbishops Davidson and Lang at Lambeth Palace, London; of Cardinal Bourne at the Archbishop's House, Westminster; and of Lord Halifax at the Borthwick Institute, York, while not definitively answering all of these questions[9], do significantly help us to better understand the circumstances behind the events of 1922. And they also hint about a new question: the extent to which Cardinal Mercier's opposition to the Flemish Movement contributed to a discrediting, in England, of the Malines Conversations.

In the middle of January 1922, Pope Benedict XV came down with influenza. His doctors were not at first alarmed. Within a few days, however, his condition grew worse. It developed into pneumonia. On January 22 he was dead.

In keeping with the Apostolic Constitution of Pope Pius X, *De Apostolica Sede Vacante*, the cardinals entered conclave ten days after Benedict's death. This was the conclave "when Merry del Val came to within single figures of the papacy"[10], and about which, during the

---

7. R. Aubert, for instance, considers the involvement of d'Herbigny and Walker *"un curieux enchaînement de circonstances ... qui ne sont pas encore bien connues"*. R. AUBERT, *Les conversations de Malines, le Cardinal Mercier et le Saint-Siège*, in *Académie royale de Belgique Bulletin de la classe des lettres et des sciences morales et politiques*, 5th Series, 53 (1967), pp. 96 and 97.

8. See B. PAWLEY and M. PAWLEY, *Rome and Canterbury through Four Centuries. A Study of the Relations between the Church of Rome and the Anglican Churches 1530-1981*, London, Oxford, 1981, pp. 265-270.

9. As observed above, note 5, important Jesuit archives are closed. Note also the letter which we received from Dr. Ivan Rebernik from the Biblioteca Apostolica Vaticana, dated September 11, 1985: "In reply to your letter of 17 July last I beg to inform you that I have made enquiries at the Vatican Archives about the possibility of consulting the documentation concerning the Malines Conversations. Only within the last few days the limits on access to the Vatican files have been extended to the end of the pontificate of Pope Benedict XV (22 January 1922), but scholars may not research beyond that date, at least for the forseeable future, so effectively the material you require could not be made available to you with the exception, perhaps, of the preliminary steps and the first of the Conversations".

10. S. LESLIE, *Cardinal Gasquet: A Memoir*, London, 1953, p. 253.

beatification process for Merry del Val, testimony was given that
Gasparri had said "during the conclave Merry del Val's ambitions
knew no bounds so much so that he incurred excommunication"[11].
Apparently Cardinal Gaetano De Lai (1853-1928) had acted as an
agent for Merry del Val during the conclave. "When his candidate
failed, (De Lai) tried to impose on Ratti the condition that he would
have Gasparri as his Secretary of State"[12]. On February 6, 1922, on the
fourteenth ballot, Ambrogio Damiano Achille Ratti was elected Pope.
He took the name of Pius XI.

Ratti, former Archbishop of Milan, was a friend of Mercier[13]. The
day after his papal election, the two friends met in private audience. We
know what they discussed because we have Mercier's handwritten *aide-
mémoire*[14] on this audience, found among his papers in the archives at
Malines. The fifth point touched on: "The idea of the Holy Father
Benedict XV: private meetings with the Anglicans ... the idea of private
meetings with the Anglicans approved by Benedict XV. A first meeting
took place on 8-10 December 1921: I explain the character and results
in order to assure myself that my superiors approve". To which
Mercier notes Pius XI's reply: "I see nothing but good from these
meetings".

Mercier returned to Malines on February 16. Shortly thereafter he
issued his Lenten pastoral letter on "The Papacy and the Election of
His Holiness Pius XI" which was an enthusiastic, albeit somewhat
exaggerated, extolling of papal power as "the most amazing power in
the world ... the accepted and cherished supremacy of one conscience
over all other consciences, of one will over all wills"[15]. We will see that
Mercier had a pressing need to stress papal power; and this need would
have a real, though indirect, impact on the Malines Conversations.

Mercier enlisted the help of Portal to get Halifax to publish the
pastoral in England. Halifax had some misgivings. "I am afraid it won't
do us much good", he wrote to his friend Athelstan Riley (1858-1945).
"Let us only hope it won't do harm. Foreigners never can understand

11. It is against conclave rules to make such advance deals. P. HEBBLETHWAITE, *John
XXIII Pope of the Council*, London, 1984, p. 105.

12. *Ibid.*, p. 106.

13. J.A. GADE, *The Life of Cardinal Mercier*, New York, London, 1934, p. 247.

14. "*Idée du Saint Père Benoît XV: réunions privées avec anglicans... Idée de réunions
privées d'anglicans approuvée par Benoît XV. Une première réunion a eu lieu les 8-10
décembre 1921: j'en expose le caractère et les résultats, afin de m'assurer que mes supérieurs
m'approuvent*". To which Mercier notes Pius XI's reply: "*Je ne vois que du bien à ces
réunions*". As R. Aubert points out in his "*Le Cardinal Mercier et le Saint-Siège*", op. cit.,
p. 132: "*Mercier avait d'abord écrit (détail révélateur de sa mentalité à l'époque): 'Sur la
conversion des anglicans'. Ces mots ont été biffés de sa main et remplacés par 'Réunions
privées avec...*'".

15. Quoted from Halifax's translation authorized by Mercier and published in Viscount HALIFAX, *A Call to Reunion*, London/Milwaukee, 1922, p. 27.

the English mind. Of course this was written for Belgians, but the translation is for us, and even I could demur to it"[16]. Halifax would end up publishing it as an *appendix* to his book: *A Call to Reunion*, London, 1922.

Meanwhile, as Halifax was working on his book, the Jesuits were getting interested in the Anglican/Roman Catholic dialogue.

Halifax and Portal, by the way, wishing to get some English Roman Catholics into their ecumenical efforts[17], had tried without success to get English Dominicans involved. The Provincial, Bede Jarrett (1871-1933) and the influential Vincent McNabb (1868-1943) sent letters of encouragement and support; but Dominican involvement hardly went further than that[18]. Neither Portal nor Halifax had thought about contacting the Jesuits.

Nevertheless — on March 6, 1922, Portal wrote to Halifax[19] that Michel d'Herbigny had contacted him about joining his Church reunion efforts with the French Jesuits. Portal was cool to the proposal. Frankly, he distrusted the Jesuits and suspected that they were in some way trying to take over the movement he and Halifax had initiated back at Madeira[20]. Today, from our better vantage point, we can see that his suspicions were well-founded[21]. We can also see that the old issue of unity by convergence vs. unity by submission was again being

16. J. G. LOCKHART, *Charles Lindley Viscount Halifax*, vol. 2, London, 1936, p. 280.

17. *"Il faut absolument que vous ayez des soutiens parmi les nôtres en Angleterre et que ce ne soient pas seulement des étrangers qui mènent campagne avec vous. Nous devons même, nous étrangers, ne pas nous mettre en évidence mais plutôt nous effacer. C'est, je crois, très important pour le succès de la nouvelle entreprise"*. BIY, The Malines Papers of Lord Halifax, Box 1, N° 52, Portal to Halifax, December, 19, 1921.

18. See for example, Halifax's Christmas letter to Portal: *"Je suis en train d'arranger des Conférences ici parmi les nôtres. Et cela fait j'écrirai au Provincial des Dominicains pour voir ce qu'il y a à faire avec les vôtres. Ce que vous dites à ce sujet est bien important"*. BIY, The Malines Papers of Lord Halifax, Box 1, N° 54, Halifax to Portal, December 22, 1921. In the same box at York we find letters from Bede Jarrett at Blackfriars, Oxford to Halifax (N° 12, November 11, 1921) "It is really to help the young to follow in such footsteps as yours, that we have come here to Oxford, to teach the truths of the Faith, to inspire the generations if we can with the ideals of courtesy, of unselfishness, of deep devotion to man and God, which your life has been consecrated to establish... We can only hope that one day our next door neighbours, Pusey House, will be isolated from us in no way at all and work to the common end under common leadership". and Vincent McNabb to Halifax (N° 99, September 22, 1922) "May the vision which has strengthened you to defy your years in a renewed youth, give youthful enthusiasm to those of us who are drawn to despair".

19. BIY, The Malines Papers of Lord Halifax, Box 1, N° 60, Portal to Halifax, March 6, 1922.

20. LOCKHART, *op. cit.*, p. 285.

21. We will not know the whole story until we can have access to the papers of Walker and d'Herbigny, as indicated above. We do know — and will demonstrate later — that Cardinal Merry del Val clearly supported and used the Jesuit Francis Woodlock in a conscious undermining of the Malines Conversations.

played out; and the Jesuits were holding firmly to the necessity of Anglican submission to Rome.

On March 6, d'Herbigny met with Cardinal Gasparri for a discussion about Roman Catholic relations with the Anglicans. Gasparri explained that Mercier had addressed a letter to Benedict XV about a conference between Roman Catholics and Anglicans. He said that he didn't know much about Mercier's proposition but that "certain steps taken by the Anglicans" had convinced him "that these interviews would be useful and productive"[22]. Gasparri was certainly thinking about the *Lambeth Appeal*. He had had direct contact with Anglicans when Davidson had sent a copy to Benedict XV. He could also have been thinking about the First Conversation at Malines; but, with the documentation currently available to us, we can only speculate[23].

Five days after his meeting with Gasparri, d'Herbigny wrote to Mercier to inform him about *Gasparri's* desires: Gasparri wanted Mercier to write down his ideas and send them in such a way that they would end up directly in Gasparri's hands. Gasparri would then make certain that they ended up in the Pope's hands[24].

On March 17, another Jesuit entered the picture — Cyril Charles Martindale (1879-1963), better known as "C.C. Martindale", the popular preacher from Campion Hall and an acquaintance of Lord Halifax[25]. He sent Halifax a long letter with his critique of the memorandum Halifax had prepared for the First Conversation. Martindale praised Halifax's "life's work" on behalf of Christian unity; but could not foresee "any likelihood or means of uniting two institutions such as the Church of Rome and that of England". The reason, he thought, was

22. Explained in letter of d'Herbigny to Mercier, AAM, The Malines Conversations, 1922, B I, March 11, 1922.

23. We believe that one can indeed speculate that Gasparri and d'Herbigny did know about the First Conversation — although it is quite possible that neither wanted the other to know that he knew. We find it unlikely that neither Benedict XV nor Pius XI would have informed the ecumenically-minded papal Secretary of State about such an important exchange. It is also unlikely that d'Herbigny would not have heard something from his Jesuit contacts (C. C. Martindale, S.J. — as indicated in his letter to Halifax, BIY, The Malines Papers of Lord Halifax, Box 1, N° 61, March 17, 1922 — knew about the First Conversation) or from his contacts in Paris. We recall that Halifax and Portal went to Paris, after their meeting with Mercier in October 1921, and discussed the upcoming First Conversation with several friends there.

24. "*Il prie Votre Éminence de bien vouloir à nouveau noter ses idées sur ce point, et d'adresser ce mémoire par telle voie qui en assurerait la remise directe entre les mains du cardinal Gasparri. Ce dernier se chargerait de le présenter à Sa Sainteté et d'assurer les conclusions*". AAM, The Malines Conversations, 1922, B I, D'Herbigny to Mercier, March 11, 1922.

25. When Ronald Knox (1888-1957) had been a house guest at Hickleton shortly before his conversion to Roman Catholicism, Halifax had arranged a meeting at Hickleton between Knox and Martindale not to encourage Knox to leave Anglicanism, but to help him at least get a clearer understanding of Roman Catholicism. See LOCKHART, *op. cit.*, p. 222.

clear: "Rome essentially *can't* alter her definitions, while the Church of England essentially *must* go back, in most substantial ways, upon her history, even if one could say that a nucleus of 'instructed' Anglicans would not have to go back upon their doctrine"[26].

While Halifax was pondering Martindale's letter and while Mercier and Portal were pondering d'Herbigny's growing interest in reunion conferences, another Jesuit, Leslie Walker, also of Campion Hall, had been having reunion discussions with the Archbishop of Canterbury's secretary G.K.A. Bell.

Walker let it be known that he was representing Michel d'Herbigny from Rome to the Archbishop of Canterbury, at Lambeth Palace. At Walker's request — "Father Leslie Walker of Oxford has kindly encouraged me to think that you may be interested in these two documents"[27]. — Bell sent Italian and Latin translations of the *Lambeth Appeal* to d'Herbigny.

On April 9, d'Herbigny wrote to Mercier that he had received the translations and that *he* would recommend that authorized Anglican delegates be sent to Rome or Malines[28]. On April 10, d'Herbigny delivered a memo to Gasparri, indicating that he had been in communication with Leslie Walker and with G.K.A. Bell and that Bell had written to him, d'Herbigny, "to ask him for suggestions about the way to achieve the unity of Anglicanism with the Catholic Church"[29]. The next day, Gasparri sent a letter to Mercier, assuring him that the Holy Father supported Mercier's ecumenical endeavors with the Anglicans: "The Holy Father has completely approved of what you have done up to this point. Try to enlighten our brothers who are in error, he had said, and thus lead them to truth and unity. To do this is to do very well the work of the apostolate. It is not only permitted but very meritorious. Apostles could do nothing otherwise"[30].

Interestingly enough, the very same day that Gasparri wrote to Mercier, April 11, 1922, Tuesday of Holy Week, Michel d'Herbigny sent a strictly confidential letter from Rome to G.K.A. Bell. D'Herbigny

26. BIY, The Malines Papers of Lord Halifax, Box 1, N° 61, Martindale to Halifax, March 17, 1922.

27. AAM, The Malines Conversations, 1922, B I, N° 3 D, Bell to d'Herbigny, March 30, 1922.

28. AAM, The Malines Conversations, 1922, B I, N° 1 A, D'Herbigny to Mercier, April 9, 1922.

29. "*Pour lui demander des suggestions sur la façon de réaliser l'unité de l'anglicanisme avec l'Église catholique*". AAM, The Malines Conversations, 1922, B I, N° 2 A, Memo, d'Herbigny to Gasparri, April 10, 1922.

30. "*Le Saint Père a pleinement approuvé ce que Votre Éminence a fait jusqu'ici. Tâcher d'éclairer nos frères qui sont dans l'erreur, disait-il, et de les amener ainsi à la vérité et à l'unité, c'est bien faire œuvre d'apostolat, non seulement permise, mais très méritoire. Les apôtres ne faisaient pas autre chose*". AAM, The Malines Conversations, 1922, B I, N° 1, Gasparri to Mercier, April 11, 1922.

thanked Bell for the translations of the *Lambeth Appeal*, and assured
Bell that though he had no authority he could say with certitude that
the signers of the *Lambeth Appeal* were held in high regard by the *Siège
Apostolique*. The letter concluded with d'Herbigny's suggestion: "It
would be useful if a representative of the reverend signers of the Appeal
or someone delegated by the illustrious Lord President could be sent
either to Rome or to Malines to Cardinal Mercier to begin to confer
about these questions with competence and authority"[31].

We note that Halifax's name had not so far appeared in any of the
correspondence generated by d'Herbigny or Walker; nor had the names
of Cardinal Bourne or l'Abbé Portal. Portal of course had removed
himself from the Jesuit activity. About Bourne, Rome seemed to be
saying — ignore him and deal with Rome or Malines. The reason for
ignoring Halifax was hinted at during a private and confidential
interview at Lambeth Palace between Walker and Bell.

During their meeting on April 26, 1922, Walker told Bell that he
understood, as we read in Bell's memorandum, that "Lord Halifax was
interested in some way in an approach to the Roman Catholic authorities,
and understood that Lord Halifax had seen Cardinal Bourne at Mrs.
Wilfred Ward's house. Walker was particularly anxious that any
conversations which might eventually take place should be of an official
and representative character as far as possible. Matters had moved
some distance since Leo XIII's Pronouncement on Anglican Orders"[32].

We recall the major criticism of Halifax, at the time of the Anglican
Orders discussions: that he did not represent the Anglican Church, only
a very small part of it. Walker was introducing the criticism again. It
would become a major criticism of Halifax's role in the Malines
Conversations, voiced especially by the Jesuit Francis Woodlock; Cardinal
Bourne; Ernest Oldmeadow, editor of *The Tablet* and Bourne's biographer; and Cardinals Merry del Val and Gasquet.

A close examination of copies of Bell's memorandum about his
meeting with Walker also reveals something, at least from Bell's
perspective, about the still tender relations between Halifax and his
Anglican Orders combatants Merry del Val and Gasquet. Bell sent
one copy of his memorandum to Halifax. We find this copy among
Halifax's Malines Conversations papers in York. Bell also gave a copy
of his memorandum to Archbishop Davidson. We find this, curiously,

31. *"Il pourrait être utile qu'un représentant des Révérends signataires de l'Appel ou un
délégué de leur illustrissime Lord Président pût être envoyé soit à Rome, soit à Malines
auprès du Cardinal Mercier, pour commencer à conférer de ces questions avec compétence et
autorité"*. BIY, The Malines Papers of Lord Halifax, Box 1, N° 65, D'Herbigny to Bell,
April 11, 1922.

32. BIY, The Malines Papers of Lord Halifax, Box 1, N° 67, Bell's "strictly private
and confidential" report of the meeting between himself and Walker, which Bell sent to
Halifax, April 26, 1922.

among Archbishop Lang's papers at Lambeth Palace. But what is most revealing is that Davidson's copy of the memorandum contains a paragraph missing in the Halifax copy. Commenting about a possible conference between Anglicans and Roman Catholics, Bell wrote: "He (Walker) knew of course that the English Romans, including Cardinal Gasquet would be somewhat opposed: also Merry del Val whose influence he said was increasing"[33].

Shortly after Walker's meeting with Bell, at which he stressed that both he and d'Herbigny were keenly interested in reunion conferences, Walker presented to Bell his own detailed "Outline of provisional scheme for a conference between representatives of the Church of England and of the Churches in communion with Rome"[34]. Some days later, Bell wrote to thank Walker for the outline and observed: "the scheme seems to me, speaking for myself, to set forth clearly and effectively the main points which would have to be considered"[35].

On May 8, 1922 d'Herbigny wrote to Mercier to inform him about Walker's visit with Bell. On May 15 d'Herbigny wrote another letter to Mercier and enclosed copies of items from the correspondence between Walker and Bell. In this letter, Michel d'Herbigny stressed that he and Walker, "persona gratissima", very much wanted to be part of any future conference with the Anglicans[36].

On May 19, Mercier wrote d'Herbigny. He thanked him for his interest but turned down his offer of involvement. Mercier told d'Herbigny that he thought it would be "imprudent" to set up parallel discussions or to involve a new group in the discussions which had already begun. He preferred to stay with the original group[37].

Jesuits can be persistent. A few days after sending his letter to d'Herbigny at Rome, Mercier received a letter from Rome — this time from Gasparri. "The Holy See has been informed by Father Michel d'Herbigny, S.J., about an exchange of letters between him and the Secretary General of the Anglican Primate of Canterbury, G.K.A. Bell,

---

33. ALPL, Archbishop Lang's papers, 1922, Bell's "strictly private and confidential" report of the meeting between himself and Walker, which he gave to Archbishop Davidson, April 26, 1922.

34. Copies of this outline can be found in ALPL, Archbishop Davidson's Papers, 1922; and in AAM, The Malines Conversations, 1922, B I, N° 31. The outline is reproduced and can be found in Appendix B.

35. AAM, The Malines Conversations, 1922, B I, N° 3, excerpt of letter from Bell to Walker, May 1, 1922, sent to Mercier by d'Herbigny on May 15, 1922.

36. Both letters in AAM, The Malines Conversations, 1922, B I.

37. "Je présume que les théologiens dont vous me parlez, les Pères Leslie Walker et d'Herbigny, ne sont pas entrés, en Angleterre, en relation avec ceux qui sont venus me trouver à Malines. Il me paraîtrait imprudent, par ailleurs, de provoquer deux séries parallèles de réunions. Alors, sauf avis contraire des autorités, je préférerais poursuivre nos premières négociations, avant d'entamer des conversations nouvelles avec un autre groupe". AAM, The Malines Conversations, 1922, B I, N° 4, Mercier to d'Herbigny, May 19, 1922.

concerning the possibility of realizing unity between Anglicans and the
Catholic Church. This exchange of letters has started after some talks
had taken place between Bell and Father Leslie Walker, S.J., from
Oxford, who wrote to the same d'Herbigny". Gasparri explained the
background and content of the exchanges (information Mercier had
already received from d'Herbigny) and observed: "Knowing the interest
that Your Eminence has for such a question (i.e. reunion conference,
JD) I thought it convenient to let you know all this so that, whenever it
is judged appropriate, you might invite, on a personal level, the
Anglican Primate to send you some delegates for a first exchange of
ideas. Of course this talk, which Your Eminence, or other people are
going to take up, should be of a strictly personal and confidential
character"[38].

At this point Mercier wrote to Portal to inform him about the
goings-on with d'Herbigny and Walker[39]. Portal immediately wrote to
Halifax, enclosing a copy of Mercier's letter to him and observing that
d'Herbigny's proposal was "ridiculous"[40].

Walker and d'Herbigny were still not ready to give up. On June 13,
1922, more than three weeks after Mercier had declined d'Herbigny's
offer to participate in a conference, Mercier received a long letter from
Leslie Walker who was at Campion Hall. We quote, at length, from
this letter because of its particular relevance. "I understand from
Fr. d'Herbigny, S.J., that Your Eminence has been approached with a
view to the holding of a conference between Catholic theologians and
representatives of the Anglican Church. Briefly the state of the question, so far as I am concerned is this: (1) I wrote two articles on the
situation in the Anglican Church for the *Gregorianum*, which are
shortly to be published. (2) In connection with these a correspondence
arose between Fr. d'Herbigny and myself, in which he suggested that an
official or semi-official conference might be possible. The idea was

---

38. *"La Santa Sede è stata testè informata dal Rev. Padre Michele d'Herbigny S.J. di
uno scambio di lettere da lui avuta con il Segretario generale del Primate Anglicano de
Cantorbery, G.K.A. Bell, circa la possibilità di realizzare l'unione degli Anglicani con la
Chiesa cattolica.*
*"Tale scambio di lettere ha avuto luogo dopo alcuni colloqui del Bell con il P. Leslie
Walker S.J., di Oxford, che ne scrisse allo stesso Padre d'Herbigny...*
*"Conoscendo il grande interesse che l'Em.zaV. Rma porta a tale questione, io ho creduto
opportuno communicarle tutto ciò, affinchè, ove Ella lo credesse conveniente, possa invitare a
proprio nome il Primato anglicano ad inviare qualche rappresentante presso di Lei per un
primo scambio d'idee. Naturalmente, l'opera di V. Em. che potrebbe essere svolta anche per
mezzo di altre persone, dovrebbe avere un carattere strettamente personale e confidenziale".*
AAM, The Malines Conversations, 1922, B I, N° 5, Gasparri to Mercier, May 31, 1922.
39. BIY, The Malines Papers of Lord Halifax, Box 1, N° 73, Mercier to Portal, June
11, 1922.
40. BIY, The Malines Papers of Lord Halifax, Box 1, N° 72, Portal to Halifax, June
14, 1922.

favorably received at Rome, and a provisional scheme, which I drew up, was also deemed satisfactory on the whole. (3) I informed the Archbishop of Canterbury through his secretary, Mr. Bell, with whom I have had several interviews and considerable correspondence in an unofficial capacity. (4) The upshot of this is that, if a request, emanating directly or indirectly from the highest authorities in Rome, is sent to the Archbishop of Canterbury, it will, I understand, be favorably received and a conference be the result". Then Walker, trying to assume the role of contact person between Davidson and Mercier, observes: "The Archbishop of Canterbury thinks (a) that since the *Lambeth Appeal* has as yet been merely acknowledged, it is fitting that the next move should be taken by us, and (b) that, if a conference is to be held, it should be a conference between *duly accredited* (our emphasis, JD) representatives on both sides. He would prefer, therefore, that the suggestion of a conference should come from the Holy Father through the Cardinal Secretary of State. Nothing has been done so far beyond unofficial pourparlers, so that no harm will arise if the scheme falls through". Later in the letter Walker made clear his own ecumenical perspective: "With respect to the possible result I should like to say quite frankly that I am not over hopeful. The Anglicans understand quite clearly that the faith-basis of reunion must be our basis, not their's; and it is on the understanding that we are not prepared to go back on past definitions of faith that they would meet us. The question here is whether they can be persuaded to accept our faith-basis, and *on other matters* (Bell's emphasis, JD) whether an accommodation can be reached which would meet their demands"[41].

Walker was apparently trying to gather support wherever he could. In August 1922, Darwell Stone (1859-1941), Anglo-Catholic theologian and Halifax's friend from Pusey House, Oxford wrote Halifax that Walker had been talking with him about "his fear of conferences other than official" because "they excite harmful suspicions among the officials of the Roman Church". Stone acknowledged to Halifax that he didn't know whether there was "anything in this" or not[42].

In Abbé Portal's mind there was. He was getting worried, and he didn't know what to do. He felt that Pius XI was too involved in Eastern Church affairs, and that the Pope was too much under the influence of Michel d'Herbigny. He was also still anxious about the fact that Archbishop Davidson had given a speech to the Anglican Convocation in February 1922, which had nothing to say about relations with Rome but had said much about the recognition of

41. AAM, The Malines Conversations, 1922, B I, N° 6, Walker to Mercier, June 13, 1922.

42. BIY, The Malines Papers of Lord Halifax, Bow 1, N° 87, Stone to Halifax, August 5, 1922.

Anglican Orders by the Patriarch of Constantinople. On November 20, 1922, Portal informed Halifax that he had decided to go see Mercier at Malines[43]. Three days later, when he had returned from Malines, Portal told Halifax that Mercier had given him the details of Walker's and d'Herbigny's activities. Portal was now convinced that someone should go to Rome to talk to the Pope and encourage him to pay a little more attention to Anglican/Roman Catholic relations. He knew, however, that neither he nor Halifax could do that because "our arrival in Rome would stir up and put in motion our enemies of the old days, (with) Cardinal Merry del Val at the head of them"[44]. Cardinals Gaetano De Lai and the Jesuit Louis Billot (1846-1931)[45], Portal believed, would also join Merry del Val and "the Pope would find himself in face of a resolute opposition"[46].

When it came to Leslie Walker and Michel d'Herbigny, Portal wanted to know "what are the real dispositions and objects of these good Fathers... Do they take part with us in order to mix up the cards (*brouiller les cartes*), or is it that they now think the future is making for us and that they wish to take possession of and guide the movement"[47].

Halifax's reply wasn't helpful. He had heard that Cardinal Bourne liked Walker and that the Roman cardinals in question were no longer opposed to reunion talks. So ... Portal again took his frustrations to Mercier: "Cardinal Bourne and the Archbishop of Canterbury seem to be animated with the best of dispositions. The Cardinal seems to have great esteem for Fr. Walker. Lord Halifax has seen him and this priest told him that the atmosphere had changed at Rome and that Cardinals Merry del Val, Gasquet, and Billot were also well disposed. I suppose that Fr. Walker has been informed by Fr. d'Herbigny and this makes me doubt the reality of the change"[48].

---

43. BIY, The Malines Papers of Lord Halifax, Box 1, N° 125, Portal to Halifax, November 20, 1922.

44. BIY, The Malines Papers of Lord Halifax, Box 1, N° 126, Portal to Halifax, November 23, 1922. This is Lord Halifax's English translation of Portal's letter. There is no indication about the location and/or existence of the French original.

45. Louis Billot (1846 1931) was a Jesuit theologian and consultor to the Holy Office. He was created cardinal by Pius X. Because of his strong sympathies for the *Action Française*, which was condemned by Pius XI in 1927, Billot was persuaded to renounce his cardinal's title.

46. BIY, The Malines Papers of Lord Halifax, Box 1, N° 126, Portal to Halifax, November 23, 1922.

47. *Ibid.*

48. *"Le Cardinal Bourne et l'Archévêque de Cantorbéry sont animés des meilleures dispositions. Le Cardinal paraît avoir beaucoup d'estime pour le P. Walker. Lord Halifax l'a vu et ce Père lui a dit que les esprits sont bien changés à Rome, que les Cardinaux Merry del Val, Gasquet, et Billot sont dans les meilleures dispositions aussi. Je suppose que le Père Walker est informé par le P. d'Herbigny et cela me fait un peu douter la réalité du changement".* AAM, The Malines Conversations, 1922, B II, N° 6, Portal to Mercier, December 1, 1922.

One could ask at this point if Portal wasn't becoming a bit paranoid. The facts would nevertheless support his suspicion. It would soon become clear that Merry del Val had not changed. And that, as we will see, even as late as January 1925, del Val would tell R. Gordon George (i. e. Robert Sencourt, "a friendly English Catholic" who often checked out rumors at the Vatican for Halifax)[49] that he would like an English Catholic at the Fourth Malines Conversation, preferably Leslie Walker or Canon James Moyes, but definitely not Bede Jarrett[50].

The day after Portal wrote to Mercier, Portal sent an anxious note to Halifax. If Bourne wants Walker, should they invite him or not? Portal was still concerned about the importance of having an English Roman Catholic participate in the Malines Conversations and about maintaining good relations with Cardinal Bourne. He really didn't know what to do. He neither trusted nor liked Walker and d'Herbigny but finally decided that they should perhaps leave the matter in Mercier's hands. Portal knew of course that Mercier preferred the original participants. In any event, they must now be prudent. Portal feared Walker and d'Herbigny because they were shaking things up and confusing the issue[51].

On December 13, Portal sent a note to Mercier that he also should be prudent about someone whose name he would reveal when they again met in person. We can only speculate about whom he had in mind[52].

In the middle of January 1923, it appeared that the Anglicans at Lambeth Palace were also having second thoughts, at least, about Walker. An extremely cautious G.K.A. Bell wrote to Halifax about a conversation the two of them had had at Lambeth Palace about Walker. Walker had previously been perceived at Lambeth Palace as a messenger with official connections at Rome. But now — January 1923 — he had become, in the mind of Bell at least, just an individual Roman Catholic. Bell sent Halifax a copy of Walker's outline for a reunion conference; and, interestingly, stressed that Archbishop Davidson did not know anything about this outline and that he should not know

49. LOCKHART, op. cit., p. 314.

50. BIY, The Malines Papers of Lord Halifax, Box 6, N° 11, Gordon George to Halifax, January 17, 1925.

51. "Le P. Walker et le P. d'Herbigny sont des agités et je les crains des brouillons qui seraient redoutables". BIY, The Malines Papers of Lord Halifax, Box 1, N° 131, Portal to Halifax, December 2, 1922.

52. Most likely Walker because he was the English Roman Catholic working so hard to become a participant in the Conversations; but we can only speculate. AAM, The Malines Conversations, 1922, B II, N° 8, Portal to Mercier, December 13, 1922. Owen Chadwick, who catalogued The Malines Papers of Lord Halifax and who also listed in his catalogue some of the papers found at Malines, noted about this letter: "Name not given d'Herbigny or Walker?"

anything about it, because "it is simply the note of an individual
Roman Catholic"[53].

The situation was getting more and more intriguing. Five days later,
Halifax received a letter from Portal warning him of Merry del Val and
also hinting at del Val's disaffection for Mercier. "You know as well as
I, that any day Merry del Val can throw sticks into the wheels he
wouldn't hesitate to do so, just for the sake of doing it and also because
of personal motives in connection with the Cardinal"[54].

In February 1923, Michel d'Herbigny published a book about Anglicanism and Eastern Orthodoxy: L'Anglicanisme et l'Orthodoxie gréco-
slave. On March 2, Halifax, in a letter to Mercier detailing his travel
plans for the next conversation, noted that d'Herbigny's book was
"very mischievous"[55] and that "Le Père d'Herbigny, like Father
Walker, S.J., seems friendly, but it is only in appearance. That, at least,
is my opinion"[56].

Mercier replied on March 4. He had thought about inviting Batiffol
but decided against it because he wanted to keep numbers of Roman
Catholic and Anglican participants equal. He also affirmed to Halifax
that there was now no question of inviting either Walker or d'Herbigny[57].

On March 8, Portal sent a final letter to Halifax criticizing inaccuracies
in d'Herbigny's book as well as d'Herbigny's exaggerated importance.
According to Portal, Fr. d'Herbigny was president of the Oriental
Institute and his influence was over-rated due to his connections with
the Superior General of the Jesuits[58].

And so it happened that the final decision about who would attend
the Second Conversation of Malines, and the decision about Jesuit

53. BIY, The Malines Papers of Lord Halifax, Box 2, N° 7, Bell to Halifax, January 9,
1923.

54. "Vous savez aussi bien que moi que le jour où Merry del Val pourra jeter des bâtons
dans les roues il n'y manquera pas et pour la chose en elle-même et pour des motifs
personnels à l'égard du Cardinal". BIY, The Malines Papers of Lord Halifax, Box 2,
N° 21, Portal to Halifax, January 16, 1923.

55. "I have just been reading a very mischievous book, called L'Anglicanisme et
l'Orthodoxie gréco-slave by Michel d'Herbigny, S.J. There cannot be a greater delusion
than to suppose that any action which may have been taken in England in regard to the
Orthodox Church has in any degree been influenced by political considerations. Anyone
who is acquainted with England would at once know how absolutely without foundation
such an idea is". BIY, The Malines Papers of Lord Halifax, Box 2, N° 94, Halifax to
Mercier, March 2, 1923.

56. Ibid.

57. AAM, The Malines Conversations, 1923, A I, N° 17, Mercier to Halifax, March 4,
1923.

58. "Le P. d'Herbigny est président de l'Institut Oriental. Il a une influence au-dessus de
sa valeur par le fait de son influence très grande sur le supérieur général des Pères Jésuites."
BIY, The Malines Papers of Lord Halifax, Box 2, N° 100, Portal to Halifax, March 8,
1923.

participation, was not made until just a few days before the participants gathered in Mercier's episcopal palace on March 14, 1923.

Before proceeding to the discussions of March 14 and 15, however, there are two more series of events which deserve our attention: (1) the publication of Lord Halifax's book in September 1922 and reactions to it; and (2) the quest for Holy See approval of reunion talks at Malines.

2. Lord Halifax's Book

We have already briefly observed that Cardinal Mercier issued a pastoral letter, on the election of Pius XI and the papal office, in early March 1922; and that he immediately enlisted the help of Abbé Portal to get Lord Halifax to translate the pastoral and publish it in England. Mercier thought that his pastoral would help the Anglicans better understand the Roman Catholic position on the papacy[59].

Halifax published the pastoral letter with reluctance, after reducing it from the main feature of an anticipated book to an appendix of his *A Call to Reunion*. In the first paragraph of the foreword to *A Call to Reunion*, we read Halifax's intentions: "I have been led to publish the following pages in the hope that they may — however imperfectly and inadequately — help, in some degree, to prepare the way towards a conference between duly authorized representatives of the Churches of Rome and England, at which the possibility of future reunion may be discussed and considered[60]. The book then gave an account of Halifax's first interview with Mercier, the text of the memorandum which had been the basis for the First Malines Conversation, a short description of the First Conversation, some observations about Mercier's pastoral letter, and finally Halifax's English translation of Mercier's letter.

A Call to Reunion, therefore, was the first public announcement of the Malines Conversations — although few people realized at the time the full import of what was being revealed. *The Tablet*[61], for instance, reacted more to a speech, "Reunion With Rome and the Holy See,

---

59. An English publication of the pastoral would also promote Mercier's image (in England, on the Continent, and particularly at Rome) as a strong supporter of the papacy. A grateful Pope would return the favor — as we shall see in section 4 — by supporting Mercier in his struggles against the Flemish Movement. It is clear from documents found in English archives that supporters of the Flemish Movement, in retaliation against Mercier, contributed, to some significant degree, to the discrediting in England of the Malines Conversations.

60. Viscount HALIFAX, *A Call to Reunion*, London, Milwaukee, 1922, p. v.

61. We note that *The Tablet*, at this time, was edited by J.B. Milburn. He had been Assistant Editor for twenty-five years and took over the editorship when J.G. Snead-Cox died in 1920. Milburn was hardly as anti-Anglican and vitriolic as E. Oldmeadow who became editor after Milburn's death in April 1923. See G.A. BECK (ed.), *The English Catholics*, London, 1950, pp. 486-487.

given by Halifax on October 9, 1922 at a meeting of the English Church Union in Sheffield than it did to the publication of his book. "A further and hardly less engaging interest attaches to Lord Halifax's speech insomuch as it discloses the fact that he has recently taken steps to arrange an informal conference between Catholic and Anglican representatives to discuss the possibilities of reunion"[62]. *The Tablet* also noted that Halifax's speech had a "pathetic interest" because it was his "farewell utterance"[63]! And when comparing the First Malines Conversation to the Anglican Orders situation of 1894, *The Tablet* noted: "This time, Lord Halifax, so far, has been more fortunate, if not in practical results, at least in his basis of operation. On this occasion he has chosen as his half-way house to Rome, not Paris, but Malines, where he had the advantage of dealing with Cardinal Mercier, one of the most learned, saintly, and sympathetic prelates of the Catholic Church"[64].

In general the Anglicans were not pleased with Halifax's publication. The participants at the First Malines Conversation had agreed, at Mercier's suggestion, not to publish anything. Halifax had sought and obtained permission from Walter Frere and Armitage Robinson to publish his brief account[65]; but neither Frere nor Robinson could agree with everything they later read in Halifax's book. Charles Gore, who at this stage was hardly an impartial observer of the goings-on at Malines, was angrily critical of the book. He called it a complete "disaster" which would create a storm of opposition, set back the Anglo-Catholic cause in England, and hinder Anglican *rapprochement* with the Orthodox[66]. Darwell Stone thought the book would arouse "a good deal of opposition and disagreement", but basically supported Halifax's publication of it, because it was good "to ventilate the subject and get it discussed"[67].

Cardinal Mercier was elated with the book and thanked God from the bottom of his heart that Halifax had published it[68]. English Roman Catholic reaction was mixed.

62. Lord Halifax's "Call to Reunion", in *The Tablet*, 140 (November 11, 1922), p. 624.

63. *Ibid.*

64. *Ibid.*

65. Years later, Halifax would also publish, to the dismay of his associates and without their permission, his account of the Malines Conversations: Viscount HALIFAX, *The Conversations of Malines 1921-1925: Original Documents*, London, 1930.

66. LOCKHART, *op. cit.*, p. 280.

67. BIY, The Malines Papers of Lord Halifax, Box 2, N° 87, Stone to Halifax, August 5, 1922.

68. BIY, The Malines Papers of Lord Halifax, Box 2, N° 87, Mercier to Halifax, September 20, 1922. In this letter Mercier was reacting to Halifax's pre-publication text. He would find out from Halifax a few days later (BIY, The Malines Papers of Lord Halifax, Box 1, N° 97, Halifax to Mercier, September 22, 1922) that the text had already

On September 24, 1922, Cardinal Bourne sent Halifax a thank you note, which curiously enough neither Halifax's nor Bourne's biographers acknowledged in their biographies: "I need not tell you that I have read with much interest what you have just written, and I rejoice that you have given to the English-speaking world the authoritative words of Cardinal Mercier... Were Cardinal Mercier's teaching on this point to be accepted by those whom you represent, then indeed a conference such as you suggest would be most useful, and with God's blessing do immense good"[69].

The November 11, 1922 edition of *The Tablet* regretted that the book gave few details about the First Conversation — "the *agenda* rather than the *acta*" — but, somewhat echoing the words of Cardinal Bourne, rejoiced that it gave the English-speaking world the inspiring words of Cardinal Mercier, which it hoped would encourage more individuals to make their submission to Rome[70].

Three weeks later, *The Tablet* again commented about the book and this time more critically observed that the Anglican Church was doctrinally divided — "Nobody could unite with the Anglican Church, as an organic whole, without facing three ways at once". — and that Halifax, by belonging to the Anglo-Catholic group, represented "a fraction of a fraction of a fraction of the English people"[71].

Vincent McNabb sent Halifax a long letter of support (sent coincidentally the same day that Bourne had sent his letter, September 24) and wished him well on his October 9 Sheffield speech: "I feel sure that when you have finished speaking the cleavage between Canterbury and Rome will be narrower than before; though still perhaps wider than you and I would wish"[72].

In the end, the chief effect of Halifax's *A Call to Reunion* was that it underscored the importance of authoritative backing — by Rome and by Canterbury — of any reunion conferences carried on at Malines.

Halifax and Mercier would interpret Pius XI's encyclical *Ubi Arcano*

---

been published. Mercier's elation was also reflected in his November 14, 1922 letter to Pius XI in which he called Halifax's introduction to his pastoral *"remarquable"*. AAM, The Malines Conversations, 1922, B I, N° 7.

69. Bourne to Halifax, September 24, 1922. The original draft of this letter is found in AAW, Cardinal Bourne's Papers, 1922. The final draft, as sent to Halifax, can be found in BIY, The Malines Papers of Lord Halifax, Box 1, N° 98. It is noteworthy that Bourne's final version was more conciliatory than his original. Where the final version has: "If I am not mistaken, you recognize that there is a fundamental difference between those who are in communion with the Holy See...", the original draft had said: "I am especially glad to see that you recognize..."

70. *The Tablet*, November 11, 1922, *op. cit.*, p. 625.

71. The "Call to Reunion", in *The Tablet*, 140 (December 2, 1922) pp. 720-721.

72. BIY, The Malines Papers of Lord Halifax, Box 1, N° 99, McNabb to Halifax, September 24, 1922.

Dei (December 23, 1922)[73] as a sign of approval. But we know of course that the quest for authoritative backing required more than a papal encyclical.

3. *Quest for Holy See Authorization*

In the middle of September 1922, when Mercier had written Halifax to thank him for *A Call To Reunion*, Mercier had also suggested the last week of October for the Second Malines Conversation. Halifax replied that, due to an impending eye operation (in 1920 and 1921, he had had three separate cataract operations), he would be unable to meet in October. If he had been able to go to Malines at the end of October, Halifax told Mercier that he would have asked him to inform the Pope about "all that has passed and has been written", and to bring before His Holiness "the possibility of carrying out what had been the first intention of Leo XIII, and to have authorized the necessary steps to secure such conferences"[74].

Mercier replied a few days later that he had already done this[75]!

---

73. *Ubi Arcano Dei* was Pius XI's first encyclical. It inaugurated Catholic Action understood at that time to mean the participation of laypeople in the hierarchical apostolate for the purpose of restoring a Christian society by permeating all aspects of public life with Catholic doctrine and morality. People like Mercier and Halifax considering this first encyclical a sign of the focus of the new papacy looked to the document and found expressions of the Pope's thinking about Church reunion, as in the excerpt quoted: *"Ex hac vero Apostolicae Sedis veluti specula et quasi arce circumspectantibus Nobis, venerabiles fratres, nimis adhuc multi occurrunt qui vel Christum penitus ignorantes vel non eius integram germanamque doctrinam, praescriptamve unitatem retinentes, necdum 'sunt de hoc ovili', ad quod tamen divinitus destinantur. Quamobrem qui Pastoris aeterni gerit vices, facere non potest quin et iisdem studiis inflammatus, easdem voces usurpet, brevissimas illas quidem sed amoris atque indulgentissimae pietatis plenas: 'Et illas (oves) oportet me adducere'; itemque memoria repetens, laetitiis omnibus excipiat eiusdem illud Christi vaticinium: 'Et vocem meam audient et fiet unum ovile et unus Pastor'. Atque ita facit Deus ut, quod Nos vobiscum, venerabiles fratres, vestroque cum coetu Christifidelium concordibus votis precibusque imploramus, hanc suavissimam divini Cordis certamque vaticinationem quamprimum videamus optatissimo eventu comprobatam"*. *Ubi Arcano Dei, Acta Apostolicae Sedis*, Annus XIV, Volumen XIV, Rome, 1922, pp. 696-697.

74. BIY, The Malines Papers of Lord Halifax, Box 1, N° 97, Halifax to Mercier, September 22, 1922.

75. *"Depuis plusieurs mois déjà, j'ai reçu, par une voie autorisée mais confidentielle, l'assurance que nos échanges de vue étaient approuvés au Vatican et que l'on y voyait de bon œil qu'ils fussent poursuivis. Mais conformément à nos déclarations, reprises d'ailleurs par vous dans votre introduction,* (i.e. A Call To Reunion, JD) *j'avais représenté nos trois aimables visiteurs à Malines les 6-9 décembre 1921 comme des personnalités privées, si haute que fût leur situation en Angleterre et dans l'Église anglicane. Cette fois, j'infère de votre lettre que les anglicans avec lesquels nous entrerions en conversation la prochaine fois seraient des* 'Anglicans named by the Archbishop of Canterbury in order to consider etc...'. *Ce langage et la publication de votre brochure* [i.e. A Call to Reunion] *me permettent de préciser mes désirs et redoublent ma confiance"*. BIY, The Malines Papers of Lord Halifax, Box 1, N° 102, Mercier to Halifax, September 29, 1922.

It is at this point that the Pawleys[76] invite us to consider why
Mercier waited so long to inform Halifax that Gasparri, in his letter
of April 11, 1922, had assured Mercier That the Holy Father had
completely approved of everything he had done up to this point[77].

We recall that Mercier at this time was involved in an active
correspondence about the possible participation of Michel d'Herbigny
and Leslie Walker in any future conferences with the Anglicans; and
also recall that d'Herbigny and Walker had all but ignored Halifax in
their meetings and correspondence. We also find it important to look
into Mercier's Belgian activities at this time in order to possibly clear-
up some of the puzzle registered by the Pawleys.

In Belgium during the five months in which he did not correspond
with Halifax, Cardinal Mercier was deeply involved in his own struggles
with the Flemish Movement[78]. To maintain his position against the
Flemish Movement[79], he needed all the support from Rome he could
get (i.e. from Pius XI, from Gasparri and his Belgian friend d'Herbigny). He would in fact not pay much attention to Halifax until
September 1922, when Halifax would again put Mercier's name before
the English and American public[80] by publishing an English translation
of the 1922 Lenten pastoral letter. That letter had conveniently supported
Mercier's attempt in early 1922 to insure Belgian Catholic backing for
his opposition to the Flemish Movement; and in the autumn of 1922 it
would again, conveniently, support his cause.

Before discussing the issues of 1922, we need to go back to the winter
of 1920. On December 18, 1920, when Mercier had met with Benedict
XV to explore his idea about inviting a small group of non-Catholic
theologians to Malines for ecumenical discussions, Mercier had also
placed before the Pope his dissatisfaction and fears about the Flemish
Movement. In fact, Mercier had expressly asked Benedict XV to issue
a letter to the Belgian episcopacy and clergy about the religious
dimension of the Flemish Movement; and Mercier had even given

76. B. PAWLEY and M. PAWLEY, op. cit., p. 267.

77. Gasparri to Mercier, April 11, 1922, op. cit.

78. For information about Mercier and the Flemish Movement, see R. BOUDENS,
Kardinaal Mercier en de Vlaamse Beweging, Leuven, 1975.

79. A movement on behalf of the linguistic and cultural rights of the Flemish (also
called the Flemish Question) arising out of the antagonism between the Flemish and
French speaking groups in Belgium. The linguistic rights of the Flemings had been
restricted after Belgium became an independent state in 1830. Part of this was due to the
fact that the Belgians had risen up against the Dutch dominated government of The
Hague and the House of Orange. In Mercier's time there was a strong movement, among
the Flemings, to have Flemish recognized and taught as one of two official Belgian
languages. Mercier saw this movement as a threat to post-World War I national unity. He
also had difficulty imagining how culture could be passed on to the next generation in the
Flemish language.

80. A Call To Reunion was published simultaneously in London and in Milwaukee.

Benedict his written suggestions about the contents of that papal letter. The letter should forbid bishops, priests, and seminarians from making any statements or engaging in any actions, public or private, which touch upon the Flemish Movement[81]. The Pope agreed to Mercier's suggestions[82].

In January 1921, a draft of the papal letter was sent to Mercier for his corrections, which he made and then returned the draft to the Vatican. The official text, *Cum Semper*, was released on February 10, 1921; and it contained "all the points which Mercier had suggested to the Pope"[83]. Mercier gave the letter wide publicity in Belgium and asked that directors of colleges and minor seminaries inform their students, before the start of Easter vacation, about "the will of the Holy Father and of their Archbishop"[84]. A few months after the appearance of *Cum Semper*, however, Mercier became concerned about the activities of the Bishop of Liege, Martin Rutten (1844-1928), whom people were starting to call "the Bishop of the Flemings"[85]. Mercier considered Rutten's actions disloyal and he feared episcopal and clerical participation in Flemish Movement activities — surely, thought Mercier, acts of disobedience to the "will of the Holy Father and of their Archbishop".

When Pius XI was elected, early in 1922, Mercier, therefore, found it opportune to issue a pastoral letter, his Lenten pastoral of 1922, to remind the Belgian bishops, clergy, and laity of "the moral power of the Papacy, the accepted and cherished supremacy of one conscience over all other consciences, of one will over all wills"[86].

We pass now to the summer of 1922, when the Bishops of Liege and Namur decided to side with the policy of the Belgian Christian Democrats, and against Mercier, about the "*vernederlandsing*" (i.e. having classes taught in the Dutch language rather than just French) of the University of Ghent. Mercier was greatly troubled by their action; and

81. "*La lettre devrait interdire au clergé et aux séminaristes de prendre une attitude dans les conflits qui passionnent et divisent les citoyens d'un même pays, de se prononcer dans la presse, dans les réunions publiques, dans l'accomplissement de leur ministère sacerdotal ou éducatif surtout, sur des questions brûlantes, qui sont étrangères à leur mission surnaturelle. Elle devrait interdire les conciliabules secrets, où l'on organise la résistance aux directions de l'autorité religieuse... La lettre serait accompagnée d'un mot confidentiel aux évêques, à l'effet d'obtenir qu'ils s'abstiennent de toute déclaration ou action publique sur la Question Flamande, avant de s'être mis d'accord entre eux, et spécialement avec leur archevêque*". BOUDENS, *op. cit.*, note 122, p. 254.

82. "*Toen de primaat van België Rome verliet, had hij de verzekering op zak dat enkele weken later een pauselijk schrijven zijn eigen visie op de Vlaamse Beweging, en op het aandeel dat de klerus erin mocht hebben, zou komen bevestigen*". BOUDENS, *op. cit.*, p. 257.

83. "*Hij bevatte alle punten die de kardinaal aan de paus voorgesteld had*". *Ibid.*, p. 257.

84. "*de wil van de H. Vader en van hun aartsbisschop*". *Ibid.*, p. 258.

85. *Ibid.*, p. 260.

86. HALIFAX, *A Call to Reunion*, p. 27.

on July 15, he sent a rather despondent letter to Gasparri: "The Church had a leader, the diocese had a leader, but the (Belgian) Church province did not"[87]. A depressed Mercier could clearly now benefit from a new infusion of international recognition — like he had received when he returned from the United States in 1919. Then it had helped him gain Vatican support for his struggles with the Flemings[88]. Now such recognition would at least boost his morale. It was therefore a happy coincidence for Mercier, and one for which he could indeed "thank God from the bottom of his heart"[89], when *A Call To Reunion* appeared in September 1922. It came at the end of what had been for Mercier an ecclesiastically long hot summer. Even Cardinal Gasquet would comment, when someone remarked about Mercier's involvement in English Church affairs: "I might as well go to Belgium and tell Mercier how to solve the Flemish Question"[90]. There was also a joke at this time about Archbishop Davidson's having made a similar statement[91].

It is an hypothesis which demands more research, but one can suspect that Halifax, perhaps unwittingly, had therefore given Mercier much moral support in the Flemish problem through the publication of the Cardinal's pastoral letter in *A Call To Reunion*. Mercier, after months of hedging with Halifax and of attending more closely — for the sake of maintaining support for his Flemish policy — with those at Rome who preferred moving Halifax out of reunion conferences, now sided with Halifax. And thus the Flemish Movement had a real though minor role in contributing to the direction in which the Malines Conversations would move.

From this point on Mercier and Halifax became closely-knit colleagues and warm personal friends in the ecumenical adventure of the Malines Conversations[92].

87. *"De Kerk had een leider, het bisdom had een leider, maar de kerkprovincie had er geen"*. BOUDENS, *op. cit.*, p. 233.

88. *"Men vond het riskant en inopportuun in de gegeven omstandigheden iets tegen hem te ondernemen"*. BOUDENS, *op. cit.*, p. 251.

89. Mercier to Halifax, September 20, 1922, *op. cit.*

90. LOCKHART, *op. cit.*, p. 286; GADE, *op. cit.*, p. 244.

91. *"Men vertelde dat de aartsbisschop van Canterbury door een reporter over het doel van zijn reis ondervraagd werd toen hij in Dover op het punt stond de boot naar Oostende te nemen. Hij antwoorde:* 'I am going to solve the Flemish Question!'" BOUDENS, *op. cit.*, p. 273.

92. The Flemish Question would more directly touch the Malines Conversations in 1924. Mrs. Bellamy Storer — we will have more to say about her in a future chapter — wrote to Halifax on June 12, 1924: "Yesterday I saw Mgr. Cerretti off. He comprehends perfectly the Catholic clergy of England and knows of their hostility against Cardinal Mercier and the Conversations at Malines. It appears that the Flemish began it and pamphlets (translated) of theirs were circulated in England". ALPL, Archbishop Davidson's papers, 1924, Storer to Halifax, June 12, 1924.

Two weeks after Mercier had informed Halifax about papal approval
of the Conversations, Halifax wrote Mercier how delighted he was and
that he had been in contact with Robinson, who suggested it would be
good if the Anglicans heard something from Mercier[93]. A few days
later, Davidson wrote Halifax that it was not enough to receive some
authorization from Mercier: "It is not for me to prescribe the exact
manner in which that authorisation should be conveyed — whether by
a letter from His Holiness the Pope, or the Cardinal Secretary of State
on his behalf, or otherwise. But it must emanate from the centre and
not from any ecclesiastical leader, however distinguished he be in
person or office"[94]. Davidson was worried that if Mercier died, the
Vatican would simply dismiss his statement of authorization as a nice
thought from a kind old man[95]. So on November 14, Mercier wrote to
Pius XI that the Anglicans and especially the Archbishop of Canterbury, and that Mercier himself wanted to see the conversations
continue. But, stressed Mercier, the Anglicans wanted some official
word of support from Rome[96].

Eleven days later, Gasparri sent the word Mercier had hoped to hear.
The Holy Father, wrote Gasparri, "authorizes Your Eminence to tell
the Anglicans that the Holy See approves and encourages your conversations and prays with all its heart that God will bless them"[97]. It is
significant that authorization came in the name of the Holy See and not
simply in the name of Pius XI[98]. This was indeed an authoritative
approval. On November 28, Mercier sent Halifax the good news, and
asked him to inform Davidson, Robinson, and Frere[99]. An enthusiastic
Halifax, believing that he and Portal were at the goal they had hoped to

93. BIY, The Malines Papers of Lord Halifax, Box 1, N° 114, Draft of Halifax to
Mercier, October 12, 1922. As received, AAM, The Malines Conversations, 1922, A I,
N° 10.

94. Davidson to Halifax, October 31, 1922, BELL, op. cit., p. 1257.

95. Ibid.

96. "Les anglicans, notamment l'archevêque de Canterbury, désirent, nous désirons nous-
même, que la Conversation reprenne. Mais les anglicans attendent qu'à leur première avance
confiante vers Rome réponde une marque de bienveillance de Rome à leur égard. Que le Saint
Père m'autorise à leur dire que le Saint-Siège approuve et encourage nos Conversations".
AAM, The Malines Conversations, 1922, B I, N° 7, Mercier to Pius XI, November 14,
1922.

97. "Autorise Votre Éminence à dire aux anglicans que le Saint-Siège approuve et
encourage vos Conversations et prie de tout son cœur le Bon Dieu de les bénir". AAM, The
Malines Conversations, 1922, B I, N° 8, Gasparri to Mercier, November 25, 1922.

98. We note, and R. Aubert has noted ("Le Cardinal Mercier et le Saint-Siège", note
1 page 101) an unfortunate mistake in J. DE BIVORT DE LA SAUDEE, Anglicans et
catholiques, vol. 1, Paris, 1948, p. 66, he has "Saint-Père" in place of "Saint-Siège".

99. "Je ne puis vous dire combien cette haute approbation et ces encouragements du
Saint-Père, — qui parle, vous le remarquez, non de l'auguste personne de Pie XI, mais 'du
Saint-Siège', — me réjouissent". BIY, The Malines Papers of Lord Halifax, Box 1, N° 128,
Mercier to Halifax November 28, 1922.

achieve thirty years earlier[100], informed his Anglican colleagues and apparently did go to visit Cardinal Bourne[101].

On November 30, 1922 Mercier wrote to Bourne to inform him about the Holy See approval[102]. This is an important letter which Bourne's biographer, Oldmeadow, failed to acknowledge in his biography. Bourne replied on December 4 that Halifax had met with him before going to Malines, that Halifax represented a very small group of Anglicans, that he thought it would be a long time before anything good could come of such conferences but that they "may well be encouraged"[103]. Bourne also sent Mercier a copy of the November 11, 1922 article in *The Tablet* about Lord Halifax's Sheffield speech[104].

On Christmas Eve 1922, Archbishop Davidson sent Halifax a note wishing that Mercier would write directly to him rather than going through Halifax: "A three cornered correspondence, though in some cases useful, is never quite satisfactory; it has always an element of possible misconception and mistake"[105]. On January 10, 1923 Mercier sent Davidson a personal letter indicating the words of the Holy See approval which had come from Gasparri[106]. And on February 2, 1923 Davidson replied to Mercier's letter of approval: "This enables our arrangements to go forward with the knowledge that the position of the members of the Church of England who take part as your guests in the discussions to which Your Eminence invites them, corresponds to the position accorded to the Roman Catholic members of the group, and that the responsibilities, such as they are, which attach to such conversations are thus shared in equal degree by all who take part in them... I need not assure Your Eminence how cordially I unite in the prayer to which expression is given on the part of the Holy See that the blessing

---

100. As Halifax expressed in a letter to Portal, LOCKHART, *op. cit.*, p.283.

101. "On Friday, 1 December 1922, Halifax wrote to Mercier: 'Only last Monday I saw Cardinal Bourne for some time and found him most kind and sympathetic'. (Archives of the Archbishopric of Malines, Dossier Conversations de Malines, 1922, A I 13)". R. AUBERT, "Cardinal Mercier, Cardinal Bourne and the Malines Conversations", in *One in Christ* 4 (1968), p. 374, note 7.

102. *"Il m'a semblé de mon devoir de mettre Votre Éminence au courant de cette correspondance. Notre prochaine entrevue, si elle a lieu, restera aussi privée. Mais le Saint Père sait qu'elle était désirée par l'archevêque de Canterbury et Votre Éminence verra dans quels termes le Saint-Siège l'approuve et daigne l'encourager"*. AAM, The Malines Conversations, 1922, B III, N° 1, Mercier to Bourne, November 30, 1922.

103. AAM, The Malines Conversations, 1922, A I, N° 2, Bourne to Mercier, December 4, 1922.

104. Mercier was very sensitive about these and other articles which were appearing, as he indicated in letters to Halifax: AAM, The Malines Conversations, 1922, AI, N° 2, December 4 1922; and to Pius XI: AAM, The Malines Conversations, 1922, B I, March 1 and 2 1922.

105. Davidson to Halifax, December 24, 1922, BELL, *op. cit.*, p.1258.

106. Mercier to Davidson, January 10, 1923, *Ibid.*, p. 1258.

of God may rest upon these conversations"[107]. It would seem then that all was set for a smooth preparation for the Second Conversation. But as far as Portal was concerned, it only seemed that way. He had a way of sensing what was in the wind; and in the middle of January 1923, he had sent a word of warning to the enthusiastic Halifax. He still did not trust Bourne and suspected the negative influence of Merry del Val and Gasquet in Rome[108]. We will see that he may have been a bit mistaken about Bourne but was certainly right about Merry del Val and Gasquet.

Towards the end of February the Anglican participants gathered at Lambeth Palace to draw up a memorandum for the Second Conversation. ("A suggestion that the Romans should prepare a similar document was never carried out"[109]). They sent a copy of this to Mercier. On March 1 and 2 Mercier drafted a letter to Pius XI which was sent on March 2. This letter informed the Pope that the next Conversation would begin at Malines on March 13. It also gave Pius XI a copy of the Anglican memorandum with Mercier's comments, and also pointed out to the Pope that *The Tablet* and *The Universe* did not look upon the conversations very kindly[110]. The next step would be the gathering at Malines. Mercier would not hear from the Pope until the end of March, thus well after the Second Conversation.

4. *At Malines, March 14 and 15*

The same six people who had gathered for the First Conversation arrived at Malines on March 13, 1923 and met for their Second Conversation on March 14 and 15. This second time, of course, the Anglicans came with the friendly backing of the Archbishop of Canterbury[111] and the Roman Catholic participants with that of the Holy See.

Before the Anglicans had left for Malines on March 13, 1923, the

107. Davidson to Mercier, February 2, 1923, *Ibid.*, p. 1259.

108. *"Le cardinal Bourne, en accusant réception au cardinal Mercier de la lettre du cardinal Gasparri, qui approuve nos Conversations, lui a envoyé l'article du Tablet. Cela marque bien la position qu'il prend. Et il faut bien être sûr que Merry del Val, Dom Gasquet, etc... vont prendre la même, si ce n'est déjà fait. La lutte d'influence va donc s'exercer à Rome sans trop tarder".* BIY, The Malines Papers of Lord Halifax, Box 2, N° 8, Portal to Halifax, January 10, 1923.

109. LOCKHART, *op. cit.*, p. 287.

110. AAM, The Malines Conversations, 1922, B I, Mercier to Pius XI, March 1 and 2 1922.

111. Davidson had warned the Anglican particpants: "Don't detract from the importance of the Thirty-Nine Articles. Don't budge an inch as to the necessity of carrying the East with us in ultimate reunion steps. Bear constantly in mind that in any admission made as to what Roman leadership or 'primacy' may mean, we have to make quite clear too that which it must not mean i.e. some of the very things which the Cardinal's Pastoral (i.e. Mercier's Lenten Pastoral of 1922, JD) claims for it". BELL, *op. cit.*, pp. 1260 and 1261.

Archbishop of Canterbury had given them some final words of advice: they should not forget the *Thirty-Nine Articles*; and they should not forget the difference between Mercier's conception of papal primacy and the Anglican position about the papal office.

The memorandum prepared by the Anglicans led to a discussion·of practical rather than dogmatic concerns: the growth of the Anglican Communion since the Reformation; how the Anglican Communion as a whole could be brought into union with the Holy See; were such a union to occur, what could be the relationship to of the Archbishop of Canterbury to the Holy See, and what would be the position of the existing Roman Catholic hierarchy in England. There were also observations about certain characteristics of Anglican rites and customs. One of the most controversial elements which surfaced was the suggestion that the Pope might be able to grant the pallium to the Archbishop of Canterbury and other Anglican metropolitans. At the end of the Second Conversation, each side agreed to draw up and submit a statement to their respective authorities. The documents were signed by their respective sponsors and by the members of the other side, as an attestation to the correctness of the text. These signatures would greatly alarm Archbishop Davidson a few days after the Second Conversation, because he thought they indicated agreement with the content of the statements.

The Roman Catholic statement, called "The French Statement", was a bit more progressive than the Anglican, or "The English Statement" as it was called[112].

---

112.   The French Statement

Cette fois, la question examinée par nous revient à ces termes: Suppose que l'assentiment des esprits soit accompli sur le terrain doctrinal, dans quelles conditions pourrait s'opérer l'union de l'Église Anglicane à l'Église Romaine?

La préoccupation dominante de l'Église Anglicane est de garder, dans la mesure du possible, son organisation et sa hiérarchie actuelles, son rite, sa discipline.

Puisqu'il s'agit non d'un retour de personnalités isolées à l'Église de Rome, mais d'un retour collectif, cette préoccupation est toute naturelle.

Il est naturel que l'Archevêque de Cantorbéry, considéré par les évêques, par le clergé, par les fidèles de l'Église Anglicane, comme leur chef, soit considéré aussi comme devant continuer à leur égard l'exercice de son autorité.

Moyennant cet exercice, les rites et la discipline seraient suffisamment maintenus. L'entrée en masse dans le giron de l'Église Romaine serait ainsi facilitée. Certaines mesures, d'ailleurs, pourraient avoir un caractère temporaire. "Alors, la question fondamentale qui se pose paraît être la suivante:

Le Saint-Siège approuverait-il que l'Archevêque de Cantorbéry, acceptant la suprématie spirituelle du Souverain Pontife et le cérémonial jugé par lui nécessaire à la validité de la consécration de l'Archevêque, fût reconnu comme le Primat de l'Église Anglicane rattachée à Rome?

Le Saint-Siège consentirait-il à accorder à l'Archevêque de Cantorbéry et aux autres métropolitains le pallium comme symbole de leur juridiction sur leurs provinces respectives?

Permettrait-il à l'Archevêque de Cantorbéry d'appliquer aux autres évêques Anglicans le

The participants left Malines happy and peaceful on March 15, 1923. Little did they imagine the storms of fear and protest their signed documents would generate in England.

cérémonial de validation accepté par l'Archevêque? Permettrait-il enfin à chaque Métropolitain de confirmer et de consacrer à l'avenir les évêques de sa province?

Tant que cette question primordiale n'aura pas été résolue, il nous serait malaisé de poursuivre nos négociations. Si elle était résolue affirmativement, la voie serait aplanie qui pourrait nous conduire à l'examen de questions ultérieures d'application.

We accept the above for submission to the respective authorities.

Halifax.
J. Armitage Robinson.
Walter Howard Frere, C.R.
+ D.-J. Card. Mercier.
E. Van Roey, vic. gén.
F. Portal, p.d.I.M.

The English Statement

The Anglican representatives being in hearty agreement with the statement drawn up by His Eminence desire on their part to sum up the position in the following terms.

As a result of the recent conversations at Malines it was agreed by those who were present that, supposing the doctrinal differences now existing between the two Churches could be satisfactorily explained or removed, and further supposing the difficulty regarding Anglican Orders were surmounted on the lines indicated in the Lambeth Appeal, then the following suggestions would form a basis of practical action for the reunion of the two Churches.

1. The acknowledgement of the position of the Papal See as the centre and head on earth of the Catholic Church, from which guidance should be looked for, in general, and especially in grave matters affecting the welfare of the Church as a whole.

2. The acknowledgement of the Anglican Communion as a body linked with the Papal See in virtue of the recognition of the jurisdiction of the Archbishop of Canterbury and other Metropolitans by the gift of the Pallium.

3. Under the discipline of the English Church would fall the determination of all such questions as: The English rite and its use in the vernacular; Communion in both kinds; Marriage of the clergy.

4. The position of the existing Roman Catholic Hierarchy in England with their Churches and congregations would for the present, at any rate, remain unaltered. They would be exempt from the jurisdiction of Canterbury, and, as at present,directly dependent on the Holy See.

Accepté pour être soumis aux autorités respectives.

+ D.-J. Card. Mercier, arch. de Malines.
E. Van Roey, vic. gén.
F. Portal, p.d.I.M.
Halifax.
J. Armitage Robinson.
Walter Howard Frere, C.R.

The French Statement and the English Statement are reproduced here as found in Viscount HALIFAX, *The Conversations of Malines, 1921-1925: Original Documents*, London, 1930, pp. 83-88. In the original texts, the words "We accept ... authorities" are in Lord Halifax's handwritting and the words *"Accepté ... respectives"* are in Cardinal Mercier's handwritting.

CHAPTER FOUR

THE THIRD CONVERSATION

Eight months elapsed between the Second and Third Conversations. They were months of building tension. Archbishop Davidson was anxious about the signed memoranda. The number of participants for future conversations was increased from six to ten. Maude Petre made a cameo appearance. The Bishop of Zanzibar sent a surprising telegram to the Pope. Lord Halifax published another book. And English Roman Catholics grew increasingly restless. The Third Conversation was a rather mild affair; but it was followed by an explosion of public outcry, occasioned by a pastoral letter from Davidson.

1. Controversy about the Signed Memoranda

Immediately following the conclusion of the Second Conversation on March 15, 1923, Robinson and Frere went to see Archbishop Davidson at Lambeth Palace[1]. The signed memoranda alarmed Davidson. He feared that the discussions had ignored an important point — discussion about *pallia* should have been preceded by a clarification of doctrinal differences. The Roman Catholic memorandum, he felt, implied absorption which was not at all the intention of the *Lambeth Appeal*. Clearly, Davidson believed, the Anglican participants at Malines had gone too far. And Charles Gore agreed: "The concessiveness of our delegation to Malines", he wrote, "apparently at the first conference and certainly at the second, seems to me more disastrous and perilous the more I think of it"[2].

When Halifax heard of Davidson's reactions, he wrote to Robinson hoping that Robinson would calm Davidson's fears; but Halifax was pessimistic. He feared "though the cases are not precisely identical, that something like the fatal mistake made by Archbishop Benson in 1894 is going to be repeated"[3]. Robinson had little success with Davidson who

1. "The Dean [i.e. Robinson] was not very handy with papers. On his outward journey to Malines he had been in trouble over his passport; now he had signed one of the memoranda in the wrong place and had mislaid important portions of his own copies; and these circumstances, combined with the misunderstanding about the counter-signatures, did not lessen the Archbishop's uneasiness". J.G. LOCKHART, *Charles Lindley Viscount Halifax*, vol. II, London, 1936, p. 288.

2. Gore to Davidson, March 19, 1923, G.K.A. BELL, *Randall Davidson*, London, New York, Toronto, 1952, p. 1267.

3. BIY, The Malines Papers of Lord Halifax, Box 2, N° 122, Halifax to Robinson, March 24, 1923.

sent at least two letters to Halifax begging him for absolute secrecy and sending him, in exchange for signed copies of the memoranda, unsigned ones.

In March, April and May, Davidson also expressed his fears in a series of letters to Mercier[4]. Davidson was courteous but cool in his insistence that there be no further discussion of administrative matters until the doctrinal matter of papal authority was settled. Mercier replied in a lengthy letter[5] that he was in agreement about the importance of addressing the doctrinal question before administrative ones, but that he would also like to know the sentiments of Davidson and Lang about the points raised in the memoranda. Mercier also gave Davidson a detailed exposition of the Roman Catholic view of papal primacy and of the origin of episcopal jurisdiction. Davidson replied that the administrative questions raised in the memoranda were too hypothetical to allow him or Lang to offer any comment.

Halifax was determined to continue pushing Davidson, as he wrote to Frere: "Let us grant that what I should like the Archbishop to do might metaphorically cost him his head. He could not lose it in a better cause"[6]. Davidson was now deadly serious. "I confess", he wrote to Halifax, "to feeling pricks of conscience as to whether in writing to the Cardinal, and even, to yourself, I have been firm enough in what I have said about the difficulties which lie ahead"[7]. And Halifax's friend, Archbishop Lang, wrote him on April 16 that he was distressed to receive in a letter Halifax's negative comments about Davidson. Lang warned Halifax about "the danger of pressing"[8]. Later that same day, Lang and Davidson met and composed, out of concern for setting the record straight, a strictly confidential memorandum "after consideration of all the documents and letters which they have seen relating to the two Conferences at Malines"[9]. And Lord Halifax pressed on.

4. AAM, The Malines Conversations, 1923, A II, Davidson to Mercier, N° 8, March 24, 1923, N° 10, April 13, 1923, N° 11, May 15, 1923.

5. ALPL, Archbishop Davidson's papers, 1923, Correspondence with Roman Catholics, Mercier to Davidson, April 11, 1923.

6. BIY, The Malines Papers of Lord Halifax, Box 2, N° 131, Halifax to Frere, March 26, 1923.

7. BIY, The Malines Papers of Lord Halifax, Box 2, N° 157, Davidson to Halifax, April 11, 1923.

8. "If, my dear old friend, you were a golfer, I would point out the danger of 'pressing', a fault which is very apt to spoil the game. But indeed I know how natural it is for you with the years shortening, to 'press'". BIY, The Malines Papers of Lord Halifax, Box 2, N° 164, Lang to Halifax, April 16, 1923.

9. BIY, The Malines Papers of Lord Halifax, Box 2, N° 166, Memorandum of the Archbishops of Canterbury and York, April 16, 1923. A copy of this memorandum is reproduced for this book is found in Appendix C.

2. *Frank Weston and Maude Petre — More Controversy*

In July 1923, Halifax wrote Mercier[10] that he realized Davidson was concerned about the Revised Prayer Book[11] issue and had to tread cautiously; that it would take some time to convince Anglicans that papal primacy was *jure divino* and not simply *jure ecclesiastico*; and that he had two new projects to help push things along. Halifax planned to publish a short defense of the *jure divino* nature of papal primacy[12]; and he would also give a major address promoting that position at a meeting of English Churchmen in London on July 27, under the chairmanship of Bishop Burge, then Bishop of Oxford. Mercier replied positively, and Halifax began working on the plans.

About this time, Davidson heard from Bishop Burge what Halifax had in mind and reacted with alarm. The Archbishop had no objection to Halifax's publication as long as it avoided "any reference to the actual conferences at Malines"[13]. Neither Davidson nor Lang and neither Frere nor Robinson could agree with Halifax's *jure divino* position; but Davidson was willing to allow Halifax to publish such a position if it were clearly seen as Halifax's own personal opinion. (Halifax, as we shall see, eventually published his opinions in *Further Considerations on Behalf of Reunion*.) When it came to the public address scheduled for July 27, however, Davidson was adamantly opposed. The last thing Davidson wanted was any public meeting

10. BIY, The Malines Papers of Lord Halifax, Box 3, N° 9, Halifax to Mercier, either July 1 or 2, 1923.

11. When Randall Davidson became Archbishop of Canterbury in 1903, one of his first acts was to persuade Prime Minister A.J. Balfour to appoint a Royal Commission known as The Royal Commission on Ecclesiastical Discipline to deal with complaints about Ritualism. The Commission ended up recommending that the Anglican Convocations embark on revising the Book of Common Prayer, which had not been revised since 1661. Nothing much happened until after the First World War. From 1920 until 1927 there was considerable debate about various proposals for revision the "Green", the "Grey", and the "Orange" books. The Prayer Book measure finally came before the House of Lords on December 12, 1927 and passed but failed to pass in the House of Commons. See: A.R. VIDLER, *The Church in an Age of Revolution*, Harmondsworth, 1981 (first published 1961), pp. 162-168.

12. In clarifying his understanding of papal primacy, Halifax relied on the theological advice of his friend from Louvain, Aloïs Janssens. We read for instance in Janssens' diary of August 20, 1923: "I had a talk with Lord Halifax in his London home... He is intellectually alert as ever, but has aged much in appearance and speaks with some difficulty. The eyes and the ears are very much affected. About his pamphlet A Call To Reunion he says: 'I wanted to make clear to our people, that we can and must admit a primacy of the Bishop of Rome, jure divino. But one has to be very careful in speaking of these things to Anglicans. The first time they hear it they are startled, the second time they find it more natural'". D. VERHELST, "Lord Halifax and the Scheut Father Aloïs Janssens", in *Ephemerides Theologicae Lovanienses* 53 (1967), p. 234.

13. BIY, The Malines Papers of Lord Halifax, Box 3, N° 11, Davidson to Halifax, July 7, 1923.

drawing attention to Church union activities. Davidson also had read and was anxious about the message of the Bishop of Zanzibar about the upcoming Anglo-Catholic Congress. The message had taken up an entire page in the June 29, 1923 issue of *The Church Times* and asserted: "It has taken us many years to escape from the spirit of party that is characteristic of British religion. We now stand for the Catholic Faith, common to East and West. We are not concerned with the shibboleths of Low Church, High Church, Broad Church, Liberal, Modernist, or even the new 'non-party' party. We stand or fall with Christ's Church, Catholic and Apostolic. And we wait patiently till the Holy Father and the Orthodox Patriarchs recognize us as of their own stock. We are not a party: we are those in the Anglican Communion who refuse to be limited by party-rules and party-creeds. Our appeal is to the Catholic Creed, to Catholic worship, and to Catholic practice"[14]. Anglican and Roman Catholic feelings were already sensitive because Charles Gore (1853-1932)[15] and Pierre Batiffol (1861-1929)[16] had been waging a paper war on the subject of papal primacy. On July 7 Davidson sent an urgent telegram and a letter to Halifax[17] begging him not to give the talk because it could create "untold mischief". Halifax reluctantly observed Davidson's request.

On July 10 Davidson had more cause for alarm. Frank Weston, the Anglican Bishop of Zanzibar and a major force behind the 1920 *Lambeth Appeal*, had, as President of the Anglo-Catholic Congress meeting in the Albert Hall, sent a telegram to Pope Pius XI: "Sixteen thousand Anglo-Catholics in Congress assembled offer respectful greetings to the Holy Father, humbly praying that the day of peace may quickly break"[18]. The telegram was actually sent to Cardinal Bourne who sent the message on to the Pope[19]. Nevertheless, Davidson was flabbergasted. Gore and others were furious.

14. Cardinal Bourne marked this paragraph in his copy of the message. AAW, Cardinal Bourne's Papers, 1923, BO III.

15. Charles Gore, a Fellow at Trinity College Oxford, had been associated with the foundation of the Community of the Resurrection in 1875. He became Bishop of Worcester in 1902 and Bishop of Oxford in 1911. At the time of the Malines Conversations, he was retired from the bishopric of Oxford. He was a well-known scholar who had introduced the science of modern exegesis into the Anglo-Catholicism. "He was politely inflexible towards the Catholic Church, and this made the somewhat timorous Archbishop of Canterbury sure of him". G. H. TAVARD, *Two Centuries of Ecumenism*, Notre Dame, 1960, p. 130.

16. Pierre Batiffol (whose name is often incorrectly spelled as Battifol) was Church historian at the *École Ste Barbe* in Paris.

17. Both sent July 7, 1923, BIY, The Malines Papers of Lord Halifax, Box 3, N° 10 and N° 11.

18. J. GOOD, *The Church of England and the Ecumenical Movement*, London, 1961, p. 110.

19. On July 31, 1923, Cardinal Gasparri sent Cardinal Bourne a thank you letter for sending the telegram to Rome. AAW, Cardinal Bourne's Papers, 1923, BO III. Charles

A few days later, increased public attention was drawn to the Malines Conversations and to the issue of papal primacy when Maude Petre, Tyrrell's friend and biographer, sent *The Guardian* an "Open Letter to Lord Halifax". Petre had written in reply to Halifax's *A Call to Reunion*, and in her letter she observed that Halifax's position held for the relative nature of theological definitions and was therefore a Modernist perspective[20]. For Halifax's relations with English Roman Catholics the timing of Petre's letter could not have been worse. The strongly anti-Modernist Jesuit Francis Woodlock (1871-1940) took up his pen with increased vigor. And from this time on, the Malines Conversations were openly tainted and haunted by Roman Catholic fears of Modernism.

Woodlock had been writing against the Anglicans in *The Church Times* and *The Guardian*. His statement: "With us the infallibility and supremacy of the Pope is a dogma which rests exactly on the same authority as does that of the Godhead of Christ" had particularly provoked and perturbed Archbishop Davidson[21].

3. *Lord Halifax's Correspondence with English Roman Catholics*

Francis Woodlock was, however, only one of several English Roman Catholics who were actively corresponding with Lord Halifax at this time. And it is noteworthy that other English Roman Catholics, especially Vincent McNabb and Bede Jarrett, did not share Woodlock's antagonistic outlook.

We noted in Chapter Three that the English Dominican, Vincent McNabb, had been unable to become actively involved in the Malines Conversations. He had nevertheless maintained a friendly correspondence with Lord Halifax. And Halifax and Portal continued to nourish hopes about English Dominican involvement in the Conversations. At the end of March 1923, for instance, Portal wrote Halifax about McNabb and the Dominicans at Oxford. He was sending Halifax a letter from Vincent McNabb. He wanted Halifax to see McNabb

Gore's biographer, ignorant of what was in the archives at Westminster, doubted that the telegram ever went to Rome: "No evidence is available to show that the famous 'telegram to the pope' was ever forwarded beyond the Roman archbishop's house at Westminster". G.L. PRESTIGE, *The Life of Charles Gore*, London, Toronto, 1935, p. 481.

20. C. F. CREWS, *The Role of Miss Maude Petre in the Modernist Movement*, Fordham University, Ph. D. Dissertation, New York, 1972, p. 302. Halifax was hardly a Modernist. He had in fact suspected Gore of being a Modernist. Halifax "disliked Gore's liberal Catholicism, which he suspected of being first cousin to Modernism". LOCKHART, *op. cit.*, p. 36. Halifax had opposed the Revised Prayer Book because "he disliked the new rubrics which he felt were designed to ease the tender consciences of Modernists at the expense of the Catholic Faith". *Ibid.*, p. 345. Nevertheless neither Halifax nor Portal nor Mercier would ever escape the suspicious accusations that they were Modernists.

21. LOCKHART, *op. cit.*, p. 294.

because it was important to establish contact with the English Dominicans who were well-disposed toward the Roman Catholic/Anglican
discussions. Certain French Dominicans were also well-disposed[22].

Vincent McNabb considered himself one of the "Roman Catholic
friends of the Anglo-Catholic movement"[23]. He had seen to it that
Batiffol's articles battling Bishop Gore were published in English
translation in *Blackfriars* and elsewhere[24]. On June 5, 1923, McNabb
sent Halifax an eleven page handwritten letter with his concerns about
possible developments within the Anglo-Catholic movement. It touched
on the tip of an iceberg. He asked about the truth of "what I hear
suggested in many quarters — that the Anglo-Catholic party has come
to a *modus vivendi* with Modernism"[25]. As Halifax was pondering
McNabb's observations, he was forced to pay closer attention again to
the English Jesuit, Francis Woodlock.

In July an anxious Archbishop Davidson wrote Halifax about Francis
Woodlock's article in *The Guardian* asserting an equal dogmatic status
for papal supremacy and the Divinity of Christ. "Nothing has happened",
wrote Davidson, "to make me think that what he there writes is other
than true, and my fear is that action on our part may be taken which is
based on a misunderstanding of the real attitude of Rome"[26]. Halifax
replied on August 9 that a response to Woodlock would be part of his
book *Further Considerations on Behalf of Reunion*[27]. When the book
came out a few days later, it did indeed contain a type of rebuttal
against Woodlock and an appendix critical of Woodlock, written by
Aloïs Janssens from Louvain[28].

22. "*Je vous renvoie la lettre du Père McNabb. Ce serait bien important que les
dominicains anglais s'intéressâssent à nos questions, et si vous pouvez voir ce supérieur
d'Oxford et vous assurer de ces bonnes dispositions ce serait parfait. La Revue des Jeunes est
dirigée par les dominicains, et le père qui la dirige se met au service de nos idées*". BIY, The
Malines Papers of Lord Halifax, Box 3, N° 124, Portal to Halifax, March 23, 1923.

23. BIY, The Malines Papers of Lord Halifax, Box 3, N° 200, McNabb to Halifax,
June 5, 1923.

24. BIY, The Malines Papers of Lord Halifax, Box 3, McNabb to Halifax, N° 168,
April 19, 1923 and N° 176, April 27, 1923.

25. BIY, The Malines Papers of Lord Halifax, Box 3, N° 200, McNabb to Halifax,
June 5, 1923.

26. BIY, The Malines Papers of Lord Halifax, Box 3, N° 28, Davidson to Halifax, July
27, 1923.

27. BIY, The Malines Papers of Lord Halifax, Box 3, N° 40, Halifax to Davidson,
August 9, 1923.

28. In "Appendix F" to Halifax's book, Janssens made a distinction which he felt
Woodlock had ignored: "That Christ is God is a fundamental, indeed the fundamental
dogma of the Christian Faith. It has always been explicitly held. There was no development in this doctrine, but only in its terminology. The terminology has become clearer
when it was found necessary to adjust and harmonize different dogmas. The infallibility of
the Pope, on the other hand, has admitted of a true development, a real doctrinal
progress. It has been held but implicitly in the first three centuries and has been doubted
afterwards, even until the time of the Vatican Council. In this sense it is not a

About Woodlock, Halifax wrote: "A comparison of Fr. Woodlock's words with these statements by Mgr. Batiffol, who was described to me in a letter from a professor of theology at Louvain as 'since the death of Mgr. Duchesne one of our ablest, if not the ablest, historian of the four first centuries', inevitably suggests the question whether the limitations and developments which apply to the Papacy have the same place in regard to the Godhead of Christ? If the answer be in the affirmative, as Fr. Woodlock's statement would seem to suggest, is not the faith of Christendom in some danger? If the answer be in the negative, are we not at least entitled to say that Fr. Woodlock's statement might have been put in a way not so obviously inspired by the desire to prejudice any attempt at corporate reunion, in the interests of individual conversions"[29]?

The day after Halifax had written to Davidson, he typed a hurried note to Portal. "A Jesuit, Father Woodlock, appears to be stirring things up here; but 'salvation from our enemies'"[30]. And nine days later in a letter to Robinson, Halifax regretted the "unfortunate intervention of Fr. Woodlock"[31].

In early September 1923, Halifax's *Further Considerations on Behalf of Reunion* came out. Francis Woodlock immediately sent Halifax a long personal letter, because he saw himself introduced in the book as "the villian of the piece"[32]. Woodlock said that he longed and prayed for reunion, could not see corporate reunion in the immediate future, and was concerned about souls living in schism. He asserted again his belief that papal supremacy and the Divinity of Christ were of equal dogmatic status and added the dogma of the Immaculate Conception. He expressed his fears about current Modernist trends which are often presented under a term he thought Halifax had used "restatement". He expressed his opinion that Halifax represented a very small group of Anglicans, that people who realized that the Anglican Church was in schism were conscience bound to convert to Rome. Woodlock was convinced that there was really no theological disagreement between himself and Janssens. And finally he said he would not go to the press

fundamental doctrine of the Christian Faith, because fundamentals do not admit of real development. Quod non fuit ab initio doctum et universaliter creditum non pertinet ad Christianae fidei fundamenta". Viscount HALIFAX, *Further Considerations on Behalf of Reunion*, London, Milwaukee, 1923, pp. 58-59.

29. *Ibid.*, p. 29.

30. *"Un jésuite, le Père Woodlock, semble vouloir embrouiller les choses ici, mais 'salus ex inimicis'"*. BIY, The Malines Papers of Lord Halifax, Box 3, N° 41, Halifax to Portal, August 10, 1923.

31. BIY, The Malines Papers of Lord Halifax, Box 3, N° 46, Halifax to Robinson, August 19, 1923.

32. BIY, The Malines Papers of Lord Halifax, Box 3, N° 74, Woodlock to Halifax, September 18, 1923.

with any comments unless someone publicly tried to assert that he and Janssens differed and his orthodoxy were challenged.

Two days later, Woodlock sent Halifax a another long letter, "as a sort of appendix to my first letter"[33]. This second letter was an exposition of Roman Catholic teaching about development of doctrine, papal infallibility, and implicit and explicit recognition of papal supremacy. "The point which appears to me to be all important", he wrote, "and which will arise to immediate prominence out of Your Lordship's thesis is whether the admission of the supremacy *jure divino* does not make a state of schism from the Pope equivalent to a state of exile from the Catholic Church". And toward the end of his letter he commented on "the Anglican idea that has been ventilated a good deal lately that it is *acceptance by the Church* (his emphasis, JD) that guarantees the infallibility of a papal utterance". This he said was the argument that could be used by the Modernists to justify their survival to the present day.

A few days later, Halifax sent Woodlock a long reply, written in "complete frankness" but "in no controversial spirit". He felt that Woodlock's way of expressing himself hindered rather than helped the cause of reunion; that he could not agree with Woodlock's observations about "restatement" even though he, Halifax, had never used that word. And Halifax raised some pointed questions about Roman Catholic theology and belief: "Let me put the matter in the form of questions: If belief in Papal Infallibility and the Immaculate Conception of our Lady rest on the same foundation as that of the Divinity of our Lord, and those doctrines, consistently with the Catholic Faith could have been denied not so long ago, could our Lord's Divinity also have been denied in the same way? If not, why not? And if the answer be, because the doctrines of Papal Infallibility and the Immaculate Conception of our Lady had not then been defined, how can you escape the conclusion that the Saints and Cardinals who had denied those doctrines had been all their lives in ignorance of important parts of the Catholic Faith? Again, in what way can such statements be reconciled with the *'quod semper, quod ubique, quod ab omnibus'*...? It would be ridiculous and presumptuous besides for one in my position to enter into any further controversy, but I may perhaps ask in conclusion whether there are not propositions in Catholic theology which seem to contradict one another, but which have nevertheless to be held in their entirety without one being allowed to diminish the force of the other"? And Halifax concluded the letter with a friendly invitation for Woodlock to visit him so that they could have "some interesting conversations"[34].

33. BIY, The Malines Papers of Lord Halifax, Box 3, N° 77, Woodlock to Halifax, September 20, 1923.

34. BIY, The Malines Papers of Lord Halifax, Box 3, N° 80, Halifax to Woodlock, September 22, 1923.

Woodlock replied to Halifax on September 24, September 30, and October 4[35]. He said he would try to "seek a less offensive way of expressing a truth" but that some "truths themselves are 'hard sayings to Anglicans'". And he thanked Halifax for his "kindness in writing so fully and so charitably to one who has *seemed* (his emphasis, JD) to hamper your efforts for corporate reunion"[36]. Woodlock further assured Halifax that his criticism of Halifax's book in *The Month*, *The Universe* and in letters to the editors of *The Church Times* and *The Guardian* were not to be taken by Halifax unkindly[37]. But Woodlock repeated and stressed his belief that "any body of Christians who were 'apart from the Pope' were by that very fact seen to be 'apart from the Church'"[38].

In the meantime, the English Dominicans Vincent McNabb and Bede Jarrett had also been corresponding with Halifax. They were both grateful for Halifax's courageous defense of papal primacy as *jure divino* but their chief concerns were about Anglican Orders. "Some of the positions you maintain ask for discussion", wrote McNabb. "I have particularly called attention to the sentence, 'Englishmen will never consent to anything which in their eyes would seem to invalidate the Orders conferred by the English episcopate'. This claim to Infallibility — this *Non Possumus* in a matter on which the English Church has changed seems, alas! to stifle all hopes of reunion! Is this the best you have to say? If so, hope seems dead"[39].

Bede Jarrett was equally firm. He could not see how one could accept the validity of Anglican Orders and he implored Halifax to convert, just as Bonner[40] had done: "He forewent his earlier judgment. Is it not possible for you, with that immense courage you have always shown as fearlessly as he, to forego an earlier judgment and find your way as he did to the Faith in peace"[41]?

At this time, as we shall soon explore in a bit more detail, Halifax was considering Mercier's desire that Bede Jarrett be a participant in the next Conversation. But he had his doubts. Nor could he help thinking about the rumor Portal had mentioned in an earlier letter. The niece of the wife of one of his friends had written him that the English

---

35. These letters are at BIY, The Malines Papers of Lord Halifax, Box 3, N° 88, N° 101, N° 106.

36. September 24, 1923.

37. September 30, 1923.

38. October 4, 1923.

39. BIY, The Malines Papers of Lord Halifax, Box 3, N° 81, McNabb to Halifax, September 23, 1923.

40. Edmund Bonner (c.1500-1569) had been chaplain to Thomas Wolsey. He ended up being the last Bishop of London to die in communion with the See of Rome.

41. BIY, The Malines Papers of Lord Halifax, Box 3, N° 86, Jarrett to Halifax, September 24, 1923.

Dominicans were only interested in the Anglicans and not at all in the Oriental Churches[42].

In the same letter, Portal also mentioned a rumor about Gasparri's *apparently* having second thoughts about Mercier and the Malines Conversations: Portal mentioned that he had seen Batiffol and that Batiffol had received a letter from a certain American lady in Rome, informing him that Gasparri had been saying alot against Mercier and against the conversations What do we make of this rumor? Perhaps nothing more than that Gasparri was trying to be diplomatic. Mercier had informed the Pope on March 1, 1923[43] about the agenda for the Second Conversation; yet Gasparri — no doubt realizing how sensitive English Roman Catholics would be to the proposed agenda — did not return the Pope's acknowledgement and words of support until the end of March 1923[44] and thus well after the Second Conversation. In no other place do we find any indications that Gasparri was ill disposed toward either Mercier or the Malines Conversations. On November 3, 1923, for instance, he had sent Halifax a friendly note thanking him for sending a copy of *Further Considerations on Behalf of Reunion*[45]. In December 1923, when the English press (and English Roman Catholics!) were buzzing about Archbishop Davidson's revelation about the Malines Conversations, Gasparri did write Mercier that he should go easy and, as much as possible, keep the press from giving the impression that the conversations had an "official character" granted by the Holy See[46]. But this was hardly a statement of opposition.

4. *From Six to Ten Participants in the Conversations*

Before the Second Conversation, both Davidson and Mercier had entertained the idea of increasing the number of participants in any future conversation. As public tensions were increasing prior to the Third Conversation — and Halifax was becoming increasingly outspoken about papal primacy — Davidson felt it important that Anglicans be

42. "*La nièce d'une dame de mes amies lui écrit que les dominicains anglais ne s'occupent que des anglicans et pas du tout des Orientaux. Elle connaît le Père McNabb*", and further "*Il m'a communiqué une lettre que lui a écrite de Rome une américaine. Elle raconte que le cardinal Gasparri parle beaucoup contre le cardinal Mercier et contre nos conférences*". BIY, The Malines Papers of Lord Halifax, Box 3, N° 198, Portal to Halifax, May 28, 1923.

43. AAM, The Malines Conversations, 1923, B I, N° 3, Mercier to Pius XI, March 1, 1923.

44. AAM, The Malines Conversations, 1923, B I, N° 5, Gasparri to Mercier, March 30, 1923.

45. BIY, The Malines Papers of Lord Halifax, Box 3, N° 135, Gasparri to Halifax, November 3, 1923.

46. "*Autant que possible il faudrait empêcher que dans les annonces des journaux les conférences prennent un caractère officiel de la part du Saint Siège*". AAM, The Malines Conversations, 1923, B I, N° 8, Gasparri to Mercier, December 30, 1923.

added to the delegation who could balance the, in some respects, very Roman theology of Halifax. On August 7, 1923, Davidson wrote to Halifax that he had received agreements from Gore[47] and Beresford James Kidd (1864-1948)[48] that they would be willing to participate in any future Malines Conversation.

As soon as Gore was appointed to the Anglican side, there was little doubt that Batiffol would be added to the Catholic side[49]. On September 10, 1923, Halifax informed Mercier about Gore and Kidd and suggested that Pierre Batiffol, Hippolyte Hemmer (1864-1945)[50] and Bede Jarrett be added to the Roman Catholic group[51]. Nearly two weeks later Mercier replied that he was inviting Batiffol and would be well disposed toward Hemmer and Jarrett[52].

And three days after Mercier's letter, Halifax heard from Portal who strongly recommended Jarrett[53]; but the very next day, Halifax wrote

47. Bishop Gore was an outspoken critic of the Roman Catholic Church; and Roman Catholics were just as outspoken about Bishop Gore. L.D. Murphy, for instance, writing in the February 1923 issue of *The Month* made the following observations about Gore: "The Advent sermons, which he delivered in Grosvernor Chapel, and which were published in three December issues of the Church Times, are of more than ordinary importance, as proving that 'Anglo-Catholicism' is radically the same as Protestantism (p. 137)... Dr. Gore seems not to know his own mind. He urges submission to proper authority, but he will have none of it himself" (p. 138).

48. B. J. Kidd was Warden of Keble College and a scholar noted for his works on the ancient Church and on the Counter-Reformation.

49. "A sharp little controversy between Bishop Gore and Mgr. Batiffol added some fuel to the fire; but at the same time in the long run it lighted the way to the future... The little controversy above mentioned seemed to indicate that Bishop Gore and Mgr. Batiffol had better argue out their case round the Cardinal's table in conference. So that would form at any rate one part of any programme that might be drawn up". W. H. Frere, *Recollections of Malines*, London, 1935, pp. 36-37. The battle between Gore and Batiffol was also reflected in Vincent McNabb's correspondence with Lord Halifax: "I have read Bishop Gore's three addresses on reunion! I can just imagine why in the hurry of speech he could preach them. But I can not imagine how such a gentleman could have printed them in the weekly press (the Church Times) or how a Christian bishop could have reprinted them in book form... I have not seen the abbé Battifol's (sic) reply to the second of Gore's addresses. It will be well worth reading". McNabb to Halifax, April 19, 1923, The Malines Papers of Lord Halifax, Box 3, The Borthwick Institute, York.

"Thanks for Bishop Gore's sermons. They make painful reading! Thanks also for Mgr. Battifol's (sic) excellent article. In substance and mode it is a striking contrast to the sermons it criticizes". McNabb to Halifax, April 27, 1923, The Malines Papers of Lord Halifax, Box 3, The Borthwick Institute, York.

50. Hemmer was Church historian at the *Institut Catholique* in Paris.

51. BIY, The Malines Papers of Lord Halifax, Box 3, N° 67, Halifax to Mercier, September 10, 1923.

52. BIY, The Malines Papers of Lord Halifax, Box 3, N° 83, Mercier to Halifax, September 23, 1923.

53. BIY, The Malines Papers of Lord Halifax, Box 3, N° 95, Portal to Halifax, September 26, 1923.

to Gore that he had second thoughts about Jarrett and was asking Mercier to delay making a decision about him[54]. What happened?

By the end of September, Halifax had decided, at least in his own mind, that the question of Anglican Orders had to be decided in favor of the Anglicans. On September 24, he had received the disappointing letter from Jarrett mentioned earlier[55] in which Jarrett saw no way that Anglican Orders could be found valid and he had even suggested that Halifax convert to the Roman Church.

A month before the Third Conversation, Portal wrote Halifax that Mercier still favored Jarrett[56]. Halifax wrote back and explained why Jarrett could not be asked. Simply stated — Halifax wanted to achieve the goal of 1895 and he could not do it with Jarrett[57].

And so because of Halifax — who ironically had always wanted English Dominican backing — Jarrett was excluded; and, as R.J. Lahey observes: "Thus Hemmer became the second new delegate and an important opportunity to reconcile English Catholic opinion was lost"[58].

5. *At Malines, November 7 and 8, 1923*

Throughout October 1923, final arrangements were made for the Third Malines Conversation.

The Anglicans met at Lambeth Palace on October 2 to receive instructions from Archbishop Davidson and to write their memoranda,

54. BIY, The Malines Papers of Lord Halifax, Box 3, N° 97, Halifax to Gore, September 27, 1923.

55. Jarrett to Halifax, September 24, 1923, *op. cit.*

56. BIY, The Malines Papers of Lord Halifax, Box 3, N° 107, Portal to Halifax, October 7, 1923.

57. It seems appropriate that we quote at length from this letter: "*Voici le point essentiel... Vous vous souvenez que nous avons eu en 1895 l'audace de mettre sous les yeux de Léon XIII certaines choses qui, mises dans une communication pontificale attireraient l'esprit et le cœur de presque toute l'Angleterre. Vous vous souvenez aussi que le Pape s'est servi de ce que nous avons osé dire, mais que la lettre a été gatée par la fin que les Catholiques Anglais ont su obtenir.*

"*Si Pie XI comme 'beau geste' dont parle le Cardinal, pouvait dire qu'il bénissait tout effort pour la réunion des Églises, notamment les conférences entreprises à Malines, etc. etc. etc., une allusion alors au rassemblement du Concile du Vatican, une autre à la Conférence de Lambeth et la lettre Encyclique des Évêques Anglicans avec une fin qu'il espérait qu'il serait possible de trouver un moyen de réconcilier les difficultés au sujet des Ordres conférés par l'Église d'Angleterre avec l'enseignement de l'Église de Rome et cela d'une manière que l'Église Anglicane pourrait accepter, le beau geste de la part de Rome aurait été donné, et de la meilleure façon. Et un beau geste de la part de l'archevêque de Cantorbéry serait facile, et un pas énorme pour la réunion aurait été pris.*

"*Vous direz que je suis fou pour penser à de telles choses, mais c'est une folie qui tient de la sagesse.*

"*Finalement pour accomplir tout ceci je doute si Dom Bede Jarrett nous aiderait beaucoup à ce moment*". BIY, The Malines Papers of Lord Halifax, Box 3, N° 110, Halifax to Portal, October 9, 1923.

58. A. HASTINGS, ed., *Bishops and Writers*, Wheathampstead, 1977, p. 89.

assisted by "a few trusted advisers"[59]. The task as the Anglicans saw it was to determine to what extent the positions of Rome and Canterbury could be reconciled on the points of Faith, Worship, Orders, and Papal Jurisdiction. They also agreed to present three important papers: one by Armitage Robinson on the position of St. Peter in the Primitive Church, one by B.J. Kidd on Petrine texts up to 461 A.D.; and another by Kidd on the repudiation of Papal authority in England at the time of the Reformation. These three papers were sent in advance to Pierre Batiffol who wrote replies to the first two. The five studies then formed the basis for the discussions at the Third Conversation in November. They were subsequently published by Halifax in 1930 in his *The Conversations at Malines, 1921-1925, Original Documents*.

As the meeting date approached, Portal and Halifax were anxious about Gore. "The conversion of Gore to our ideas is the chief point at the moment", Halifax had written to Portal[60]. They even discussed the possibility of Gore's being able to sleep at Mercier's house so that he could be "charmed by the Cardinal"[61]. Mercier too was anxious about Gore and he was fearful about becoming involved in any conflict at Malines between Gore and Batiffol. In fact in September Mercier had suggested to Halifax that there be a special meeting — which he would not attend — prior to the Third Conversation to take care of any controversial discussions between the two publicly known contenders about the papacy[62]. Davidson was absolutely opposed to such a meeting and it never took place. Mercier's fears no doubt explain why he gave the impression of "retiring a little into the background" during the Third Conversation[63].

When the ten representatives met at Malines on November 7 and 8,

---

59. Among them were the Bishop of Ripon, Canon Storr, Canon Quick, and Dr. Jenkins. LOCKHART, *op. cit.*, p. 299.

60. Halifax to Portal, October 3, 1923, quoted in LOCKHART, *op. cit.*, p. 299. Gore's reaction to Halifax's Further Considerations on Behalf of Reunion had been strongly negative, as he wrote to Halifax: "With your argument on behalf of the de jure divino position of the See of Peter at Rome and (generally) what you say about the Eastern Church of early time I disagree rather profoundly. Some of your sentences seem to me the reverse of the truth". BIY, The Malines Papers of Lord Halifax, Box 3, N° 76, Gore to Halifax, September 20, 1923.

It is interesting to note, however, that even before the Second Conversation Halifax would have been willing to have Gore as an Anglican representative, as he had explained in a letter to Portal: "Do you think I am mad? But what would you say if we should be able to bring Gore with us to Malines for our next meeting? It is dangerous, but it is necessary to take risks. To get Gore on our side would be tremendous. He is quite the most distinguished bishop we have...". BIY, The Malines Papers of Lord Halifax, Box 2, N° 60, Halifax to Portal, February 10, 1923.

61. LOCKHART, *op. cit.*, p. 300.

62. BIY, The Malines Papers of Lord Halifax, Box 3, N° 66, Mercier to Halifax, September 10, 1923.

63. LOCKHART, *op. cit.*, p. 301.

the newcomers actually took the forefront in the discussions. The Catholics and the Anglicans formulated separate conclusions about the discussions of the five papers and then tried to determine to what extent their conclusions might agree. The outcome was "far from spectacular"[64] because there was no real conclusion. The Anglicans could not accept the phrase "universal jurisdiction" as applied either to St. Peter or the Roman Church. Robinson proposed the terms "spiritual leadership" or "general superintendence". Gore had difficulty with these — much to the annoyance of Lord Halifax — and proposed "spiritual responsibility" to describe the Papal office. Hemmer composed a list of points which he thought the Catholic participants as well as the Anglicans could agree on and proposed that all participants sign it. The Anglicans, recalling the difficulties resulting from the signed documents of the Second Conversation — as well as Davidson's warnings prior to their departure for the Third Conversation[65] — would not sign anything. In the end, both sides did agree on the importance of frank discussions and they decided that they would have to meet again for more such open conversation; and they concluded the Third Conversation, with Mercier's blessing, in a spirit of friendly optimism[66].

64. B. PAWLEY and M. PAWLEY, *Rome and Canterbury Through Four Centuries*, London, Oxford, 1981, p. 271.

65. When Davidson had met with the Anglican participants in October 1923, he warned them to be faithful to the Anglican tradition. "It ought to be made clear on the Anglican side, beyond possibility of doubt, that the great principles upon which the Reformation turned are our principles still, whatever faults or failures there may have been on either side in the controversies of the sixteenth century. It would be unfair to our Roman Catholic friends to leave them in any doubt as to our adherence, on large questions of controversy, to the main principles for which men like Hooker or Andrews or Cosin contended, though the actual wording would, no doubt, be somewhat different today. What those men stood for we stand for still; and I think that in some form or other that ought to be made immediately clear". FRERE, *op. cit.*, p. 77.

66. A Roman Catholic summary was formulated as follows:

"I. There are abundant indications in the Synoptic Gospels and in the Gospel of St. John that Peter fulfilled a peculiar function of service towards Jesus and among His disciples. The cause of this is to be found neither in the fact that he was the first that was called by Jesus, nor in the forcefulness of his character, but in a determination of the will of Jesus. The Savior manifests more explicitly this His will by the words 'Thou art Peter' of St. Matthew, 'Strengthen thy brethern' of St. Luke, and 'Feed my lambs' of the Fourth Gospel.

II. This will discloses itself in the Acts by the fact that Peter appears and acts as the head of the primitive community (leader of the Church); and Paul, who claims the apostolate of the Gentiles, recognizes Peter as the apostle of the Circumcision, and never attempts to deny to Peter a more extended mission.

III. We hold that the sayings of the Gospel notably the Tu est Petrus and the Pasce agnos express a prerogative of Peter as the foundation of the Church and the principle of its unity.

We consider that the events of history have thrown light on these texts which has brought out more clearly their true significance.

IV. The Vatican Council defines as of the Catholic Faith the primacy of universal

A few days later, B.J. Kidd wrote Mercier about "the wonderful atmosphere of good will" during the Third Conversation and that they "reached an agreement limited, of course, but real, such as I hardly dared to expect"[67]. And even Gore, who on one occasion during the conversation had been "almost wrangling"[68] with Mercier, was a bit elated [69-70]. Years after The Malines Conversations, W.H. Frere would look back at the discussions of the Third Conversation with a bit more objective theological perspective. "My own impression at the time was that our biblical argument had not been really faced; apparently one or two texts concerning St. Peter had hypnotized the Roman Catholics in their outlook, to the exclusion of the scriptural description of the Church itself; and a re-reading of the documents confirms me in this"[71].

jurisdiction conferred on Peter, grounding itself on the two texts Tu es Petrus and Pasce oves. It declares that the denial of the primacy is contrary to the plain sense of Holy Scripture as the Catholic Church has always understood it.

The Council does not indicate the numerous testimonies which prove the tradition in the interpretation of the text, and which are to be found in the patrology and ancient Christian literature". The closest formulation to approach an Anglican summary took this shape:

"I. That the Roman Church was founded and built by St. Peter and St. Paul, according to St. Irenaeus (Adv. Haer. iii. 3. 2).

II. That the Roman See is the only historically known Apostolic See of the West.

III. That the Bishop of Rome is, as St. Augustine said of Pope Innocent I, president of the Western Church (Contra Iulianum Pelagianum, i, 13).

IV. That he has a primacy among all the Bishops of Christendom; so that, without communion with him, there is in fact no prospect of a reunited Christendom.

V. That to the Roman See the churches of the English owe their Christianity through 'Gregory our father' (Council of Clovesho, A.D. 747) 'who sent us baptism' (Anglo-Saxon Chronicle, Anno 565)". Viscount HALIFAX, The Conversations at Malines, 1921 1925: Original Documents, London, Milwaukee, 1930, pp. 48-49.

67. AAM, The Malines Conversations, 1923, A III, N° 8, Kidd to Mercier, November 12, 1923.

68. PRESTIGE, op. cit., p. 483.

69. "Je ne puis qu'exprimer quoique c'est presque inexprimable le sens de votre bonté envers nous Anglicans avec lequel je suis revenu de Malines. Ce n'est pas seulement que vous avez été un hôte si généreux, mais c'est que vous avez réussi en faisant nous autres hérétiques se sentir si pleinement chez soi dans votre maison, qu'on a pu oser de parler parfaitement franchement même des choses les plus désagréables. J'ai senti jusqu'au cœur même votre 'tolerantia perseverantissima', et je demande pardon si j'ai parlé un seul mot qui n'était pas nécessaire pour expliquer la position. Quel que peut s'éventuer de ces conférences j'espère que nous pouvons tous sentir que c'est bon de s'entretenir et de se comprendre". AAM, The Malines Conversations, 1923, A III, N° 7, Gore to Mercier, November 10, 1923.

70. Mercier replied that there was no need for any apology and that it had been "un fait bien remarquable, que nous ayons pu, pendant deux longues journées, échanger librement notre manière d'apprécier la Primauté de Pierre, sans aboutir à une conclusion négative qui eût mis fin à nos communes espérances". PRESTIGE, op. cit., p. 484.

71. FRERE, op. cit., p. 302.

6. *The Question of Publicity*

Immediately after the Third Conversation, there was a felt need to go public with more information about the Malines Conversations. Roman Catholics were curious, fearful and angry. And so were the Anglicans, whose lives were already greatly agitated by the progress of the Revised Prayer Book issue. "I have had much trouble about the Malines business", Davidson wrote to Archbishop Lang in the middle of December 1923[72]. Halifax wanted to publish another book with complete details of everything that had so far taken place[73]. Davidson and the other Anglican participants thought otherwise. There would be no official Malines Conversations report, but Davidson would acknowledge and comment about the Conversations in a circular letter to the Archbishops and Metropolitans of the Anglican Communion. A draft of this letter was sent to the Anglican participants in the Conversations and to Cardinal Mercier. There were several criticisms. Mercier, in particular, wanted Davidson to omit a direct quote of the statement of Holy See approval for the Conversations[74]. This response from Mercier surprised Davidson, who said that obviously Mercier had "taken a little freight", but he complied[75].

Mercier was of course concerned about English Roman Catholic public reaction. He had apparently made the suggestion to Davidson on his own accord because it was not until after the publication of Davidson's letter that Gasparri had written to Mercier to ask him, in the letter of December 30 which we have already mentioned, to downplay the issue of papal support for the Conversations at Malines. Later Mercier explained with better clarity what his intention had been — to distinguish between official and confidential approval: "Rome neither approved nor disapproved officially but approved, encouraged, approves and encourages confidentially"[76].

Davidson's letter came out at Christmas 1923 in the form of a report

---

72. ALPL, Archbishop Lang's papers, 1923, Davidson to Lang, December 19, 1923.

73. LOCKHART, *op. cit.*, pp. 302-303.

74. AAM, The Malines Conversations, 1923, A II, N° 17, Mercier to Davidson, December 15, 1923; copy also found in BIY, The Malines Papers of Lord Halifax, Box 3, N° 170.

75. "I had a letter from the Cardinal who has, I think, taken a little fright and I imagine thinks that he has perhaps gone further than the Vatican approves. He bid me certainly not publish the wording of the message from the Pope, which he says is quite accurate but was private... I have at his request, cut out the footnote giving the words of the Pope's message, and have merely said that I had satisfied myself about the Pope's cognizance of what was happening". ALPL, Archbishop Lang's papers, 1923, Davidson to Lang, December 19, 1923.

76. "*Rome n'approuvait ni désapprouvait officiellement, mais approuvait, encourageait, approuve, encourage confidentiellement*". BIY, The Malines Papers of Lord Halifax, Box 4, N° 28, Mercier to Halifax, February 7, 1924.

about the response that had been received to the *Lambeth Appeal* of 1920. Nearly half of the second part of that letter dealt with the Conversations at Malines[77].

Davidson explained his conviction that the *Lambeth Appeal* of 1920 could not be reconciled with "an attitude of apathy or sheer timidity as to our touching the Roman Catholic question... We there express our readiness to welcome any friendly discussion between Roman Catholics and Anglicans for which opportunity may be given". He stressed that "our visitors to Malines were not likely to forget what the historical Anglican position and claims have been in the past, as set forward for example by the great theologians of the sixteenth and seventeenth centuries — a position which we have no thought of changing or weakening today". He further stated that the discussions were very much in "a quite elementary stage", that the Anglican participants had his encouragement, that one could not say what the final result of the discussions would be; but that "there has been no attempt to initiate what may be called 'negotiations' of any sort".

On December 31, 1923, The English Dominican, McNabb, sent Davidson an appreciative note. "The courtesy and charity with which your words are charged have quickened unto hope what was a seemingly Utopian desire"[78]!

The reaction from other English Roman Catholics — as well as from most Anglicans — however, was fierce and negative. As we will see in the next chapter, 1924 was not just a winter but an entire year of malicious maneuvers and discontent.

---

77. See Appendix D for Davidson's letter.

78. ALPL, Archbishop Davidson's papers, 1923, McNabb to Davidson, December 31, 1923.

CHAPTER FIVE

THE FOURTH CONVERSATION

Eighteen months separated the Third and Fourth Conversations —
five hundred and fifty-five long days of public meetings, heated articles,
letters to editors, pastoral letters from Davidson, Mercier and Bourne,
and behind-the-scenes intrigues and maneuverings. For the aging Halifax
— he was then eighty-five — they seemed like an eternity. Halifax often
doubted that he would see the ultimate reconvening at Malines. For
English Roman Catholics, the interim was a period of rapidly-growing
overt propaganda and covert in-house wrangling, because English
Roman Catholics, at this time, were hardly unanimous in their opposition to the Malines Conversations. Even Cardinal Bourne remained
supportive until after the Fourth Conversation.

1. *Rumblings within English Roman Catholicism*

By early January 1924, the English Roman Catholic press was
"beginning to repeat the familiar manifestations of 1894"[1]. On January
4, Halifax sent Portal a packet of newspaper clippings, which included
a long letter to the editor of the *Times* written by Francis Woodlock.
"You will see", wrote Halifax, "that our English Catholics haven't
learned anything"[2]. He then went on to report that the Rome corres-
pondent for the *Times* while not absolutely lying had certainly given a
false impression by reporting that Gasparri had told him the Conversations did not have authoritative Vatican backing.

The following day Halifax again wrote Portal that clearly, Merry del
Val and Gasquet were at it again[3]!

It was also on January 5 that *The Tablet* launched into the new year
with a stinging editorial "Ring Out The False", in which E. Oldmeadow
fulminated against the "false hopes" raised by Archbishop Davidson's
Christmas letter. "We ring out the false... Not only are there innumer-
able Protestants but also thousands of High Churchmen (deceiving

---

1. J.C. LOCKHART, *Charles Lindley Viscount Halifax*, vol. 2, 1936, p. 308.
2. BIY, The Malines Papers of Lord Halifax, Box 4, N° 5, Halifax to Portal, January
4, 1924.
3. "*Vous avez remarqué, je l'espère, ce qu'a dit le correspondant du Times écrivant de
Rome à propos des Français et des Belges qui avaient la présomption de s'occuper des
affaires ecclésiastiques d'Angleterre, et que jamais le Pape ne se serait permis de se servir de
leurs interventions en de telles affaires. C'est Mgr Merry del Val et Gasquet encore*" BIY,
The Malines Papers of Lord Halifax, Box 4, N° 6, Halifax to Portal, January 5, 1924.

themselves by the name 'Anglo-Catholic') whom *The Tablet* believes to be in good faith. To many of these High Churchmen last week brought a Boxing Day indeed. The box which Dr. Davidson handed to them seemed heavy with accomplishment, although it contained nothing more solid than a false hope. Over the cold remains of more than one turkey last Thursday High Anglicans glowed warm in the belief that 'the Italian mission in Britain' is about to be snubbed and snuffed out of existence; that Gallicanism is on the eve of a tardy but triumphant vindication; that the Patriarch of the West is proposing to toe the line with the dubious ex-Patriarch of Constantinople, with the distracted Orthodox Patriarch of Jerusalem, and with their inconclusive brother of Cyprus, in contradicting Leo XIII by recognizing Anglican Orders; and in short that corporate reunion (or, at the very least, Anglo-Roman intercommunion) has been brought a long step nearer... With every desire to be courteous we say that a four-card trick is being played in the name of the *Lambeth Appeal*"[4]. In the same issue, Canon Moyes gave a summary of the progress to date of the Malines Conversations, he stressed that the Rome correspondent of the *Times*, "who is no doubt instructed from higher quarters", gives the assurance that it is a misconception if anyone believes that "the Vatican had any official cognizance, or gave any encouragement to the Conferences at Malines"[5].

A copy of Fr. Woodlock's letter to the editor of the *Times*, which Halifax had mentioned in his letter to Portal, was also printed in this issue of *The Tablet*. Woodlock could not have been more blunt: "The fiasco which caused such disillusionment, disappointment, and bitterness in 1895 and 1896 could have been avoided, had a group of men more representative of average Anglicanism accompanied Lord Halifax when he visited the French ecclesiastics and spoke to them of the readiness of the English Church for corporate reunion. Leo XIII was misled by these foreigners"[6].

And it was again on January 5 that Portal wrote to Halifax that Batiffol was corresponding with Canon James Moyes. Moyes, we recall, had been a major collaborator with Merry del Val and Gasquet in securing the papal condemnation of Anglican Orders. In 1924, he was Cardinal Bourne's personal theologian. Portal wasn't certain about the implications of the Moyes/Batiffol correspondence, but he suspected the worst. He had also heard rumors that Bourne was writing against the conversations[7].

4. *The Tablet* 143 (January 5, 1924), pp. 3 and 4.
5. "The Conferences at Malines", in *The Tablet*, 143 (January 5, 1924), p. 5.
6. *Ibid.*, p. 6.
7. "*Tavernier m'écrit que le Cardinal Bourne a fait paraître une lettre sur nos affaires et qu'il a paru différentes notes dans les journaux. Je ne sais rien de tout cela. Je suis ici perdu dans la neige*". BIY, The Malines Papers of Lord Halifax, Box 4, N° 7, Portal to Halifax, January 5, 1924.

On January 6, Mercier wrote to Gasparri that the English Catholics were uneasy and suspicious about the Conversations. (He would repeat the same message to the Pope on January 30, when he would ask for "two lines of encouragement")[8].

Finally on January 18, in reply to "strong blasts of disapproval"[9] from England, and because he was not satisfied with Davidson's report about the Conversations[10], Mercier issued a pastoral letter: *Les Conversations de Malines*. The letter explained Mercier's involvement in the Malines Conversations right from the start. In response to the question of why he had become involved, Mercier told his clergy that he could not have turned down an opportunity to perform an act of "brotherly charity and Christian hospitality". He would never want one of the "separated brothers" to ever be able to say that he had knocked at the door of a Roman Catholic bishop and had been turned away[11].

The Anglican participants at Malines had mixed feelings about Mercier's letter. They were not pleased about the general context in which Mercier explained the Conversations — the de-Christianization of the masses which Mercier said was more common in Protestant countries than Catholic. The Anglicans felt that Mercier still did not understand their situation in England. As Frere said: "The largeness of his heart embraced us all, but his head did not seem to take in our position"[12]. Halifax, however, along with Portal, was delighted with Mercier's strong rebuke of their critics, which they thought would put the English Catholics in their place. We quote here from an English translation of Mercier's pastoral which was made by his secretary Chanoine Dessain: "A great nation was, for more than eight centuries, our beloved sister; this nation gave the Church a phalanx of saints whom to this day we honour in our liturgy; astonishing reserves of Christian life have been maintained in its vast empire; from it number-less missions have gone out far and wide; but a gaping wound is in its side. We Catholics — kept safe by the grace of God in the whole truth — we weep over the criminal sundering which tore it away, four centuries ago, from the Church our Mother. And forsooth there are Catholics who would that, like the Levite in the parable of the Good

8. AAM, The Malines Conversations, 1924, B I, N° 1, Mercier to Gasparri, January 6, 1924. AAM, The Malines Conversations, 1924, B I, N° 3, Mercier to Pius XI, January 30, 1924.

9. W. H. FRERE, *Recollections of Malines*, London, 1935, p. 49.

10. See LOCKHART, *op. cit.*, pp. 303-309.

11. *"Pourquoi? Tout d'abord, parce que je n'ai pas le droit de me dérober à une occasion qui vient à moi de faire un acte de charité fraternelle et d'hospitalité chrétienne. Pour rien au monde, je ne voudrais autoriser un de nos frères séparés à dire qu'il a frappé de confiance à la porte d'un évêque catholique romain et que cet évêque catholique romain a refusé de lui ouvrir"*. From Part II of Mercier's pastoral titled *Pourquoi ces conversations?* See Appendix E for the entire pastoral.

12. FRERE, *op. cit.*, p. 50.

Samaritan, a Catholic bishop should pass his way, superbly unfeeling, and refuse to pour oil in this gaping wound, to tend it, and try to lead the invalid to God's house whither God's mercy calls him. Oh! I must needs plead guilty had I been so cowardly. I know well that those who misjudge us will not deny our charitable intentions, but they consider our interference inopportune or ineffective. Inopportune, because they think it is wiser to let the separated Churches go to complete decay, the contrast between truth and error to become sharper; then evil carried too far will strike terror, and the hour of triumph will ring for truth. Ineffective, because, so it seems, we do not adopt the right method of apostolate, i.e., the appeal to individual conversions"[13]. Mercier also assured his clergy, as Davidson had done in his pastoral letter, that the Conversations were private, were not negotiations, and that neither Church was committed to the positions expressed by the participants. Mercier also stressed, however, that he was acting "in agreement with the supreme Authority, blessed and encouraged by it"[14].

Halifax was so excited about Mercier's pastoral that he considered writing an open letter to Cardinal Bourne to gain greater support from those English Catholics somewhat well disposed toward the Conversations and "to put the others in their place"[15]. Halifax later, and wisely, decided against his open letter.

On February 2, Oldmeadow wrote to Canon Moyes that he was sending him Dessain's translation of the pastoral. "I think you will agree with me", he observed, "that it is a prolix and futile document. His Eminence has either avoided or overlooked the crucial point; namely, whether he did or did not encourage the colleagues of Lord Halifax to believe that the 'Anglo-Catholic' minority in the Church of England could somehow expect an ecclesiastical conjuring-trick amounting to corporate reunion"[16].

The editor of *The Universe*, Herbert Dean, was also upset about Mercier's pastoral. He sent a quick note to Cardinal Bourne. He hoped Bourne could do something "in Rome" about the Conversations. He said the situation in England had been "troublesome enough" after Davidson's letter but now it had been made "unhappily, far worse" by Mercier's letter. He said that Mercier had sent him and Oldmeadow English translations of the pastoral with requests that they publish it. Dean said he would publish it, but "the effect will be most unfortunate. The document throws no light whatever upon what went on, but is in

13. *The Tablet*, 143 (February 9, 1924), p. 177.
14. *Ibid.*
15. BIY, The Malines Papers of Lord Halifax, Box 4, N° 17, Halifax to Portal, January 25, 1924.
16. AAW, Cardinal Bourne's papers, 1924, BO III, Oldmeadow to Moyes, February 2, 1924.

substance an attack upon the English Catholic body, who are accused of 'exclusivism', with a reference, by way of illustration, to the Levite in the Parable of the Good Samaritan. Apart from the merits or demerits of the affair, this sort of thing is most distressing and disheartening to the English Catholic clergy and public, who are laboring so hard to get conversions and know from daily experience how it can be done and how it cannot"[17].

Cardinal Bourne's reaction to Mercier's pastoral took his fellow English Catholics by complete surprise. Cardinal Bourne was in Rome at the time Mercier's pastoral had come out, staying with the Redemptorists. The Redemptorist priest, A. Sordet, had received a copy of the pastoral from Mercier and it was he who showed it to Bourne. On February 6, Bourne sent the following instructions to Oldmeadow: "You will no doubt have a copy of Cardinal Mercier's letter to his clergy *Les Conversations de Malines*. Give it the most sympathetic and cordial treatment, and quote largely from it. In a sense the most important words are on page 7: 'For us it was enough to know that we were acting in accordance with the Supreme Authority and blessed and encouraged by it', which reveal the fact, known to me in confidence all along, that the conversations were held with the knowledge, approbation, and encouragement of the Holy See"[18].

Bourne had called special attention to the phrase about the encouragement and blessing of the supreme authority because of its obviously important contents but also because *l'Osservatore Romano* had suppressed that phrase when it published an Italian translation of Mercier's pastoral. In Rome at the time this happened, Bourne had been concerned about the blunder and had tried, apparently without much success, to get to the bottom of it. R. Aubert proposes that the blunder was deliberate and part of an Integrist plot to subvert the Malines Conversations. We still do not know the whole story about this intriguing incident[19].

In any event, On February 9, 1924, *The Tablet* published the entire text of Dessain's translation of Mercier's pastoral letter; but in the same issue, editor Oldmeadow also included an editorial, "More About Malines", in which he observed: "It is plain, however that the Catholics

17. AAW, Cardinal Bourne's papers, 1924, BO III, Dean to Bourne, February 4, 1924.
18. *"Il nous suffisait de savoir que nous marchions d'accord avec l'Autorité suprême, bénis et encouragés par Elle"*. AAW, Cardinal Bourne's papers, 1924, BO III, Bourne to Oldmeadow, February 6, 1924.
19. *"Si l'on peut soupçonner à l'origine de la 'gaffe' de l'Osservatore une intervention du clan intégriste hostile aux Conversations de Malines au sein du Sacré Collège, on manque de raisons positives pour supposer que l'intervention était venue de plus haut et que Gasparri ne disait pas la vérité lorsqu'il écrivait à Mercier que le Saint-Siège était 'totalement étranger' à ce procédé peu élégant"* R. AUBERT, "Les Conversations de Malines" (1967), p. 115. For Aubert's complete discussion of this incident see pages 112-117.

at Malines were misinformed, as foreigners naturally may be, as to the present situation in England"[20].

It was also in February that Archbishop Davidson gave an address about the Malines Conversations to the Upper House of Convocation. Fearful about the outcome of the Prayer Book Revision, Davidson hoped to calm Anglican fears about the Conversations. "Let me repeat", he said on February 6, 1924, "for the reiteration of it seems to be necessary, that there have been no negotiations whatever. We are not at present within sight of anything of the kind. Cardinal Mercier emphasizes this as strongly as I do. There are whole sentences about it in his pastoral. They were private conversations about our respective history and doctrines and nothing more"[21]. Davidson's speech helped him regain much Anglican support but left Catholics cold. Oldmeadow, writing in *The Tablet*, called it "Much Ado About Almost Nothing"[22]. While Halifax was studying the issue of *The Tablet* which contained Mercier's pastoral and Oldmeadow's denigration of Davidson's Upper House address, he received a letter from Mercier, in which Mercier emphasized again that Gasparri was supportive of their endeavors; but that the Holy See did not want to take an "official position" at this time[23].

On February 15, Portal wrote to Halifax that he had learned from Chanoine Dessain, that several English Catholics — bishops, priests, and lay — had written Mercier letters of support which demonstrated that the sentiments of *The Universe* were not shared by all in England. Vincent McNabb had sent Mercier "one of the nicest letters he had ever received". And there had even been a congratulatory note from a group of "Catholic cadets"[24].

Such positive reinforcement from English Catholics was soon offset however by other events and revelations.

20. E. OLDMEADOW, "More About Malines", in *The Tablet*, 143 (February 9, 1924), p. 168.

21. Viscount HALIFAX, *The Conversations of Malines 1921-1925: Original Documents*, London, 1930, Appendix II, p. 56.

22. *The Tablet*, 143 (February 9, 1924), p. 169.

23. "*De Rome, j'ai reçu une excellente lettre privée du Cardinal Gasparri: cette lettre confirme les encouragements de la première lettre, mais le S. Siège désire, jusqu'à présent, ne pas prendre une attitude officielle. La chose s'explique d'elle-même*". Mercier also summarized his opinions about the reactions of the Catholic press to his pastoral letter. "*l'Osservatore Romano, la Civiltà Cattolica, et aussi le 'Church of England'* [Here Halifax added a note that Mercier meant the Church Times, JD] *sont très distinctement marche en arrière. Bon indice. The Universe et The Tablet ont promis de publier ma lettre intégralement. Je regrette que le Times ait refusé de la publier, d'autant plus qu'il a insinué que Rome désapprouvait nos conférences. Rome n'approuvait ni désapprouvait officiellement, mais approuvait, encourageait, approuve, encourage confidentiellement*". BIY, The Malines Papers of Lord Halifax, Box 4, N° 28, Mercier to Halifax, February 7, 1924.

24. BIY, The Malines Papers of Lord Halifax, Box 4, N° 41, Portal to Halifax, February 15, 1924.

In February the English Jesuit publication *The Month* carried an article by Joseph Keating, S.J., who was later to become editor of *The Month*, which was strongly critical of the Malines Conversations. The article was reminiscent of the Ultramontane English Catholic journalism in the days of Cardinal Vaughan. Keating pointed out the impossibility of corporate reunion, "the inevitable barrenness of the *Lambeth Appeal*", and "the unfortunate inclusion of the well-known Abbé Portal amongst the Catholic interlocutors at Malines ... who has apparently learnt nothing since 1896"[25]. Keating would continue his assault the following month when he accused Halifax of deliberately distorting Mercier's pastoral letter as implying "the duty of English Roman Catholics to consider how they can assist in bringing about the corporate reunion of the Church of England with the Holy See, rather than merely considering how best to secure individual conversions". Halifax had made the statement in a letter to the editor of the *Church Times*, dated February 22, 1924 and Keating thought it smacked of heresy. He said it would not surprise him to hear that Portal had made such a statement but he would not expect it from Mercier, who would be "the last man to countenance the heresy that the one church is visibly divided ... though his assessor, the Abbé Portal, is still ill-advised enough to speak of the Anglican Church as 'the daughter of Rome' and as actually 'belonging to the Patriarchate of the West'. The theologian who rules the Archdiocese of Malines could never use expressions so savouring of heresy"[26].

Aloïs Janssens again publicly entered the reunion debates at this time with an article in *Ephemerides Theologicae Lovanienses* titled "Anglo-Catholicism and Catholic Unity". The main point of his article was that the visible Roman Catholic Church needs and has a visible head, the Pope. Janssens stressed that Charles Gore had misunderstood and misrepresented the papal office in his *Catholicism and Roman Catholicism* (London, 1923). He also observed that Batiffol had not correctly understood Gore's use of the term "Roman". Batiffol applied it to the local Church of Rome, while Gore applied it to the Catholic Church in communion with the Church of Rome. Janssens concluded his article with praise for Mercier and for Halifax who had taken a courageous public stand on behalf of *jure divino* papal jurisdiction: "This, I believe,

---

25. J. KEATING, "Clearing the Air", in *The Month*, 143 (February 1924), pp. 105 and 101.

The Month had also attacked Portal in the November 1923 issue because he had negatively criticized Michel d'Herbigny's book about Anglo-Catholicism and Orthodoxy. Portal saw the attack as he expressed in a letter to Halifax on November 22 (BIY, Box 3, N° 150) as a clear indication that his and Halifax's "old friends" were out to make as much trouble for them as possible.

26. J. KEATING, "Malines and Corporate Reunion", in *The Month*, 143 (March 1924), p. 261.

no Anglican leader ever did since the time of the Elizabethan settlement. His is a powerful voice, calling for peace and union"[27].

On February 12, 1924, H. Barton-Brown, the Rector of St. Charles,
Hatfield, Herts, a house of studies for convert clergyman, wrote
Mercier to complain that all the public discussion about the Malines
Conversations had cutt-off his supply of students. He usually registered
about fifty a year. Now he had none! Apparently, he said, Anglican
clergy interested in converting to Rome were now in a holding pattern
waiting to see what further developments the Conversations would
bring[28].

Mercier soon learned about an even more distressing English Catholic
development. Portal had received a note from Vincent McNabb who
reported that everything he wrote about Church reunion was now being
denounced at Rome. McNabb wanted Portal to ask Mercier to intercede
for him[29].

Apparently someone or someones at Rome were starting a crack-
down on English Catholics supportive of the Malines Conversations.
This fact would also be reinforced years later by the English Jesuit
Albert Gille who, under the name of "Father Jerome", published a
book on reunion *A Catholic Plea for Reunion* (London, 1934). The
most interesting part of the book was Gille's revelation that Mercier
had many English Roman Catholic supporters and that they were
under pressure to keep their mouths shut. "Every Catholic apologist
vehemently asserts that the Anglican Church is not schismatic but
heretical. He must rub it in! And he often adds that only foreigners
hold the contrary view. I know of no such foreigners; neither Cardinal
Mercier nor Mgr. Battifol (sic) held that view; they only held that
charity unites faster than logic, and there are many English priests,
both secular and religious, who share the same opinion and firmly hold
that Cardinal Mercier's move was the only sane, sensible and hopeful
effort towards regaining the Anglican Church; only these priests are not
allowed to express their opinion in print. The censors see to that... If
you gag all the British who differ from you, it is plain that only
foreigners will be left to share their opinion. The best witnesses have
been made 'safe'"[30].

27. A. JANSSENS, "Anglo-Catholicism and Catholic Unity", in *Ephemerides Theologicae Lovanienses* 1 (1924) 66-70.

28. AAM, Cardinal Mercier's papers, 1924, Pastoral II, N° 24, Barton-Brown to
Mercier, February 12, 1924.

29. AAM, The Malines Conversations, 1924, B II, N° 2, McNabb to Mercier,
February 18, 1924.

30. Father JEROME, *A Catholic Plea for Reunion*, London, 1934, p. 31.
The book begins, by the way, with a "note" in which the author observes: "I am no
more Father Jerome than Archangel Raphael was Azarias, son of the great Ananias, but
Catholic priests, like Archangels, may sometimes find it convenient to hide their identity".

Near the end of February 1924, Portal explained the McNabb problem to Halifax. He mentioned first that the French Dominican publication *La Revue des Jeunes* was going to publish up to three thousand copies of Mercier's pastoral letter and distribute them to bishops, seminaries, and elsewhere; and Portal hoped this would help correct any false impressions about the pastoral created by the blunder in *l'Osservatore Romano*. He then went on to explain, in a bit more detail, what was happening to McNabb. The English Dominicans could not do so much. Rome had ordered McNabb not to write anything on reunion[31].

On March 1, 1924, the English Roman Catholic Bishops of Birmingham, Clifton, Shrewsbury, and Plymouth — the four dioceses in the Province of Birmingham — issued a joint letter to their clergy warning of the dangers of various schemes of "organized Christianity" working for social betterment. "We have the gravest fears", wrote the Bishops, "that all this is nothing but Modernism in action, on a large scale; nor are our fears diminished in the least by the assurance that 'the Church of England has given a lead'"[32]. This letter was a subtle indication of a current of thought, among one group of English Roman Catholics, which would find a fuller expression four years later in *Mortalium Animos*. Apparently at this time, however, Cardinal Bourne did not share the alarm of this group of his episcopal colleagues. On March 8, *The Tablet* published Cardinal Bourne's Lenten Pastoral for 1924: "The Union of Christendom". It was a generally positive ecumenical document which evidenced none of the fears of Modernism or of inter-Church cooperation found in the letter from the Bishops of Birmingham Province. Bourne said that he was sympathetic toward the reunion movement, that "unfortunately there are some who, separated from us, are apparently not prepared to give us credit for this sympathetic attitude". He announced that "there is not a bishop among us who would not gladly resign his see and retire into complete obscurity if thereby England could again be Catholic. The Catholic Church is used to sacrifice for principle or for the common good". He then gave the example of how the bishops of France had given up dioceses, dwellings, colleges, etc., for the sake of religion in their country. Bourne also stated that it was a "matter of rejoicing that members of the Establishment, to whatever school of thought they may belong, should seek from representative Catholics whether they be in France, or in Belgium, or

31. *"Cette Revue est dirigée par les Dominicains et je suis bien content qu'ils entrent dans la mêlée. Je regrette que les Dominicains anglais n'en fassent pas autant. Le P. McNabb à qui j'en avais écrit m'a répondu qu'il avait reçu défense d'écrire quoique ce soit sur la réunion sans une permission spéciale du supérieur général, qui est à Rome, comme vous le savez. Et je crois que tous les Dominicains anglais sont logés à la même enseigne"* BIY, The Malines Papers of Lord Halifax, Box 4, N° 82, Portal to Halifax, April 13, 1924.
32. "Our Common Christianity", in *The Tablet*, 143 (March 1, 1924), p. 294.

here at home, or in any other country, a more complete understanding
of what the Catholic Church really teaches"[33].

Ironically — and as a further indication that not all English Catholics were unanimous in their sentiments about the reunion movement —
the same issue of *The Tablet* which carried Bourne's pastoral also
carried a feisty article by Francis Woodlock who had attended "An
Anglican Reunion Lecture" and found it a hotbed of Modernism. He
accused the Anglican speaker of "deliberate and habitual falsehood"
but admitted that certain Roman Catholics were attracted to such
Anglicans. "Besides the obvious criticism that it is fallacious to draw
universal conclusions from a few particular cases, it may be noted",
wrote Woodlock, "that the few covert Modernists and Gallicans who
probably do exist in the Church, even at the present day, are just the
kind of people to seek out anti-papalist Anglicans and pour their
doubts and grievances into their sympathetic ears"[34].

From across the Atlantic, Jesuit reaction to Bourne's Lenten pastoral
was supportive and appreciative. Wilfrid Parsons, S.J., writing in
America on April 5, observed that Cardinal Mercier's letter to his clergy
"seemed to hint at certain disagreements of procedure between his
Eminence and English Catholics. Now the leader of the English Catholics
in a dignified official way puts the world right on this point, and at the
same time explains dispassionately the conditions of the union of
Christendom". Parsons also complimented the English Jesuit Joseph
Keating for his clear statements in *The Month* that Anglicans hereti-
cally believe they belong to the Church[35].

On March 22, 1924 Mercier wrote McNabb that he supported all he
wrote but that he was powerless to change what was happening at
Rome[36]. Perhaps Mercier had already gotten wind of what Portal
would soon reveal to Halifax.

In April 1924, Portal reported to Halifax that he had made more
discoveries about a campaign to mold English Catholics into unanimous opposition to the Conversations. Clearly the forces which had
worked against him and Halifax at the time of Leo XIII were now
working against them again, by trying to give the impression that all
English Catholics were opposed to the conversations[37].

33. Cardinal BOURNE, "The Reunion of Christendom", in *The Tablet*, 143 (March 8,
1924), p. 309.

34. F. WOODLOCK, "At An Anglican Reunion Lecture", in *The Tablet*, p. 307.

35. W. PARSONS, "Canterbury and Malines", in *America* (April 5, 1924), p. 587.

36. AAM, The Malines Conversations, 1924, B III, N° 4, Mercier to McNabb, March
22, 1924.

37. "*Il faut que nous tenions compte de la campagne que mènent et que mèneront les
catholiques anglais*". Portal saw the developing scenario as a repeat of earlier history.
"*Vous vous souvenez qu'ils ont eu pour but de nous isoler et par le fait d'isoler Leon XIII et
puis, après un an, ils l'ont retourné. Ils reprennent la même tactique. Le P. McNabb a
défense de rien publier sur nos affaires sans la permission du supérieur général qui est à*

2. An Informal Gathering at Malines

By early spring 1924, Halifax was getting restless and feared he had little time remaining to work for reunion and probably would not be able to attend the next Conversation. He had already thought about his successors and had begun grooming his son Edward and his friend Lord Hugh Cecil to carry on his life's work. At the end of April he decided to organize a mini-conversation at Malines; and on April 29 he, Edward, Cecil, and Portal traveled to Malines for two days of informal and unofficial — but not secret — conversations with Mercier. Later Halifax recorded most of the events of this meeting in a memo which we find among his papers at the Borthwick Institute in York.

At Malines in April, Portal, Halifax and Mercier agreed to schedule the Fourth Conversation for early October 1924. We know of course that — due to the Anglican Prayer Book revision controversies, Robinson's poor health, and strong desires from Bourne and Davidson for a cooling-off period following the revelations after the Third Conversation — the Fourth Conversation was not held until May 1925. But in April 1924, the following October had seemed a good time to reconvene because Mercier had told his friends that he would be going to Rome in November 1924 and would be able personally to fill-in the Pope and Gasparri about the discussions. Mercier also told the group that he had already been in communication with Pius XI and had told him about the unfavorable reactions of some English Catholics. He also said, as Halifax recorded, that "an allusion to the subject of reunion directly intended to refer to the Cardinal's (i.e. Mercier's, JD) communication had been made by the Pope at the recent consistory, a fact which was directly communicated to the Cardinal by Cardinal Gasparri who added that the Cardinal would be pleased to hear what he had to tell him". Mercier also told the April delegation that Cardinal Bourne, while stopping in Rome during his spring pilgrimage to the Holy Land, had objected to the *l'Osservatore Romano* suppression of the now famous sentence from Mercier's pastoral. He also added that as far as the Conversations were concerned, Bourne "had been more sympathetic after he had seen the Pope".

Halifax, Mercier and Portal also committed themselves to making special efforts at eliminating "much ignorance and misapprehension" on both sides. Halifax said that he would be willing to gather a group of Anglicans for discussions at Hickleton and that he would also stop by Westminster and invite Cardinal Bourne to send some English Catholics to join the dialogue at Hickleton. Interestingly, Halifax noted

Rome. Les catholiques anglais apparaîtront donc comme ayant un avis unanime et contraire à notre action" BIY, The Malines Papers of Lord Halifax, Box 4, N° 82, Portal to Halifax, April 13, 1924.

that Mercier and Portal thought "that if I did so, Cardinal Bourne would assent to my wish"[38].

One thing which Halifax did not mention in his memo, however, was a small conversation between him and Mercier when they were alone. Years later — July 18, 1928 — he told his Louvain friend Aloïs Janssens about it. We quote now from Janssens' diary: "Lord Halifax told me this morning — he spoke an hour and a half with me: This is confidential and no one knows. Once, when I was at Malines, Portal left the room. Seeing we were alone Mercier said: 'May I ask something of you?' Lord Halifax: 'Nothing would give me more pleasure, than to have you treat me with all confidence'. Mercier: 'Well then I think you ought to make your submission'. Lord Halifax (I remember his exact words) 'Your Eminence it would be quite useless. Newman was a giant in his day, he made his submission. What came of it? Nothing. If I made my submission it would be meaningless. It would not affect the English people in the least. It would not make any change in my life or in my belief'"[39]. The reader will recall that in 1890 at Madeira Portal had asked Halifax to make his submission and that Halifax's refusal had led to Portal's ecumenical conversion.

In early May 1924, Halifax wrote Archbishop Davidson that he had been to Malines[40]. Later in the month he went to London to meet with Davidson to discuss the April 29-30 visit in a bit more detail; to secure Davidson's support for a private meeting at Hickleton; and to make plans for the next Conversation. Halifax found that Davidson "was inclined to think further conferences at Malines had better be postponed for the moment and that he deprecated such meetings at Hickleton as I had contemplated"[41].

Halifax also visited Cardinal Bourne at this time and left us a written report[42] which deserves reproduction in its entirety: "I had as it happened an opportunity of seeing Cardinal Bourne the next morning before leaving for Devonshire, and I found that for various reasons, some not very dissimilar to those influencing the Archbishop of Canterbury, he did not think the moment propitious for any immediate action, or for such action in regard to private discussions as I had in my

38. BIY, The Malines Papers of Lord Halifax, Box 4, N° 93, Halifax's Memo I on April meeting in Malines, April 29 and 30, 1924, pp. 2 and 3.

39. D. VERHELST, "Lord Halifax and the Scheut Father Aloïs Janssens", in *Ephemerides Theologicae Lovanienses* 43 (1967), p. 242. The same incident is reported in LOCKHART, *op. cit.*, pp. 215-216 and 310.

And it is reported somewhat cynically in E. OLDMEADOW, *Francis Cardinal Bourne*, vol. 2, London, 1940, p. 376.

40. BIY, The Malines Papers of Lord Halifax, Box 4, N° 99, Halifax to Davidson, May 6, 1924.

41. BIY, The Malines Papers of Lord Halifax, Box 4, N° 93, Halifax undated memorandum of his meeting with Davidson, p. 1.

42. *Ibid.*

mind, or indeed, if I remember rightly, for other conversations in England such as had taken place at Malines between Roman Catholics and ourselves as I had contemplated. There was, he said, at the moment a good deal of irritation on the subject; that Cardinal Mercier who was simplicity and goodness itself was apt to get into difficulties, e.g., such as had met him in Belgium in regard to the Walloons and the Flemish, such as he had encountered when he had mixed himself up in Irish affairs; that this was felt even by some Belgians, that one Belgian[43] entitled to speak on the subject had, as I understood, mentioned Cardinal Mercier's name to him with some disapprobation, and that admirable and excellent as Cardinal Mercier was and great as was the position he occupied, his reward and his greatness were likely to be better recognized and appreciated in the next world rather than in this. In a word that a pause was desirable now till existing irritation was allayed".

Halifax had also planned on visiting Bourne in November 1923 but that visit had never materialized[44].

3. The Calm before the Next Storm

The May 10, 1924 issue of The Tablet carried a brief tribute to Cardinal Mercier in honor of his golden jubilee and, in its "News and Notes" column observed: "Although Malines Conversations are no longer discussed with eagerness by the people at large, editors are still finding room for belated articles concerning them"[45]. For the remainder of the year, however, the pages of The Tablet were unusually quiet about the Malines Conversations.

"People at large" may not have paid that much attention to the Malines Conversations during the second half of 1924; but a handful of letters found in various archives hint that there was, in fact, considerable behind-the-scenes maneuvering going on.

In June, Halifax heard from his American friend Mrs. Bellamy Storer. She had been talking with her friend Cardinal Cerretti who "comprehends perfectly the Catholic clergy of England and knows of their hostility against Cardinal Mercier". Storer reported Cardinal

---

43. It could have been the Belgian priest Maurice Emmanuel Carton de Wiart. Cardinal Bourne was acquainted with him, went on the 1924 Holy Land pilgrimage with him, and later, as we will demonstrate in the next chapter, corresponded with him in negative fashion about Dom Lambert Beauduin.

44. "J'ai écrit une longue lettre au Cardinal pour lui demander s'il ne serait pas utile que je visse le Cardinal Bourne et lui dise, avec prudence bien entendu, un peu de ce qui s'est passé à Malines. Je crois qu'il serait utile d'avoir une telle conversation, mais je ne voudrais pas m'y engager sans savoir ce que pense le Cardinal Mercier d'un tel projet". BIY, The Malines Papers of Lord Halifax, Box 3, N° 142, Halifax to Portal, November 13, 1923.

45. "News and Bits", in The Tablet, 143 (May 10, 1924), p. 621.

Cerretti's somewhat exaggerated judgment about the origins of English hostility toward Mercier — mentioned briefly in an earlier footnote — "It appears that the Flemish began it and pamphlets (translated) of their's were circulated in England"[46].

Obviously, as is more than clear by now, the Flemish cannot be blamed for English Roman Catholic antagonism toward Cardinal Mercier and the Malines Conversations! It is plausible that some Flemings, living in England, and out of reaction against Mercier's stance regarding the Flemish Question, did write and publish pamphlets in England against Mercier and the Malines Conversations. We can only speculate about who. We do know that in 1920 the editor-in-chief of the *Tongerloo's Tijdschrift*, Rombout Jordens was so outspoken against Mercier that Mercier had him fired from the paper and banned to England. Jordens remained in England until he heard about Mercier's death in 1926, at which time he said he wanted to return to Belgium because "Those who wanted to kill the child are dead"[47]. Was Jordens one of the Flemings whose "pamphlets" were circulated around England?

In October Michel d'Herbigny's name reappeared in correspondence between Gore and Halifax. Gore wrote that he had met with Batiffol in late September and that Batiffol had suggested inviting d'Herbigny to participate in the next Conversation[48]. Halifax replied that he was dubious about d'Herbigny: "I am also wondering about d'Herbigny. As you probably know, he is a Jesuit, concerned in Oriental and other affairs, and one whose intervention I should not have thought would be likely to make for peace"[49].

Apparently when Halifax heard about d'Herbigny he must have immediately written to Portal, because on October 6 Portal wrote Halifax that he was astonished at Batiffol's suggestion. He knew that Batiffol had visited England; but, regardless, Mercier did not want any Jesuits[50]. D'Herbigny was not invited!

46. ALPL, Archbishop Davidson's Papers, 1924, Storer to Halifax, June 12, 1924.

47. R. BOUDENS, *Kardinaal Mercier en de Vlaamse Beweging*, Leuven, 1975, p. 203.

48. BIY, The Malines Papers of Lord Halifax, Box 5, N° 37, Gore to Halifax, October 2, 1924.

49. BIY, The Malines Papers of Lord Halifax, Box 5, N° 38, Halifax to Gore, October 3, 1924.

50. BIY, The Malines Papers of Lord Halifax, Box 5, N° 40, Portal to Halifax, October 6, 1924. Dom Lambert Beauduin loved to tell the story about the Jesuits and priests' retreats in Malines. "The Jesuits by tradition had been charged with the clergy retreats in Malines. When Mercier became cardinal he announced that henceforth the Benedictines would preach the retreats. (Because of Marmion, his confessor, Mercier had developed a great admiration for the Benedictine spirituality.) But the formerly all-powerful Jesuit Fathers were not about to surrender so easily to the Benedictines. They wrote to Rome and the father general asked the cardinal to reconsider his decision. He replied: 'This year I will preach the retreat myself in order to become familiar with all the

On November 5, Portal wrote Halifax that he had received a letter from Batiffol who suggested that he read an article in the October 1924 issue of *Contemporary Review* titled "Rome and Reunion"[51]. The article had been written by an English Roman Catholic layman who was an acquaintance of Halifax: R. Gordon George[52]. George had been critical of the attitude of some English Roman Catholics toward the Malines Conversations. Later in November he was taken to task for his opinions by E. Oldmeadow, who complained about him in *The Tablet*: "The writer is evidently much under the spell of that small group of Continental reunionists who are bemused by the illusion that the Catholics of England are so embittered by bigotry and by the memories of the penal laws (obsolete for nearly a century!) that they are constitutionally incapable of the charity and reasonableness desired and required for the discussion of reunion with Anglicans... To say that the Continental bishops, clergy, or faithful are more patient with the sixteenth century heresies than we are is surely to do them a grave injustice[53].

Halifax's curiosity about what Batiffol might be up to remained and he sensed the need for a brief public relations campaign in France, on behalf of the Malines Conversations. In the third week of November he went to Paris, for three days (November 19, 20 and 21). There he met with Batiffol, Hemmer, Portal, several other theologians, Auxiliary Bishop Chaftal, and several French editors and journalists, trying to spread the good news about the Conversations and to enlist support against the accusations of some of the English Catholics[54]. The new year would also witness a pro-Malines Conversations public relations campaign conducted by Gordon George.

4. *The Personal Diplomacy of R. Gordon George*

The year 1925 was a Holy Year — a special time for unlocking doors. As Pope Pius XI was solemnly knocking at the *Porta Sancta* at

priests of my diocese'. He preferred additional work to bowing before the Jesuit general". S.A. QUITSLUND, *Beauduin A Prophet Vindicated*, New York, Paramus, Toronto, 1973, p. 199.

51. BIY, The Malines Papers of Lord Halifax, Box 5, N° 61, Portal to Halifax, November 5, 1924.

52. R. Gordon George was really Robert Sencourt (1890 1969), a somewhat eccentric critic, biographer, and historian. He wrote several books, among them: *The Genius of the Vatican* (1935) and *Life of Newman* (1947). The author of this book had a couple opportunities to visit with him in 1964 when he was on a lecture tour throughout the United States, speaking about his friend "Tommy" (i.e. T.S.) Eliot.

53. E. OLDMEADOW, "A Layman on Malines", in *The Tablet*, 144 (November 22, 1924), p. 660.

54. In the three days, Halifax met with at least twenty-four people. The complete list is found in Portal's handwriting as well as in typed form at BIY, Box 5, N° 77.

St. Peter's, R. Gordon George was contemplating his own campaign
of knocking at religious doors — a type of personal ecumenical
diplomacy.

On Christmas day 1924, Gordon George had written to Halifax to
tell him that he had seen Bourne and found him "extremely sympathetic",
and willing to send an English priest to Malines "if the initiative came
from Malines as something agreeable to the Holy See". George thought
it would be good to somehow involve Bourne more in the Malines
Conversations "on account of his personal sympathy" and "because he
would silence 'Papist' criticism in England"[55]. On the Feast of the
Epiphany 1925, Gordon George again wrote to Halifax. This time he
reported that he had met with Mercier. The Cardinal had disclosed to
him the Holy Father's "large and sympathetic view towards the Church
of England". George said that Mercier had discussed the subject of
corporate reunion with the Pope, and, as he phrased it in his letter to
Halifax "This is what Cardinal Mercier wants me to write you. You
will understand that the highest authority would be prepared to suggest
some kind of corporate reunion with the Church of England, and
perhaps even to make a definite proposal, if they felt sure that the
propitious moment had arrived and a favourable acceptance was
assured". George then went on to observe that both the Pope and
Cardinal Gasparri were well disposed toward Halifax's reunion view
and again that Cardinal Bourne "is by no means unsympathetic".
Interestingly George then went on to report: "That, on the whole, the
English priests in Rome are almost deliberately ignorant of the mind of
the Holy Father, is, I fear too true, and I have not yet reason to think
that either Cardinal Merry del Val or Cardinal Gasquet have fought
themselves free of the influence of small minds"[56].

Later in January, Gordon George went knocking at the doors of
Merry del Val, Gasparri, and Archbishop Davidson. He summarized
his discoveries in a letter to Davidson on January 11. Merry del Val
who had had a reputation of being "most intransigeant" was in
Gordon's mind very understanding! He and Merry del Val had discussed
Anglican Orders and Merry del Val "even said that the Church of
England had retained the priesthood but not the *sacerdotium* in the
hierarchical sense in which Rome understands it". Here Merry del Val
— as we shall see in the next chapter of this book — was playing word
games with the theologically uninformed Gordon George.

About Gasparri, George reported to Davidson that "His Eminence
has given me full authority to write that any suggestion coming from

55. BIY, The Malines Papers of Lord Halifax, Box 5, N° 111, Gordon George to
Halifax, December 25, 1924.
56. BIY, The Malines Papers of Lord Halifax, Box 6, N° 6, Gordon George to
Halifax, January 6, 1925.

Your Grace directly to him of cooperation or even of corporate
reunion whether immediate or remote would be received in the most
courteous and sympathetic manner by the Holy See and answered
so"[57].

On the same day that George wrote to Davidson, George also wrote
to Halifax that Merry del Val wanted an English Catholic participating
in the Malines Conversations and that he would prefer Leslie Walker or
Canon Moyes[58].

Three days later Halifax again heard from Francis Woodlock. Woodlock was concerned about the dangers of Modernism in the Anglican
Church, he was pleased to read that Halifax was going to publish his
addresses before the English Church Union, because he had heard that
the English Church Union was about to publish "anti-modernist literature by good men"[59]. A few days later, an article written by Woodlock,
"Modernism and a United Christendom", appeared in *The Tablet*. In
his article Woodlock warned about the growth of Modernism within
the Anglican communion. "The Church of England is fast approaching
a crisis in her history. The increasing strength of the opposing parties,
Modernist and Anglo-Catholic, must issue in a conflict that, even
before Disestablishment comes, will produce a schism. In this conflict
all our sympathies must be with the Anglo-Catholics. Though they have
some Modernists in their midst — camp followers of ritualistic temperament but rationalistic mentality — they do stand for very many
Catholic truths and are firm in their belief in Our Lord's divinity"[60].
He also warned about the Modernist fallacy of some Anglo-Catholics
who rely on religious experience to prove the Catholicity of their belief.
Coincidentally, at the time of the nineteenth century Anglican Orders
debates, Halifax and others had argued for validity because of the
experience of graced encounters with the Lord through the ministrations of Anglican clergy.

In the last week of February, on Ash Wednesday, Halifax again
heard from Gordon George, who repeated for Halifax's benefit, the
statement from Merry del Val about Anglican Orders: "They have the
priesthood but not the *sacerdotium*". George thought the statement left
an open door for some type of new consideration of Anglican Orders
which might please Anglicans, and that it showed that the sentiment of

57. BIY, The Malines Papers of Lord Halifax, Box 6, N° 9, Gordon George to
Davidson, January 11, 1925.
58. BIY, The Malines Papers of Lord Halifax, Box 6, N° 11, Gordon George to
Halifax, January 17, 1925.
59. BIY, The Malines Papers of Lord Halifax, Box 6, N° 12, Woodlock to Halifax,
January 20, 1925.
60. F. WOODLOCK, "Modernism and a United Christendom", in *The Tablet*, 146
(January 24, 1925), p. 101.

the Roman Curia toward Anglicans was one of generosity and concilia-
tion[61].

On February 26, Halifax sent Portal a very brief note. Lord Shafts-
bury had seen Pius XI and Cardinal Gasparri and was pleased with
their attitude. Francis Woodlock had been Halifax's house guest at
Hickleton for three days. Halifax thought he had been able to soften
Woodlock a bit; but he could not trust either the Jesuits nor Merry del
Val[62]. Gordon George's name does not appear again until after the
Fourth Conversation, when Merry del Val in one of his letters to
Francis Woodlock would reveal that he had no respect for George.

5. *An American Interest in the Conversations*

In our brief survey of the Anglican Orders debates, we made mention
of the fact that Lord Halifax had given serious consideration to
involving Americans in those discussions. It is also clear that he and
other Anglicans gave consideration to involving Americans in the
Malines Conversations, after they had been approached by the American
Hoffman Nickerson[63].

On January 22, 1925, Nickerson wrote to W.H. Frere. He had visited
Frere two years earlier to discuss what was happening at the Malines
Conversations, now he was writing about the possibility of American
Episcopalians becoming directly involved in the Conversations. "You
may remember my call upon you two years ago to talk about Malines.
Since that time (largely through the Archbishop of Canterbury's public
statements) the American Church has become greatly interested in what
is going on. Our local Romans being difficult to deal with, it seems best
to associate ourselves with your enterprise. I recently had a talk with
the Archbishop, and told him that the American Church would very
much welcome the opportunity of participating, as a sister Church, in
future conferences. He readily agreed that in principle American participation is desirable and said that he would consult with others, and
particularly with you, as to the best means of bringing it about without
seeming to give the whole Malines business a more formal and official
air than he was willing to"[64].

At the end of January, Nickerson reported to Halifax that he had

61. BIY, The Malines Papers of Lord Halifax, Box 6, N° 31, Gordon George to
Halifax, February 25, 1925.

62. *"J'ai eu le Père Woodlock ici pour trois jours. Il est parti je crois un peu adouci, mais
je ne me fie ni aux jésuites ni au Cardinal Merry del Val"*. BIY, The Malines Papers of
Lord Halifax, Box 6, N° 32, Halifax to Portal, February 26, 1925.

63. Hoffman Nickerson wrote an article "On Alliance with Rome" which appeared in
the very first issue of *Commonweal* (November 12, 1924) pp. 6-7. He argued primarily for
cultural reasons that it was time for Christians to reunite with Rome.

64. BIY, The Malines Papers of Lord Halifax, Box 6, N° 14, Nickerson to Frere,
January 22, 1925.

had a very good conversation with the Archbishop of Canterbury, at Windsor Castle in the home of Lord Stamfordham, the King's private secretary. He had also met with Abbé Portal, in Paris. He found Portal "delighted to hear of the chance of American participation and said he would present me to the Parisian reunionists"[65]. Halifax had sent Portal a letter of introduction about Nickerson earlier in the month, assuring Portal that Nickerson was very interested in the Conversations and in very close contact with all of the Episcopalian bishops in the United States[66].

In February and March, Nickerson and his wife made the rounds in Europe, talking with Roman Catholics, and especially with Mercier, Portal, Batiffol, and Hemmer, about reunion.

At the end of March, Nickerson sent Halifax a long report about his discussions. It contained a surprising revelation about the state of Mercier's thinking just two months before the Fourth Conversation. In Nickerson's words: "I told the Abbé Portal that his Eminence had thrown out all my calculations by saying that to make a 'uniat' Anglican Communion would disturb 'the good Catholic order' of things — that now that Cardinal Bourne had publicly announced the willingness of the English R. C. hierarchy to quit their sees in the course of reunion if the Anglicans came over it would be better to leave only one hierarchy in England and that the present Anglican one. He said the 'uniat' communions in the East were due to special circumstances, that differences of rite could easily be arranged for, that 'if the R. C. Church wished to do so', then a dual hierarchy could be set up and then repeated that such a proceeding would trouble good Catholic order". And Nickerson further noted that Portal could not make "head nor tail" of what it all meant[67]. None of the Malines Conversations participants knew at this time of course — as we will touch on later in more detail — that Mercier had requested and received from Dom Lambert Beauduin a study of the possibility of a uniate patriarchate of Canterbury. Beauduin had sent this to Mercier on January 31, 1925[68].

---

65. BIY, The Malines Papers of Lord Halifax, Box 6, N° 19, Nickerson to Halifax, January 30, 1925.

66. BIY, The Malines Papers of Lord Halifax, Box 6, N° 15, Halifax to Portal, January 22, 1925.

67. BIY, The Malines Papers of Lord Halifax, Box 6, N° 39, Nickerson to Halifax, March 30, 1925.

68. R. Aubert points out that Mercier had approached Beauduin in October 1924 about writing some observations for use at the Malines Conversations. We quote Aubert about the results of that request: "Dom Lambert, rentré à Rome, où il enseignait alors à Saint-Anselme le traité de l'Église, se mit à l'œuvre et spontanément donna à son travail un développement beaucoup plus considérable que prévu, dépassant la simple étude historique pour esquisser tout un plan éventuel de réunion où l'Église anglicane, réunie à Rome par l'intermédiaire de son primat, conserverait sa personnalité et une grande autonomie interne,

It appears Mercier was using the American Episcopalian to test out reactions to Beauduin's proposal before Mercier's reading of it during the Fourth Conversation.

Mercier had also given Nickerson a letter of introduction to Gasparri who he said could arrange a papal audience for him.

In early April, Nickerson again wrote Halifax that he had not yet been able to get to Rome but that he wondered if any arrangements had yet been made for American participation in the next Conversation. He also reported that he had heard a rumor from a friend in London that Cardinal Bourne planned on sending two English Catholics to the next Conversation[69]. A few days later Halifax wrote to Kidd that it looked like the English Roman Catholics were divided on Malines. He also asked him about Nickerson's participation[70]. Kidd replied that the coming Conversation would be critical and that it would not be wise to invite Nickerson or any new members to participate in it[71]. In the end his view prevailed. Curiously, Hoffman Nickerson does not appear again — in any of the correspondence we have surveyed — until four months after the Fourth Conversation. Then, writing to Halifax from his New York City address, Nickerson reported that his trip to Rome had been disappointing. He had found Gasparri and Gasquet cool and evasive, and he had been unable to see the Pope. Nickerson also reported that he had spent three days in Rome talking with American, French, and English ecclesiastics and found that Gasquet was still considered an expert on Anglican affairs but that he advanced "nothing new since the unhappy arguments of thirty years ago"[72].

On May 9, 1925 *The Tablet* carried an article by another of the participants in the "arguments of thirty years ago", Canon Moyes. His article, "An Anglican 'Call to Action'", outlined the growing dissatisfaction of Broad and Low Church Anglicans about the activities of the Anglo-Catholics. Moyes' purpose was to portray the Anglican Church as a disunited house — the same tactic that he and others had used at the time of the Anglican Orders debates. He said he hoped that from all of the Anglican in-house fighting some good would come. He hoped that all Anglicans would come to realize that a unified Church could only result from "glad and wholehearted discipleship of the Catholic

dans la ligne des anciens patriarcats. C'est le 31 janvier 1925 qu'il envoya son rapport à Mercier". R. AUBERT, *op. cit.* (n. 19), p. 120.

69. BIY, The Malines Papers of Lord Halifax, Box 6, N° 41, Nickerson to Halifax, April 6, 1925.

70. BIY, The Malines Papers of Lord Halifax, Box 6, N° 49, Halifax to Kidd, April 16, 1925.

71. BIY, The Malines Papers of Lord Halifax, Box 6, N° 49, Kidd to Halifax, April 17, 1925.

72. BIY, The Malines Papers of Lord Halifax, Box 7, N° 61, Nickerson to Halifax, September 18, 1925.

Church"[73]. Moyes, by the way, would later comment about the Malines Conversations: "Perhaps the best thing that comes of such attempts is the lesson that nothing ever comes of them"[74]. The same issue of *The Tablet* which carried Moyes' article also carried a strongly hagiographic biography of Cardinal Merry del Val, written by the paper's Rome Correspondent, in honor of del Val's silver jubilee. *The Tablet* admitted that Merry del Val was sometimes depicted as "intransigent", "Ultra-montane", "Jesuitical", and even "Machiavellian", but insisted that he was "gentleness, kindness itself" and that all should be grateful for "the never-ceasing vigilant work" of his Holy Office[75].

6. *At Malines, May 19 and 20, 1925*

When the ten participants from the Third Conversation returned to Malines for the Fourth — and really final — Conversation, held May 19 and 20, 1925, they gathered in Mercier's house in "the added warmth of pure friendship"[76]. The Conversation would see another eruption between Gore and Batiffol but also, as Frere recalls, "plenty of chaff and fun between the meetings"[77].

Frere, in fact, delighted in telling about one of their good natured jokes on Mercier: "I remember going out with Bishop Gore for a short walk before our morning meeting; as we got outside we found a Rogationtide procession on its way through the parish, so we joined in and followed for some time until it was time to get back to our gathering. At *déjeuner* subsequently Batiffol said to the Cardinal, 'Eminence, do you know that there were two Anglican Bishops following in the Rogationtide procession this morning?' The Cardinal in his grave way said, 'Then indeed we are coming nearer to unity'. 'Yes', said Batiffol, 'but does your Eminence know that they didn't follow the procession the whole way?' 'Ah?' said the Cardinal. 'No, they left just before the prayer for the Pope'. This scandalous misstatement was drowned in roars of laughter; in fact we had left in the middle of the invocations of the Virgin Martyrs"[78].

At the Fourth Conversation both the Catholics and the Anglicans had prepared papers which they had shown to each other ahead of time. Van Roey read a paper on "The Episcopate and the Papacy from the Theological Point of View"[79]. Kidd responded with a paper on the

73. Mgr. MOYES, "An Anglican 'Call to Action'" in *The Tablet*, 146 (May 9, 1925) p. 618.
74. E. NORMAN, *Roman Catholics in England*, Oxford, New York, 1985, p. 128.
75. "Cardinal Merry del Val", in *The Tablet*, 146 (May 9, 1925), pp. 625 and 626.
76. FRERE, *op. cit.*, p. 52.
77. *Ibid.*
78. *Ibid.*, pp. 52-53.
79. It was a paper "*qui était très nuancé par rapport à la théologie classique du temps et*

same subject. Hemmer read his long study on "The Agreement of the Pope and Bishops from the Historical Point of View". Gore replied with "Unity in Diversity", stressing that in Anglican and Orthodox Churches as well as in some Protestant Churches certain elements of primitive Christianity had been preserved which the Roman Church had more or less abandoned. This led to a heated discussion between Gore and Batiffol about fundamental and non-fundamental doctrines. Gore had asked for instance: "with a sense of my audacity in asking it", whether the idea is wholly impossible that, with a view to the corporate reconciliation of the Orthodox Communion and the Anglican Communion, the Roman Church could be content to require not more than the acceptance of those articles of faith which fall under the Vincentian Canon, in other words, what Gore considered "fundamental"[80]. But as Prestige observes in his biography of Gore, "The discussion concluded with the resolve to commit to future reflection the task of maturing decisions on this difficult subject"[81].

The most significant event of the Fourth Conversation was the totally unexpected reading by Mercier of a paper, "*L'Église Anglicane Unie non Absorbée*" which Mercier said had been written by a "Canonist". It was subsequently revealed by Van Roey, in 1930, that the author was Dom Lambert Beauduin (1873-1960) of the Benedictine Community of Amay[82]. The event marked the second time that Mercier had taken a conference by surprise and introduced the novel ideas of Beauduin[83]. This time, as W.H. Frere put it, the surprise "took our breath away"[84].

laissait pressentir en plusieurs points la position adoptée par Vatican II". R. AUBERT, "L'histoire des Conversations de Malines", in *Collectanea Mechliniensia* 52 (1967), p. 52.

80. FRERE, *op. cit.*, p. 117.

81. G.L. PRESTIGE, *The Life of Charles Gore*, London, Toronto, 1935, p. 488.

82. Dom Lambert Beauduin was born in 1873 near Liège. He was ordained in 1897 and joined the *Aumôniers du Travail* in 1899. He left these "Labor Chaplains" and entered the Benedictine Abbey of Mont César at Louvain in 1906. In 1909 in September he gave the famous talk on liturgy at the National Congress of Catholic Works at Malines. The following November the first issue of Liturgical Life was published at Louvain. In 1912 his plans for a liturgical institute collapsed due to lack of funds. In 1914 he was Mercier's special messenger to the Belgian bishops. In 1915, Beauduin, a member of the Belgian underground, escaped to England where he came into contact with the leading Anglican ecumenists. In 1919 he was named sub prior of Mont César at Louvain. In 1921 he was appointed professor of fundamental theology at Sant' Anselmo in Rome. In 1924 Pius XI issued *Equidem Verba*, encouraging the Benedictines to begin ecumenical monastic foundations. In 1925 Beauduin became prior at Amay. The following year *Irénikon* was founded. He was exiled from his monastery by Roman authority in 1931. In 1945 Angelo Roncalli, then nuncio to Paris, restored him to good graces with Roman authorities; and in 1951 Beauduin returned to his community now at Chevetogne. He died in 1960. — For Beauduin's text, see Appendix F.

83. As mentioned above, at the Catholic Congress of Malines in 1909, Mercier surprised everyone by calling on Beauduin to make a report "The True Prayer of the Church" which marked the start of the Mont César based liturgical movement.

84. FRERE, *op. cit.*, p. 56.

Dom Lambert Beauduin's proposal was an echo of the 1841 ecumenical proposal of Ambrose Phillips de Lisle; basically what Beauduin said was that in the pre-Reformation Church the Archbishop of Canterbury had had a type of patriarchal status. He spoke about the current position of Uniate Churches in the Catholic Church and suggested that there could be a similar type of arrangement for the Anglican Church — a patriarchate of Canterbury, in communion with Rome, which would have its own liturgy and canon law. The Archbishop of Canterbury would become a fifth patriarch and the existing Roman Catholic sees in England would be suppressed.

Years later when the paper was made public it created an understandably hostile reaction from English Catholics; nevertheless Albert Gille would reveal in 1934 that it "still embodies the secret ambitions of many a Catholic in England"[85].

The Fourth Conversation ended with a nearly unanimously felt desire to meet again in the near future. Only Gore had come to the conclusion that there was no point in a future meeting. In accordance with Mercier's request, and with the full agreement of Davidson, there was to be no publication of the proceedings.

Later in May Mercier went to Rome and Gasquet could write in his diary: "May 24: Cardinal Mercier has arrived, his conversations with the Anglicans finished. It is said that they are agreed that nothing practical can be done. No compromise on doctrine being possible". And the next day he wrote that Cardinal Mercier had found the English ecclesiastics in Rome "chilly over his Anglican venture"[86].

85. Fr. JEROME, op. cit., p. 31.
86. S. LESLIE, Cardinal Gasquet: A Memoir, London, 1953, p. 255.

CHAPTER SIX

FINAL EPISODES

After the Fourth Conversation, May 19-20, 1925, enthusiasm for the Malines Conversations gradually dissipated. In October and November of 1925, Mercier would nearly create an international ecclesiastical incident by angrily snapping at Francis Woodlock and enchanging barbs with Cardinal Bourne; but then two months later, Mercier would be in his grave. Four months after that Portal would also be gone. And already in January of 1926, it would be clear that Pius XI had cooled toward Malines. The tide was changing. Even the King of England would wish an end to the Malines Conversations. A Fifth Conversation, of sorts, would be held in October of 1926; but it was a melancholic affair — a business meeting for going over past documents and gathering materials for final reports.

For Halifax, it would seem like an eternity before those reports would be published. Batiffol and Van Roey would in fact try to scuttle their report. Halifax would end up publishing his own report to the dismay of just about everyone. A frustrated Cardinal Bourne would make an uncharacteristic attack on the Anglican Church in Archbishop Lang's see city of York. The Prayer Book revision would go down defeated in the Commons — the Malines Conversations would be blamed.

In 1928 Pius XI would close the door on further Roman Catholic ecumenical activity with his strong disciplinary encyclical: *Mortalium Animos*. In the same year a worn-out Archbishop Davidson would retire; and he would be dead within two years. Within a year of Davidson's retirement, two less than enthusiastic observers of the developments at Malines, the participant Batiffol and the critic Gasquet, would also be in their graves.

The English/Spanish curialist Cardinal Merry del Val would carry-on an extensive — and revealing — correspondence with the English Jesuit Francis Woodlock, but then he too would be gone in 1930. Gore would go in 1932. Robinson would be gone in 1933.

Lord Halifax, nearly deaf and nearly blind, would continue his ecumenical journey right to the end. His travels — promotion as well as fact-finding missions — would take him again to Rome, Paris, and Louvain. In 1934 he would oversee the union of his English Church Union and the Anglo-Catholic Congress, and he would be elected one of the co-presidents of the new ecumenical body. A few days later,

however, he would come to the end of his *caminho novo*. And Cardinal
Bourne would die the same year.

1. *From the Fourth Conversation to the Death of Cardinal Mercier*

Immediately after the Fourth Conversation, as we noted in the last
chapter, Cardinal Mercier went to Rome. On May 29, he was interviewed
by *La Nation Belge* and reports of that interview appeared in the
paper's June 3 edition. When asked about the contents of the just
concluded Conversation, Mercier had said that he could not make
anything public until the official reports had been prepared; but that he
was "very satisfied with the new discussions" and could indicate two
important results of the Conversations: (1) that for the fourth time,
eminent Anglicans and Catholic theologians could meet for friendly
discussions about "the problem of the reunion of the Churches"; and
(2) that the atmosphere had become more enlightened.When asked
about any future Conversations, Mercier replied "it is now an institution" and that, God willing, they would be meeting again during the
coming year at his house in Malines[1]. That interview — no doubt due
to the already tense Prayer Book situation — greatly ruffled the
feathers of George Grahame, the British Ambassador to Belgium, and
of George V (1865, 1910-1936) the King of England.

Grahame, on the same day that the interview appeared in *La Nation
Belge,* sent an angry note to Lord Stamfordham, the King's private
secretary: "It is extraordinary that our Church representatives do not
see the game of the Roman Catholics in this matter... In my humble
opinion, the sooner these pourparlers between Cardinal Mercier or his
representatives and Anglican theologians with the authority of the
Archbishops are stopped the better for us. Cardinal Mercier is well-
known here to be intolerant in religious matters, and furthermore, not
long since, over the Irish question showed marked hostility to Great
Britain"[2]. Two days later, Stamfordham sent Grahame's note to Archbishop Davidson, with a cover note: "The King thinks you should see
the enclosed from the Ambassador in Brussels. His Majesty is very
uneasy about these interviews with Cardinal Mercier"[3]. Davidson

1. *"C'est d'abord un fait significatif que, pour la quatrième fois, des hommes éminents du
protestantisme anglican de la 'High Church' soient venus, sous le patronage de leurs deux
archevêques de Canterbury et d'York, passer trois jours à l'archevêché de Malines pour y
rencontrer des théologiens catholiques et examiner amicalement avec eux le problème de la
réunion des Églises... Et je puis en noter un autre, c'est que les entretiens que nous venons
d'avoir ont permis de constater que depuis l'année dernière, suivant l'expression même de nos
visiteurs, l'atmosphère s'est éclaircie".* ALPL, Archbishop Davidson's papers, unclassified
newspaper clipping, *La Nation Belge*, June 3, 1925.

2. ALPL, Archbishop Davidson's papers, unclassified letter, Grahame to Stamfordham,
June 3, 1925.

3. ALPL, Archbishop Davidson's papers, unclassified letter, Stamfordham to Davidson,
June 5, 1925.

replied on June 6 that the matter would have to be handled delicately. They would have to go around the Foreign Office, because the Under-Secretary in the Foreign Office, Sir William Tyrrell, was a Roman Catholic. But he was certain he could "deal effectively" with the situation and that "the outcome may well be that the Malines Conversations may have come to an end"[4].

By the end of June, as B.J. Kidd reported to Halifax, the problem had been at least temporarily resolved. Kidd had found the English reaction to the interview unfortunate, thought it had helped "queer the pitch", but could report that Davidson had been able to reassure the King. In a word, they could proceed with plans for a future meeting[5]. News about developments within the English Roman Catholic community also reached Halifax in June. Portal wrote that he had received a letter from his friend, the auxiliary bishop of Nice, who had reported that the English Roman Catholics were making a case against the Conversations "because of the decreased number of individual conversions". Portal also made two important observations: first — that the Pope was not yet negatively affected by the English Catholic argument. And in connection with this point, Cardinal Gasquet's diary entry for October 24, 1925 is also supportive: "I had an audience with the Holy Father. We discussed the question of the Malines Conference but though I spoke very plainly he still approved of the fact that conversations in private could do no harm. I replied that unfortunately they were regarded as semi-official. He said he did not put any value on the alleged falling-off of conversions"[6].

Portal's second observation was a word of warning, at the end of his letter about the connection between Batiffol and Moyes[7]. Halifax replied that he was not surprised about Moyes because Moyes was simply being true to himself[8]. It was also in the spring of 1925 that Francis Woodlock sent Cardinal Merry del Val a copy of his "Farm Street Lectures". He was preparing them for publication and wanted del Val to read them. On July 3, Merry del Val sent him a "confidential" letter thanking him for the pages and indicating that he found

4. ALPL, Archbishop Davdison's papers, unclassified letter, Davidson to Stamfordham, June 6, 1925.

5. BIY, The Malines Papers of Lord Halifax, Box 6, N° 100, Kidd to Halifax, June 27, 1925.

6. S. LESLIE, *Cardinal Gasquet: A Memoir*, London, 1953, p. 255. We also note Leslie's summation of the situation: "So Gasquet found himself back again with the questions of reunion and Anglican Orders after thirty years. It was strange to find Mercier in Rampolla's place trying to find a way of squaring the ecclesiastical circle and making valid the invalid", p. 255.

7. "*Les rapports avec Moyes sont toujours à surveiller*". BIY, The Malines Papers of Lord Halifax, Box 6, N° 87, Portal to Halifax, June 1, 1925.

8. "*Quant au Chanoine Moyes il reste ce qu'il a toujours été*" BIY, The Malines Papers of Lord Halifax, Box 6, N° 90, Halifax to Portal, June 7, 1925.

"nothing to object to and much to admire" in the pages he had read.
He complained about the "extraordinary *'ignoratio elenchi'* on the
continent regarding the situation in England". He could not understand
how Catholics could speak of "re-uniting the English Church of today,
because that Church, if a Church it is in any real sense, was never
united, being a new institution, with different and heretical doctrines,
different and invalid orders in our sense, (and) different and invalid
constitution". And he thought that Leo XIII had made all of this clear
in *Satis Cognitum*[9].

In *The Tablet* of July 4, 1925, there was a brief announcement about
the annual meeting of the Converts Aid Society in London, indicating
that during the meeting Cardinal Bourne had asked for continued
support for the society and for converted Anglican clergymen. "It is no
use allowing their attention to be diverted", announced the English
Cardinal, "by transient incidents such as the Conversations at Malines"[10].
Francis Woodlock also spoke up at this annual meeting; and he
sounded like a prophet. Soon, he said, there would be more converts
and "within the next ten days many people would be amazed and
astonished at things which would be said at the Anglican Convention in
Albert Hall in connection with the Church and the Pope"[11]. He was
speaking of course about rumors that Halifax was about to make a
major announcement. On July 9, Halifax gave an important speech
— approved ahead of time by the Archbishop of Canterbury[12] —
before the Anglo-Catholic Congress at Albert Hall. Early in his speech,
Halifax stressed that he was speaking on his own behalf, not for
Davidson nor for any of the Anglican participants at Malines. But then
Halifax — without indicating the source — went on to announce and
advocate what had been the major point of Dom Lambert Beauduin's
proposal which Mercier had read at the Fourth Conversation! "Now in
considering this aspect of the question of reunion", said Halifax, "it is
well to bear in mind that for the space of a thousand years Rome and
England were one... For it must be remembered that reconciliation
with Rome does not imply any denial of the historic claims of Canterbury, nor involve the absorption of the Church of England into the
Church of Rome, but rather the union of the two Churches under the
primacy of the successor of St. Peter, which is quite another thing"[13].

9. AEPSJ, Woodlock papers, BH/6, Merry del Val to Woodlock, July 3, 1925.

10. "Converts Aid Society Annual Meeting", in *The Tablet* 146 (July 4, 1925), p. 14.

11. *Ibid.*

12. Halifax had sent Davidson a draft of his proposed address. Davidson did not
agree with the contents, but would not object to Halifax's expressing such ideas as long as
Halifax clarified that the ideas were his and not those of his Anglican colleagues at
Malines. See J. LOCKHART, *Charles Lindley Viscount Halifax*, vol. 2, London, 1936,
p. 320.

13. Viscount HALIFAX, *Reunion and the Roman Primacy*, London, Milwaukee, 1925,
pp. 34 and 35.

Woodlock had been in a box at Albert Hall throughout Halifax's speech. Afterwards, he "betook himself to the warpath"[14].

The day after Halifax's speech, Woodlock wrote Halifax to "remove a misunderstanding on the all important 'reunion' question". He was concerned that someone might think that Mercier supported Halifax's erroneous "branch" theory. "No Roman Catholic", wrote Woodlock, "could possibly hold these claims to be true, and if Cardinal Mercier were to put such views forward, Cardinal though he is, I am sure that he would promptly be told to retract them... Anglicans are not Catholics, their Church has not got Apostolic Succession and this is the doctrine taught by every theologian of the Church. Malines cannot make any difference to this Catholic truth"[15]. Eight days later, Canon Moyes took Halifax to task in *The Tablet*, in an article titled "What Does Lord Halifax Mean?" Moyes was clear about what he and his English Roman Catholic sympathizers meant: "All that we have been thus supposing would be a complete and genuine absorption of the Church of England into the fold of the Catholic Church, and that is not in the least what Lord Halifax or any bulk of even the Anglo-Catholic party have in their minds and aspirations"[16]. The same issue of *The Tablet*, by the way, carried the full text of Halifax's speech.

Three days after the appearance of Moyes' article, Woodlock was again at his typewriter with a new message for Halifax. Halifax had written to him that his previous letter was "one long misunderstanding from beginning to end". Woodlock now replied that he was "puzzled" at such a comment from Halifax, because Woodlock thought it was all perfectly clear where Halifax stood. Nevertheless, Woodlock was alarmed that an article in the *Church Times* "contrasts my doctrine with that of Cardinal Mercier" and he thought "it is owing to his Eminence to contradict this attack upon his orthodoxy, and I have written a strong letter to the *Church Times* on the point". But the most revealing part of Woodlock's letter came near the end when he wrote: "I know that copies of last week's *Church Times* have reached Rome and the result may be that the 'Conversations' at Malines will come to be regarded as disseminating rather than as dissipating misunderstandings"[17]. What Woodlock never revealed to Halifax was that he himself had sent the articles to Cardinal Merry del Val. Del Val would later send him a thank you note[18]. A few days after Woodlock's letter, however, Halifax

14. LOCKHART, *op. cit.*, p. 320.
15. BIY, The Malines Papers of Lord Halifax, Box 7, N° 9, Woodlock to Halifax, July 10, 1925.
16. J. MOYES, "What Does Lord Halifax Mean?", in *The Tablet*, 146 (July 18, 1925), pp. 74 75.
17. BIY, The Malines Papers of Lord Halifax, Box 7, n° 14, Woodlock to Halifax, July 21, 1925.
18. AEPSJ, Woodlock papers, BH/6, Merry del Val to Woodlock, July 28, 1925.

did receive a short letter from Portal, warning about Woodlock's
Roman connections: "A word especially about Father Woodlock ... it
is important to avoid all controversy with him and especially all
comparison between him and Cardinal Mercier... There is no doubt
that Cardinals Merry del Val and Gasquet are linked with Woodlock
and they are urging him on. The Pope and Cardinal Gasparri are
certainly favorably disposed toward Mercier; nevertheless, it is the
same old story – and we very well know how it ended in 1896"[19].

The day after Portal's letter, an exasperated Halifax sent a feisty
letter to Woodlock, accusing Woodlock of being a trouble-maker and
of deliberately changing the meaning of Halifax's words[20]. Halifax then
sent all of Woodlock's letters to Portal with the observation: "For the
most part, English Catholics are truly impossible"[21].

It was also about this time that the editor of *The Tablet*, Ernest
Oldmeadow, went to Rome and conferred with Cardinal Merry del Val.
As Oldmeadow describes it: "He (Merry del Val) spoke strongly about
the 'Reunionists" methods and commended to my study the plain
words of the Holy See, dated September 16, 1864, by which English
Catholics were forbidden to join or remain in 'the Association for
Promoting the Unity of Christendom'. On that occasion, Rome objected
to such movements because they are 'pervaded by the idea that the true
Church of Jesus Christ consists partly of the Roman Church spread
abroad and propagated throughout the world, partly of the Photian
schism and of the Anglican heresy; and that the two latter have equally
with the Roman Church, one Lord, *one faith* (original emphasis, JD)
and one baptism'". Merry del Val asked Oldmeadow to reprint that
papal document of 1864 in *The Tablet*; but Oldmeadow decided not
to because "doing so at a tense moment would have been deemed
provocative"[22].

19. "*Un mot seulement à propos du P. Woodlock ... il faudrait éviter toute controverse
avec lui et surtout toute comparaison entre lui et le card. Mercier... Il n'y a pas de doute que
les cards. (sic) Merry del Val et Gasquet sont avec le P. Woodlock et le poussent. Bien qu'ils
sachent très bien que le Pape et le card. Gasparri sont favorables au card. Mercier, c'est de
la vieille histoire mais nous savons très bien comment elle a fini en '96*". BIY, The Malines
Papers of Lord Halifax, Box 7, N° 17, Portal to Halifax, July 27, 1925.

20. "You invest my words with a meaning of your own, you attach to them a
significance which is not theirs, and having done me this injustice you make it patent to
everyone by your own letters that you are influenced by the fear that the conversations at
Malines, instead of facilitating individual conversions, may promote the corporate
reunion of the Church of England with the Holy See... Do not the words of the Psalm: 'I
labour for peace but when I speak unto them thereof they make them ready to battle' sum
up the situation between us?" BIY, The Malines Papers of Lord Halifax, Box 7, N° 18,
Halifax to Woodlock, July 28, 1925.

21. "*Les Catholiques Anglais pour la plupart sont vraiment impossibles*". BIY, The
Malines Papers of Lord Halifax, Box 7, N° 19, Halifax to Portal, July 28, 1925.

22. E. OLDMEADOW, *Francis Cardinal Bourne*, vol. 2, London, 1944, p. 364, note 1.

At the end of July, Merry del Val wrote Woodlock that no one in Rome "would dream of countenancing the suggestions made by Lord H." and he hoped that Cardinal Bourne and the English bishops would "take occasion to make a clear statement and sweep away this false doctrine". He said he knew that Gasquet was ready to do just that. And then del Val hinted at a bit of the struggle that was going on at the Vatican when he said: "I would do so myself if I were not Sec. of the Holy Office and unable therefore to make a public statement otherwise than officially and if the question is officially presented. I cannot on my personal initiative take part in a local controversy". The Cardinal concluded his letter by encouraging Woodlock to look up and write about certain documents: the document of 1864 which he had mentioned to Oldmeadow; *Apostolicae Curae*; and — because of the "lines still continued by Lord H. and others" — Leo XIII's letter to the Archbishop of Paris suppressing Abbé Portal's *La Revue Anglo-Romaine*[23].

On August 1, 1925, Halifax sent a final letter to Woodlock: "You do not believe in the possibility of corporate reunion and what you desire are individual conversions. I do believe in corporate reunion and I do not desire individual conversions. That sums up the whole matter between us and there it must stop. I am glad to know that all your co-religionists are not of your way of thinking"[24].

In August, Woodlock took his arguments to the pages of *The Month* in which he offered "critical and historical notes" about Halifax's Albert Hall speech[25]. And in the same issue, Joseph Keating reported — what he thought was good news — that there was a rumor that Mercier had told certain Milan journalists that the Malines Conversations had already ended in failure. Keating then told his readers that Halifax had not learned anything at Malines, because he still believed "in the continuity theory, that hoary historical fallacy which generations of Catholic writers have exploded, which the Elizabethans, killing, racking and plundering the adherents of 'the old religion', never dreamt of, to which the existing Catholic Church in this country, heir to the faith, if not to the possessions, of the martyrs, daily gives the lie". Keating then launched into an impassioned complaint against the Roman Catholic participants at Malines: "In loyalty to our glorious dead, as well as to the truth for which they died, we must protest against that false implication and, in so far as it seems to be endorsed by our brethren abroad, we must make bold to deny the competence of foreigners to understand our intimate history better than ourselves"[26].

23. AEPSJ, Woodlock papers, BH/6, Merry del Val to Woodlock, July 28, 1925.

24. BIY, The Malines Papers of Lord Halifax, Box 7, N° 24, Halifax to Woodlock, August 1, 1925.

25. F. WOODLOCK, "Miscellanea: Critical and Historical Notes. A Speech by Lord Halifax", in *The Month* 146 (August 1925), p. 156.

26. J. KEATING, "A Last Word on Malines", in *The Month* 146 (August 1925), p. 163-167.

It was also in August 1925 that Halifax received at least two letters from R. Gordon George who rambled on about his travels, his ecumenical hopes, about the terrible things being said against Halifax and against the Conversations in *The Tablet*, and about finding a way around *Apostolicae Curae*. Most interesting was George's comment that Cardinal Pietro La Fontaine (1860-1935), the Patriarch of Venice, was supportive of the Conversations and that the Patriarch had told him the Holy See was still supportive[27].

In spite of all the negative press coverage, Mercier and Davidson were still determined to move ahead with plans for the next Conversation, though Mercier did think that Davidson was becoming a bit too careful and slow to act. In early August, Mercier received a long letter from Davidson in which the Archbishop said he was convinced that the Conversations had so far been "fruitful of good". In fact, said Davidson, they were the "piers which would be useful if we were able to construct the bridge". Davidson, however, was not pleased with a phrase suggested by Mercier that the participants at Malines had made "progress in agreement". Nevertheless, Davidson said he shared Mercier's opinion that "those who have met under your presidency should meet again", and he was willing to leave the choice about discussion topics to the "decision of those who take part in the Conversations"[28]. Mercier's reply was delayed until the end of October — for reasons which we will soon touch on. He said that when he first read Davidson's letter he was touched by "*un certain malaise*" but that perhaps it should have been expected. Mercier was in agreement with Davidson that there should be a compilation of points of agreement and points for further discussion, but he stressed that they should focus on points in favor of union. And then, no doubt giving expression to his emotional state at the moment, Mercier concluded his letter with a bit of stark realism, reminding Davidson that the ones who plant the seeds, often with tears, are often not the ones who harvest the crop[29].

27. BIY, The Malines Papers of Lord Halifax, Box 7, N° 33, Gordon George to Halifax, August 9, 1925 and N° 46, August 25, 1925.

28. Davidson to Halifax, October 25, 1925, published in G.K.A. BELL, *Randall Davidson. Archbishop of Canterbury*, London, New York, Toronto, 1952, pp. 1293 1296.

29. "*Au dehors, quand nous prêtons l'oreille à ceux qui nous suivent, nous constatons des impatiences qu'il n'est pas en notre pouvoir de satisfaire et il peut en résulter pour nous, j'entends pour moi-même et pour Votre Grandeur, des impressions d'inquiétude ou de fatigue auxquelles il n'est pas toujours aisé de se soustraire.... Fidèles à notre point de départ, nous avons à mettre progressivement au jour ce qui est de nature à favoriser l'union; ce qui y fait obstacle doit être écarté ou différé.... Moissonneurs d'âmes, nous avons à semer à la sueur de notre front, et, le plus souvent, dans les larmes, avant que sonne l'heure de la moisson; et quand sonnera cette heure bénie, un autre vraisemblablement aura pris notre place. 'Alius est qui seminat, alius est qui metit'. (Joan. iv. 37)*". Mercier to Davidson, October 25, 1925, published in Viscount HALIFAX, *The Conversations at Malines: 1921-1925*, 1928, pp. 61-68.

As far as ecumenical developments were concerned, August 1925 was indeed a busy month. After years of preparation, it was from August 19-30, at Stockholm, that the first meeting of the Universal Christian Conference on "Life and Work" was held under the joint presidency of the Archbishop of Canterbury, Randall Davidson; the Patriarch of Constantinople, Germanos Strenopoulos; the Archbishop of Upsala, Nathan Söderblom; and the Rev. William Adam Brown, D.D. (1865-1943), from New York. Six topics formed the basis for discussions at the Conference:

1. The Purpose of God for Humanity and the Duty of the Church.
2. The Church and Economic and Industrial Problems.
3. The Church and Social and Moral Problems.
4. The Church and International Relations.
5. The Church and Christian Education.
6. Methods of Cooperative and Federative Efforts by the Christian Communions[30].

The liberalism of the discussions and the spectre of an international federation of Churches, including Canterbury, separate from Rome shocked the Pope. Stockholm 1925 contributed much to the hardening of ecumenical attitudes at Rome in 1925 and its "pan-Christian" orientation would be denounced in Pius XI's *Mortalium Animos* in 1928.

At the end of August, Kidd sent Halifax a letter, indicating that he had given up on English Roman Catholics. He found them terribly "hampered by their passion for individual conversions", but could also understand their opposition to corporate reunion. "In truth", he wrote, "they must know that it would leave them out in the cold, or perhaps be effective at the price of their extinction"[31].

From our perspective, we can see Kidd's perceptive observation as the fuse of an approaching Roman Catholic explosion; and Francis Woodlock was ready to ignite it.

The first issue of *The Tablet* to appear in September 1925 carried a book review of the newly released collection of Woodlock's Farm Street lectures — the essays he had sent to Merry del Val — under the title of *Modernism and the Christian Church*. *The Tablet* lauded the author for clearly pointing out that "Anglo-Catholics remain out of communion with Catholics ... yet they remain in communion with anti-sacerdotalists and Modernists"[32]. Woodlock's ideas were also featured in the

---

30. G.K.A. BELL, *The Stockholm Conference of 1925*, London, 1926, p. 2.

31. BIY, The Malines Papers of Lord Halifax, Box 7, N° 49, Kidd to Halifax, August 28, 1925.

32. *The Tablet* again called attention to the danger of Anglo-Catholics bringing Modernism into the Church, if any reunion plan were to succeed. In a review of F. Woodlock's *Modernism and the Christian Church*, the reviewer observed: "Anglo-Catholics remain out of communion with Catholics ... yet they remain in communion

September issue of *The Month*, which published his letter which had appeared in the the *Church Times* on August 21 as well as the personal letter Halifax had sent Woodlock afterwards. Woodlock then gave a detailed critique of Halifax's words noting in conclusion that Halifax had clearly accused him of "conscious dishonesty"; but, said Woodlock, "As I am a Jesuit, I suppose I must not be surprised at this"[33]. And in mid-September Woodlock was at it again in *The Tablet*, pointing out the fallacy of the Anglo-Catholics who "believe in the mass and 'feel sure' of the validity of their orders ... on account of their experience of God's graces given them on the occasions of their devout approach to their Eucharist"[34].

A few days later, Portal summarized for Halifax what was happening: the English Jesuits were apparently now fighting a battle against the Malines Conversations[35]. But then Portal tried to lift his old friend's spirits by reminding him of a new ecumenical adventure and a new group of supporters: the Benedictines of Dom Lambert Beauduin.

In early 1925, the Belgian Benedictine, Beauduin, had received permission to found his ecumenical community the *Moines de l'Union*. Though he did not yet have a site for the monastery (later the Belgian locality Amay), he enthusiastically set out to gather support for his dream by "capitalizing on the providential publicity that the Malines Conversations created for Christian unity"[36]. In the autumn of 1925, he organized a series of unity days in Belgium: at Brussels, September 21-25; at Liège and Verviers, November 11-15; and at Louvain, November 19.

Beauduin was not timid about "drawing the eminent personalities associated with the Malines Conversations into his own projects"[37]. Thus during the unity days at Brussels, Abbé Portal gave two talks about Archbishop Wake and concerns about Christian unity in the nineteenth century Anglican Church. Beauduin also explained the Catholic position on unity in the light of Vatican I and concluded

with anti-sacerdotalists and Modernists". "Farm Street Lectures" in *The Tablet* 146 (September 5, 1925) p. 305.

33. "Lord Halifax and Father Woodlock", in *The Month* 146 (September 1925), p. 260.

34. F. WOODLOCK, "An Anglican Bishop on Anglican Ordinations", in *The Tablet* 146 (September 12, 1925), pp. 342-343: "Anglo-Catholics believe in the mass and they 'feel sure' of the validity of their orders... Most of them really believe on account of their experience of God's graces given them on the occasions of their devout approach to their eucharist".

35. "*Il semble que les jésuites anglais engagent une vraie bataille contre les Conversations de Malines*". BIY, The Malines Papers of Lord Halifax, Box 7, N° 60, Portal to Halifax, September 13, 1925.

36. S. QUITSLUND, *Beauduin. A Prophet Vindicated*, New York, Paramus, Toronto, 1973, p. 125.

37. *Ibid.*

that, when properly understood, the First Vatican Council did not compromise the work for unity. Lord Halifax and Portal also spoke at the Louvain unity day in November and created quite an uproar. We will touch on that a bit later[38].

By October 1, Portal was back in the South of France and delighted about his experiences during the Brussels unity days. He wrote Halifax that he was convinced that the Belgian Benedictines had begun an important Church unity movement and it reminded him of his and Halifax's efforts in 1894. And he said he was hopeful about the success of their efforts, because apparently the Benedictines had the backing of the Belgian bishops. And he added that the bishops were on the side of Mercier; and were against Merry del Val, Gasquet, the English Catholics, and the Jesuits[39]! As far as the Jesuits were concerned — it would only be a matter of days before one Jesuit in particular would be on the attack against Portal, as well as Halifax and Mercier.

The Jesuit was Francis Woodlock. The occasion was his letter to the editor of *The Tablet* on October 10, 1925. This was the letter that brought the explosion which pitted Mercier and Bourne against each other and which significantly contributed to Pius XI's later disenchantment with the Malines Conversations. The turmoil provoked by this letter was indeed, as G. Tavard has observed, "a troublesome episode" which "cast a shadow over the Malines Conversations in 1925 and 1926"[40]. In the situation, Woodlock, completely loyal to his Roman advisor and blinded by his solidly Ultramontane theology, revealed a stubborn and disagreeable side of his character. For one thing he was still peeved that Mercier had ignored a letter he had sent to him in July asking for some clarifications as to the Cardinal's position — a letter, by the way, which Woodlock had sent at the suggestions of the Belgian Carton de Wiart and Cardinal Merry del Val[41]. Nevertheless, we find Tavard's assessment of him —"Father Woodlock was poorly informed, incompetent, and uncivil"[42], — a bit extreme.

What prompted Woodlock's letter was the appearance of an article in the *Green Quarterly*, an Anglo-Catholic publication, which reported about Abbé Portal's speeches during the unity days in Brussels. The article enraged Woodlock.

We find it important now to excerpt major sections of Woodlock's

38. For more background on the unity days in Belgium, see QUITSLUND, *op. cit.*, pp. 123-129.

39. "*Les évêques marchent d'accord avec le cardinal; tous savent qu'ils vont contre les card. Gasquet (et) Merry del val, contre les catholiques anglais, et contre les jésuites*". BIY, The Malines Papers of Lord Halifax, Box 7, N° 72, Portal to Halifax, October 1, 1925.

40. G. TAVARD, *Two Centuries of Ecumenism*, Notre Dame, 1960, p. 164.

41. OLDMEADOW, *Francis Cardinal Bourne*, p. 382.

42. TAVARD, *op. cit.*, p. 164.

letter, because it had such an impact on the Malines Conversations. And in a moment, we will do the same with Mercier's response.

Woodlock: "Appropos of your note last week on the matter of the Malines Conversations, may I draw your attention to a passage in the current issue of the *Green Quarterly* — the Anglo-Catholic organ. We are told that: 'The position of ourselves (i.e. the Anglo-Catholics) to the Papacy is, to some extent, simplified because we are all more conscious than before that the difficulty is concentrated in the doctrine of the Papal claims. Remove that, and no other obstacles would be unsurmountable. We are so used to our charming Anglican characteristic of comprehension and vagueness that it is odd to find the difficulty in this issue lies rather in the uncertainty of the Roman Catholic interpretation. Our English Roman friends are, for the most part, uncompromisingly Ultramontane, while at Malines the explanation of the Papal claims has differed quite as much from the Ultramontane as an Anglo-Catholic interpretation of the *39 Articles* differs from that, say of a moderate and married parish priest'".

To which Woodlock observed: "Anglicans will not realize that since the Vatican Council 'Ultramontanism' and Catholicism are one in the acceptance of the clear sense of the dogmatic definition". And then Woodlock got to his main point: the supposition, which he thought Mercier did nothing to remove, that English Roman Catholics and the Catholics at Malines held different interpretations of the Papal office. "One cannot complain of the non-acceptance of the decree by Anglicans, but we have a genuine grievance against the policy of insinuation which during the last two and a half years has suggested that English theologians have presented a different theory of infallibility from that held by their Continental — and less Ultramontane — brethren.

"Cardinal Mercier has been faithful to the undertaking that no account of what passed at Malines should be published until the final minutes agreed upon should be issued to the public. The Abbé Portal appears to have been less reticent, with the result that his alleged announcement of agreement on the basis of the Council of Trent was at once denied by Bishop Gore. One unfortunate result of Cardinal Mercier's silence has been that Anglicans have been enabled to assert confidently that his version of supremacy and infallibility is not the 'English' one. I have myself been called 'an extremist' by the *Church Times*, and accused by the *Guardian* of 'uttering crude theological defiances', when I set forth the clear and universally accepted meaning of the Vatican definition. In a leader in the *Church Times* last July, just after Lord Halifax's Albert Hall speech, we read appropos of the present claim of Anglicanism to be today part of the Catholic Church in spite of its state of schism from the Papacy: 'We will certainly not perpetrate the blunder of committing the Roman Church to the utterance of an individual preacher' (i.e. myself), 'but there is certainly enough in these utterances to justify an inquiry: Which of the two represents most nearly the prevailing Roman spirit; is it the benevolent and venerable Cardinal at Malines or is it the Jesuit in our midst?' It is to be noted that no 'utterance' of Cardinal Mercier on this matter has been made public; yet it is strongly insinuated that His Eminence and I hold different doctrines as to the necessity of communion with the Pope as a condition of Catholicity. It is chiefly the mystery as to what passes at Malines that causes all the mischief. For us there is no mystery as to the nature of the doctrines held by Cardinal Mercier and the Continental theologians, for they are orthodox Catholics and share in our common faith. But Anglicans, with their experience of how 'Anglo-Catholics' explain the *39 Articles* so as to make them express Catholicism and how Modernists 'interpret' the Creed so as to make it mean the opposite to what it expresses, hope that some similar method is at work at Malines and that an 'interpretation' of Papal Infallibility and Supremacy is being concocted there which may be acceptable to those who reject the definition as English Theologians present it.

"We in this country are suspected of heaping up unnecessary obstacles to 'reunion'. I have been accused of 'fearing' lest it should be brought about at Malines. Are we suspected of a jealous fear lest some day a 'uniate' Canterbury should overshadow by its historic glories and 'incomparable' English liturgy the Latin Church of Westminster in an England once more brought into communion with the Pope by the tactful charity of Continental Catholics?

"Seeing that the chief result of the Malines Conversations up to date has been to discredit the teaching of English theologians with regard to the dogma of Papal supremacy, and foreseeing the disappointment which will result when the publication of the minutes of the 'Conversations' makes it clear that there is only one Catholic doctrine after all, in which all Catholics agree, whether Belgian, French, or British, I feel no penitence for my lack of optimism and enthusiasm with regard to the well-intentioned effort of Cardinal Mercier, by which he hoped to bring Anglicans into communion with the Pope and thus make Catholics of them"[43]. This same issue of *The Tablet* mentioned the appearance of another book from Halifax: *Reunion and the Roman Primacy*, but passed it off with the brief observation that "the venerable President of the English Church Union appears to have profited little by his many hours at Malines"[44].

The following week the unnamed author of the *Green Quarterly* article replied to Woodlock via *The Tablet*: "Should Father Woodlock deny the possibility of these differences of interpretation, I can only reply that several Roman Catholic theologians, English as well as

43. F. Woodlock, in *The Tablet* 146 (October 10, 1925), pp. 484-485.
44. *Ibid.*, p. 468.

foreign, have admitted that they exist, and in some cases have expressed their opinion"[45]. The unknown writer from the *Green Quarterly* and Francis Woodlock exchanged barbs in *The Tablet* for three weeks; but the most important reaction to Woodlock came from Mercier. On October 26, 1925, Mercier wrote a letter to Woodlock which he sent to *The Tablet* for publication. On the same day he also sent a copy of the letter to Halifax with the suggestion that, if Halifax was in agreement, it be published in the *Times*[46]. Mercier was angry and his letter was cutting[47].

45. *The Tablet* 146 (October 17, 1925), p. 523.

46. BIY, The Malines Conversations Papers of Lord Halifax, Box 7, N° 107, Mercier to Halifax, October 26, 1925.

47. "*Une première fois, le 22 juillet, au lendemain du discours du vénéré Lord Halifax à l'Albert Hall, une lettre de vous me parvint qui m'invitait à ratifier une appréciation tendancieuse que vous aviez donnée d'un passage de la conférence.*

Lord Halifax se vit obligé de vous écrire que vous aviez commis une injustice à son égard. Vous lui aviez fait dire ce qu'il n'avait pas dit; vous vous insurgiez contre une interprétation qui était vôtre et qu'il désavouait.

J'ai cru ne pouvoir mieux faire que d'opposer à votre lettre du 22 juillet un silence dont je croyais que vous auriez compris la signification.

Une seconde fois, dans le n° du Tablet, du 10 octobre, vous me mettez en cause. Un journaliste a prêté à l'Abbé Portal des paroles invraisemblables que l'Abbé Portal n'a pas prononcées; sans attendre le texte authentique du discours, vous partez de nouveau en guerre contre les 'Conversations de Malines', contre 'le mystère' dont elles s'entourent et vous n'êtes pas éloigné de nous faire un grief de ne pas bénéficier de votre expérience et de vos directives.

Je récuse votre tutelle, mon Révérend Père, et n'entends aucunement m'associer à vos procédés de polémique. Aussi bien, ces procédés se retournent contre vous-même et jettent sur votre enseignement un discrédit dont, bien à tort, vous cherchez à nous endosser la responsabilité.

À l'intention de ceux qui seraient tentés de nous juger à travers vos insinuations, je demande au Tablet de pouvoir vous opposer les trois déclarations que voici.

1. Les théologiens catholiques qui ont pris part aux 'Conversations de Malines' et moi-même connaissons, aussi bien que vous, je pense, la doctrine du Concile du Vatican sur la Primauté et l'infaillibilité du Pape. Aucun de nous n'est disposé à la trahir.

2. Ce qui s'est dit au cours de nos réunions, nous le révèlerons au public qu'au moment ou nous le jugerons opportun.

3. Dans la conclusion de votre article du Tablet, vous avertissez le grand public que, tout en voulant bien ne pas suspecter la droiture de mes intentions, vous assistez sans enthousiasme à l'humble effort tenté par nous pour aider à la réalisation du vœu de Notre Divin Sauveur: 'Ut unum sint'.

Vous écrivez: 'I feel no penitence for my lack of optimism and enthusiasm with regard to the well-intentioned effort of Cardinal Mercier by which he hoped to bring Anglicans into communion with the Pope and thus make Catholics of them'.

Veuillez m'en croire, mon Révérend Père, je me passe sans trop de chagrin de votre approbation et de vos encouragements, que je n'ai, d'ailleurs, jamais espérés. Ceux de ma conscience, confirmés par la parole auguste du Souverain Pontife me suffisent.

Vous avez perdu de vue, sans doute, l'appel si paternellement affectueux du Souverain Pontife à nos frères dissidents qu'il voudrait tant serrer dans ses bras, 'quam vehementer eos amplexari aveamus'; vous avez oublié ce passage de Son Allocution Consistoriale du 24 mars, 1924.

'Nous adressons l'expression de Notre plus vive reconnaissance à tous les catholiques qui,

When Mercier's letter arrived in London at *The Tablet*, editor Oldmeadow went immediately to see Bourne, who told him that it would be "a grave error of judgment" to publish the letter[48]. Bourne then wrote to Mercier.

"Your Eminence has kept honourably the silence imposed upon or accepted by you. But it is manifest that the same discretion is not being observed by Anglicans, and they openly declare that the views on the Holy See held at Malines are not the same as those taught by us in England. The Abbé Portal is allowed to speak in Belgium, and we are not allowed even to have an accurate account of what he actually said. The Anglicans are treated as friends — we, the Catholics of England, apparently as untrustworthy.

"I am powerless to intervene, for Your Eminence has thought well to leave me — who after all am the principal Catholic prelate in this country and your colleague in the Sacred College — absolutely in the dark. It would have surely been but right and seemly that Your Eminence should have stipulated from the outset that there should be no secrets from me. Yet, with the exception of Your Eminence's communication at the end of 1923, I have been treated as if I did not exist. The Archbishop of Canterbury has been given the fullest information of the proceedings at Malines — I have been excluded from all such knowledge and thereby a grave wrong has been done both to me and to the interests of the Catholic Church in England. Out of respect and affection for Your Eminence I have been patient and have kept silence, with the result that I am quite unable either to correct or to control free-lances like Fr. Woodlock who has many sympathizers here and in Rome".

It is important to point out that Bourne, in his letter to Mercier, was not censuring the Malines Conversations. As we have already seen, for instance, Bourne had been delighted with Mercier's Pastoral and had told Oldmeadow to give it "cordial and sympathetic treatment". Bourne had also said to Oldmeadow early in 1924 that it was a "fact, known to me in confidence all along, that the conversations were held with the knowledge, approbation, and encouragement of the Holy

---

sous l'impulsion de la grâce divine', se tournent vers leurs frères dissidents et s'appliquent à leur 'frayer la voie du retour à l'intégrité de la Foi, en dissipant leurs préjugés, en leur exposant dans son entièreté la doctrine catholique et, surtout, en leur donnant un exemple vivant de la caractéristique des disciples du Christ, la charité'".

BIY, The Malines Papers of Lord Halifax, Box 7, N° 106, Mercier to Woodlock, October 26, 1925.

Woodlock also published "À propos des Conversations de Malines", in *Études* 184 (1925), pp. 304-310; and "Un épilogue aux 'Conversations de Malines'", pp. 569-573.

This whole Woodlock/Mercier affair is detailed in a sarcastic manner in OLDMEADOW, *Francis Cardinal Bourne*, pp. 382-390.

48. OLDMEADOW, *Francis Cardinal Bourne, op. cit.*, p. 383.

See". Even Bourne's Lenten Pastoral of 1924 had been supportive of
the Malines Conversations. Bourne's complaint then — and for it he
had some justification — was that he had not been given further
information to which he felt he had a right. As R. Aubert and R. Lahey
have stressed[49], Bourne saw himself as the logical counterpart to
Davidson; but Mercier had a different perspective — which as we have
seen had been clearly supported right from the time of the *Lambeth
Appeal* by Gasparri at Rome — that the logical counterpart to the
Anglican Primate was the Holy See.

We must also note the role played by E. Oldmeadow in this unfortunate affair. As R. Lahey has pointed out: "Bourne's stand has been
misconstrued not only by Halifax, who later wrote of 'the machinations
of Cardinal Bourne and the English Roman Catholics', but even by the
Cardinal's own biographer, Ernest Oldmeadow, who tended to project
onto his subject some of his own strong opposition to the Conversations"[50]. In 1924, in fact, Bourne had written to Oldmeadow from
Rome asking that further comment (i.e. in the pages of *The Tablet*) on
the conversations be held up[51]. And our final observation about
Oldmeadow is that there is no doubt in anyone's mind that, throughout
the time of the Malines Conversations, he had worked hand-in-hand
with Moyes, Merry del Val, and Gasquet to subvert the actions of
Halifax and Portal[52].

In reaction to Bourne's letter, Mercier sent Halifax a telegram on
October 30 asking him not to publish his letter. The same day,
Mercier's secretary Dessain sent Halifax a letter of explanation:
"Cardinal Bourne has written asking His Eminence not to publish the
letter, and in deference to this wish, His Eminence wishes to reflect and
so prefers that no publication should occur now"[53]. Dessain also wrote
Portal to tell him the news. Portal thought the letter should have been
published, as he explained to Halifax in November[54].

---

49. Up to the present, the best explanations of Cardinal Bourne's activities regarding
the Malines Conversations have been: R. AUBERT, "Cardinal Mercier, Cardinal Bourne,
and the Malines Conversations", in *One in Christ* 4 (1968) 372-379, and R. LAHEY,
"Cardinal Bourne and the Malines Conversations", in *Bishops and Writers*, edited by
A. HASTINGS, London, 1976, pp. 81-106.

50. LAHEY, *Bishops and Writers*, p. 86.

51. "Cardinal Bourne wrote from Rome asking that further comment on the Conversations be held up". This undated note in Oldmeadow's handwriting is found on the proof
of an unpublished article found in AAW, Cardinal Bourne's papers, BO III/124/4.

52. Oldmeadow's connections with Moyes, Merry del Val, and Gasquet and their
common antagonism toward Halifax and Portal are clearly indicated in the chapter on the
Malines Conversations in Oldmeadow's *Francis Cardinal Bourne, op. cit.*, pp. 353-414.

53. BIY, The Malines Papers of Lord Halifax, Box 7, N° 115, Dessain to Halifax,
October 30, 1925.

54. "*Je lui écris que je regretterais beaucoup que la lettre ne fut pas publiée*". BIY, The
Malines Papers of Lord Halifax, Box 7, N° 119, Portal to Halifax, November 2, 1925.

A few days after Bourne's letter to Mercier, Oldmeadow traveled to Malines to confer with Mercier. It was not a helpful meeting, and Oldmeadow found it "worse than futile"[55].

There was another exchange of letters between Mercier and Bourne in which they exchanged barbs, with Mercier finally writing that in the interests of peace he would not push *The Tablet* for any further comment[56]. We note as an aside that at one point in mid-November, Oldmeadow had even suggested to Bourne that a draft editorial, which would probably not be printed but "which it might be well to set up in type", be sent to Mercier to force him to "awaken to the mess he is in"[57].

While Mercier and Bourne were corresponding, Halifax had received a letter from his American friend, Maria Longworth Storer (Mrs. Bellamy Storer). She reported that she had seen Cardinal Cerretti and had given him newspaper clippings about the troubles with English Roman Catholics. Cerretti said he regretted the unkindness toward Halifax, that he backed the reunion movement, and that he would defend Halifax at Rome[58].

Cerretti was fond of Halifax and supportive of his efforts[59]. He had considered Halifax's Albert Hall speech, in which Halifax had expressed Beauduin's ideas, "another important step", in the Church union movement[60]. On November 13, 1925, Halifax went to Paris where he had "encouraging conversations"[61] with Cerretti and other dignitaries. On November 17, he and Portal traveled to Malines where they met with Mercier and discussed the publication of a report about the Conversations; and on November 19, both of them were guest speakers at Louvain for Dom Lambert Beauduin's unity day. "The session at Louvain", as Beauduin later wrote to a friend, "was a great success. Lord Halifax and Abbé Portal provoked a veritable enthusiasm, and they especially accentuated that our work for the union of Churches is for the West and England as well as for the Orient. I especially wanted

55. OLDMEADOW, *Francis Cardinal Bourne*, p. 385.

56. AAW, Cardinal Bourne's papers, BO III/124/4: Mercier to Bourne, November 8, 1925; Bourne to Mercier, November 17, 1925, Mercier to Bourne, December 7, 1925.

57. AAW, Cardinal Bourne's papers, BO III/124/4, Oldmeadow to Bourne, November 14, 1925.

58. BIY, The Malines Papers of Lord Halifax, Box 7, N° 92, Storer to Halifax, October 19, 1925.

59. Bonaventura Ceretti (1872-1933) was nuncio to Paris at this time. He was supportive of the ecumenical efforts of Halifax and Portal and distrusted by Cardinal Merry del Val.

60. "*Il discorso di Lord Halifax è un altro passo notevole, ma quello del Vescovo di Londra è una doccia fredda*". Scheut Fathers Louvain, Aloïs Janssens papers, unclassified letter, Cerretti to Storer, July 22, 1925.

61. LOCKHART, *op. cit.*, p. 324.

this affirmation — and I am above all eager through them to join our efforts to a still greater and more universal Oxford Movement"[62].

Before returning to England, Halifax also met with the Archbishop of Cambrai, Jean Chollet (1862-1952), "who showed a sympathetic interest in the Conversations and offered his good services with the French episcopate"[63]. And to all appearances, events seemed to be shaping-up for the next Conversation.

On December 9, Archbishop Davidson wrote Mercier: "It gives me real satisfaction to know that, on Your Eminence's hospitable invitation, the interrupted 'conversations' are to be resumed at Malines on January 25". He then went on to express his concerns about clearly publishing their disagreements about the nature of Papal authority, in any report about the Conversations. He said he knew something about the Church and People of England, and he had no hesitation in saying that to publish a record or summary of the discussions without making reference to that great unremoved mountain of difficulty would be worse than useless[64].

On December 15, 1925, Cardinal Bourne met with the Pope and discussed the Malines Conversations. Bourne's *aide de memoire*[65] for his private audience reveals that the Conversations were the chief item he wished to discuss and that he had five points to bring to the Pope's attention:

1. Setting aside the English Roman Catholic hierarchy.
2. Re-opening the issue of Anglican orders.
3. Effacing of Papal infallibility.
4. If Anglican orders were recognized and teaching authority placed into the episcopacy, the Anglicans would have gained all they wish.
5. The Archbishop of Canterbury as *Papa alterius orbis*.

Bourne's December 1925 meeting with Pius XI was the turning point. Bourne may not have expressed a personal opposition to the Conversations (Portal and Cerretti, who had their ears turned toward Rome, thought he didn't), but Bourne had apparently raised enough grave questions in the Pope's mind to get the Pope to reconsider his own support. Anglican Orders had been one of the issues, we recall, about which the Pope had told Gasquet in October of 1925 no compromise was possible. It seems to us that the situation with Pius XI was now

62. QUITSLUND, *op. cit.*, p. 124.

63. LOCKHART, *op. cit.*, p. 324.

64. Davidson to Mercier, December 9, 1925, quoted in BELL, *Randall Davidson*, pp. 1925-1926.

65. On December 14, 1925, Bourne, at Rome, received a note from Caccia the Pope's *Maestro di Camera*, informing Bourne that his audience with Pius XI would be on the following day at 10:30 in the morning. On the back of this note, Bourne wrote down the items he wished to discuss with the Pope. AAW, Cardinal Bourne's papers, BO III/124/4, Caccia to Bourne, December 14, 1925.

similar to the situation with Leo XIII in 1895 when Merry del Val
finally got through to him that Rampolla and Gasparri (and Portal and
Halifax) had been giving him an incorrect impression of the actual state
of affairs with the English Church. From this time on — and before the
death of Mercier — Portal would indicate to Halifax that the future of
the Conversations was in the Papal balance and it was a question of
which group would be strong enough to sway him to its position[66].
And it was on the day of Mercier's death, but before Portal had read
the news in the evening papers, that Portal would report to Halifax
that Cardinal Cerretti and Hippolyte Hemmer had told him the same
thing[67].

Before we examine the January events immediately preceding Mercier's
death however, we would like to call attention to two more letters of
December, sent after Bourne's papal audience.

On December 21, 1925, Mercier wrote to Halifax about his *malaise*
but he hoped that he would be able to attend the next Conversation. If
unable, Mercier said Van Roey would preside in his place[68]. On the
following day, Mercier wrote basically the same message to Davidson
and expressed his agreement with Davidson's wish that the various
positions about the Papal office should in some way be published[69].

And it was also on December 22 that Halifax received a letter from
Francis Woodlock — his Christmas greetings! "May I in spite of our
controversies this year", he wrote, "join with your many friends in
wishing and praying for every best grace and blessing at this season of
peace. I am sure that Our Lord will bless you for your wonderful effort

---

66. "*Il me semble que tout dépend du S. Père. Les opposants sont très nombreux et très
fort et Lui seul peut dominer la situation*". BIY, The Malines Papers of Lord Halifax, Box
8, N° 21, Portal to Halifax, January 22, 1926.

67. Speaking about Cerretti, Portal wrote: "*D'après lui nous devrions poser le fait de la
continuation sous la présidence de quelqu'un d'influent... Le cardinal Mercier était un
colosse m'a-t-il dit*". And about Hemmer: "*Il croit que le cardinal Bourne acceptera de
s'occuper des conversations mais il croit aussi que malgré toute sa bonne volonté il sera
débordé et que nos adversaires l'emporteront*". In the same letter, Portal also disclosed why
he thought Batiffol was collaborating with Merry del Val: "*Il se fait toute une campagne
en faveur de Merry del Val que l'on veut faire considérer comme le futur Pape*". And as far
as Merry del Val was concerned, Portal was convinced that del Val still had a grudge
against him: "*Son Éminence manifeste à mon égard une rancune tout à fait espagnole. Bien
espagnole aussi l'idée que j'aurais recherché dans les conversations de Malines une revanche
de l'affaire des ordinations anglicanes, comme il l'a dit au cardinal Mercier*". At the end of
this letter to Halifax, Portal attached a post script that the evening papers had just
announced the death of Mercier. BIY, The Malines Papers of Lord Halifax, Box 8, N° 22,
Portal to Halifax, January 23, 1926.

68. BIY, The Malines Papers of Lord Halifax, Box 7, N° 160, Mercier to Halifax,
December 21, 1925.

69. Mercier to Davidson, December 22, 1925, quoted in BELL, *Randall Davidson*,
pp. 1298-1299.

to bring us, where we should be, together around his altar in one
communion"[70].

In early January Portal and Halifax sent heart-broken letters to each
other about Mercier's worsening condition.

On January 21, Halifax, Portal, and Hemmer were at Mercier's
bedside for what Hemmer has called "*les suprêmes conversations de
Malines*"[71]. And shortly after this final meeting, Mercier dictated his
last letter to Davidson: "'That they all may be one' this is the supreme
wish of Christ and of the Supreme Pontiff. It is your's and mine. Would
that it be realized in its fullness"[72].

Mercier, in his last days, had also received two kind letters from
Cardinal Bourne, who recalled their Louvain days together, their
organizing help for refugees from Belgium during the German occupation — a time when several friendly letters had passed between them[73].
Mercier was greatly pleased by Bourne's letters. "He feared", Dessain
had written to Bourne at the time, "Your Eminence might have been
pained by the recent incident and was so pleased to know that the
long-standing affection which united him to Your Eminence was
unchanged"[74].

It was later in the day on January 21, that Mercier gave Halifax his
episcopal ring. At first Halifax was reluctant to accept it; but then
Portal said it would be an important memento for him and for his son
Edward. The ring was subsequently given to Halifax by Mercier's
family. Halifax wore it on a chain around his neck until his death, when
it was set into a Flemish chalice for use at York Minster — Oldmeadow
would make an unfortunate issue of this gesture in later years[75].

Halifax returned to Hickleton on January 21. On January 23 he
received word that Mercier had died. Cardinal Bourne wrote Halifax
the following day — Halifax had written him earlier about arranging a
meeting to discuss the next Conversation: "I am indeed grateful for

70. BIY, Malines Papers of Lord Halifax, Box 7, N° 163, Woodlock to Halifax,
December 22, 1925.

71. H. HEMMER, *Monsieur Portal. Prêtre de la mission*, Paris, 1947, p. 208.

72. "'*Ut unum sint*', *c'est le vœu suprême du Christ, le vœu du Souverain Pontife; c'est le
mien, c'est le vôtre. Puisse-t-il se réaliser dans sa plénitude*". Mercier to Davidson, January
21, 1926, quoted in BELL, *Randall Davidson*, p. 1299.

73. OLDMEADOW, *Francis Cardinal Bourne*, p. 389.

74. *Ibid.*, p.390.

75. "*Lord Halifax me disait: Je me suis procuré une petite chaîne en or. J'y ai mis
l'anneau du Cardinal et je le porterai toujours au cou. C'est une relique du plus grand prix
que je ne quitterai jamais et qui sera pour moi la source de ce qui importe le plus dans la vie.
Et, un jour, j'osai lui demander de me montrer cet anneau. Il déplaça sa chemise. Et je vis
l'anneau, suspendu par une chaînette, qui oscillait sur son cœur. Après sa mort l'anneau fut
donné par son fils à la cathédrale d'York et enchâssé dans le calice eucharistique*".
J. GUITTON, in "*Dialogue avec les précurseurs*". *Journal œcuménique 1922-1962*, Paris,
1962, p. 118.

your letter and for your great kindness in telling me so fully of your visit to our dear friend, Cardinal Mercier. It is just 43 years since I began to know him, when I was studying under him at Louvain, and every year since then has added to our intimacy and friendship... It will be a great pleasure to see you whenever you are able to call"[76].

On January 28, Halifax was back in Malines for Mercier's funeral. Afterwards he met with Van Roey who told him that, in keeping with the Cardinal's wish, he would preside at the next Conversation[77].

2. Cardinal Mercier: the Man

Cardinal Mercier was given a state funeral attended by King Albert, the Crown Prince, and Marshal Foch: a final national tribute for a memorable Belgian hero. But what about Mercier the man?

It is not our concern to probe in depth the psychology of Cardinal Mercier. We do find it important, however, to consider some outstanding elements of his character because they are the qualities which helped shape the Malines Conversations. The spirit of Mercier was the guiding spirit at Malines; and his death was a mortal loss for the Conversations.

What strikes us most about Cardinal Mercier, as we survey his life, is that he was primarily a creative thinker in the Aristotelian tradition of Thomas Aquinas — a philosopher more than a theologian or historian. Moreover, his thinking was especially open and courageous at a time when his anti-Modernist Church was exceptionally closed and fearful about new ideas.

As founder and first president of *L'Institut Supérieur de Philosophie* at Louvain, Mercier raised eyebrows at Louvain and at Rome with his stress on the importance of psychology and the natural sciences as well as by his suggestion that some classes should be taught in French rather than Latin. His novel approach combined with his popularity among students and his strong-willed authoritarianism also brought him into conflict with Mgr Abbeloos, rector of the university. But when he was

---

76. BIY, The Malines Papers of Lord Halifax, Box 8, N°23, Bourne to Halifax, January 24, 1926.

77. "Halifax returned to Belgium with Dr. Kidd for the funeral on the 28th, when the Cardinal was laid to rest in his own cathedral. His body was borne through the crowd-packed streets of Brussels in a great black and gold hearse, with all the pageantry of sorrow. Princes and cardinals, soldiers and ambassadors followed on foot. Cannon (sic) were booming and bands were playing the Funeral March. Next day, the body was brought to the cathedral. Halifax, now nearly eighty-seven, walked with head uncovered through the rain for an hour and stayed through the long service.

"When all was over he saw Mgr. van Roey, who told him that by the Cardinal's wish he would preside at the next Conversation. Halifax returned to England with this grain of comfort and, as but to be expected after the emotional and physical strain he endured, was laid up in bed for several days". LOCKHART, *op. cit.*, p.328.

convinced about something, Mercier had courage and energy in abundance[78].

Mercier had not been fearful, for instance, about calling the American Episcopal bishops his "brothers in the Christian Faith", nor did he regret his action even after being reprimanded by Benedict XV for recognizing "pseudo-bishops". Mercier had been willing to give the Modernist Tyrrell asylum in his diocese, even though the action would make him even more suspect at Rome among the Integrists; and Mercier came to the defense of Lagrange and of his professors at Louvain, van Hoonacker and others, when they had been accused of Modernist tendencies. Mercier was hardly faultless — R. Boudens and others have explored his lamentable shortcomings in regard to the Flemish Question[79], — but in his thinking he clearly, and rather successfully, embodied his favorite adage from Lacordaire: "St. Thomas must not be a boundary-mark for us but a guiding light"[80].

As Boudens, Aubert, and others have observed, Mercier's thinking, and the ecumenical actions flowing from it, made him a Churchman "ahead of his time"[81]. Were he living today, the popular Catholic press would probably have called him a Vatican II bishop!

There is yet another dimension of Mercier's character which strikes us as we look at his life and at the role he played in the Malines Conversations: his ability to change and grow. This is especially noteworthy when we consider the fact that Mercier was, throughout his life, a strong-willed, powerful, and occasionally overbearing clergyman[82]. Earlier, we noted the irony of the fact that during the post World War I negotiations leading to the Treaty of Versailles Mercier had taken the initiative of approaching Clémenceau with a view to obtaining the Palestinian mandate for Catholic Belgium, in a desire to preserve the Holy Places from Protestant England and especially from Zionism which was beginning to make itself felt"[83]. Mercier's trip to

---

78. For important background about Mercier's Louvain career, see R.BOUDENS, "*Le Saint-Siège et la crise de l'Institut Supérieur de Philosophie à Louvain 1895-1900*", in *Archivum Historiae Pontificiae* 8 (1970) 301-322.

79. R. BOUDENS, *Kardinaal Mercier en de Vlaamse Beweging*, Leuven, 1975.

80. R. AUBERT, *Cardinal Mercier. A Churchman Ahead of His Time*, city and date not indicated, p. 4.

81. *Ibid.* and R. BOUDENS, *op. cit.*, p. 264: "*Op sommige punten was hij zelfs zijn tijd voor*".

82. As briefly mentioned earlier, Mercier's strong will was evidenced early in his academic career at Louvain when he tangled with the Rector of the University, Mgr. Abbeloos, about the independent status of his Higher Institute of Philosophy. Aubert comments: "Mercier, like all people with great plans, was not an easy person to get on with, especially during the first few years of his career". *Cardinal Mercier. A Churchman Ahead of His Time*, p. 8. Later during the First World War, Mercier took a strong position in pastoral letters and public action against the German Governor General.

83. AUBERT, *Cardinal Mercier. A Churchman Ahead of His Time*, p. 14.

the United States had later opened his eyes to Anglicanism and forced him to greatly modify his thinking.

Another example: In 1924 Mercier had asked Halifax to make his submission to Rome; yet in 1925 he read during the Fourth Conversation, and apparently supported, Beauduin's proposal for the corporate reunion of the Anglican Church as a separate rite.

We find one of the finest examples of his growth, however, in a letter to Halifax written in 1925: "It is a fact that from the time of Saint Augustine until the sixteenth century the Church of England formed part of the same body with the Roman Church. In fact even today is it not implicitly united to Rome? If on both sides of the barrier our consciences were to analyse themselves more deeply, would they not find, with the help of the Holy Spirit, that they were wrong to consider themselves to be immutably separated? Historical influences, errors of interpretation, ill-founded fears, may they not have created and maintained superficial divergences which, without our being aware of it, cover and hide from a profound conscience those truths in which we believe? For my part I believe this to be so"[84].

The freedom to think and the courage to grow, these then are the personal qualities which Cardinal Mercier brought to and stimulated at the Conversations he hosted in Malines. They were also, by the way, the personal qualities of Abbé Portal[85], whose death would follow Mercier's by just a few months.

3. *The Death of Abbé Portal and the Fifth Conversation*

In February 1926, *The Antidote*, a Roman Catholic ecumenical newsletter published in the United States, carried a feature article about Lord Halifax's Louvain address of November 1925. The American publication called attention to the fact that Halifax had reminded the Louvain audience: "Your coreligionists in England unfortunately make the mistake of refusing to see anything good in the Anglo-Catholic Movement ... they never will restore the old union that lasted one thousand years, to which we owe all our past glory and triumphs"[86].

At the same time, however, that American Catholics were reading in *The Antidote* about Halifax's assessment of English Catholic difficulties with Anglicans, the English Catholic, Francis Woodlock, was in Rome criticizing Modernist tendencies within Anglicanism. *Corriere d'Italia* of

---

84. *Ibid.*, pp. 27-28.

85. Fr. Gratieux who knew both Portal and Mercier: "In certain respects the Cardinal could have been compared to Fr. Portal: the same desire to bring Catholic thought up-to-date with the contemporary world; the same broad-mindedness and the same uprightness, the same love of young people and the same ability to attract people". AUBERT, *Ibid.*, p. 24.

86. "Lord Halifax at Louvain", in *The Antidote* 8 (February 1926), p. 39.

March 2 reports that at the end of February, Woodlock gave a
conference at the Biblical Institute on "Anglican Progress Towards
Reunion"[87]. Woodlock alerted his audience to the dangers of Modernism in the Anglican Church and to the fact that the Anglican Modernists were now pushing strongly for a reunited Church.

In mid-March 1926, it was announced that Ernest Van Roey would
be appointed to the vacant see at Malines. On March 19, Portal wrote
Halifax about the news and commented that he had heard that Bourne,
the Jesuits, and "all of our usual adversaries were lined up strongly
against" Van Roey's appointment. Unfortunately Portal did not reveal
the source of his information nor make any further comment[88]. Six
days later, Portal could again write Halifax that he had received a letter
from Van Roey, who had written Portal that he would be happy to
host the next conversation at Malines[89]. It was also during this same
month that: the Anglican participants were busy working on their
reports from the previous meetings; the English Roman Catholics — at
least the ones in England — were rather quiet; and a provisional date
for the next Conversation was set for the end of June 1926.

April brought a series of interesting developments, which served to
emphasize the variety of English Catholic positions about Church unity
and to clarify a bit more clearly the position of Cardinal Bourne. It also
brought a new ecumenical involvement on the part of Abbé Portal.

On April 7, Cardinal Gasparri sent Francis Woodlock a thank you
letter, on behalf of the Holy Father for certain books written by
Woodlock which he had sent the Pope. The letter was a pro forma type
of Vatican response; and we see no reason for making a point of the
fact that it came from Gasparri. He was afterall Secretary of State. The
titles of the books however are revealing and show the type of message
Woodlock, and certainly Merry del Val, were trying to get across to
Pius XI. They were: *Modernism and the Christian Church; Catholicism
the True Rationalism; Constantinople, Canterbury, and Rome*, and *La
Chiesa Anglicana e l'unione della Christianità*[90].

The day after Gasparri wrote his letter to Woodlock, Cardinal
Bourne received a letter from the English Jesuit W.N. d'Andria.

D'Andria wrote that he had the approval of his superiors in the
English Province of the Society of Jesus to "propagate" the Church
Unity Octave on behalf of Fr. Paul of the Society of the Atonement in

87. AAW, Cardinal Bourne's papers, unclassified newspaper clipping, Corriere d'Italia,
March 2, 1926.

88. BIY, The Malines Papers of Lord Halifax, Box 8, N° 70, Portal to Halifax, March
19, 1926.

89. BIY, The Malines Papers of Lord Halifax, Box 8, N° 78, Portal to Halifax, March
25, 1926.

90. AAW, Cardinal Bourne's papers, BO III/124/4, Gasparri to Woodlock, April 7,
1926.

New York. His request: "Knowing that Your Eminence has always approved of and encouraged the observance of the Octave, those engaged in this work have decided to ask your Eminence whether there is any likelihood of the approval of the entire Hierarchy being given or even whether it is wise to seek it". On the top of d'Andria's letter Bourne wrote the substance of his response: while he approved of the devotion he noticed some "very serious objections" to the title "Church Unity Octave"[91].

In the middle of April, B.J. Kidd wrote Halifax with news about the next conversation. He had received "an important communication" from Batiffol who had reported that Van Roey had asked him, Portal, and Hemmer "to make preparations for our next Conversation at Malines". Kidd also mentioned that he had received a letter from Frere who had reported that the Papal Nuncios in Brusssels and Paris had written Van Roey to "proceed with preparations" for the next Conversation. "I take this to mean", noted Kidd, "that Rome wants to get on with the business"[92].

It was also in April 1926 that Portal directed his energies to his last ecumenical activity. He suggested to Dom Lambert Beauduin, whose monastery at Amay had now been open for a few months, that what he and his new community needed was a review. We know that Portal had a special interest in reviews! And so it was that Beauduin's *Irénikon* was born, with Abbé Portal "in large part responsible for its inception"[93]. The purpose of the review was expressed in the first issue: "In response to Pius XI's call, it is an organ of the movement for reunion, to promote the spiritual reconciliation of minds and hearts that must precede official and juridical reunion"[94]. Within its first three years, *Irénikon* was threatened with suppression three times by Roman authorities[95]. Ironically, one of the review's earliest supporters was the man who eventually signed the papers condemning Beauduin — Eugenio Pacelli.

In May the English Roman Catholic layman Lord Fitzalan began to respond to a new ecumenical overture from Halifax. Lord Halifax had written to him about gathering a group of English Roman Catholics for theological discussions, something Halifax had wanted to organize years earlier. Fitzalan met with Bourne who apparently had no opposition and who also said he intended to send two English Roman Catholics to the next Malines Conversation. On May 2, Fitzalan wrote

91. AAW, Cardinal Bourne's papers, BO III/124/4, d'Andria to Bourne, April 8, 1926.
92. BIY, The Malines Papers of Lord Halifax, Box 8, N° 99, Kidd to Halifax, April 16, 1926.
93. QUITSLUND, *op. cit.*, p. 135.
94. *Ibid.*, p. 136.
95. *Ibid.*

168 CHAPTER SIX

Bourne about the contents of a letter he would be sending Halifax. The letter reveals that Bourne, more than four months after his meeting in Rome with the Pope, was still not opposed to another Conversation. "I have purposely mentioned what you told me as to the two you intended for Malines", wrote Fitzalan, "because I thought it might appeal to Lord Halifax as proof of your willingness to continue the discussions"[96]. On May 7, Fitzalan wrote Halifax. He said he was "impressed by the importance" of Halifax's proposal for a gathering of English Catholics, and that he had met twice with Cardinal Bourne whom he found "very sympathetic to the idea". Bourne, wrote Fitzalan, had also supported Halifax's suggestion that Fitzalan chair such a gathering. Then Fitzalan turned to the Malines Conversations and he reported that Bourne "in the event of his being approached with a view to a renewal of the Malines Conferences ... had contemplated sending Bishop Bidwell and Canon Myers". Bidwell was Auxiliary Bishop in the Westminster Diocese and Myers the President of St. Edmund's College[97].

Halifax was delighted about Fitzalan's response but, as he expressed in a confidential letter to Frere[98], he was "troubled" about "certain matters in regard to our future conversations". He was anxious about "deficiencies" in Robinson's draft *compte rendu* of previous meetings and he did not trust Batiffol. "I never have trusted him completely; and, though I think he is to be used, and that extracts from things he has published can be made good use of, I feel sure that he is not to be depended on".

Halifax's last comments in a long and restless letter, were about the "two classes" of English Roman Catholics — those who were sympathetic and friendly to "our affairs" and those who were hostile.

On May 19, Halifax heard from Batiffol. Batiffol mentioned that he was looking forward to the next conversation, but toward the end of his letter he grew critical of unnamed people who were still asking for a reconsideration of Anglican Orders and he was also critical of the proposal read by Mercier at the Fourth Conversation by "an alleged Roman canonist"[99].

Apparently Batiffol had earlier sent a similar letter to Portal, because it was also on May 19 that Portal wrote to Halifax about it. He thought

96. AAW, Cardinal Bourne's papers, BO III/124/4, Fitzalan to Bourne, May 2, 1926.
97. BIY, The Malines Papers of Lord Halifax, Box 8, N° 109, Fitzalan to Halifax, May 7, 1926.
98. BIY, The Malines Papers of Lord Halifax, Box 8, N° 108, Halifax to Frere, May 7, 1926.
99. BIY, The Malines Papers of Lord Halifax, Box 8, N° 117, Batiffol to Halifax, May 19, 1926.

it was a typical Batiffol letter: "Wherever he is, he divides and breaks up. It would greatly be worth our efforts to restrict his evil action"[100].

At the end of May, Portal wrote Halifax that Canon Myers, who had been recommended by Bourne as a future participant at Malines, had been in Paris. He had met with Portal's *protégé* Martel, who later had told Portal that he had some doubts about where Myers stood in regard to the reunion movement. In any event, Portal wrote Halifax that he had written a letter to Van Roey suggesting that it would be better not to have an English Catholic at the next Conversation[101]. Quite simply, at this point, Portal had heard so many rumors about English Catholics that he did not know what to do. We recall that he had been in a similar quandary when there had been considerations about Leslie Walker and Michel d'Herbigny. And we must also remember that at this point Portal was not well.

In April Portal had been taken ill and had had a seizure one morning on his way to mass; but at the time thought little of it. In May he had seemed somewhat better; but on June 19, Halifax received a letter from Martel, the young *protégé*, that Portal had had another seizure and would be unable to attend the next Conversation. A day later, Halifax received a telegram that his old friend Etienne Fernand Portal — his "best and dearest friend"[102] — had died.

"The Abbé's death clouds everything", Halifax wrote to his son, "First the Cardinal, then Portal, and the next should be me I am sure — death always goes by threes and that third would make the trio complete"[103].

Portal had said very little during the Malines Conversations. For all his theological experience and talents, he had not even contributed a memorandum. Portal was opinionated but had never interfered with Mercier's conducting of the Conversations. Nevertheless, as his colleague and friend H. Hemmer has observed[104], Portal should be credited with infusing Mercier with his ideas and was probably responsible for Mercier's transformation from seeking individual conversions to accepting the possibility of corporate reunion.

Because of Portal's death, the Fifth Conversation was pushed back to October 11 and 12, 1926. When the participants finally met, they had decided to not invite any newcomers since their purpose was now to review and record what had been said earlier. In fact, it was a truncated

100. *"Partout où il est, il divise et désagrège. Nous aurons beaucoup de peine à empêcher son action malfaisante"* BIY, The Malines Papers of Lord Halifax, Box 8, N° 118, Portal to Halifax, May 19, 1926.

101. BIY, The Malines Papers of Lord Halifax, Box 8, N° 121, Portal to Halifax, May 26, 1926.

102. LOCKHART, *op. cit.*, p. 331.

103. *Ibid.*, pp. 330 331.

104. H. HEMMER, *Fernand Portal Apostle of Unity*, London, 1961, p. 168.

group which met for the final session at Malines. On the Anglican side, Halifax, Kidd, and Frere were in attendance; and on the Roman Catholic side, Van Roey, Batiffol, and Hemmer. Apparently even at the last minute there had been some consideration given to inviting Mario Besson (1876-1945), the Bishop of Fribourg, and Lambert Beauduin to join the Catholic side, but, for reasons already stated, nothing came of it[105].

The business of the Fifth Conversation, which after the deaths of Mercier and Portal — according to J.C. Lockhart — took on "the depressing atmosphere of a liquidation"[106], was to discuss the memoranda which the Anglicans and Roman Catholics had prepared in view of their future publication. On October 11, the Anglican statement was studied, amended, and approved. The next day, the Roman Catholic statement, a summary of points of agreement which had been written by Hemmer, was discussed and approved in similar fashion.

The Anglicans and Catholics also agreed that each document should be published in its original language and in translation and that the various papers read at the Conversations would not be part of the published report.

At the conclusion of the Fifth Conversation, a somewhat contented Halifax returned to his home, expecting to see the published report out by Christmas. Ecclesiastical politics within both Churches would, in fact, delay publication until 1928.

4. *From the Fifth Conversation to Mortalium Animos*

In January and February 1927, Lord Halifax pushed Anglicans and Roman Catholics, without success, to get their statements published. The Anglicans were reluctant to move toward publication because of the impending Prayer Book revision. Roman Catholics, as far as Halifax could determine, were apparently being slowed down by Rome.

Opinions at Rome, however, were at this time still unclear, as we learn from a letter Merry del Val sent Francis Woodlock at the end of March 1927.

Merry del Val wrote Woodlock on March 31, asking him to "report here (i.e. to Rome, JD) the true purport and doctrinal value of the Prayer Book revision". Why? Because some people in Rome thought the Prayer Book revision was a sign that the Church of England was moving toward acceptance of Roman Catholic teaching! In Merry del Val's words: "Here generally the situation is not in the least under-

105. "*Il avait été question de demander à Mgr Besson, évêque de Fribourg, et à Dom Beauduin, O.S.B., prieur d'Amay-sur-Meuse, de combler les vides du côté catholique. En réalité, ni l'un ni l'autre n'y furent présents*". J. DE BIVORT DE LA SAUDÉE, *Documents sur le problème de l'union anglo-romaine*, Paris, 1949, p. 173.

106. LOCKHART, *op. cit.*, p. 332.

stood... Many believe that the present revision means the acceptance of Catholic doctrine, that the English Church is on the way to assimilate the doctrine of transubstantiation and all other Catholic teaching, that the National Church is in schism, but freeing herself from heresy and is therefore moving towards Rome"[107].

So there were various viewpoints; but apparently by early April, the Holy See had decided there would be no more Conversations.

On April 12, 1927 Pierre Batiffol sent a letter to Pius XI. He said that Van Roey had written to him and Hemmer to inform them that "the Holy See intends that there not be a resumption of the 'Malines Conversations' and that nothing which was discussed during the said conversations should be published". Batiffol assured the Holy Father that he would follow the orders of the Holy See absolutely, but he suggested that it might be good to publish both statements side-by-side. Batiffol reminded the Pope that Mercier had promised a report; it would be dangerous for the Holy See to appear to repudiate what Mercier had done; and, Batiffol suggested, the report could also show critics of the Conversations that the Anglicans had made several concessions to Rome. And a final reason for publishing the report would be that it would make an important Roman Catholic point before the July ecumenical conference in Lausanne[108].

The following day Batiffol wrote to Van Roey that he had been well-received by the Pope in private audience and that they had discussed at some length the Malines Conversations. Batiffol then expressed to Van Roey the Holy Father's wishes and feelings in regard to the Conversations: there would be no more Conversations because of "God having called Cardinal Mercier to Himself", the Conversations must remain what they were, "Discussions without any official character — private discussions". Pius XI told Batiffol he was not offended that the Anglicans had gone to Mercier rather than to someone else, because "a person has every right to select his own confessor"; but he did not like the speeches of Lord Halifax, "the ones which were sharply criticized by Father Woodlock". As to the matter of publication of the Anglican and Roman Catholic statements, Batiffol stressed that they could not give any indication of being official and that therefore there could be no cover letter, as Halifax wanted, written by the Archbishop of Canterbury[109].

If Batiffol was, in some sense at least, concerned about public relations and not creating difficulties with the Anglicans, Cardinal

107. AEPSJ, Woodlock papers, BH/6, Merry del Val to Woodlock, March 31, 1927.

108. "*La publication de ces deux documents serait un coup de barre à droite qui engagerait l'anglicanisme, à la veille de la World Conference protestante, qui se tiendra à Lausanne en juillet prochain*". Batiffol to Pius XI, April 12, 1927, quoted in DE BIVORT DE LA SAUDÉE, *op. cit.*, pp. 276-277.

109. Batiffol to Van Roey, April 13, 1927, *Ibid.*

172 CHAPTER SIX

Bourne at this time did not seem to share his sentiments. On Easter Sunday, April 17, 1927, he went to York to commemorate the thirteen hundredth anniversary of York Minster's foundation and the baptism of Edwin, King of Northumbria, by St. Paulinus, Archbishop of York. Bourne's sermon, which he preached in St. Wilfrid's Church, was a surprise attack on the Anglican Church.

At York Cardinal Bourne, in fact, sounded more like Cardinal Vaughan: "I assert", he proclaimed, "that the Church of England, established by law in England — and no where else, I believe, in the world — is in no way connected in faith or in ecclesiastical law or authority with the Catholic Church which, from the days of Paulinus until the religious upheaval of the sixteenth century, was the sole spiritual teacher and guide of the people of this city and of this country". Bourne admitted that there might be a "fiction of continuity" between the pre-Reformation Catholic Church and the Anglican Church, due to English law, but that in fact there was no continuity of doctrine or hierarchical government. The Archbishop of Westminster then went on to extoll the great devotion of English Roman Catholics for the Mass and the Real Presence and noted that the religious devotion of the Anglicans "began by casting down, desecrating, and defiling the altar-slabs consecrated for and by the Mass". And he concluded by reminding his congregation that Anglican Orders were invalid regardless what some people were saying[110].

A week after publishing Cardinal Bourne's sermon, E. Oldmeadow continued the attack in *The Tablet*. "That there is dismay among professional Protestants over Cardinal Bourne's reception in York does not surprise us... Not at the professional No-Popery-men alone has the Cardinal's week-end in York dealt a heavy blow. It has proved to the more perspicacious sort of High Anglicans that the English people, who were badly gulled in the sixteenth century, are less easy to hoodwink in the twentieth. Brought out into the sunny streets, the Anglican demand that Englishmen shall recognize the Establishment as the Catholic Church of Old England has melted like snowflakes in June"[111].

Halifax was himself now getting angry and agitated. He wanted all the more to get the final statements published. Toward the end of May he received a letter from Emmanuel Boyreau[112] who wrote that he was in complete agreement with Halifax that everything which had happened at Malines had to be published. He also noted that Cardinal Bourne and Cardinal Gasquet were working together, but that Bishop Besson

110. F. BOURNE, "York: The Thirteenth Centenary of King Edward's Baptism", in *The Tablet* 149 (April 23, 1927), p. 555.
111. E. OLDMEADOW, "Continuity Continued", in *The Tablet* 149 (April 30, 1927), p. 573.
112. Emmanuel Boyreau was one of the circle of French friends with whom Portal and Halifax stayed in contact.

might be able to clear up some of the problems created by Bourne's sermon at York as well as positively influence opinions at Rome[113].

At about the same time, Halifax also received a letter from Gore, who had just returned from Paris. "I have seen Batiffol and Hemmer in Paris", he wrote. "I gather from them that since Cardinal Mercier's death, the cause for which he stood and the sympathy of the Pope with the Malines Conference have gone back and Cardinal Bourne is in the ascendant". He also reported that Batiffol was "clearly very nervous" and wanted the Roman Catholic — i.e. Hemmer's — statement suppressed and no letter from the Archbishop of Canterbury in the Anglican statement. Interestingly, Gore noted that Batiffol's opinion "was not quite Hemmer's view". Gore also reported that he had met with Davidson and Davidson didn't want anything published until after the Prayer Book issue had been resolved[114].

On June 3, 1927, Halifax wrote Kidd to find out why the Anglican statement from the Fifth Conversation was not yet ready for publication. Kidd had been entrusted with that project by the participants at Malines. Two days later Kidd replied. He had had everything ready for publication in January! Hemmer had taken longer than expected with the French translation, but the real hold-up had been Van Roey who had not yet returned a draft copy sent him for final approval. And then Kidd also reported that he had heard from a friend in Rome that Batiffol and Hemmer had gone to Rome and that "things were awkward there". "I am afraid", Kidd concluded his note, "that there is fear on both sides — not of each other, but of external authorities"[115].

A few days after Kidd's letter, Halifax heard from Hemmer who reported that he had been in Rome and that the atmosphere there about the Malines Conversations had greatly changed since the death of Mercier. And he asked Halifax to try and intercede with Bourne[116].

On June 17, Halifax, now eighty-eight years old, went to Paris to find out for himself what was happening. When he returned to England he gave Davidson a full report which we quote at length because it will help the reader understand later actions taken by Halifax: "The situation at Rome, owing to Cardinal Bourne and Cardinal Gasquet's action (I should say intrigues) is that the Pope's mind has been changed and that a message has been sent Archbishop van Roey that the Conversa-

---

113. "*Mgr. Besson est le plus remarquable de nos évêques de langue française. Je crois qu'il serait possible de lui faire comprendre l'erreur du point de vue du Cardinal Bourne et, par lui, on pourrait convaincre Rome où il est très écouté*". BIY, The Malines Papers of Lord Halifax, Box 9, N° 15, Boyreau to Halifax, May 20, 1927.

114. BIY, The Malines Papers of Lord Halifax, Box 9, N° 17, Gore to Halifax, May 31, 1927.

115. BIY, The Malines Papers of Lord Halifax, Box 9, N° 21, Kidd to Halifax, June 5, 1927.

116. BIY, The Malines Papers of Lord Halifax, Box 9, N° 26, Hemmer to Halifax, June 10, 1927.

tions at Malines must cease and that those (the Frenchmen) who took part in them must not publish their report as had been agreed to at our last meeting at Malines and which, if there had not been all these delays, would have been in the hands of the public by now. The French, Hemmer (who is friendly — and much annoyed) wished *both* accounts, their's and our's to appear together as had been agreed, said quite clearly they could publish nothing themselves. Privately I think Hemmer for one would not be sorry if someone took the bull by the horns and published what they are forbidden to do... The other Frenchmen I saw were all most sympathetic and did not conceal their annoyance at and dislike of the action at Rome. The new Archbishop of Malines, though an excellent man, was not one, they all said *'qui combattrait'* or would concern himself much about anything outside his own diocese... They all agreed that it was imperative that there should be an authoritative and complete statement of the result of the conversations at Malines with a view not only to the present but to the future"[117].

On June 23, 1927, as a matter of fact, Halifax had written his son that he had already decided to publish the statements: "I shall say nothing and do it". People who stood in his way were "owls" and "traitors"[118].

It was also at the end of June that Halifax received another series of gossip-filled letters from R. Gordon George, whose most significant bit of news was that the English Roman Catholic bishops were upset about an article in *Irénikon* which had openly advocated the branch theory. The English Roman Catholic Bishops said George were therefore out to discredit both Dom Lambert Beauduin's monks as well as his review[119].

On June 28 and 29, 1927, Cardinal Van Roey, Cardinal Bourne, Pierre Batiffol — and of course a great many other dignitaries — were in Louvain for a festive celebration of the fifth centenary of the University of Louvain (for various reasons the celebration had been delayed for eighteen months). Batiffol had ample opportunity to speak to both Cardinals about the publication of the Anglican and Roman Catholic statements.

On June 30 Batiffol, writing from Louvain, sent Halifax a terse set of orders: Van Roey had given him the Anglican statement which he had sent to Kidd. The statement, since it had been primarily written by Robinson, could be published under Robinson's signature only and must not contain any letter or word from the Archbishop of Canterbury. Any publication had to affirm that the Anglican statement was

117. BIY, The Malines Papers of Lord Halifax, Box 9, N° 37, Halifax to Davidson, June 25, 1927.

118. LOCKHART, *op. cit.*, p. 335.

119. BIY, The Malines Papers of Lord Halifax, Box 9, N° 40, Gordon George to Halifax, June 26, 1927; N° 46, June 28, 1927; N° 47, June 29, 1927.

the result of private conversations. The Roman Catholic statement would not be published. And finally Batiffol said that Cardinal Bourne was in agreement with what he had proposed and that if Halifax wanted to know more about Bourne's position he should perhaps go talk to him[120]. A few days later, B.J. Kidd wrote Halifax that he also had received a letter from Batiffol. The message was the same[121].

On July 8, and just before the Lausanne Conference, Cardinal Merry del Val's Holy Office issued a reminder of Benedict XV's regulations about Roman Catholic participation in ecumenical assemblies: that Catholics must not take part in "congresses, meetings, lectures, or societies which have the scope of uniting into a religious confederation all who in any sense whatever call themselves Christians"[122], — the spirit of Pius XI's *Mortalium Animos* was already in the air. And Halifax was ready to publish.

On August 5, 1927, Lord Halifax wrote to Kidd with suggestions for revisions in the Anglican statement; but his main concern was to explain the course he had decided to follow: "You will remember the publication of both memorandums was agreed to, even almost the form of the publication, if I remember right, by both French and English at our last Conversation in 1926, at which Mgr. Van Roey presided, and this so definitely that I don't for a moment admit that any fresh permission to publish is the least necessary"[123].

On August 13, 1927, R. Gordon George wrote Halifax from Amay with bits of news he had picked up from Dom Lambert Beauduin: The English bishops were trying to get Lambert Beauduin suspended and *Irénikon* put on the *Index*. There were rumors that Merry del Val and Bourne were not in complete agreement. Beauduin wanted Halifax to go to Rome to find out the truth[124].

Halifax resolved to go to Rome. But before making his travel plans, he wrote Van Roey on August 17 that he was going to publish both the Anglican and the Roman Catholic statements. "To this slightly minatory letter Van Roey made no reply"[125].

At the end of August, Dom Lambert Beauduin wrote Halifax about the importance of his trip to Rome. He repeated what Gordon George had said about Bourne's opposition to his work and his review. Bourne was "irritated" because of articles in *Irénikon* about patriarchates and

120. BIY, The Malines Papers of Lord Halifax, Box 9, N° 49, Batiffol to Halifax, June 30, 1927.

121. BIY, The Malines Papers of Lord Halifax, Box 9, N° 54, Kidd to Halifax, July 2, 1927.

122. J. HOLMES, *The Papacy in the Modern World*, New York, 1981, p. 29.

123. BIY, The Malines Papers of Lord Halifax, Box 9, N° 70, Halifax to Kidd, August 5, 1927.

124. BIY, The Malines Papers of Lord Halifax, Box 9, N° 80, Gordon George to Halifax, August 13, 1927.

125. LOCKHART, *op. cit.*, p. 336.

because Beauduin had ignored publishing anything about Bourne's "regrettable speech" at York but had published an address by Archbishop Lang. This was the event which prompted Bourne to ask the Bishop of Namur to condemn *Irénikon*. In his letter to Halifax, Beauduin also commented that Batiffol was behind Bourne. "Unfortunately, he (Bourne) is under the influence of Batiffol who has completely changed". Then Beauduin directed his attention to the Pope. "The Holy Father – has he changed? In his official acts nothing has changed. But it is certain that he has heard alot of criticism, alot of reproaches, and his drive has begun to weaken a bit"[126].

Over the next few weeks, Halifax worked on Davidson to get him to agree to publication of both statements. Finally Davidson gave in on the condition that the Roman Catholic participants be informed about publication and be given three weeks in which to offer their veto[127].

On September 18, 1927 Halifax wrote Hemmer that he was going to publish both statements and observed: "From things I have heard in various quarters both in England and from abroad, I cannot help feeling that the attitude of the Vatican has been misrepresented to us. Has the Pope ever desired that the French account of the proceedings at Malines should not be published? I am told on good authority that he is still as anxious as ever to further the cause of reunion, but that Cardinal Bourne and other English Catholics have been making hostile representations to him, as to what has been done at Malines, and that (what very particularly affects our affairs) the attitude of Mgr. Batiffol has completely changed"[128].

By the end of September none of the Catholic participants at the Fifth Conversation had vetoed Halifax's plan to publish, so on October 10 Halifax sent a letter to the *Times* which announced the imminent publication of "the report of the Malines Conversations". "That publication", wrote Halifax, "will take place at once... That report will be complete and will contain both the English and French memorandums in full"[129].

On October 15, Fr. Dessain, now Cardinal Van Roey's secretary, wrote Halifax: "His Eminence is somewhat astonished to see a report in the papers stating that the publication you are about to undertake will comprise not only the Anglican report but also the 'French'

---

126. BIY, The Malines Papers of Lord Halifax, Box 9, N° 88, Beauduin to Halifax, August 24, 1927.

127. LOCKHART, *op. cit.*, p. 336.

128. BIY, The Malines Papers of Lord Halifax, Box 9, N° 109, Halifax to Hemmer, September 18, 1927.

129. AAW, Cardinal Bourne's papers, unclassified newspaper clipping, *The Times*, October 12, 1927.

report... His Eminence does not see his way to authorise such a publication ... and is convinced that it will do no good"[130].

Halifax ignored Dessain's letter. At Davidson's request he did agree to postpone publication until after the December Prayer Book vote in Parliament.

In November Halifax and his chaplain Fr. Painter went to Rome. Cardinal Cerretti and his friend Mrs. Storer had made all the arrangements. Cerretti had told the Pope about Halifax's visit and the Pope had asked for a written statement from Halifax. Halifax wrote down his comments in English and French and Cerretti delivered them to Pius XI[131]. Halifax and the Pope never had a discussion. The Pope did give Halifax his personal blessing — a gesture which Halifax, whether correctly or not[132], interpreted to mean, as he wrote to Davidson that his work on behalf of reunion "what I cared for more than anything else in my life ... had received the Pontifical blessing"[133].

On his way back to England, after his trip to Rome, Halifax visited various people in Paris, Brussels, and Malines. He learned that Hemmer had been to Brussels to see Abbé van den Hout "to complain of Mgr. Batiffol's attitude, who had been speaking not very kindly of Cardinal Mercier"[134]. In fact, Halifax had heard that Batiffol "had said contemptuous things about Cardinal Mercier's mental attitude in regard to reunion"[135]. From Cerretti he learned that Bourne had been "doing all he can to prejudice Cardinal Mercier's attitude about reunion both in Rome, Milan, Freiburg, where the Bishop is a very important person, and also in Paris"[136]. He learned that in July of 1927 Batiffol had sent Bourne documents from the Malines Conversations — which documents we don't know. And finally, Halifax saw Cardinal Van Roey, who, he found "had certainly been influenced by Cardinal Bourne and Mgr. Batiffol"[137].

130. BIY, The Malines Papers of Lord Halifax, Box 9, N° 130, Dessain to Halifax, October 15, 1927.

131. This is all explained in a letter to Halifax from Cerretti. BIY, The Malines Papers of Lord Halifax, Box 9, N° 129, Cerretti to Halifax, October 15, 1927.

132. E. Oldmeadow made a big issue of this papal blessing, asserting that it was not what Halifax had said. Cerretti and Mrs. Bellamy Storer maintained that the Pope had given Halifax a personal blessing. They also tried to keep some of the bad press coverage of the event from Halifax, working through his chaplain Fr. Painter. BIY, The Malines Papers of Lord Halifax, Box 9, N° 150, Storer to Painter, November 25, 1927; N° 151, Ceretti to Painter, November 26, 1927.

133. BIY, The Malines Papers of Lord Halifax, Box 9, N° 143, Halifax to Davidson, November 19, 1927.

134. *Ibid.*

135. BIY, The Malines Papers of Lord Halifax, Box 9, N° 144, Halifax to Kidd, November 19, 1927.

136. BIY, The Malines Papers of Lord Halifax, Box 9, N° 143, Halifax to Davidson, November 19, 1927.

137. BIY, The Malines Papers of Lord Halifax, Box 9, N° 144, Halifax to Kidd, November 19, 1927.

Concerning Cardinal Bourne's attitude at this time, we find some interesting hints, in Archbishop Davidson's papers, that Bourne was not entirely negative.

Sir James Marchant of the publishing house Longmans had a special interest in the reunion movement. In October 1927 he had, in a series of letters to the *Times*, praised the movement toward reunion and the work of the Monks of Amay; but he had also stressed that: "The Benedictine monks of Belgium, who are exploring the ground of reunion between Rome and Constantinople, would be well advised not to intervene in the English conversations (i.e. any unity talks between Anglicans and Roman Catholics, JD), which no foreigner, however sympathetic, can adequately understand. They may pray for us, but we must work out our own salvation, and there is sufficient good will and knowledge in the English hierarchy for this high purpose. For the same reason it is probably well that the Malines Conversations should cease. No country long enjoys foreign encouragement to do its religious duty. But we can all pray for the will to reunite"[138].

In November 1927, Marchant visited Cardinal Bourne; and then he went to Lambeth Palace to tell Davidson what he had learned. He gave Davidson the impression that Bourne had been misunderstood and that Bourne was under a lot of pressure about the Malines Conversations. We read in Davidson's notes that Marchant had said: "The Cardinal's (Bourne's) eyes were filled with tears when he spoke to me of his longing desire to see more friendly relations established (i.e. between the two Churches, JD) and his constant prayer for reunion... Cardinal Bourne from his somewhat rigid and even hard way of expressing himself on these matters had been largely misunderstood"[139]. A few days later, in fact, Bourne wrote Davidson that he would be willing to meet with him and discuss the Malines Conversations with him when he returned from a trip to Rome[140].

On December 15, 1927, the Revised Prayer Book was defeated by the House of Commons. Some of the blame for its defeat was placed on the Malines Conversations, because Kidd and Frere had had important roles in the Prayer Book committee. Archbishop Davidson asked Halifax to wait about publication of the statements, but Halifax declined; and *The Malines Conversations* appeared on January 19, the second anniversary of Portal's death. However...

It was on January 6, 1928 that Pius XI issued his encyclical *Mortalium Animos* which was widely interpreted as an expression of disapproval

138. AAW, Cardinal Bourne's papers, unclassified newspaper clipping, Marchant to The Times, October 3, 1927.

139. ALPL, Archbishop Davidson's papers, Reunion III, Davidson's Memorandum, November 22, 1927.

140. ALPL, Archbishop Davidson's papers, Reunion III, Bourne to Davidson, December 6, 1927.

for the Malines Conversations and was clearly a warning to Catholics about their participation in the Faith and Order movement[141].

According to *Mortalium Animos*, the ecumenical movement was too much associated with doctrinal relativism and indifferentism in ecclesiology. The encyclical condemned what it called a "Pan Christianity", in which "congresses, meetings, and addresses are arranged, attended by a large concourse of hearers, where all without distinction, unbelievers of every kind as well as Christians, even those who unhappily have rejected Christ and denied his divine nature or mission, are invited to join in the discussion ... the Apostolic See can by no means take part in these assemblies, nor is it in any way lawful for Catholics to give to such enterprises their encouragement or support ... the unity of Christians can come about only by furthering the return to the one true Church of Christ of those who are separated from it"[142].

On January 21, *l'Osservatore Romano* announced that there would be no more Conversations at Malines.

5. *Lord Halifax: Last Publications and at Journey's End*

Ironically, on the very same day that *Mortalium Animos* appeared, Halifax had also published a small pamphlet titled *Notes on the Conversations at Malines*. The pamphlet described Halifax's trip to Rome, his receiving the papal blessing on his life's work; and it offered some "points of agreement" between Anglicans and Roman Catholics[143]. The appearance of *The Conversations at Malines: 1921-1925* a few days later, somewhat eclipsed the impact of Halifax's *Notes*, but the pamphlet clearly upset Merry del Val and Gasquet at Rome.

On January 15, 1928, Cardinal Merry del Val sent Francis Woodlock a thank you letter for sending him a copy of Halifax's *Notes on the Conversations at Malines*. Del Val was surprised about the "points of agreement". "How", he asked, "could Catholics present at the Conversations agree upon those points as expressed in their incomplete and

141. As R. Aubert observes: "Furthermore, as far as the Vatican was concerned, the desire of the Pope and his Secretary of State to reach a negotiated settlement of the Roman question made it necessary to give certain pledges to the intransigent wing of the Sacred College, the group around Merry del Val". R. AUBERT, *The Church in a Secularized Society*, New York, Toronto, London, 1978, pp. 603-604. See Appendix G.

142. HOLMES, *op. cit.*, p. 29.

143. In the introduction to his book, Halifax had written: "It was with the greatest satisfaction that I returned homeward with the knowledge that the attitude of the Holy See had not changed from that which had always existed during the life-time of Cardinal Mercier. Before returning to England I paid a visit to Cardinal Van Roey at Malines, who expressed his willingness, at a suitable date, to preside at such future conversations as might be arranged on similar lines to those held under the presidency of Cardinal Mercier". Apparently Halifax had misunderstood Van Roey, because Van Roey later said that he had told Halifax that he *"ne voyait pas la possibilité de reprendre les Conversations"*. E. OLDMEADOW, *Francis Cardinal Bourne*, p. 395.

misleading way?" And then he expressed his annoyance about Halifax's comments about his trip to Rome. "Halifax was not granted a private audience, nor do I believe for a moment that H. H. 'extended his blessing to his work for reunion'. I do not believe either that the Holy See requested a 'paper' from him as he says in his Introduction. I suspect that Cardinal Cerretti, who knows little of these matters, asked him to write a statement, especially in view of his not having obtained a private audience"[144]. Halifax may indeed have exaggerated the "audience" dimension of the papal visit; but del Val's statement about the 'paper' is contradicted by a letter Cerretti had sent to Halifax in which Cerretti said: he, Cerretti, had spoken to the Pope about Halifax's visit and that the Pope had asked Cerretti to suggest to Halifax that he should send a written statement before the trip to Rome[145].

Apparently Cardinal Bourne had also sent Merry del Val a copy of Notes, because on January 20, Merry del Val sent Bourne a thank you letter for sending him a copy of the little pamphlet. Merry del Val called the Notes "most misleading and mischievous and unsound". He also sent Bourne a copy of the l'Osservatore announcement that there would be no more Conversations. Del Val said it had been published "by order of His Holiness". About Halifax's 'paper', Merry del Val said: "What happened was that when he applied for an audience, which the Holy Father did not think suitable, especially after his letter in The Times about setting aside the English Hierarchy, he was told that he might write what he had to say, thus sparing himself the journey". Del Val then blamed part of the problem on Cerretti who he said was "not fully acquainted with the situation"[146].

Four days later, Merry del Val was writing again to Woodlock. This time to thank him for sending a copy of The Conversations at Malines: 1921-1925. Del Val also mentioned his struggles about the publication of Mortalium Animos hinting at the lack of unanimous opinion at Rome: "I thank God for the encyclical... It has been anxious work and I hardly hoped to reach the goal amidst the confusion of those who raised the dust, the failure to understand the situation on the part of many and the ignorance of the facts". Del Val said again that he found Notes "misleading", and The Conversations at Malines "most ambiguous" and full of "half-truths". He then criticized Cardinal Mercier one of whose letters to Davidson had been published in The Conversations at Malines: "With all respect", wrote Merry del Val, "I consider Cardinal Mercier's letter to Canterbury deplorable. He writes on equal terms as

144. AEPSJ, Woodlock papers, BH/6, Merry del Val to Woodlock, January 15, 1928.
145. BIY, The Malines Papers of Lord Halifax, Box 9, N° 129, Ceretti to Halifax, October 15, 1927.
146. AAW, Cardinal Bourne's papers, BO III/144/4, Merry del Val to Bourne, January 20, 1928.

from Church to Church, which is censured in the encyclical"[147]. The question of what really happened to Lord Halifax when he was in Rome would linger on for months. Even as late as the end of April 1928, Mrs. Bellamy Storer would be writing to Cardinal Van Roey protesting that the English Catholic press was very unfair to Lord Halifax and that she had learned from Cardinal Cerretti that the source of the malicious and untrue stories in the English press was Cardinal Gasquet and his secretary Philip Langdon[148].

Woodlock must have been a busy man in January 1928. On January 26, he received a thank you letter from Cardinal Gasquet — thanking him for sending a copy of *The Conversations at Malines*. "I have been through the whole book and am astonished how very little there is in it except the very vague Anglican ideas. The Catholics seem almost as vague and uncertain as the rest who met there... But the pathetic thing is the figure of poor old Halifax, who seems to have no distinct views on any subjects"[149].

In February, an article on "The Upshot of Malines", written by Woodlock appeared in *The Month*. There Woodlock again strongly criticized the Malines Conversations in view of the two most recent publications from Halifax: *Notes* and *The Conversations at Malines*. Woodlock's criticism also conveyed the sentiments of his highly placed Roman collaborators: "It must be remembered", wrote Woodlock, "that 'Malines' was working professedly for 'corporate reunion': that what was being there discussed was the possibility of bringing the *Churches* (original emphasis, JD) together... One wonders whether ... the 'Anglo-Catholics' explained to their Belgian friends how firmly Modernism has taken root in the Established Church and how the recital of the Creeds is no guarantee of belief in their articles". In his article Woodlock also stressed that there were passages in *Mortalium Animos* which were so "extraordinarily apropos that it will be hard to show they were not written with reference to Malines as well as to Stockholm and Lausanne"[150].

Following *Mortalium Animos*, there were also reverberations at Dom Lambert Beauduin's Amay, where some "defections" occurred. Apparently three monks had at least announced their intentions of becoming Orthodox; one took the step. And one who had converted to Catholicism returned to his original Church. "These events received undue publicity. Cardinal Bourne, as spokesman for the English hierarchy,

147. AEPSJ, Woodlock papers, BH/6, Merry del Val to Woodlock, January 24, 1928.

148. AAM, Cardinal Van Roey's papers, unclassified letter, Storer to van Roey, April 29, 1928.

149. AEPSJ, Woodlock papers, BH/6, Gasquet to Woodlock, January 26, 1928.

150. F. WOODLOCK, "The Upshot of Malines" in *The Month* 149 (February 1928), pp. 158-161.

took full advantage of the unfortunate circumstance. D'Herbigny, increasingly powerful in Rome, also had cause for complaint"[151].

In May 1928, Cardinal Bourne gave a talk at Wolverhampton about the "Tragic Failure of Re-Union Negotiations". Bourne indicated that he thought the Malines Conversations had not amounted to much — "I do not think that anyone who has watched these negotiations (sic) can maintain that anything really substantial has been attained". But what we find especially remarkable about his address was his denial that he had been opposed to them! "With reference to the Malines Conversations", he said, "I will only say this, that those of our countrymen who have not hesitated to say that we, the Catholics of England, whether the episcopate or the clergy or the faithful, were hostile or to some extent unsympathetic to such intercourse, when they say that they are not speaking with accuracy"[152]. We know of course — and will later touch on some of the documentation about it — that Cardinal Bourne would later endorse another round of Anglican/Roman Catholic conversations under the leadership of James Marchant in 1931. Bourne clearly was more than the mouthpiece for Merry del Val and Gasquet, when it came to ecumenical relations.

We pass now to July 1928, when the Belgian theology professor from the Scheut house of studies at Louvain, Aloïs Janssens, was a house guest at Hickleton and told Halifax what he had hoped to hear. Halifax had felt that more of what went on during the Conversations should be made available to the public. On July 20, Janssens wrote in his "*Notae Commenorativae VIII*", "I tried to convince him of the necessity of publishing his report, separately. The history of the Malines Conversations must come afterwards. Now is the time for the full report. He would think it over. I offered to make the Latin translation"[153].

By September 1928, Halifax had decided to publish his report. In October "he made a semi-secret journey to Brussels and to Amay"[154] where he met with Dom Lambert Beauduin and others to discuss his plan to publish the full proceedings of the Malines Conversations.

It was also in October 1928 that Halifax again got into trouble with *The Tablet* because he very clumsily published under the title *Rome and Reunion* a manuscript he had received from Abbé Calvet with permission to print it in 1921. The manuscript — *Le problème catholique et l'union des Églises* — was a collection of sermons on reunion. Their publication raised eyebrows because Halifax gave the impression that he had just received the manuscript and that it therefore had been

151. QUITSLUND, *op. cit.*, p. 142.

152. AAM, Cardinal Van Roey's papers, unclassified newspaper clipping, The Universe, May 18, 1928.

153. D. VERHELST, "Lord Halifax and the Scheut Father Aloïs Janssens", in *Ephemerides Theologicae Lovanienses* 43 (1967), p. 245.

154. LOCKHART, *op. cit.*, p. 154.

written not only after the Malines Conversations but after *Mortalium Animos*. Oldmeadow was upset, Bourne was upset, and Calvet, who knew nothing about the thing, because publication had been arranged through an agent, was upset; and there was a great protest against Halifax in *The Tablet*, and other papers. The publishers were even at each other's throats: Oldmeadow of *The Tablet* and the publisher of the book, Philip Allan, whose director was Halifax's later biographer J.G. Lockhart, were nearly at the point of taking each other to court[155]. Interestingly however, there was also a great swelling of popular support for Halifax from English Roman Catholics — much to Oldmeadow's dismay. The *Church Times*, noted, for instance: "We desire to make no comment on the repeated attacks on Lord Halifax that have recently appeared in *The Tablet* except to say that we have received many assurances that they do not represent the feeling of the majority of English Roman Catholics. We do not suppose that Lord Halifax has ever imagined that they did"[156]. The battles about the Calvet affair dragged on into the new year; but Halifax tried to distance himself from them and continued working quietly on his next book, with his chaplain Fr. Painter making arrangements to secure a publisher.

On January 13, 1929, Pierre Batiffol died, true to his death to what he had said about the Malines Conversations in 1923 — but few then had paid much attention to it: "It is no use thinking of a reconciliation of the Anglican Church. That would be utopian; but we can draw nearer to the Anglo-Catholic movement, encourage and enlighten it, perhaps help to detach it from the political or Modernistic elements in Anglicanism. That is the perspective in which we must direct our work: conversations without any immediate aim, but helping to make Anglo-Catholic opinion advance in a Catholic direction"[157].

On April 4, 1929 Cardinal Gasquet died, maintaining to the end his fight against the validity of Anglican Orders. In early May, 1929, Dom Lambert Beauduin sent a circular letter to about fifteen people announcing his idea of conducting ecumenical discussions by mail among a small group of interested participants. Beauduin had been inspired by the model of the Malines Conversations. Somehow, one of the letters ended up in Cardinal Bourne's hands; and Bourne "immediately interpreted it as a secret continuation of the Malines Conversations. Supported by the tone and content of *Mortalium Animos*, instant cries of outrage were raised"[158]. Bourne would later play a role in the Roman condemnation of Amay.

155. The correspondence about the Calvet affair can be found in the Bourne papers at Westminster. Oldmeadow also devotes a few pages to it in his *Francis Cardinal Bourne*, pp. 398-404.
156. "Catholics and Lord Halifax", in *The Tablet* 151 (April 7, 1928), p. 466.
157. DE BIVORT DE LA SAUDÉE, *op. cit.*, p. 81.
158. QUITSLUND, *op. cit.*, p. 170.

In early January 1930, a little book came out by the Anglican scholars White and Knox *One God and Father of All* which immediately caught the attention of Francis Woodlock who sent it to Merry del Val. Merry del Val was angered by the book because it asserted that, among other things, Leo XIII had been swayed by Cardinal Vaughan and the English Catholics to take a position contrary to the position of his Roman theologians. On January 16, 1930, Merry del Val sent a seven page typed letter to Woodlock justifying the position he and others had taken and pointing out the errors of White and Knox. He encouraged Woodlock to use his letter for background for an article refuting the position of *One God and Father of All*[159].

On February 3, 1930, English Catholic attention was drawn to another book. A brief notice appeared in the *Times*; but it provoked a major storm:

"The original documents, French and English, read at the four Conversations (1921-1925) held at Malines under the presidency of Cardinal Mercier, together with the summary of the Conversations written by the French members, are about to be published by Lord Halifax...". If the notice had stopped there it probably would not have attracted that much attention. It was the focus of the next paragraph however which provoked immediate responses on both sides of the channel. The article pointed out that one important document, not published in 1928 by Halifax, was now being made public: "It was read at the fourth Conversation in May, 1925, by the Cardinal, and bears the title *'L'Église anglicane unie non absorbée'* but the authorship is not revealed. It puts foreword on the part of Rome a formula of union which would allow for Anglican autonomy under the suzerainty of Rome. It contemplates, among other provisions, the re-establishment of the Archbishop of Canterbury, after receiving the *pallium* from the Pope, as Patriarch of the Anglican Church, with the rights appertaining to that office, including the nomination and consecration of bishops; the maintenance of an Anglican liturgy, and of all the ancient historic sees of the Anglican Church, and the suppression of the new Catholic sees, created since 1851. 'Union not absorption', would, as the writer says, appear to be the formula of reconciliation"[160].

Lord Halifax, "with a magnificent disregard of the law of copyright and in face of the objections of his old companions"[161], had published *The Conversations at Malines: 1921-1925 Original Documents*.

On February 4, Maurice Emmanuel Carton de Wiart, writing from

159. AEPSJ, Woodlock papers, BH/6, Merry del Val to Woodlock, January 16, 1930.
160. AAM, Cardinal Van Roey's papers; unclassified newspaper clipping, *The Times*, February 3, 1930.
161. LOCKHART, *op. cit.*, p. 339.

the Archbishop's House in Westminster, sent Cardinal Van Roey newspaper clippings about the forthcoming publication[162].

On February 7, Merry del Val, deplored the publication in a letter to Cardinal Bourne: "It is indeed astonishing and deplorable", he wrote. "Though what was to be expected from such 'representatives'(?) as Portal, Batiffol, and Hemmer, with poor Cardinal Mercier in a dream and all at sea over the history of the Reformation in England and of the real state of religion in the 'Anglican Church'". He also deplored the suggestion that the Archbishop of Canterbury could receive a special jurisdiction "under the Roman suzerainty". He thought Bourne should write directly to the Pope and suggested that the climate at the Vatican would be receptive because, as Merry del Val noted: "I understand that Cardinal Gasparri is leaving his office in a few days". Del Val, we know, had never held Gasparri in much esteem. In February 1925, he had written to Canon Moyes that Gasparri was "all at sea" about Anglican/Roman Catholic relations and that "his position today makes his attitude more mischievous, for he does what he likes"[163]. Now, in February of 1930, he had repeated the old accusation and added that Gasparri had nursed "extraordinary delusions" about the Anglicans. At the conclusion of his letter, Merry del Val also revealed a bit of his fabled wit: "Just imagine", he wrote about what could happen if Beauduin's proposal were implemented, "the Cardinal Patriarchs with precedence over all others and Mrs. Canterbury with precedence too and English Catholics handed over to his and her authority"[164].

The Pope, by the way, had accepted Gasparri's request to resign on February 7, 1930, the same day that Merry del Val had written to Bourne.

On February 9, 1930, Hippolyte Hemmer, wrote Cardinal Van Roey to protest Halifax's impending publication and to ask him to do something about it. He especially feared the reactions at Rome and in England to L'Église anglicane unie non absorbée. We note with special interest that Hemmer wrote about Beauduin's proposal as though Beauduin's authorship were already common knowledge[165].

162. AAM, Cardinal Van Roey's papers, unclassified letter, Carton de Wiart to Van Roey, February 4, 1930.

163. AAW, Moyes papers, unclassified letter, Merry del Val to Moyes, February 14, 1925.

164. AAW, Cardinal Bourne's papers, BO III/124/4, Merry del Val to Bourne, February 7, 1930.

165. "Cette élucubration de Dom Beauduin est de nature, je crains, à faire fâcheuse impression à Rome et avec les catholiques anglais". AAM, Cardinal Van Roey's papers, unclassified letter, Hemmer to Van Roey, February 9, 1930. As to when Beauduin suspected that Van Roey knew he was the author of the proposal, see QUITSLUND, op. cit., p. 75.

At about this same time the book came out. On February 11, Van Roey wrote a letter of protest to Halifax, deploring especially the inclusion of Beauduin's proposal[166]. And on February 22, Cardinal van Roey sent a disclaimer to the *Libre Belgique* which was subsequently printed in the *Sunday Times*. Van Roey's main points were: (1) that Halifax had published the book contrary to the agreement of the participants at Malines; (2) the printed reports still did not give the whole picture of what had happened at the Conversations; and (3) that the anonymous document did not reflect the position of Rome or of Cardinal Mercier but "of Dom Lambert Beauduin the Benedictine monk of Amay"[167].

On February 22, 1930 B.J. Kidd also felt compelled to issue a public disclaimer, which he sent to the *Times* and also to Cardinal Van Roey: "On behalf of the English colleagues of Lord Halifax at Malines, I am requested to disclaim all responsibility for the recent publication of documents concerning them. At the final meeting at Malines, when the official report had been passed for publication, it was 'agreed not to publish the memoranda nor our minutes; but a writer might publish his own paper, if he did so independently of the Conversations'. Whatever we may think of the wisdom of publication or the reverse we have felt ourselves bound by that agreement"[168].

As Oldmeadow, and others would be quick to point out, Halifax's book had failed to include one important paper — Bishop Gore's, as Lockhart explains: "Halifax had either mislaid or had originally omitted to procure a copy of Gore's paper 'On Unity with Diversity' (which subsequently appeared in Dr. Frere's book), and Gore indignantly refused to supply it"[169]. Halifax later sent Fr. Painter to look for a copy among Portal's papers in Paris but he could not find it.

As to the publication itself, Halifax defended his action because of "the conspiracy of silence which certain people in authoritative quarters had set up against the Conversations"[170].

On February 26, 1930, a major conspirator against Anglican Orders and against the Malines Conversations, Cardinal Merry del Val, was dead. About his passing, *The Tablet* noted, in what was certainly a classic understatement, that he had been "one of the most active and influential Churchmen of his time"[171].

---

166. LOCKHART, *op. cit.*, p. 339.

167. "*Il est de la plume de Dom Lambert Beauduin, moine bénédictin d'Amay, dont il représente par conséquent les idées*". AAW, Cardinal Bourne's papers, unclassified newspaper clipping, *Libre Belgique*, February 22, 1930.

168. AAM, Cardinal Van Roey's papers, unclassified letter, Kidd to *The Times*, February 22, 1930, sent to Van Roey on February 23, 1930.

169. LOCKHART, *op. cit.*, p. 340.

170. *Ibid.*, p. 339.

171. *The Tablet* 155 (March 1, 1930) p. 262.

In March 1930, del Val's *protégé* Francis Woodlock published a surprisingly mild article about *The Conversations at Malines: 1921-1925: Original Documents*, in which he expressed his gratitude that Halifax had finally "given us the full and official record of what passed at Malines". Woodlock was even positive about the Roman Catholic participants in the Conversations, assuring his readers that Halifax's book proved that "our continental co-religionists were, throughout the meetings, orthodox, loyal, and completely intransigeant and uncompromising in the matter of the dogmatic requirements for union with the Catholic Church". We suspect Merry del Val would not have been pleased with this article! And finally, when speaking about Lambert Beauduin's proposal, Woodlock briefly observed: "There is nothing to suggest that this anonymous paper was inspired by a 'high personage at the Vatican' and everything to lead us to the conclusion that Rome was not even cognizant that the suggestion was to be put forward at Malines"[172]. And he left it at that.

On May 25, 1930 Randall Davidson died. Later in the year, the Lambeth Conference, over which he had presided in 1920, would summarize the current state of affairs after the Malines Conversations and after *Mortalium Animos*. It issued a statement to "express its conviction of the value of such Conversations and conferences", and its regret that the Vatican could no longer allow Catholics to participate in them. "This regret", said the Conference, "is shared by many members of the Church of Rome". The Conference went on to express a further regret "that in the encyclical the method of 'complete absorption' has been proposed to the exclusion of that suggested in the Conversations, as, for example, in the paper read at Malines, '*L'Église anglicane unie non absorbée*'"[173]. It was also in 1930 that Halifax published his last book: *The Good Estate of the Church* a little book which did not attract much attention but gave expression to some thoughts he had not yet expressed after "seventy years during which ecclesiastical matters have been my greatest interest"[174].

In the new year, however, attention would be focused again on Dom Lambert Beauduin and his connections with England.

On January 13, 1930 Beauduin was called to Rome to answer a series of charges. On January 14, Michel d'Herbigny, President of the Pontifical Commission for Russia, sent a letter from Rome, marked "*urgente*", to Cardinal Bourne in London. D'Herbigny informed Bourne that the monks of Amay were being examined because of

172. F. WOODLOCK, "The Malines Conversations Report", in *The Month* 151 (March 1930), pp. 238 and 241.

173. H. HENSON, *The Church of England*, Cambridge, 1939, p. 237.

174. Viscount HALIFAX, *The Good Estate of the Church*, London, New York, Toronto, 1930, p. 1.

certain actions of Dom Lambert Beauduin in regard to the return of "*dissidenti*" to the unity of the Church. Bourne was to send immediately any documents he had about the activities of Beauduin[175].

Bourne's reply was sent on January 27, 1931. He sent a copy of Beauduin's letter about the "conversations by mail", and some newspaper clippings about "the extraordinary letter which Dom Beauduin wrote to the Protestant self-styled Benedictines at Alton"[176]. The letter from Beauduin had been signed "Your brother in St. Benedict", and it had created an uproar in England when someone leaked it to the *Times*[177].

On January 30, the commission which had been established to examine Beauduin's activities, rendered its decision. Michel d'Herbigny, the president of the commission — and the man who had years earlier worked so feverishly to become one of the participants in the Malines Conversations — read the verdict to Beauduin: "Here is the will of the Holy Father that I am charged to communicate to you. An equivocation exists that must disappear. Amay is opposed to the conceptions of the Holy See. This name, the spirit it incarnates, the methods it represents, even the place and the thing must disappear. Nothing can remain of Amay"[178]. Throughout this entire Beauduin affair, Cardinal Van Roey remained silent, even though it had been his revelation of Beauduin as author of the famous Fourth Conversation proposal that had no doubt helped precipitate the actions against the Belgian monk[179].

We don't know where — or if — it fits into the decision against Dom Lambert Beauduin, and Quitslund in her book *Beauduin A Prophet*

175. AAW, Cardinal Bourne's papers, BO III/124/4, d'Herbigny to Bourne, January 14, 1931.
176. AAW, Cardinal Bourne's papers, BO III/124/4, Bourne to d'Herbigny, January 27, 1931.
177. QUITSLUND, *op. cit.*, p. 172.
178. *Ibid.*, p. 175.
Quitslund raises the question of whether the Pope really knew what was happening in this judgment: "Ordinarily in such a hearing as Beauduin's the decision represents the majority vote of the members of the commission. In this case, however, the decision seems to have resulted from the report that d'Herbigny supposedly made to the pope. If he told the commission that it was the pope's decision, the case would be considered closed and there would be no cause for further action. In short, a vote was not necessary, and it appears that Beauduin's fate depended exclusively on d'Herbigny's report to the pope. (If in fact d'Herbigny simply attributed to the pope his own wishes in this matter, it was not the only such instance)".
179. Quitslund comments about Van Roey's involvement: "But with Van Roey's disclosure in the public press of Beauduin's authorship, the whole controversy broke out anew. His choice of words 'Dom Lambert Beauduin, prior of Amay' — immediately implicated Amay. Extremely concerned, Beauduin went to Van Roey with a written statement for the press. He argued that Amay had been unfairly implicated on two counts: (1) the Proposal had been written in Rome before the conception of Amay, and (2) Beauduin had Mercier's letters of approval. When Van Roey asked the monk not to publish the reply (because it contradicted the cardinal on these two points), Beauduin tore up his text and threw it in the cardinal's wastepaper basket". QUITSLUND, *op. cit.*, p. 171.

Vindicated makes no mention of it; but we know that at some point in 1931, Cardinal Bourne had prepared two pages of "Notes for Monsignor Carton de Wiart" about the activities of Dom Lambert Beauduin. It was in fact a list of things Beauduin had done or was alleged to have done which annoyed Bourne. A major concern of Bourne's touched on Anglican Orders: "It is now being said", wrote Bourne, "definitely that Dom Bauduin (sic) is encouraging Anglican clergymen to believe that the *irreformable* decision of Leo XIII on Anglican Orders may be revised and that he places a room in his priory at their disposition to enable them to celebrate therein the Anglican communion service"[180].

In the spring of 1931, came the irony of ironies, a new set of Anglican/Roman Catholic conversations — held at the Thackeray Hotel in London with the cognizance of Archbishop Lang, now Archbishop of Canterbury, and Cardinal Bourne! They were held under the chairmanship of the Roman Catholic publisher James Marchant. Our knowledge of these discussions is scant[181]; but they apparently lasted with little notice from June to October 1931 and then ended without much attention having been given to them, perhaps because of the attitude of one of the observers of the conversations, the English Jesuit Alban Goodier, one time Archbishop of Bombay. In October 1931, Goodier sent Bourne an Anglican memorandum which had come out of the conversations, some letters from Marchant about the Thackery conversations, and his own, i.e. Goodier's, evaluation of the conversations. Apparently Bourne had asked him to write an evaluation "for the use of those at Rome". As to the contents of Goodier's evaluation: he thought the conversations had been a failure. As he said, "I have especially tried to show that the idea of 'conversion' to the Catholic Church never so much as entered once in the discussions; all that was sought for was recognition by Rome, on the ground that they were already just as Catholic as ourselves. The more I have thought of the outcome of these conversations, the more I am disappointed, not to say annoyed. I see now yet more clearly what Fr. Woodlock has long since said: that Anglicanism is to be met not by sympathy, which is only exploited, but by clear and emphatic definitions"[182].

That apparently was the end of the Thackery Hotel conversations.

180. AAW, Cardinal Bourne's papers, BO III/124/4, Bourne's undated "Notes for Monsignor Carton de Wiart".

181. AAW, Cardinal Bourne's papers, BO III/124/4, Thackeray Hotel conversations correspondence: Anglican Memorandum, June 18, 1931; letter, Marchant to Archbishop Lang, June 19, 1931; letter, Marchant to Bourne, July 1, 1931; letter, Goodier to Bourne, October 28, 1931.

182. AAW, Cardinal Bourne's papers, BO III/124/4, Thackeray Hotel conversations, Goodier to Bourne, October 28, 1931.

Nevertheless, the very fact that they had been allowed by Bourne to take place, and this after *Mortalium Animos*, showed once again that Bourne was more open to ecumenical dialogue than many critics have suggested.

But as we said at the start of this chapter, the Malines momentum was slowing down.

In January 1932, Charles Gore died; and when Halifax heard that Gore had asked to be cremated, Halifax wrathfully exclaimed "I could shake the life out of him with my own hands"[183]!

In 1933 a liaison committee was set up to work toward the amalgamation of the English Church Union and the Anglo-Catholic Congress.

On January 1, 1934, the amalgamation was complete and Lord Halifax was elected one of two presidents of the new ecumenical body. He had been an ecumenical pioneer right to the end of his life's journey, which came on January 19 at half past seven in the evening.

Lord Halifax was buried on January 22, the eighth anniversary of Cardinal Mercier's death.

"Halifax was seized by the idea of reunion. He remained so throughout his life. He may have been unrealistic according to the ecumenical standards of his time; but he never gave up. Two years before his death, he wrote to his friend in Louvain, Alois Janssens: 'To be discouraged is a cowardice. And in my heart of hearts I know that the object for which, in different ways, we are struggling will one day and in God's good time be accomplished'"[184].

And it was also in "God's good time", that Cardinal Bourne died, twelve months after Halifax, on December 31. Perhaps Halifax had never seen him in his true light. Regardless —Bourne had not only witnessed but in his own way had supported a warming of relations between the two English Churches. After his death, the English Roman Catholic Church would continue its slow and often painful ecumenical evolution.

183. LOCKHART, *op. cit.*, p. 364.

184. R. BOUDENS, "Lord Halifax: An Impression", in *Ephemerides Theologicae Lovanienses* 60 (1984), p. 452. Professor Boudens gave this address at Malines in the presence of Dr. Habgood, Anglican Archbishop of York during a commemoration of the fiftieth anniversary of the death of Lord Halifax.

CONCLUSION

Contrary to what had been the general understanding of the situation in England at the time of the Malines Conversations, English Roman Catholics were not unanimous in their opposition to the Conversations. English Roman Catholics in favor of the Conversations, however, were not well represented in the English Catholic press and were gradually forced into virtual silence by directives from Rome. Throughout the years of the Malines Conversations, there were clearly two groups at Rome struggling about the Conversations: a group favorable to the Conversations and symbolized in Cardinal Gasparri, and a group hostile toward the Conversations and symbolized in Cardinal Merry del Val. After the death of Cardinal Mercier, the Merry del Val group gained control.

Cardinal Bourne's theological advisor James Moyes, who had been on Cardinal Vaughan's Anglican Orders Commission, as well as Ernest Oldmeadow, editor of *The Tablet*, worked hand-in-hand with Cardinal Merry del Val and Cardinal Gasquet to discredit the Malines Conversations.

Those English Roman Catholics opposed to the Malines Conversations, were opposed initially because of the involvement of Lord Halifax and Abbé Portal, who were identified with the party favoring the validity of Anglican Orders.

The fear of Modernism remained a strong undercurrent among the opposition to the Conversations: Merry del Val suspected both Portal and Mercier of Modernist tendencies. He felt that Bourne was not strong enough in his opposition to suspected Modernists; and he used the anti-Modernist Francis Woodlock in his campaign against English Modernism and the Malines Conversations.

Toward the end of the Malines Conversations, the issue of corporate reunion as opposed to individual conversions became the central issue among those opposed to the Conversations, because: (1) it was seen by them as implying the validity of Anglican Orders, (2) it questioned the existence of the English Roman Catholic sees established after 1850, and (3) it raised fears of Anglican Modernists being brought into the Roman Church as part of the package.

Cardinal Bourne, up until shortly before the death of Cardinal Mercier, remained surprisingly open toward the Conversations. And after the death of Mercier, and even after *Mortalium Animos*, Bourne remained surprisingly ecumenical. He was clearly mis-represented by his biographer and mis-understood by Halifax and Portal, who were somewhat battle-scarred by their experiences with Cardinal Vaughan and the nineteenth century decision against the validity of Anglican Orders.

Cardinal Bourne, in fact, ended up being a symbol of English Roman Catholic reactions to the Malines Conversations. He was positive and negative. He wanted to be involved yet was fearful about involvement. He wanted to be open to the Anglicans but found himself bound to defend, sometimes against the Anglicans, important elements of English Roman Catholic history since the sixteenth century. He looked for understanding and yet was often not understood. He was a tragic figure not a hero.

Francis Bourne was the restless leader of a restless Church which was slowly edging out of the narrow Ultramontanism it had been confined to by his predecessors at Westminster.

APPENDICES

AN APPEAL TO ALL CHRISTIAN PEOPLE
From the Bishops assembled in the Lambeth Conference of 1920*

We, Archbishops, Bishops Metropolitan, and other Bishops of the Holy Catholic Church in full communion with the Church of England, in Conference assembled, realizing the responsibility which rests upon us at this time, and sensible of the sympathy and the prayers of many, both within and without our own Communion, make this appeal to all Christian people.

We acknowledge all those who believe in our Lord Jesus Christ, and have been baptized into the name of the Holy Trinity, as sharing with us membership in the universal Church of Christ which is His Body. We believe that the Holy Spirit has called us in a very solemn and special manner to associate ourselves in penitence and prayer with all those who deplore the divisions of the Christian people, and are inspired by the vision and hope of a visible unity of the whole Church.

I. We believe that God wills fellowship. By God's own act this fellowship was made in and through Jesus Christ, and its life is in His Spirit. We believe that it is God's purpose to manifest this fellowship, so far as this world is concerned, in an outward, visible, and united society, holding one faith, having its own recognized officers, using God-given means of grace, and inspiring all its members to the world-wide service of the Kingdom of God. This is what we mean by the Catholic Church.

II. This united fellowship is not visible in the world today. On the one hand there are other ancient episcopal Communions in East and West, to whom ours is bound by many ties of common faith and tradition. On the other hand there are the great non-episcopal Communions, standing for rich elements of truth, liberty and life which otherwise have been obscured or neglected. With them we are closely linked by many affinities, racial, historical and spiritual. We cherish the earnest hope that all these Communions, and our own, may be led by the Spirit in to the unity of the Faith and of the knowledge of the Son of God. But in fact we are all organized in different groups, each one keeping to itself gifts that rightly belong to the whole fellowship, and tending to live its own life apart from the rest.

III. The causes of division lie deep in the past, and are by no means simple or wholly blameworthy. Yet none can doubt that self-will ambition, and lack of charity among Christians have been principle factors in the mingled process, and that these, together with the blindness to the sin of disunion, are still mainly responsible for the breaches of Christendom. We acknowledge this condition of broken fellowship to be contrary to God's will and we desire

---

* CONFERENCE OF BISHOPS OF THE ANGLICAN COMMUNION (Lambeth Palace July 5 to August 7, 1920), *Encyclical Letter*, London, 1920, pp. 7-24.

frankly to confess our share in the guilt of thus crippling the Body of Christ and hindering the activity of His Spirit.

IV. The times call us to a new outlook and new measures. The Faith cannot be adequately apprehended and the battle of the Kingdom cannot be worthily fought while the body is divided, and is thus unable to grow up into the fullness of the life of Christ. The time has come, we believe, for all the separated groups of Christians to agree in forgetting the things which are behind and reaching out towards the goal of a reunited Catholic Church. The removal of the barriers which have arisen between them will only be brought about by a new comradeship of those whose faces are definitely set this way.

The vision which rises before us is that of a Church, genuinely Catholic, loyal to all Truth, and gathering into its fellowship all "who profess and call themselves Christians", within whose visible unity all the treasures of faith and order, bequeathed as a heritage by the past to the present, shall be possessed in common, and made serviceable to the whole Body of Christ. Within this unity Christian Communions now separated from one another would retain much that has long been distinctive in their methods of worship and service. It is through a rich diversity of life and devotion that the unity of the whole fellowship will be fulfilled.

V. This means an adventure of goodwill and still more of faith, for nothing less is required than a new discovery of the creative resources of God. To this adventure we are convinced that God is now calling all the members of His Church.

VI. We believe that the visible unity of the Church will be found to involve the whole-hearted acceptance of:-

The Holy Scriptures, as the record of God's revelation of Himself to man, and as being the rule and ultimate standard of faith; and the Creed commonly called Nicene, as the sufficient statement of the Christian faith, and either it or the Apostles' Creed as the Baptismal confession of belief:

The divinely instituted sacraments of Baptism and the holy Communion, as expressing for all the corporate life of the whole fellowship in and with Christ:

A ministry acknowledged by every part of the Church as possessing not only the inward call of the Spirit, but also the commission of Christ and the authority of the whole body.

VII. May we not reasonably claim that the Episcopate is the one means of providing such a ministry? It is not that we call in question for a moment the spiritual reality of the ministries of those Communions which do not possess the Episcopate. On the contrary we thankfully acknowledge that these ministries have been manifestly blessed and owned by the Holy Spirit as effective means of grace. But we submit that considerations alike of history and of present experience justify the claim which we make on behalf of the Episcopate. Moreover, we would urge that it is now and will prove to be in the future the best instrument for maintaining the unity and continuity of the Church. But we greatly desire that the office of a Bishop should be everywhere exercised in a representative and constitutional manner, and more truly express all that ought to be involved for the life of the Christian Family in the title of Father-in-God. Nay more, we eagerly look forward to the day when through its acceptance in a united Church we may all share in that grace which is pledged to the members of the whole body in the apostolic rite of the laying-on of hands, and in the joy and fellowship of a Eucharist in which as one family we may together, without any doubtfulness of mind, offer to the one Lord our worship and service.

VIII. We believe that for all the truly equitable approach to union is by the way of mutual deference to one another's consciences. To this end, we who send forth this appeal would say that if the authorities of other Communions should so desire, we are persuaded that, terms of union having been otherwise satisfactorily adjusted, Bishops and clergy of our Communions would willingly accept from these authorities a form of commission or recognition which would commend our ministry to their congregations, as having place in the one family life. It is not in our power to know how far this suggestion may be acceptable to those to whom we offer it. We can only say that we offer it in all sincerity as a token of our longing that all ministries of grace, theirs and ours, shall be available for the service of our Lord in a united Church.

It is our hope that the same motive would lead ministers who have not received it to accept a commission through episcopal ordination, as obtaining for them a ministry throughout the whole fellowship.

In so acting no one of us could possibly be taken to repudiate his past ministry. God forbid that any man should repudiate a past experience rich in spiritual blessings for himself and others. Nor would any of us be dishonouring the Holy Spirit of God, Whose call led us all to our several ministries, and Whose power enabled us to perform them. We shall be publicly and formally seeking additional recognition of a new call to wider service in a reunited Church, and imploring for ourselves God's grace and strength to fulfil the same.

IX. The spiritual leadership of the Catholic Church in days to come, for which the world is manifestly waiting, depends upon the readiness with which each group is prepared to make sacrifices for the sake of a common fellowship, a common ministry, and a common service to the world.

We place this ideal first and foremost before ourselves and our own people. We call upon them to make the effort to meet the demands of a new age with a new outlook. To all other Christian people whom our words may reach we make the same appeal. We do not ask that any one Communion should consent to be absorbed in another. We do ask that all should unite in a new and great endeavour to recover and to manifest to the world the unity of the Body of Christ for which He prayed.

The Lambeth Conference of 1908 passed the following resolution (No.78) "The constituted authorities of the various Churches of the Anglican Communion should, as opportunity offers, arrange conferences with representatives of other Christian Churches, and meetings for common acknowledgement of the sins of division, and for intercession for the growth of unity".

In another part of this Report it is shewn that in many countries, particularly in the United States of America, in India, and in Africa, this course has been very largely followed. But the urgency of the present world situation, and the wide and deep longing for unity which these Conferences have revealed, and which fills the hearts of Christian people throughout the world, seem to us to call for further and more responsible action. We ask the Conference to recommend that the authorities of the Churches of the Anglican Communion should, in such ways and at such times as they think best, formally invite the authorities of other Churches within their area to confer with them as to the possibility of taking definite steps to co-operate in a common endeavour, on the lines set forth in the Appeal, to restore the unity of the Church of Christ. It may be that these approaches will meet with some rebuffs and disappointments. Special circumstances may be urged as shewing that such conferences would be premature. Some doors seem for the present to be shut. But many doors in all parts of the world are open. There are already movements in progress for a closer union of Communions separated from us and from one another. With the spirit and hopes of these movements we would associate ourselves, heartily desiring their success and trusting that they may forward the cause of the ultimate union of the universal Church. Yet the historical traditions and the spiritual sympathies of the Anglican Church seem to lay upon us a special duty, which at this present time we ought to accept as a definite call of God. May He in His mercy forgive and take from us any spirit of self-satisfaction! We have need frankly to acknowledge and humbly to confess our manifold sins and shortcomings as a Church. In all our approaches to our fellow Christians of other Churches we shall try to make it plain that we only desire to be permitted to take our part with them in a cause to which the Lord Whom we serve is at this time most manifestly calling the members of His Church.

Here it will not be out of place to draw the attention of our fellow-churchmen to some important results of the extension and development of the Anglican Communion, and the bearing of these upon the question of reunion and upon our attitude and duty towards it.

At the date of the first Lambeth Conference, 1867, this Communion had taken the form of a federation of self-governing Churches, held together for the most part without legal sanctions by a common reverence for the same traditions and a common use of a Prayer Book which, in spite of some local variations, was virtually the same. Our missionary workers were then planting churches among nations very different from the Anglo-Saxon race and from one another, but as yet these had shewn but little growth. In the interval between that time and the present there have grown up indigenous Churches in China, in Japan, in East and West Africa, in each of which the English members are but a handful of strangers and sojourners, some engaged in missionary work, some in secular business. In India the Church includes large numbers both of British and of Indian members: the emergence of a National Church, claiming freedom to regulate its own affairs, is only a matter of time. Consequently the Anglican Communion of today is a federation of Churches, some national, some regional, but no longer predominately Anglo-Saxon in race, nor can it be expected that it will attach special value to Anglo-Saxon traditions. The blessing which has rested upon its work has brought it to a new point of view. Meanwhile, it might also be said that its centre of gravity is shifting. It already presents an example on a small scale of the problems which attach to the unity of a Universal Church. As the years go on, its ideals must become less Anglican and more Catholic. It cannot look to any bonds of union holding it together, other than those which should hold together the Catholic Church itself.

While this development has been going on, another has kept pace with it. Our Communion has taken into itself, tried, and found valuable many elements which were not to be found in any effective condition in the Church of England one hundred or even fifty years ago. The bearing of these on the problem of reunion is so important that we deem it worth while to notice here some examples. In most parts of our Communion the Episcopate does not even present the appearance of autocracy or prelacy. Various arrangements have been adopted by which the Bishop is elected by the Diocese over which he is to preside. The affairs of the Diocese are managed by the Bishop in conjunction with a Diocesan Synod or Council. The bishops and their Dioceses are further correlated in Provincial and General Synods, Conventions or Assemblies. Thus, Episcopacy among us has generally become constitutional, and the clergy and laity have attained to a share in the government of the Church. Again, in many parts of our Communion systems of patronage have been adopted which recognize the right of congregations to take part in the selection of their ministers. We draw attention to these matters as evidencing our recognition, not only in word but in deed, of the value of some of those elements of Church life which those now separated from us have developed with marked success. We urge further on our own fellow-churchmen that it is one of the most pressing and most important steps towards a reunion that they should develop in every place, according to its own circumstances and the genius of its people, the well-tried principles of constitutionalism in the government of the Church, and of the full employment of every member in its life, and the Committee venture to submit a Resolution to this effect to the Conference.

There are other signs of similar expansion from within, which have made our Communion more representative of the varying phases of Christian life and devotion. The development of mission services and missions of many kinds, the use of various additional forms of prayer, of ex tempore prayer, of silent prayer, and again of various kinds of ceremonial and elaboration of liturgical worship, testify quite apart from the merits of any of them, to the increasing recognition of the diversity of the temperaments of men and of the duty of the Church to make them all feel at home in the family of God. We welcome the spirit of that expansion which has brought one part or another of our Communion nearer to those who are separated from us. We look forward hopefully to the far greater variety in the expression of the one faith and of devotion to the one Lord, which must necessarily ensue when the Churches of men who are strangers in blood, though brothers in Christ, come to fuller age and to more characteristic development. We call upon our fellow-churchmen in every branch of our Communion to accept ever more fully the standard of the universal Church and its necessary inclusiveness, so that they will not feel strange when they are called upon to live in the fellowship of the re-united universal Church.

Meanwhile, the needs of the whole world lay upon Christian men and women everywhere the obligation to manifest the fellowship which they already possess as believers in the one Lord, and as the soldiers and servants of His Kingdom, by praying and working together for the vindication of the Christian Faith and the extension of the rule of Christ among all nations and over every region of human life. We therefore recommend that, where it has not already been done, Councils representing all Christian Communions should be formed within such areas as may be deemed most convenient, as centres of united effort to promote the physical, moral and social welfare of the people and the spread of the Kingdom of God and of His righteousness among men. Such co-operation will, we are confident, both strengthen the desire and prepare the way for a fuller spiritual union of life and worship.

OUTLINE OF PROVISIONAL SCHEME FOR A CONFERENCE
between representatives of the Church of England
and of the Churches in communion with Rome*

Note: the following scheme has been drawn up by an individual, is in no way sanctioned as yet by either party, and is subject to indefinite modification; in short, is a mere suggestion of a possible scheme which may or may not be approved.

I. The FAITH-BASIS.

Acceptance of the Scriptures as the inspired Word of God, of Catholic tradition as guided by God, of the Creeds as expressing in brief the content of the Christian revelation, and of the general principle that neither party shall be called upon to renounce anything that they hold to be *de fide*, i.e. to pertain to the essence of the Christian revelation:

Main problem: to discover whether there is any sense in which the documents which the Churches in communion with Rome regard as *de fide* can be interpreted, so as to render them, without doing violence to the "plain meaning" of the statement therein contained, acceptable alike to all parties, notable in the case of the decrees of the Council of Trent and the Council of the Vatican.

II. The BASIS FOR WORSHIP.

Acceptance of the general principle that the liturgy and worship of the Church, its *lex orandi*, must adequately express its *lex credendi*, and (ii) that, in so far as it is possible, the rites of all countries should be such that members of any nation may join in and appreciate them.

Main problem: to discover by what means the usage of the Church of England, inherited from the past but modified at the time of the Reformation, could be rendered acceptable to the Churches in communion with Rome, particularly
  (a) with respect to the Eucharist
  (b) with respect to the seven sacraments
  (c) with respect to presence and worship of our Lord in the reserved sacrament
  (d) with respect to communion in one or two kinds.

III. The BASIS FOR ORDERS.

Acceptance of the principle enunciated at the Lambeth Conference that a way must be found whereby the ministrations of the Church of England clergy may become acceptable to other Churches, so that "we may without any

---

* AAM, *The Malines Conversations*, 1922, B I, N° 31.

doubtfulness of mind, offer to the one Lord our worship and service".
Main problem: to discover a way of accomplishing this (i) with respect to
Apostolic Succession, and (ii) with respect to the Ordinal.

IV. PAPAL JURISDICTION, AND CHURCH ADMINISTRATION.

Basis: acceptance of the hierarchic constitution of the Church with the Bishop
of Rome as Summus Pontifex, and of the general principle that the communion
of members with members and of members with the head must be as intimate
and effective as possible.

PROBLEMS:

(1) How far the present system of government, as exercised by the Roman
    Curia, would be acceptable to, and applicable in England, with special
    reference to
    (a) Papal decrees
    (b) The decrees of Roman Congregations and Commissions
    (c) The appointment of bishops and other dignitaries.
    (d) The control of public pronouncements in matters of faith and
        morals, and in the matter of Scripture.
    (e) The control of teaching in seminaries.
    (f) Dispensations and reservations
(2) The relation of the Church to the State.
(3) The relation of the Church of England, in the event of reunion, to the
    Church in England which is already in communion with Rome.
(4) The applicability of the present Code of Cannon law, with special reference
    to
    (a) the Celibacy of the Clergy
    (b) the use of the Breviary
    (c) the position of the religious orders
    (d) Marriage: impediments etc. divorce.
(5) The teaching of Moral Theology.

APPENDIX C

MEMORANDUM
BY THE ARCHBISHOPS OF CANTERBURY AND YORK
18th April, 1923, after consideration of all the documents
and letters which they have seen relating to the two Conferences at Malines*

It is, we believe, sufficiently clear from the two papers signed at Malines, and the comptes rendus of the actual conversations, that the provisional suggestions made about possible procedure following upon any attained basis of doctrinal agreement are simply suggestions as to points which may appropriately be discussed seriatim at the proper time. They are not notes of points of agreement which have been even provisionally reached as yet. Of course we have throughout assumed — and the language of both the Memoranda entitles us to assume — as common ground the position that, before any scheme of union is possible, agreement must have been reached on the large doctrinal questions which at present are under the Church of England from the Roman Catholic Church. These doctrinal questions include such subjects of vital importance as the dogmas respecting Transubstantiation and the Immaculate Conception of the Blessed Virgin and most markedly, the underlying question of the doctrine held respecting the position and authority of the Pope. But upon this last point we have thought and said that it would be premature even to discuss the administrative points mentioned in the Memoranda until it has been the subject to fuller conference. It is true that upon this point Cardinal Mercier and Monsignor Van Roey and the Abbé Portal have all, in the papers or letters, given expression to some opinion or have described opinions held. The Cardinal has done this with great fullness. But it has not in our judgement been as yet sufficiently discussed. We have accordingly said that while we are willing that these administrative points should be the subject of further conference this must be conditional upon immediate and full conference first taking place on the question of the Papacy.

It is in our judgement important that this Memorandum should be on record lest, if any of these documents became known in isolated parts or in inaccurate quotations, it might be supposed that the representatives of the Church of England had committed themselves, even provisionally, to any of the suggestions thus made. This is in full accordance with the intimations we have already endeavoured to give both to the Cardinal and to the Anglican representatives who took part in the conversations at Malines.

18th April, 1933.

---

* Original found among Archbishop Davidson's papers at Lambeth Palace Library, London.

LETTER FROM THE ARCHBISHOP OF CANTERBURY
to the Archbishop and Metropolitans of the Anglican Communion*

Lambeth Palace.
Christmas 1923.

My Dear Archbishop,

More than three years have passed since the Lambeth Conference of 1920, and I am told on many sides that it would be a good thing that I should send to the Metropolitans of our Communion a brief summary of the position, as I view it, of the Reunion question, which has during these years been astir.

This letter is not in any strict sense official. It is merely a brief summary of what seems to me personally to be the present features of the scene or 'movement' viewed from an advantageous standpoint. You will pardon me if, for the sake of clearness, I go over some very familiar ground.

I. Start from Lambeth Conference of 1920. Its Report, with special emphasis upon the 'Appeal to All Christian People', to which we had agreed with almost complete unanimity, was, as you know, circulated in many languages and in many lands. The Metropolitans throughout the Anglican Communion have no doubt, in accordance with the request of the Conference, taken steps within their respective areas to confer upon the subject with the local leaders of other churches. Besides this, it was my privilege to send copies officially to the heads of other leading churches throughout the world, and the replies from every quarter. Eastern and Western, and from the English-speaking Churches and Denominations at home and overseas, were uniformly courteous and were sometimes even eager in their expressions of cordiality and hope.

Much has passed during these years with regard to Reunion, and not all of it bears directly upon the Lambeth 'Appeal', but that 'Appeal' has in all cases formed a background to what has been done and said.

2. I would remind you that here in England, within a few weeks of our transmitting the Appeal to the authorities of the different Free Churches, a series of Conferences began to be held at Lambeth between leaders officially appointed by the Federal Council of Evangelical Free Churches and a number of English Bishops. I think I am not exaggerating when I say that these Conferences in their composition, their character and their purpose, have no precedent in the history of the Church in these Islands. The Archbishop of York has throughout taken lead in the discussions, and I cannot sufficiently express the debt owed by the whole Church to the wisdom, determination, and patience with which he has guided the spokesmen on the different sides and assisted them in their efforts to reach agreement in the truth.

You will remember that the first Report of the subjects discussed and agreed upon at these Conferences was issued in May 1922, over the joint signatures of

* G.K.A. Bell, *Documents on Christian Unity*, London, 1955, pp. 130-140.

the two Archbishops and the Moderator of the Federal Council. It treated the crucial topics of the Nature of the Church, the Ministry, and the Place of the Creed in a United Church, and was published by S.P.C.K. under the title of *Church Unity*. On the basis of that Report, and with the full co-operation of the Federal Council, further Conferences have taken place during the past twelve months on the 'Status of the Existing Free Church Ministry'. The Anglican members of the Joint Conference, after repeated discussion with the Free Church representatives and with one another, presented a long Memorandum on that subject to the Federal Council, which in its turn issued last September a statement of the Free Church position, and again expressed the desire that the Conference should be resumed. The whole of these documents have now been issued in a single pamphlet published by S.P.C.K. under the title, '*Reunion. The Lambeth Conference Report and the Free Churches*'.

In addition to this I myself addressed the Wesleyan Conference at Bristol this year on the subject of Christian Unity; and the Archbishop of York has personally commended the '*Appeal*' to the Annual Assemblies of the Baptist Union, the Presbyterian Church of England, and also the Wesleyan Conference. All these Churches, as well as others, have passed Resolutions of general welcome to the 'Appeal'. The Wesleyan Conference has adopted a considered reply of its own.

3. In Scotland the Church of Scotland and the United Free Church of Scotland have been, and are still, engaged on their own union movement, and the time is not yet ripe for the initiation of the formal communications with ourselves, which they have expressed their readiness to take in hand in due course. Meantime I have had the honour, together with the Primus of the Scottish Episcopal Church and the Bishop of Peterborough, of addressing the General Assembly of each Church, after consideration in Committee, adopted a careful and friendly response to the 'Appeal'.

It seems to me therefore that we have a right, with thankfulness to Almighty God, to regard the position, in Great Britain itself, as fraught with abundant hope. There can be no question that the leaders upon all sides, and through them the officers, clerical and lay, of the respective Churches are disposed in quite a novel degree to appreciate one another's position and to look forward to a yet nearer approach.

4. From overseas, reports steadily reach Lambeth, sometimes from the Metropolitans themselves, sometimes in other ways, showing the eager welcome which the 'Appeal to All Christian People' has received both in non-Episcopal and in Episcopal Churches. To remind you of only a few instances: In South India negotiations of a searching kind are in progress between the South India United Church and the Anglican Church. In America, in addition to all the work relating to the proposed World Conference of Faith and Order, the preparations for which are proceeding apace, the Protestant Episcopal Church has shown a remarkable readiness for new opening in its dealings with the members of many European Churches who have come to live in the United States. I have appreciated highly the encouraging news which reaches me from Australia of Conferences at Sydney and at Cronulla between representatives of our own Communion and of the Presbyterian, Methodist, and Congregational Churches. And so I could go on. It seems to me quite clear that in almost every part of the world where the Anglican Communion is found — in Canada,

Australia, New Zealand, East Africa, West Africa and also in Japan, in China, in Egypt, in Palestine, and in many parts of the Continent of Europe — a new spirit of fellowship, a new readiness for understanding and co-operation have been revealed during these eventful years.

5. It will not be forgotten that the Church of Sweden gave a cordial welcome to the Resolutions which the Lambeth Conference adopted with regard to it. In September 1920, the Bishops of Durham and Peterborough, by invitation of the Archbishop of Upsala, took part in the Consecration of two Swedish Bishops in Upsala Cathedral. In April 1922, the Bishops of the Church of Sweden issued a full reply to our Resolutions which was published in the S.P.C.K. magazine *Theology* in July 1922.

6. I pass to the Eastern Orthodox Church and our relations thereto. As you will remember, an important Delegation, officially sent by the Patriarchate of Constantinople, was welcomed by the Lambeth Conference in 1920 and attended meetings of a special Committee which we appointed for the purpose. On its return to Constantinople the Delegation produced a Report which was officially presented to the Holy Synod and was subsequently printed in the *The Christian East* for March 1922. This Report is an important document and raises a number of interesting questions, with some of which our regularly constituted Eastern Churches Committee (appointed at the request of a previous Lambeth Conference) has been invited to deal. Side by side with it a treatise on 'Anglican Ordinations' was published by the late Professor Komnenos, one of the most prominent theologians of the Orthodox Communion, himself a member of the Delegation. In that scholarly treatise the validity of the Anglican Orders is clearly upheld. And, as is now well known, in August 1922 the Patriarch and the Holy Synod of Constantinople issued an official Declaration on Anglican Ordinations in the form of a letter from Patriarch Meletios IV to myself. This document states that 'as before the Orthodox Church, the Ordinations of the Anglican Episcopal confession of Bishops, priests and deacons, possess the same validity as those of the Roman, Old Catholic, and Armenian Churches possess, inasmuch as all essentials are found in them which are held indispensable from the orthodox point of view for the recognition of the "Charisma" of the priesthood derived form Apostolic succession'. I communicated the Declaration formally to the Convocation of Canterbury in full Synod last February, and explained fully its meaning and limitations in a speech which was subsequently translated into Greek. The Address in English and Greek is published in pamphlet form. The Constantinople Declaration was shortly afterwards endorsed by the Patriarch of Jerusalem and by the Church of Cyprus.

7. These are not small matters in the contemporary history of the Church of Christ, and you will, I feel sure, pardon me for thus bringing them to your notice or recollection in a consecutive form. A volume is now in the Press under the title *Documents on Christian Unity*, 1920-4 (Oxford University Press), which will contain not merely the Reports and papers to which I have here referred, but other information on the subject.

8. In addition to all this there remains the question — a question which has features of paramount importance — of the relation of the Church of England to the Church of Rome. You will agree with me in regarding that subject as separated from other reunion problems, not only by the history of centuries of

English life but by present-day claims and utterances. And the plain fact confronts us that in relation to that subject there exist both at home and in the overseas Dominions passions, dormant or awake, which are easily accounted for but which, when once aroused, are difficult to allay. I have myself been repeatedly warned that to touch that subject is unwise. Men urge that 'even if the opportunity be given' it is easier and safer to let it severely alone. That may be true, but you and I are party to the 'Appeal to all Christian People', and I, at least, find it difficult to reconcile that document with an attitude of apathy or sheer timidity as to our touching the Roman Catholic question. Not only are we pledged to the words and spirit of the 'Appeal' itself, but we have before us what was said on the subject by the Committee of the same Lambeth Conference in 1920. We there express our readiness to welcome any friendly discussion between Roman Catholics and Anglicans for which opportunity may be given[1]. I have no right to say that the utterances of the Lambeth Conference have influenced Roman Catholic opinion, but I am certain that they have increased our own responsibilities in the matter. I was accordingly glad when I learned two years ago that a private conference or conversation was about to take place at Malines, between Cardinal Mercier, the venerated Archbishop of Malines, and a few Anglicans, who were to meet under his roof, with a view to the discussion of outstanding and familiar barriers between the Church of England and the Church of Rome. Though I had no responsibility for this arrangement, nor even any official knowledge of it, I was courteously informed of the proposed visit and was furnished with the names of those who were to take part in the informal discussions[2]. The substance of the Conversation which took place was reported to me both by the Cardinal and by my Anglican friends. It necessarily turned in large part upon the position and claims of the Roman See, or in other words, the Primacy of the Pope. A Memorandum upon that and kindred subjects which had been prepared on behalf of the Anglican group was discussed, and the Lambeth Conference 'Appeal to All Christian People' was, I understand, considered paragraph by paragraph. It was suggested that, with a view to a second visit, the two English Archbishops might informally nominate delegates and might suggest the outline of discussion to be followed. I did not see my way to doing this, but in the correspondence which ensued I expressed my readiness to have official cognizance of the arrangements, provided that a corresponding cognizance were given by the Vatican. Satisfied, after correspondence, with regard to that point, I gave what was described as friendly

1. The words are as follows: 'Your Committee feels that it is impossible to make any Report on Reunion with Episcopal Churches without some reference to the Church of Rome, even though it has no Resolution to propose upon the subject. We cannot do better than make our own the words of the Report of 1908, which reminds us of "the fact that there can be no fulfilment of the Divine purpose in any scheme of reunion which does not ultimately include the great Latin Church of the West, with which our history has been so closely associated in the past, and to which we are still bound by many ties of common faith and tradition". But we realize that — to continue the quotation — "any advance in this direction is at present barred by difficulties which we have not ourselves created, and which we cannot of ourselves remove". Should, however, the Church of Rome at any time desire to discuss conditions of reunion we shall be ready to welcome such discussions'.

2. On the Anglican side Dr. Armitage Robinson, Dean of Wells, Dr. Walter Frere and Lord Halifax; and on the Roman Catholic side, His Eminence the Cardinal, Monsignor van Roey, Vicar General, and the Abbé Portal.

cognizance to a second visit of the Anglican group to Malines in March 1923. They again received the kindly hospitality which has been courteously given and gratefully welcomed. The conversation on that occasion turned in part on certain large administrative problems which might arise, if and when a measure of agreement had been reached on the great doctrinal and historical questions sundering the two Churches.

It was agreed that a third Conference should take place. A wish was expressed on both sides that the number of participants should be enlarged, and I took the responsibility of definitely inviting Dr. Charles Gore, late Bishop of Oxford, and Dr. Kidd, Warden of Keble College, Oxford (both of whom had given special attention to the Roman question), to join the Anglican group. This increased my responsibility in the matter, and I found myself in concurrence with His Eminence the Cardinal, as well as with the members of the original group, in pressing the point that prior to any discussion upon the possible administrative questions which might arise, attention should be concentrated upon the great doctrinal and historical issues at stake between the two Churches. Certain memoranda were prepared and circulated[3], and I had the advantage of personally conferring at Lambeth with the five Anglicans who were to take part in the third Conference, together with a few friends and counsellors of my own whom I had invited to meet them. I have always considered it important that our representatives at Conference which take place, whether with Free Churchmen, or Orthodox, or Roman Catholics, should remember that, while each individual remains free to express his own opinions, what is in question is not what any individual may think but what the great Anglican body has in the past maintained or is likely to maintain in the future. I found, as I anticipated, that our visitors to Malines were not likely to forget what the historical Anglican position and claims have been in the past, as set forward for example by the great theologians of the sixteenth and seventeenth centuries — a position which we have no thought of changing or weakening today. It seemed to me to be fair to the Roman Catholic members of the Malines Conference, now augmented by the addition of Monsignor Batiffol and the Abbé Hemmer, that the firmness and coherence, as we believe, of our Anglican doctrine and system should be unmistakably set forward.

Thus arranged, the third Conference was held at Malines a few weeks ago, under the same kindly hospitality as before. There has not yet been time to weigh adequately the record of the conversations which took place, still less the unresolved differences which they exhibit, but I may say at once that, as was inevitable, the discussions are still in a quite elementary stage, and that no estimate, so far as I judge, can yet be formed as to their ultimate value. Needless to say, there has been no attempt to initiate what may be called 'negotiations' of any sort. The Anglicans who have, with my full encouragement, taken part, are in no sense delegates or representatives of the Church as a whole. I had neither the will nor the right to give them that character. This

3. To prevent misunderstanding I ought perhaps to explain that Lord Halifax's second pamphlet, entitled *Further Considerations on Behalf of Reunion*, was published independently, to express his personal view on certain points relating to the origin and growth of the Papacy. That view, as their writings show, is not shared by his Anglican companions at Malines.

is well understood on both sides. They have sought merely to effect some re-statement of controverted questions, and some elucidation of perplexities. And to me it seems indubitable that good must in the Providence of God ensue from the mere fact that men possessing such peculiar qualifications for the task should, in an atmosphere of goodwill on either side, have held quiet and unrestrained converse with a group of Roman Catholic theologians similarly equipped. No further plans are yet prepared, but it is impossible, I think, to doubt that further conversations must follow from the careful talks already held. At the least we have endeavoured in this direction, as in others, to give effect to the formal recommendation of the Lambeth Conference that we should 'invite the authorities of other Churches to confer with [us] concerning the possibility of taking definite steps to co-operate in a common endeavour ... to restore the unity of the Church of Christ'.

I have stated all this somewhat fully, though there is, of course, a great deal more which might be said. Indeed, I hope myself before long to have an opportunity in Convocation or elsewhere of speaking further upon the subject. From the nature of the case the proceedings have of necessity been private. To attempt them publicly would have been obviously futile. For what has been done I am bound to accept full personal responsibility. I have not thought it right, or indeed, practicable, to involve others in that responsibility, though I have confidentially informed all our Diocesan Bishops, and especially the Archbishop of York, of every step that has been taken. The difficulties are immense. You know them as clearly as I do. They may prove to be, for some time to come, insuperable. Paul may plant and Apollos water, it is God who giveth the increase.

9. In this letter, my dear Brother, I have recounted facts and endeavours with some of which you are, I am glad to know, familiar. With all that is astir in the world today, there may be some — you I am sure are not among them — who think that we are devoting too much time and effort to questions of reunion within the Church of Christ.

To us it seems certain that upon the Church of Christ must rest a chief responsibility for every forward step that can be taken towards the healing and the bettering of a distracted world. If the Church is to fulfil such a function in the world, its effort is infinitely weakened so long as it is obliged to go forward in scattered and independent detachments, and not as one body. It is in simple and wholehearted reliance upon the guidance of God the Holy Spirit that we are emboldened to nourish hope and to shape resolve. The vision which our Lord, as we believe, has set before us points the road to reunion. The road may not be short, but we believe it will be sure.

I remain, as always,
My dear Archbishop,
Your faithful brother and servant in our Lord Jesus Christ,
Randall Cantuar.

LETTER FROM CARDINAL MERCIER TO HIS CLERGY

LES "CONVERSATIONS DE MALINES"*
Lettre de S.E. le Card. D.J. Mercier à son Clergé.

Malines, le 18 janvier 1924
Fête de la Chaire de saint Pierre à Rome

Chers confrères et dévoués collaborateurs,

Voilà deux années, et davantage, que je suis en relations intimes avec quelques personnalités du monde Anglican auxquelles je porte une estime profonde et une affection sincère. Nous nous sommes rencontrés plusieurs fois; nous avons échangé avec elles des correspondances au sujet de ce que nous avons le plus ardemment à cœur, les intérêts de l'Église Catholique notre Mère.

Il ne nous serait pas venu à la pensée de vous mettre au courant de ces relations, pour la raison fort simple que leur objet est, de sa nature, confidentiel et que nous nous sommes engagés, au surplus, de part et d'autre, à n'en rien livrer au public sans un accord préalable.

Cet accord a été gardé. L'Archevêque de Cantorbéry n'a rien révélé de ce qui forma le thème de nos conversations et de leurs conclusions, mais il a jugé l'heure venue pour lui de fixer ses coreligionnaires sur l'attitude qu'il avait prise à l'égard de nos conférences. C'était, de sa part, un acte de loyauté auquel nous accordâmes, d'ailleurs, notre plein acquiescement. C'était aussi un acte de courage, car, étant donné l'état d'esprit, déclaré ou sourd, très répandu encore dans les milieux Anglais non catholiques, et que l'on désigne souvent d'un mot, "l'antipapisme", il était aisé de prévoir qu'un témoignage de déférence, ne fût-il qu'implicite et indirect, à un évêque, à un Cardinal de l'Église de Rome, attirerait à son auteur autre chose que des sympathies et des compliments.

Dans une Lettre datée de Noël 1923, adressée aux archevêques et aux métropolitains de la communion anglicane, le Dr. Randall Davidson, archevêque de Cantorbéry, fait allusion aux "Conversations de Malines" et déclare que, sans y avoir officiellement engagé son autorité, il ne les a pas ignorées, y a pris intérêt, et en espère des résultats heureux.

Les milieux protestants et un certain nombre de catholiques s'émurent fort de cette révélation. Pendant plusieurs semaines, les journaux et les revues y ont vu un thème à vives controverses, dont l'écho a passé la Manche; le désir du public d'avoir chaque matin des nouvelles à sensations, l'ardeur des journalistes à lui en fournir qui allassent crescendo, créèrent autour de nos paisibles réunions de Malines une atmosphère d'agitation factice, à laquelle il est de mon devoir de les soustraire.

Je vous dirai les faits, à l'effet de les rétablir dans la simplicité de leur vérité.

Je vous en fournirai les raisons déterminantes.

Et, puisque l'occasion heureuse m'en est offerte, j'essaierai d'en tirer, Chers

* G.K.A. BELL, *Documents On Christian Unity*, London, 1955, pp. 141-157.

Confrères, pour vous et pour nous un enseignement qui fait loi dans le ministère pastoral.

I
Les Faits.

Les autorités religieuses, les hommes d'ordre attentifs à l'évolution des idées et des événements, s'effraient de la déchristianisation des masses et de la rapidité avec laquelle la disparition de la Foi au surnaturel mène à la négation de toute religion. Le phénomène est général, mais il est plus grave, plus saillant chez les nations protestantes qu'en pays catholiques.

Déjà Newman, en 1877, l'écrivait: "J'ai toujours pensé, disait-il, que nous sommes arrivés à une époque où l'infidélité se répand partout. En fait, pendant ces dernières années, les eaux se sont élevées comme un déluge. J'entrevois, pour après ma mort, le moment où seuls les sommets des montagnes apparaîtront comme des îles dans le désert des eaux". Et il ajoutait: "Je parle surtout du monde protestant"[1].

Oui, "surtout dans le monde protestant", parce que, là, les divergences doctrinales des "confessions" ou "dénominations" qui s'y multiplient privent les consciences religieuses du spectacle lumineux et réconfortant de l'unité dans la Foi. La désagrégation de la communion protestante conduit au libéralisme en matière religieuse, c'est-à-dire, à cette sorte de croyance vague que toutes les religions représentent des opinions libres qui se valent, pour la raison qu'aucune d'elles ne peut invoquer à son profit les preuves d'une Révélation positive et divine; alors, l'indifférentisme religieux lui-même conduit inévitablement à l'irréligion, au sectarisme antireligieux.

Les Protestants clairvoyants virent se réaliser les prédictions de Newman. Ceux d'entre eux qui ont gardé la Foi à la divinité du Christ et de son Église, ceux qui prient pour eux-mêmes et pour les âmes dont ils ont la charge, discernent le péril, se sentent le devoir de s'appliquer à le conjurer. Eux aussi croient à la parole des Actes des Apôtres: "Il n'y a de salut que dans le Christ", *"Non est in alio aliquo salus"*[2].

C'est un groupe de ces hommes de Foi, une élite intellectuelle et morale, que la divine Providence a conduite vers nous et que nous eûmes la consolation d'accueillir.

Nos deux premiers visiteurs furent Lord Halifax, que toute l'Angleterre, sans distinction de religion, ni de parti, vénère et affectionne, et M. l'Abbé Portal, fils de saint Vincent de Paul, prêtre de la Mission, ancien Supérieur de Grand Séminaire, et qui fut intimement mêlé, sous Léon XIII, à la question de la validité des Ordinations anglicanes; il exerce aujourd'hui auprès de la jeunesse universitaire de Paris un apostolat de premier plan.

Ils nous procurèrent, en octobre 1921, l'occasion de faire personnellement leur connaissance et nous revinrent les 6, 7 et 8 décembre de la même année, accompagnés de deux Anglicans de marque, le Dr. Armitage Robinson, doyen de Wells, ami intime de l'Archevêque de Cantorbéry, et le Dr. Frere, supérieur de la communauté religieuse des Résurrectionnistes, devenu depuis lors évêque

---

1. Wilfrid WARD, *The Life of Newman*, ii, p. 416.
2. Act. Ap. IV, 12.

de Truro, l'un et l'autre auteurs de publications hautement appréciées sur des sujets scripturaires et d'ancienne littérature chrétienne.

Pour leur donner accueil, nous invitâmes à se joindre à nous M. l'Abbé Portal, et notre savant et dévoué Vicaire Général, Mgr Van Roey, Maître en théologie de l'Université de Louvain.

Il fut, dès l'abord, entendu que l'objet et les résultats éventuels de nos entretiens resteraient privés, jusqu'au jour où, de commun accord, nous jugerions utile et opportun d'en publier les conclusions.

Les deux groupes se retrouvèrent à Malines en mars 1923.

En novembre de la même année, eut lieu une troisième réunion à laquelle prirent part, cette fois, outre le doyen Robinson et le Dr. Frere, le célèbre Dr. Charles Gore, ancien évêque d'Oxford, sorti du ministère actif pour se vouer exclusivement à ses travaux de science religieuse, et le Dr. Kidd, Préfet du Keble College, un des hommes les plus considérés d'Oxford.

Mgr Batiffol, chanoine de Notre-Dame de Paris, si universellement estimé pour ses travaux sur les origines chrétiennes, et M. l'Abbé Hemmer, curé de Saint-Mandé, qui professa jadis l'histoire à l'Institut Catholique de Paris, avaient bien voulu venir se joindre à nous et nous apporter leur précieux concours.

Tels étaient nos hôtes: voici quel fut le caractère de nos réunions.

Celles-ci, de la première à la dernière, furent *privées*: c'étaient des *conversations* dans un salon privé.

Ce n'était donc pas la rencontre d'autorités ecclésiastiques envoyant l'une vers l'autre leurs délégués officiels.

Cette déclaration que nous émettons ici, l'archevêque de Cantorbéry l'a formulée nettement dans son message à ses Métropolitains; on semble n'avoir pas voulu le remarquer. Il savait, certes, ses amis en relation à Malines avec des membres du clergé catholique; il suivait avec un sympathique intérêt le développement de nos entretiens, mais, dès l'abord, il avait tenu à affirmer, comme nous même d'ailleurs, que nous n'engagions d'aucune façon, ni les communautés auxquelles nous appartenons, ni l'autorité que, dans une certaine mesure, nous représentions.

Nos échanges d'idées ne furent donc pas des "négociations". Pour négocier, il faut être porteur d'un mandat et, ni de part ni d'autre, nous n'avions de mandat. Aussi bien, en ce qui nous concerne, n'en avions-nous pas sollicité: il nous suffisait de savoir que nous marchions d'accord avec l'Autorité suprême, bénis et encouragés par Elle.

Nous nous mîmes à l'œuvre, animés d'un même désir de mutuelle compréhension et d'aide fraternelle.

Évidemment, sur plusieurs questions fondamentales le désaccord des deux groupes était notoire; de part et d'autre, on en avait conscience. Mais, nous nous disions que, si la vérité a ses droits, la charité a ses devoirs; nous pensions que, peut-être, en parlant à cœur ouvert et avec la persuasion intime que, dans un vaste conflit historique, qui a duré des siècles, tous les torts ne sont pas d'un seul côté; en précisant les termes de certaines questions en litige, nous ferions tomber des préventions, des méfiances, dissiperions des équivoques, aplanirions les voies au bout desquelles une âme loyale, aidée de la grâce, découvrirait s'il pouvait plaire à Dieu, ou retrouverait la vérité.

Le fait est qu'à l'heure de clôture de chacune de nos trois réunions les membres se sentaient plus étroitement liés, plus confiant les uns dans les autres, qu'à leur prise de contact. Nos hôtes nous l'ont dit; nous l'ont écrit; nous leur avons tenu le même langage; je suis heureux de le répéter ici.

Cependant, l'on pense bien que, lorsque surgirent des questions essentielles — telle la Primauté du Pape définie par le Concile du Vatican, et qui fut la première et la dernière à l'ordre du jour — ni mes amis ni moi n'eûmes, un instant, la pensée de sacrifier à un désir insensé d'union à tout prix un seul article du Credo catholique, apostolique et romain.

Nos rencontres furent donc des conversations privées; elles n'engageaient que notre responsabilité personnelle; elles eurent un caractère amical; j'ajoute qu'elles furent instructives et édifiantes.

Aucun livre ne vaut un commerce oral. La conversation est révélatrice de choses intimes qui ne passent pas dans la lettre imprimée.

Les hommes sont faits pour s'aimer les uns les autres; il n'est pas rare que des cœurs mutuellement étrangers qui auraient pu, à distance, se croire ennemis, goûtent, à se comprendre, un charme pénétrant qu'ils n'auraient pas soupçonné.

Nos compagnons, à leur départ, avaient l'âme dilatée. C'est peut-être la première fois, depuis quatre cents ans, disait l'un d'eux, que des hommes d'études, protestants et catholiques, aient pu s'entretenir, avec une franchise entière, pendant des heures et des heures, sur les sujets les plus graves qui intellectuellement les divisent, sans qu'un instant la cordialité de leurs rapports en ait été troublée ni leur confiance dans l'avenir déconcertée.

Assurément, le rapprochement des cœurs n'est pas l'unité dans la Foi, mais il y dispose.

Des hommes, surtout des groupements d'hommes qui ont vécu longtemps étrangers les uns aux autres, dans une atmosphère chargée de méfiances sinon d'animosités, ancrées dans les profondeurs des consciences par une tradition quatre fois séculaire, sont mal préparés à se rendre aux argumentations, si serrées soient-elles, que veulent leur imposer leurs contradicteurs.

Avant de définir la justification chrétienne, le Concile de Trente ne dit-il pas que, pour s'y disposer, il faut préparer les cœurs à écouter la parole de Dieu: "*Praeparate corda vestra Domino*"[3]?

Si la Providence divine a conduit vers nous, plutôt que vers d'autres plus directement mêlés à des controverses religieuses, certains chrétiens dissidents, ne serait-ce pas parce que, à raison même de notre isolement, il nous était possible d'accomplir, dans une atmosphère plus sereine, une tâche toute préliminaire à des négociations et à des déterminations qui devraient éventuellement se poursuivre et se conclure ailleurs?

Au milieu même du bruit qui se faisait autour de la Lettre de l'Archevêque à ses Métropolitains, le membre de nos réunions auquel je faisais allusion à l'instant m'écrivait: "Il serait malaisé à qui n'habite pas l'Angleterre de mesurer l'importance que prendra dans l'opinion publique le résultat qui vient d'être acquis. Même si le succès immédiat est peu considérable, je crois qu'il marquera pour beaucoup un point de départ vers de nouveaux progrès et que nous aurons les meilleures raisons d'en rendre grâces à Dieu"[4].

3. I Regum, vii. 3.
4. Avec la permission de l'auteur nous citons l'original: "It is hard for any one outside

Au surplus, à l'issue de chacune de nos conférences nous prîmes congé les uns des autres en nous promettant de prier, de faire prier nos ouailles pour le succès de la cause sainte qui nous avait réunis.

Il me souvient que le Dr. Kidd, au début de notre dernier entretien, me disait, et j'espère qu'il ne trouvera pas indiscret que je le redise: "J'ai prié avec mes élèves avant de quitter Oxford et je sais qu'ils invoquent en ce moment l'Esprit Saint pour le succès de nos travaux".

Quant à nous, mes chers Confrères, nous savons que, dans son Encyclique "*Provida Matris*" du 5 mai 1895, le Pape Léon XIII, de sainte mémoire, demanda aux catholiques du monde entier des prières spéciales à l'Esprit Saint, "pour la réconciliation, qu'il espérait avec une "ferme confiance, de nos frères séparés". Nous savons que, reprenant avec plus d'ampleur encore, dans son Encyclique "*Divinum illud munus*" du 9 mai 1897, la même pensée, il prescrivait une neuvaine de prières, à laquelle vous restez fidèles chaque année, de l'Ascension à la Pentecôte, afin de hâter la réalisation bénie de l'unité chrétienne, "*ad maturandum christianae unitatis bonum*".

Le Pape Benoît XV, n'a-t-il pas encouragé une octave de prières, du 18 janvier, fête de la chaire de Saint Pierre, au 25 janvier, fête de la conversion de saint Paul, pour obtenir le retour de nos frères séparés à l'unité de l'Église?

Et notre Père bien-aimé, le Pape Pie XI, ne nous révèle-t-Il pas les sentiments de charité et de piété de sa grande âme lorsque, dans son Encyclique si paternelle "*Ecclesiam Dei*", Il invite Latins et Orientaux à se mieux comprendre et prie ceux-ci de ne pas rendre l'Église Romaine responsable des préjugés, des torts personnels de ceux-là; lorsque aux uns et aux autres. Il demande de prier, afin que se réalise l'accord de tous les peuples dans l'unité oecuménique, "*haec populorum omnium in oecumenica unitate consensio*"?

Tel est donc l'exposé rapide des faits.

Voici le pourquoi de nos "conversations".

II
Pourquoi ces conversations?

Pourquoi? Tout d'abord, parce que je n'ai pas le droit de me dérober à une occasion qui vient à moi de faire un acte de charité fraternelle et d'hospitalité chrétienne.

Pour rien au monde, je ne voudrais autoriser un de nos frères séparés à dire qu'il a frappé de confiance à la porte d'un évêque catholique romain et que cet évêque catholique romain a refusé de lui ouvrir.

Une grande nation fut, pendant plus de huit siècles, notre sœur aimée; elle donna à l'Église une phalange de saints que nous honorons encore aujourd'hui dans notre liturgie; elle a gardé au sein d'un vaste empire des ressources étonnantes de vitalité chrétienne, elle exerce un rayonnement immense sur d'innombrables missions, mais elle porte au flanc une blessure; nous, catholiques, maintenus par la grâce de Dieu dans la vérité intégrale, nous nous lamentons sur le déchirement criminel qui l'arracha, il y a quatre siècles, à

England to understand how serious the step will appear in the public mind, both among those who care deeply and among those who do not. Even if we get but little further at present, I believe that this will mean a new outlook for very many, and that we shall have good reason for true gratitude to God.

l'Église notre Mère; et, ce sont des catholiques qui voudraient qu'à l'exemple du Lévite et du Prêtre de la Loi ancienne réprouvés par notre divin Sauveur dans la parabole du Samaritain un évêque catholique passât à côté de ce grand blessé, dans une indifférence superbe, refusât de verser une goutte d'huile dans sa plaie béante, de la bander, et de s'essayer à amener l'infirme à l'hôtel-Dieu où l'appelle la divine Miséricorde!

Je me serais jugé coupable si j'avais commis cette lâcheté.

Oh! je le sais, ceux qui nous jugent de travers ne voudront pas méconnaître nos intentions charitables, mais ils estiment notre intervention inopportune et inefficace.

Inopportune, parce qu'il vaut mieux, selon eux, laisser les églises séparées aller à une décomposition complète, s'accuser plus fort le contraste entre l'erreur et la vérité: arrivé aux extrêmes, le mal épouvantera, et ce sera l'heure du triomphe de la vérité.

Inefficace, parce que, semble-t-il, je n'emploie pas la bonne méthode d'apostolat, celle des conversions individuelles.

Pesons, un instant, ces deux griefs.

Je ne trouve nulle part préconisée ni approuvée dans l'Évangile la politique du pire. J'y lis, au contraire, qu'il ne faut pas étouffer la mèche qui fume encore.

Que des protestants croyants tombent dans le libéralisme en matière religieuse, que ses victimes deviennent indifférentes à toute religion positive, aboutissent à l'irréligion, aillent grossir les rangs de l'athéisme, et, bientôt après, ceux de l'anarchie: c'est un mal, un grand mal.

Des chrétiens sincères se sentent impuissants — ne le sommes-nous pas nous-mêmes dans une moindre mesure? — à enrayer ce mal, font appel à notre aide secourable, nous invitent tout au moins à nous concerter avec eux pour enrayer l'irréligion, et il se trouverait des esprits outranciers pour nous l'interdire!

Voilà donc, déjà, un premier service positif à rendre à nos frères séparés, une première raison de les accueillir à cœur ouvert.

Soit, dira-t-on peut-être, mais là n'était pas votre objectif principal: il s'agissait, avant tout, d'exercer une action directe sur des croyants, membres de "la Haute-Église", afin de les ramener à l'Église de Rome.

L'objectif principal! Qu'en savez-vous? Nous n'avons jamais sérié, par ordre d'importance, les motifs inspirateurs de notre conduite.

Nous avons considéré une situation d'ensemble où nous apparaissaient des âmes, soucieuses à la fois d'elle-mêmes et de leur influence sociale. Nous avons eu la confiance de penser que nous pouvions rendre un service d'aide spirituelle à nos frères et trouvé là une seconde raison de converser avec eux.

Mais vous jugez que nous nous y prenons mal pour dénouer cette situation: notre méthode de travail est, selon vous, maladroite; l'expérience vous a appris qu'il faut renoncer à agir sur les collectivités; il faut ne viser que les individus.

De quel droit limitez-vous l'action de la divine Miséricorde? Agissez, tant que vous le pouvez, sur les individus; éclairez, de votre mieux, chacune des âmes que Dieu met sur votre chemin, priez pour elle, dévouez-vous à elle: parfait; nul ne pourrait songer à vous en blâmer.

Mais, qu'est-ce qui vous autorise à écarter les collectivités? C'est votre exclusivisme qui est condamnable.

Laissez-moi rafraîchir vos souvenirs. Écoutez la grande voix de Léon XIII, qui, le 14 avril 1895, dans sa Lettre Apostolique "*Amantissimae Voluntatis*", s'adressait, non aux individus, mais à la masse du peuple anglais, "*ad Anglos*". Relisez cette Encyclique, elle a pour destinataire la nation appelée par le Pape "*gens Anglorum illustris*"; et quand, au moment de conclure, le saint Pontife pressent les objections que des pessimistes opposeront à son optimisme, il écrit: "Des difficultés, il y en a, oui, mais elles ne sont pas de nature à ralentir le moins du monde notre charité apostolique, ni à décourager vos volontés". "*Difficultates, si quae sunt, non sunt tamen ejusmodi ut aut caritatem nostram Apostolicam omnino iis retardari, aut voluntatem vestram deterreri oporteat*". "Sans doute, les révolutions et une séparation plusieurs fois séculaire ont enraciné des dissentiments dans les cœurs: mais, est-ce une raison de renoncer à tout espoir de réconciliation et de paix?" "*Esto, quod rerum conversionibus ac diuturnitate ipsa dissidium convaluerit: num idcirco reconciliationis pacisque remedia respuat omnia*"? "Nullement, s'il plaît à Dieu". "*Nequaquam ita, si Deo placet*".

"Pour évaluer les résultats que peut promettre l'avenir, il ne faut pas se baser seulement sur des calculs humains, il faut surtout tenir compte de la puissance et de la miséricorde de Dieu". "*Sunt eventus rerum non provisione humana tantummodo sed maxime virtute pietateque divina metiendi*".

"Lorsque nous sommes aux prises avec une œuvre vaste et laborieuse", — c'est toujours le Pape qui parle — "ayons une intention droite et le cœur généreux; et Dieu alors sera avec nous; c'est à triompher des obstacles que se révèle avec le plus d'éclat la beauté de l'action de la divine Providence". "*In rebus enim magnis atque arduis, si modo sint sincero et bono animo susceptae, adest homini Deus, cujus Providentia ab ipsis inceptorum difficultatibus capit quo magnificentius eluceat*".

Une année et demie plus tard, en septembre 1896, le Pape se voit obligé d'infliger aux Anglicans une déception amère: il proclame l'invalidité de leurs ordinations. Va-t-il abandonner ses larges espoirs et ne préconiser plus que la propagande d'individu à individu? Au contraire, il conclut sa Lettre Apostolique "*Apostolicae curae*" par un appel direct aux ministres qu'il a eu la douleur de peiner et il conjure les individus et la masse de s'inspirer ensuite de l'exemple de leur conversion.

"Nous ne cesserons pas, dit-il, de travailler, autant que nous le pourrons, à leur réconciliation avec l'Église; les individus et les groupes trouveront alors en eux, c'est notre ardent désir, de puissants exemples à imiter". "*Nos quidem, quantum omni ope licuerit, corum (religionis ministrorum) cum Ecclesia reconciliationem fovere non desistemus; ex qua singuli et ordines, id quod vehementer cupimus*, multum capere possunt ad imitandum*".

C'est que, mes chers Confrères, aujourd'hui encore, en dépit de toutes les déclamations emphatiques sur les progrès intellectuels des masses populaires, sur l'indépendance de leur pensée et la souveraineté de leurs initiatives, le peuple ne précède pas, il suit, il ne commande pas, il obéit. Même en démocratie, le régime social reste oligarchique. Des tribuns démagogues, d'une part, des élites, d'autre part, se disputent l'hégémonie des foules, les premiers pour prêcher la violence et soulever les révolutions, les secondes, pour sauvegarder l'ordre et la discipline.

Si donc il est dans le plan de la divine Providence que nos frères séparés de nous depuis Luther, Henri VIII et la reine Élisabeth, rentrent un jour dans le giron de l'Église, il appartient aux élites d'ouvrir les voies à ce mouvement de

retour. Que des autorités morales respectées de tous entrent dans une conception plus sereine des relations voulues par le Christ entre les fidèles, l'épiscopat
et la Papauté, un grand pas sera fait dans le sens de l'unité catholique. C'est ce
que Léon XIII déclarait si nettement dans sa Lettre *"ad Anglos"*; c'est ce dont,
à la suite de cet illustre Pontife, nous avons essayé de nous pénétrer dans nos
"conversations de Malines".

Si, après cela, vous nous demandez quelles étaient, quelles sont encore
aujourd'hui nos espérances, nous ne pouvons que vous répondre, avec Notre
Saint-Père le Pape Pie XI, que "l'unité des peuples dans la Foi catholique est,
avant tout, l'œuvre de Dieu", *"Haec populorum omnium in oecumenica unitate
consensio opus in primis est Dei ..."*[5]. La Providence universelle la réalise dans le
temps avec force et douceur, *"Attingit ... ad finem fortiter et disponit omnia
suaviter"*[6], mais l'heure des résultats est son secret. Il y emploie les causes
secondes; aux apôtres de son divin Fils Il daigne demander leur collaboration:
de personne Il ne réclame, à personne Il ne promet le succès.

III
Un enseignement.
La condition essentielle de la fécondité de l'apostolat.

Cette condition, le Vicaire du Christ nous l'a rappelée dans cet avertissement:
"Les grands événements religieux de l'histoire ne se peuvent évaluer par des
calculs humains".

Dans une œuvre dont le résultat est le salut des âmes, le facteur essentiel n'est
ni la sagesse humaine, ni la sagacité des tacticiens, c'est la bonne simplicité
évangélique, la foi à la divine miséricorde, à la toute-puissance de la grâce qui
suppléera, au besoin, à l'insuffisance des procédés.

Cette foi ardente est à l'origine, au milieu, au terme de tout effort d'apostolat.

Seule, elle est capable de soutenir la constance du missionnaire; seule elle lui
assurera, quoi qu'il advienne, sa récompense.

Dans le domaine surnaturel, "ce n'est", dit saint Paul, "ni de vouloir, ni de
courir qui importe, c'est de se fier à la miséricorde de Dieu". *"Neque volentis,
neque currentis, sed miserentis est Dei"*[7].

"Vous aurez beau planter", dit-il encore, "arroser vos plantations, un seul a
le pouvoir de donner aux organismes vivants la croissance, c'est Dieu". *"Neque
qui plantat est aliquid, neque qui rigat, sed qui incrementum dat, Deus"*[8].

Vous vous impatientez, le succès est lent à venir, vos peines vous semblent
perdues. Soyez sur vos gardes; la nature et ses empressements vous égarent: un
effort de charité n'est jamais perdu. Mais "les fruits de salut réclament une
longue patience:" *"fructum afferatis in patientia"*[9].

Ne voyez-vous pas comment la Providence conduit les causes secondes? Dans
l'ordre de la nature, le laboureur jette les graines dans ses sillons laborieusement
creusés, puis il laisse passer les frimas de l'hiver, il attend le soleil du printemps,
les chaleurs de l'été, et ce n'est qu'après cette longue attente, faite d'alternances

---

5. Encycl. *Ecclesiam Dei.*
6. Sap. viii, 1.
7. Rom. ix. 16.
8. I Cor. iii. 7.
9. Luc. viii. 15. Cfr. 2 Cor. vi. 4.

de craintes et d'espoirs, qu'il a enfin la joie de récolter et d'engranger ses moissons.

Nous aussi, moissonneurs d'âmes, le Christ nous en a prévenus, nous avons à semer à la sueur de notre front, et, le plus souvent, dans les larmes, avant que sonne l'heure de la moisson; et quand sonnera cette heure bénie un autre vraisemblablement aura pris notre place.

"*Alius est qui seminat, et alius est qui metit*"[10]. "*Qui seminant in lacrymis, in exultatione metent. Euntes ibant et flebant mittentes semina sua. Venientes autem venient cum exultatione, portantes manipulos suos*"[11].

Conclusion.

Mes bien chers Confrères, je conclus. Si j'ai pris aujourd'hui la parole pour vous mettre au courant d'un effort qui, dans ma pensée, devait rester secret, c'est parce que je me suis aperçu que plusieurs de nos confrères d'Outre-Manche, égarés par des informations fantaisistes et des commentaires hasardés de la presse, interprétaient erronément mon action et s'en offensaient; c'est aussi parce que, dénaturée à vos yeux, cette action eût pu, non seulement me priver d'un pieux concours que j'attends de vous en ceci comme en tout ce qu'il m'est donné d'entreprendre à la gloire de notre Dieu, mais fausser même la conception spirituellement désintéressée que vous devez vous faire de l'apostolat.

J'espère avoir réussi à dissiper le léger nuage de poussière qui, un instant, s'est interposé entre nos amis d'Angleterre et nous-mêmes.

J'espère aussi avoir avivé vos sympathies pour la cause sainte de l'unité de l'Église, en réponse au vœu suprême du Pasteur des pasteurs, *le* Pasteur par excellence, Notre Seigneur Jésus: "*Ut omnes unum sint*" "Que tous ne fassent qu'un!"

"Je suis *le* bon Pasteur", dit-Il; "je connais (d'une connaissance toute chargée d'amour) les brebis qui sont miennes, et celles qui sont miennes me connaissent, de même que mon Père me connaît (et m'aime) et que je connais (et que j'aime) mon Père. Aussi donne-je ma vie pour le troupeau (confié à mes soins). "*Ego sum Pastor bonus: et cognosco oves meas et cognoscunt me meae, sicut novit me Pater et ego agnosco Patrem*".

Mais aussitôt, Il ajoute: "Puis, j'ai d'autres brebis encore". — Il ne dit pas: "Je les aurai", ni "Je les voudrais avoir", Il dit: "Je les ai, elles sont à moi, *habeo*"; — oui, "J'ai d'autres brebis encore qui, présentement, ne font pas partie de mon bercail; il faut me les amener, et alors, quand vous me les aurez amenées, proche de moi, et qu'elles entendront ma voix, il n'y aura plus qu'un seul bercail et un unique Pasteur". "*Et alias oves habeo, quae non sunt ex hoc ovili: et illas oportet me adducere, et vocem meam audient, et fiet unum ovile et unus pastor*"[12].

Vous l'avez entendue, mes chers Confrères, la parole du Maître:
"Oportet", "il faut me les amener".

Allez donc dans les broussailles, le long des sentiers rocailleux, sous le soleil brûlant du désert, allez partout où il y a des brebis à découvrir et à sauver.

---

10. Joan. iv. 38.
11. Ps. cxxv. 5-6.
12. Joan. x. 14-16.

Ne vous préoccupez pas du succès; Dieu ne l'exige pas de vous; ce qu'Il réclame de vous, dit saint Bernard, c'est le soin des malades, Il se réserve de les guérir: *"Curam exigeris, non curationem"*[13].

À travers tout l'exercice de votre ministère pastoral, priez, peinez, donnez, dépensez-vous; commencez, tenez bon, persévérez; fidèles toujours au mot de saint Bernard, ne perdez jamais confiance; à vous le travail, à Dieu le succès, *"Noli diffidere, curam exigeris, non curationem"*.

Votre tout dévoué in X°,
† D.J. Card. MERCIER, *Archev. de Malines.*

---

13. *De Consideratione*, Lib. iv, Cap. ii.

L'ÉGLISE ANGLICANE UNIE NON ABSORBÉE*

INTRODUCTION

1. À ne considérer que le droit divin, tous les évêques sont égaux entre eux: un seul, le successeur de Pierre, l'évêque de Rome, est établi le chef suprême du corps épiscopal et de l'Église catholique universelle. Sa juridiction épiscopal s'étend à toutes les Églises particulières sans exception: *Episcopus catholicus*.

2. Mais le droit humain, soit coutumier, soit positif, a admis entre les évêques une hiérarchie de juridiction qui a créé entre eux des rapports de supériorité et de subordination: patriarches, primats, archevêques, suffragants. Pour être légitimes et conformes au droit divin, ces pouvoirs doivent être ou établis explicitement, ou admis implicitement, ou légitimés *post factum* par le pouvoir suprême dont nous avons parlé au numéro 1.

3. Ces deux principes ont reçu leur parfaite application dans l'établissement et toute l'histoire de l'Église anglicane pendant les dix premiers siècles de son existence (594-1537). D'une part, la constitution de cette Église en un organisme d'une autonomie très accentuée grâce à la dépendance de tout l'épiscopat anglais sous la juridiction très effective et très étendue du patriarche de Cantorbéry. D'autre part, la reconnaissance théorique et pratique la plus explicite de la juridiction suprême des Pontifes romains, et la subordination sans équivoque du pouvoir patriarcal de Cantorbéry au siège de Pierre, qui a fait de l'Église anglicane *l'Église la plus foncièrement et fidèlement romaine* de l'Occident et de l'Orient.

4. En d'autres termes, d'une part l'Église anglicane apparaît dans toute son histoire, non comme une juxtaposition de diocèses rattachés à Rome, sans liens hiérarchiques efficaces et sérieux entre eux, mais comme un corps fortement organisé, comme un tout compact et unifié sous l'autorité des successeurs de saint Augustin; organisation si conforme aux aspirations de cette nation autonome et insulaire, éprise de "*self-governement*" et de "*splendid isolement*".

Et d'autre part, aucune Église aussi romaine dans ses origines dans ses traditions, dans son esprit, dans son histoire; aucune si rattachée au siège apostolique, à l'Église-mère et maîtresse de toutes les autres, au point qu'après quatre siècles de séparation, un écrivain a pu dire: "L'Angleterre est une cathédrale catholique habitée par des protestants".

5. Large autonomie interne et fidèle dépendance romaine: telles sont les deux caractéristiques de son histoire; telles sont peut-être aussi les possibilités de la réconciliation. Notre rapport a pour but d'envisager ce double aspect.

Premier paragraphe: Démonstration historique de ce double caractère: Point d'histoire.

Deuxième paragraphe: Possibilité d'un statut catholique actuel de l'Église anglicane s'inspirant de ces données historiques: Point de droit canonique.

Conclusion

* *L'Église anglicane unie non absorbée*, Malines, 1977, pp. 11-24.

§ 1. Point d'histoire

1. Dès l'origine, saint Augustin de Cantorbéry a été constitué chef de l'Église d'Angleterre par saint Grégoire le Grand, revêtu par lui du pallium, insigne des pouvoirs patriarcaux (*usum tibi pallii in ea ac sola missarum solemnia aganda concedimus...*) (*Epist. ad Augustinum* citée par le vénérable Bède, *Hist. Eccles. Anglorum* M.L., t. XCV, col. 69), comportant une juridiction effective sur tous les évêques présents et futurs du royaume d'Angleterre: "*Britanorum vero omnium episcoporum tuae curam Fraternitati committimus, ut indocti doceantur, infirmi persuasione roborentur, perversi auctoritate corrigantur*". (*Epist. ad Aug.* M.L., t. LXXVII, col. 1192.)

2. Aucun doute n'est possible sur la portée effective de cette juridiction patriarcale. En effet, saint Augustin voulut obtenir des précisions et demanda si son pouvoir s'étendait également sur les évêques des Gaules qu'il fréquente sans doute à l'occasion de ses voyages à Rome. Saint Grégoire lui écrit: *In Galliarum episcopos nullam tibi auctoritatem tribuimus, quia ab antiquis praede-cessorum temporibus pallium Arelatensis episcopus recepit, quem nos privare auctoritate percepta minime debemus... Ipse autem auctoritate propria episcopos Galliarum judicare non poteris sed suadendo, blandiendo, bona quoque tua opera eorum imitationi monstrando... Britannorum vero omnium episcoporum tuae curam fraternitati committimus etc...* Il n'est donc pas question d'une préséance d'honneur ou d'une influence fraternelle: l'évêque d'Arles en Gaule et l'évêque de Cantorbéry en Grande-Bretagne jouissent sur toutes les Églises de leurs pays des pouvoirs patriarcaux.

3. Cette juridiction patriarcale est conférée par un symbole aussi vénérable que significatif, l'imposition du *pallium*; et pour comprendre les documents utilisés dans cette enquête, il faut bien saisir toute la portée de ce rite d'investiture auquel jadis on attachait tant d'importance. Le *pallium* est un vêtement, large écharpe de laine, qui protégeait le cou et les épaules. Le *pallium* des Pontifes ne tarda pas à s'enrichir d'une signification plus haute: il symbolisa le pouvoir du bon Pasteur qui prend sur ses épaules la brebis égarée et la tient enlacée autour de son cou. Aussi pour communiquer à un prélat la participa-tion au pouvoir du suprême Pasteur, quoi de plus naturel que de le *revêtir* du *vêtement* symbolique du successeur de Pierre, du *pallium*: c'est *l'investiture* pontificale. Déjà ancien sous saint Grégoire le Grand [voir la lettre à saint Augustin citée plus haut: *ab antiquis temporibus*], ce symbole était en grande vénération au moyen âge: confectionné avec la laine d'agneaux solennellement offerts à l'autel, il est béni par le Pape dans la Basilique vaticane en la fête de saint Pierre; on le dépose ensuite sur la Confession du Prince des Apôtres en attendant qu'il soit donné. Il est ensuite postulé, délivré, imposé dans trois cérémonies successives: c'est le signe de l'investiture d'un pouvoir supra-épisco-pal qui ne peut avoir pour origine que le tombeau du successeur de Pierre: "*in quo est plenitudo pontificalis officii cum archiepiscopalis nominis appellatione*".

Aussi en imposant le *pallium* à Augustin, saint Grégoire lui disait-il: *Tua vero fraternitas non solum eos episcopos quos ordinaverit, neque hos tantummodo qui per Eboracae episcopum fuerunt ordinati, sed etiam omnes Britaniae sacerdotes habeat de Domino Nostro Jesu-Christo autore subjectos*". (Beda. *Hist. Eccl.* Lib. I cap. 29. M.L., t. VC, col. 69.)

4. Dans les chroniques des archevêques de Cantorbéry, on retrouve fréquemment la mention de cette origine romaine du pouvoir patriarcal de Cantorbéry. On lit entre autres: "*Effimus Lippe (†959) successor Odoni ... ille petenli palii causa Romam tendens ubi Alpes conscendit, nimio evectus frigore interiit*". (Mabillon, *Annales lib.*, 46, Luca [1739], t. III, p. 518.) Le récit de la vie de son successeur Dunstan débute ainsi: *Dumstanum pallii causa Romam proficiscentem ... (Ibidem*, p. 518.) Depuis Augustin jusque Cranmer tous les archevêques de Cantorbéry ont reçu leur pallium des Souverains Pontifes; la plupart même, selon l'antique règle, ont fait eux-mêmes le voyage de Rome pour le recevoir des mains du Pape lui-même. Avant d'avoir reçu cette investiture, l'archevêque ne jouit d'aucun droit patriarcal: le *pallium* imposé par le Pape est comme le sacrement de sa juridiction supra-épiscopale. C'est ainsi qu'un archevêque ayant reçu le *pallium* d'un antipape, ne fut pas reçu en Angleterre comme patriarche (Edwin Burton, *The Catholic Encyclopedia*, Vol III, p. 301).

5. Ce pouvoir patriarcal de Cantorbéry conféré par saint Grégoire à Augustin devint dans la suite le principe unificateur de l'Église anglicane. En 668, le Pape Vitalien nomma à ce siége Théodore, moine oriental de Tharse en Cilicie, qui avait passé de longues années à Rome, illustre par sa science des choses divines et humaines. Au dire de son illustre contemporain, le vénérable Bède (675-735) (cf. *Hist Eccl. Anglorum lib.*, 4 M. L., t. 95, col. 171), il fut pendant près d'un quart de siècle (668-690) un des plus grands archevêques de Cantorbéry et établit fortement le pouvoir patriarcal; créant de nouveaux diocèses, nommant ou révoquant les évêques, visitant les diocèses, convoquant en concile patriarcal les différentes provinces ecclésiastiques; bref organisant sur le modèle des Églises orientales et avec le constant appui de Rome la juridiction très effective et très étendue du patriarche.

6. Deux siècles plus tard, le Pape Formose III (†896), dans une lettre célèbre adressée aux évêques d'Angleterre, confirme solennellement ces pouvoirs patriarcaux et menace des peines ecclésiastiques les évêques qui tenteraient de se soustraire à cette juridiction pleinement légitime. (Allusion à l'archevêque d'York qui aurait voulu soustraire sa métropole à cette juridiction). Vu l'importance de ce document, il faut en citer ici le passage principal: (*Bullarium. Editio Taurinensis* 1857, t. I, p. 369): *...Quis autem inter vos principatum tenere debeat, quaene sedes episcopalis ceteris praepolleat, habeatque primatum, abantiquis temporibus notissimum est. Nam ut ex scriptis Beati Gregorii ejusque successoribus tenemus, in Dorobernia civitate* (Cantorbéry) *metropolim, primamquem sedem episcopalem constat regni Anglorum, cui venerabilis Frater noster Pleigmundus* (890-914) *nunc praeesse dignoscitur; cujus honorem dignitates nos ullo pacto imminui permittimus; sed ei vices apostolicas per omnia gerere mandamus, et sicut Anglorum episcopos esse subjectos constituit; sic nos praenominato Fratri Dorobernae seu Canterberiae archiepiscopo, ejusque successoribus legitimis eamdem dignitatem confirmamus mandantes et auctoritate Dei et beati Petri apostolorum principis praecipientes, ut ejus canonicis dispositionibus omnes obediant et nullus eorum quae ei suisque successoribus apostolica auctoritate concessa sunt, violator existat...*

7. Au siècle suivant, au Concile de Brandenford, en 964, tout l'épiscopat approuve le décret du roi Édouard qui met fin aux lois persécutrices de son prédécesseur et rapelle saint Dunstan sur le siège de Cantorbéry *ut Ecclesia Christi in Dorobernia aliarum Ecclesiarum regni nostri mater sit et Domina et*

cum suis omnibus perpetualiter sit ubique libera (Mansi, A.C.C., t. 18-A, col. 476).

8. Toute la vie de saint Anselme (†1109) atteste cette même vérité. Tout l'épiscopat anglais assiste à son sacre en 1093 et le proclame *totius Britaniae Primatem*. (On verra que ce n'est pas là un titre purement honorifique). [Cfr. Mansi, A.C.C., t. 20, col. 792].

Au Concile de Rockingham en mars 1094 (*ibidem*, col 791) dans le discours où saint Anselme expose à tout l'épiscopat réuni son conflit avec le roi, il dit: ... *nam cum nuper licentiam adeundi Urbanum sedis Apostolicae praesulem*, juxta morem antecessorum meorum pro pallii mei adeptione *ab ipso postulassem...*

Au Concile de Bari (1098), Urbain II fit asseoir Anselme près de lui et de son archidiacre, en disant: "Qu'il fasse partie de notre cercle, lui qui est en quelque sorte le Pape de l'autre partie du globe": *Includamus hunc in orbe nostro, quasi alterius orbis papam.* (Mansi, A. C. C., t. 20, col. 948). Un fait plus significatif encore et qui montre combien était effective et étendue cette juridiction prima-tiale, Gérard, évêque d'Hereford, est promu en 1107 au siège métropolitain de York, le premier siège de Bretagne après Cantorbéry et qui cherchait à s'affranchir de sa dépendance. Anselme veut exiger du nouvel élu une nouvelle profession explicite d'obéissance et de soumission, ne se contentant pas de celle émise par Gérard pour entrer en possession du siège d'Hereford. De là un conflit auquel le roi trouva heureusement une solution conciliatrice: sans faire une profession nouvelle l'élu rappellerait explicitement celle faite pour Here-ford: *Annuit Anselmus; et Gerardus sua manuu imposita manui Anselme, interpo-sita fide sua pollicitus est se eamdem subjectionem et obedientaim ipsi et successo-ribus suis archiepiscopatu exhibiturum quam Herefordensis Ecclesiae ab eo sacrandus antistes promiserat* (cfr. Mansi, A.C.C., t. 29, col. 1229).

9. Et vraiment rien ne manquait à la réalité de cette juridiction patriarcale. De nombreux bénéfices ecclésiastiques étaient soustraits à la dépendance de l'évêque du lieu et relevaient directement du siège de Cantorbéry. C'était l'exemption actuelle mais au profit du patriarche. À l'époque de saint Anselme, il y avait environ 80 bénéfices exempts dans le sens que nous venons de dire. Plusieurs monastères suivaient la même loi.

10. Sous le pontificat d'Alexandre III (1159-1181), les droits patriarcaux du siège de Cantorbéry furent vivement attaqués par les archevêques de York et de Londres; et le roi, soucieux d'amoindrir le patriarche pour mieux asservir l'Église (comme le fera plus tard en Russie Pierre le Grand en substituant au patriarche de Moscou le Saint Synode), le roi soutint toutes ces prétentions. L'archevêque Thomas, qui devait mourir bientôt victime de son zèle, vengea les droits de son Église, excommunia les évêques insubordonnés et le roi lui-même. Alexandre III, par plusieurs bulles, confirma tous les droits et privilèges de l'Église de Cantorbéry: *sicut a temporibus beati Augustini praedecessores tuos habuisse Apostolicae Sedis auctoritate constat*" (Cfr. Mansi, A.C.C., t. XXI, col 871-872 jusque 899).

11. Ces quelques faits historiques que nous venons de rappeler et qu'on pourrait multiplier n'établissent-ils pas à l'évidence les deux règles que nous avons signalées au début? Église fortement unifiée et organisée sous l'autorité patriarcale très effective de l'archevêque de Cantorbéry, l'Église anglicane est une réalité historique et catholique qui constitue un tout homogène: elle ne peut être absorbée et fusionnée sans perdre le caractère propre de toute son histoire.

Et d'autre part cette Église est fortement rattachée depuis ses origines au siège de Pierre. Investi du manteau symbolique du prince des apôtres, l'archevêque de Cantorbéry participe à la juridiction apostolique non seulement sur les fidèles mais aussi sur les Pasteurs. Comme jadis Élisée revêtit le pallium de son Maître et y trouva les effluves de son esprit, ainsi aussi Augustin et tous ses successeurs sans exception viennent chercher à Rome, par l'imposition du pallium, l'investiture de leur juridiction patriarcale. Et cette constatation historique est tellement évidente qu'il faut dire en toute vérité qu'une Église anglicane séparée de Rome est avant tout une hérésie historique.

Bref: Une *Église anglicane absorbée par Rome* et une *Église anglicane séparée de Rome* sont deux conceptions également inadmissibles. Il faut chercher la vraie formule dans la voie moyenne, la seule historique: Église anglicane *unie* à Rome.

§ 2. ESSAI DE STATUT CATHOLIQUE SELON CES DONNÉES

Selon le droit ecclésiastique *occidental* actuel, le titre de Patriarche ou de Primat est purement honorifique et ne comporte par lui-même aucune juridiction spéciale (Can. 271). Il n'en fut pas toujours ainsi. Historiquement, jusqu'au XIIe siècle environ (et plus encore pour certains sièges), la fonction patriacale ou primatiale comportait une juridiction effective et très étendue tant sur différentes provinces ecclésiastiques que sur les diocèses. Cette juridiction, participée du pouvoir du Primat de toute l'Église du Christ, a-t-elle porté le même nom et surtout a-t-elle été aussi étendue dans l'Église latine que dans l'Église byzantine? La proximité plus grande de Rome et le titre de patriarche d'Occident que le Souverain Pontife porte encore officiellement aujourd'hui, diminuèrent l'utilité et l'importance de ce grade hiérarchique et amenèrent graduellement son atrophie. Mais il est incontestable que, sous le nom différent de Primat, la chose a existé en Occident comme en Orient, et tout particulièrement, comme nous l'avons vu, dans l'Église d'Angleterre.

Voyons d'abord à ce point de vue le statut actuel des Églises orientales unies à Rome.

Nous verrons ensuite l'application qu'on en peut faire à l'Église d'Angleterre.

I. L'ORGANISATION INTÉRIEURE DES ÉGLISES ORIENTALES UNIES

L'organisation patriarcale est encore en vigueur, comme on sait, dans les Églises orientales. On peut même dire qu'elle est plus effective dans les Églises unies à Rome que dans les Églises séparées où les ingérences du pouvoir civil et de l'élément laïc la rendent souvent illusoire.

Pour concrétiser, voyons l'organisation patriarcale de l'Église melkite catholique. La juridiction du Patriarche, Mgr. Cadi, s'étend sur tous les fidèles melkites qui habitaient l'empire ottoman en 1894, date de cette concession par Léon XIII.

Le Patriarche melkite d'Antioche (qui administre en même temps les deux patriarcats de Jérusalem et d'Alexandrie) compte dans son patriarcat cinq métropoles et sept évêchés, soit douze diocèses, en tout 170.000 fidèles environ.

1. Dès que le synode des évêques a élu le nouveau Patriarche, celui-ci écrit au Souverain Pontife une profession de foi détaillée et lui demande *le pallium patriarcal* comme signe d'investiture apostolique. Avant d'avoir reçu cette investiture, l'élu ne jouit d'aucun pouvoir patriarcal.

2. Le choix des évêques se fait de la manière suivante: Le Patriarche propose trois candidats parmi lesquels les prêtres séculiers doivent faire un choix. Le nouvel élu est ensuite confirmé et sacré par le Patriarche, sans aucune intervention de Rome qui n'est même pas informée de l'élection et du sacre. Aussi aucun évêque oriental n'est-il proclamé au Consistoire. Quant aux évêques titulaires, leur choix et leur consécration dépendent du Patriarche seul, sans aucune intervention ni information romaine.

3. Le Patriarche convoque à des époques déterminées les archevêques et évêques en synode patriarcal, qu'il préside et dirige. Les décrets et décisions sont ensuite soumis à l'approbation du Saint-Siège.

4. Le Patriarche a un droit d'inspection et de visite dans les différents diocèses. Pour les mesures plus graves, comme serait la démission d'un évêque, l'approbation du Synode est requise.

5. L'exemption de quelques grands monastères de la juridiction épiscopale est au profit du Patriarche. On les appelle stavropégiaques, c'est-à-dire qui dépendent directement du Patriarche. Chez les Melkites orthodoxes, sur 17 monastères, cinq sont stavropégiaques.

6. Les Églises patriarcales ont leur droit et leurs coutumes propres, réglés par les Synodes, leur liturgie, leurs œuvres; bref elles constituent, sous l'autorité patriacale, des institutions autonomes, jouissant d'une organisation propre; mais en communion et dépendance de l'Église romaine.

7. Loin de porter préjudice à cette organisation intérieure autonome, Rome a assuré aux Églises orientales la conservation de cette large autonomie. Le premier article du code de droit canonique déclare que la législation occidentale ne les atteint pas et que l'Orient catholique conserve son Droit et ses institutions propres. Il en est de même pour la Liturgie et pour toute l'organisation ecclésiastique. Léon XIII a formulé à merveille dans son encyclique *Praeclare* du 20 juin 1894 et dans la Constitution *Orientalium dignitas* du 30 novembre 1894 la ligne de conduite fondamentale de l'Église romaine: "La véritable union entre les chrétiens est celle que l'auteur de l'Église, Jésus-Christ, a instituée et qu'il a voulue: elle consiste dans l'unité de la foi et du gouvernement. Ni Nous ni Nos successeurs ne supprimerons jamais rien de votre Droit, ni des *privilèges de vos Patriarches*, ni des coutumes rituelles de chaque Église. Il a été et il sera toujours dans la pensée et la conduite du Saint-Siège de se montrer *prodigue de concessions à l'égard des origines et des mœurs propres de chaque Église*".

II. APPLICATION À L'ANGLETERRE

1. Il existe donc une formule catholique d'union des Églises qui n'est pas une absorption mais qui sauvegarde et respecte l'organisation intérieure autonome des grandes Églises historiques, tout en maintenant leur parfaite dépendance vis-à-vis de l'Église romaine, principe d'unité de l'Église universelle.

2. Or, s'il est une Église qui par ses origines, son histoire, les mœurs de la nation a droit à ces concessions d'autonomie, c'est bien l'Église anglicane. Nous

l'avons suffisamment démontré dans notre enquête historique. Le principe affirmé par Léon XIII et qu'il applique aux Églises orientales: "Il a été et il sera toujours dans la pensée et la conduite du Saint-Siège de se montrer prodigue de concessions à l'égard des origines et des mœurs propres de chaque Église"peut également trouver son application pour l'Église anglicane.

3. Pratiquement, l'archevêque de Cantorbéry serait rétabli dans ses droits traditionnels et effectifs de Patriarche de l'Église anglicane. Après avoir reçu son investiture du successeur de Pierre, par l'imposition historique du *pallium*, il jouirait de ses droits patriarcaux sur toute l'Église d'Angleterre: nomination et sacre des Évêques; convocation et présidence des conciles inter-provinciaux; inspection des diocèses; juridiction épiscopale; bref organisation intérieure de l'Église anglicane unie, calquée sur l'organisation sanctionnée et maintenue par Rome pour les Églises orientales unies.

4. Le code de droit canonique de l'Église latine ne serait pas imposé à l'Église anglicane; mais celle-ci, dans un synode inter-provincial, fixerait son droit ecclésiastique qui serait ensuite soumis à l'approbation du Saint-Siège et sanctionné pour l'Église anglicane. On sait que le droit oriental est totalement différent du droit ecclésiastique latin, sauf évidemment dans les points de droit naturel et divin. Par exemple, si la chose était jugée opportune par l'Église anglicane, je n'hésiterais pas à ne pas imposer le célibat ecclésiatique en Angleterre pas plus qu'en Orient.

5. L'Église anglicane aurait aussi sa liturgie propre, la Liturgie romaine des VIIe et VIIIe siècles telle qu'elle la pratiquait à cette époque, et telle que nous la retrouvons dans les sacramentaires gélasiens. Déjà aujourd'hui, il y a un grand mouvement dans l'Église anglicane pour ressusciter cette belle liturgie romaine classique, qu'hélas Rome n'a pas conservée, et que l'Église anglicane remettrait en honneur. Comme le culte de Notre-Dame et des Saints est moins exubérant dans cette liturgie classique que dans la liturgie romaine actuelle, il y aurait là un heureux tempérament qui faciliterait singulièrement la transition.

6. Évidemment, tous les anciens sièges historiques de l'Église anglicane seraient maintenus et les sièges catholiques nouveaux, créés depuis 1851, seraient supprimés à savoir: Westminster, Southwark, Portsmouth, etc. Évidemment c'est une mesure grave; mais qu'on se rappelle que Pie VII lors du Concordat français supprima les diocèses existants et demanda la démission de tous les titulaires (plus de cent).

7. Une grosse question de préséance se poserait: les patriarches ont-ils la préséance sur les cardinaux. Question grave qui pourrait envenimer et compromettre les négociations, si l'on ne se décide pas à la résoudre d'après les données historiques, dont nous indiquons ici quelques points.

a) Il a été décrété solennellement par plusieurs conciles oecuméniques (4e de Constantinople (869) au can. 21e (Denziger 341) et 4e concile de Latran (1215) can. 5 (Denziger 436) que les quatre Patriarches *effectifs*, à savoir Constantinople, Alexandrie, Antioche et Jérusalem avaient droit aux quatre premières places, dans l'ordre indiqué plus haut, immédiatement après le Souverain Pontife de Rome. Si donc on rend à Cantorbéry la plénitude effective de la fonction patriarcale, il devrait prendre rang dans cette catégorie et occuper le cinquième rang parmi les Patriarches, immédiatement après le Pape, avant les Cardinaux. Bien entendu, il ne s'agit que des grands Patriarches, ceux qui avaient jadis leur résidence patriarcale à Rome, quand ils y venaient; de là le nom des cinq Basiliques patriarcales: le Latran était la résidence du Patriarche œcuménique, le Pontife suprême et universel; à Saint Pierre était la résidence du Patriarche de Constantinople; à Saint Paul, celle du Patriarche d'Alexandrie; à Sainte Marie Majeure, celle du Patriarche de d'Antioche; à Saint-Laurent hors les murs, celle du Patriarche de Jérusalem. Tous ces usages antérieurs au schisme devraient être repris: et l'archevêque de Cantorbéry devrait être assimilé à ces quatre Patriarches. Or il est incontestable qu'avant le schisme, les grands Patriarches avaient le pas sur les Cardinaux.

b) Mais vu les idées régnantes à partir du XIe siècle, il sera difficile d'appliquer ces anciennes pratiques. On pourrait alors s'inspirer d'une règle qui a été appliquée à certaines époques pour de hauts personnages princiers: ils prenaient rang immédiatement après le doyen du Sacré-Collège. La préséance était accordée au Corps du Sacré-Collège en la personne de son Doyen.

c) Enfin un autre système qui a prévalu à certaines époques: les grands Patriarches prenaient rang après les cardinaux évêques, avant les cardinaux prêtres et diacres.

d) Une solution élégante serait de créer l'ordre des cardinaux-patriarches, comme on a créé au VIIIe siècle l'ordre des cardinaux- évêques, plusieurs siècles après l'institution des cardinaux-prêtres et diacres. Cette solution a le défaut d'être neuve, dans un domaine surtout où l'Église est justement traditionnelle; mais pour être neuve la solution respecte la ligne de la tradition.

Quoi qu'il en soit, n'oublions pas que ces questions de préséance, à cause des principes qu'elles symbolisent, ont une grande importance et doivent être envisagées selon les principes traditionnels.

CONCLUSIONS PRATIQUES

1. Union non absorption, telle est donc, nous semble-t-il, la formule de la réconciliation. D'une part une société religieuse, l'Église anglicane, jouissant de son organisation intérieure propre, un corps moral jouissant de son autonomie, de ses institutions, de ses lois, de sa liturgie propre, sous l'autorité de son chef, le Patriarche de Cantorbéry; mais manquant, si elle reste isolée, du principe d'unité et du fondement infaillible de la vérité, que le Christ veut dans l'Église qu'il a fondée: *unum ovile et unus Pastor*. D'autre part, l'Église romaine, qui elle aussi a ses Institutions, son droit, sa liturgie, en un mot, son organisation intérieure latine; mais qui en plus et surtout possède en son chef le principe d'unité, le fondement de vérité et d'apostolicité, la Pierre inébranlable sur laquelle toute l'Église du Christ est fondée. Il faut donc nécessairement, si l'Église anglicane veut appartenir à cette société unique et visible du Christ, qu'elle établisse entre elle et l'Église romaine ce lien de dépendance et de soumission au successeur de Pierre; en d'autres termes, il faut qu'elle devienne non *latine* mais *romaine*; et qu'en conservant toute son organisation intérieure, toutes ses traditions historiques et sa légitime autonomie, à l'instar des Églises orientales, elle établisse fortement ce lien indispensable de subordination à l'Église universelle dont le principe d'unité est à Rome.

2. Si les principes généraux indiqués dans ce rapport pouvaient servir de base à une entreprise pour l'union des Églises, il serait nécessaire évidemment de développer ce travail et d'en établir scientifiquement les différentes assertions

historiques et canoniques. Vu l'opposition inévitable et probablement très vive que ces idées trop neuves pourront soulever, il est nécessaire, avant de les rendre publiques, de les appuyer de considérations et de développements qui, au point de vue théologique et historique, sont inattaquables, et de leur donner une forme précise et détaillée, de façon à éviter toute équivoque. Pareil travail ne pourrait se faire que grâce au concours de plusieurs qui pourraient élaborer ensemble une œuvre complète.

3. Que pensera Rome de ce projet? Évidemment, il pose un principe de décentralisation, qui n'est pas conforme aux tendances actuelles de la curie romaine, principe qui pourrait trouver dans la suite d'autres applications. Ne serait-ce pas un bien et un grand bien? Mais Rome sera-t-elle de cet avis? Rien ne peut faire prévoir quelle sera la réponse à cette question. Si des faits minimes peuvent quelquefois trahir de grands desseins, deux choses peuvent être notées:

a) Dans la lettre apostolique au cardinal Pompili du 5 mai 1924 (A. A. S. 1924, p. 233), Pie XI, en rappelant les gloires de la Basilique du Latran dont il annonçait le treizième centenaire, évoquait explicitement le souvenir du sacre du moine Augustin par Grégoire le Grand et ajoutait: "Cet illustre pontife imposa ensuite le *pallium* à Augustin, en fixant par un décret que toutes les Églises d'Angleterre déjà fondées alors ou fondées dans la suite seraient sous la juridiction de l'Église primatiale de Cantorbéry".

b) Un autre fait significatif est que de *tous* les Primats de l'Église catholique, le primat catholique de Westminster, le cardinal Bourne, bien que ce titre soit d'institution toute récente, est le *seul* à jouir de privilèges vraiment patriarcaux dans les différentes provinces ecclésiastiques d'Angleterre, en vertu de la Constitution apostolique *Si qua est* du 26 novembre 1911 (A.A.S. 1911, p. 554); il préside de droit les synodes inter-provinciaux d'Angleterre; il a préséance dans tout le pays sur les autres métropolitains, même dans la propre province de ceux-ci; peut porter le *pallium*, ériger son trône et faire porter la croix devant lui dans toutes les églises de l'Angleterre: il est le représentant officiel de toute l'Église d'Angleterre auprès de la Cour impériale. "Tel privilège, dit un auteur, par ce qu'il a de singulier, d'insolite, d'énorme, ressort mieux comme une exception". (Cfr. Gromier, *Prérogatives archiépiscopales*. Bruxelles (1924) p. 16)

Ces faits, peu importants en eux-mêmes, peuvent-ils être interprétés comme une suggestion, une avance, une disposition bienveillante? Je ne sais; en tout cas, ils peuvent servir sinon de base au moins d'excuse à l'exposé qui été fait dans ces lignes.

MORTALIUM ANIMOS
Encyclical Letter
on Fostering True Religious Union of Our Most Holy Lord*

Venerable Brethren, Health and Apostolic Benediction

Never perhaps in the past have the minds of men been so engrossed as they are today with desire to strengthen and extend for the common good of mankind that tie of brotherhood — the result of our common origin and nature — which binds us all so closely together. The world does not yet fully enjoy the fruits of peace; on the contrary, dissensions old and new in various lands still issue in rebellions and conflict. Such disputes, affecting the tranquil prosperity of nations, can never be settled without the combined and active goodwill of those who are responsible for their government, and hence it is easy to understand — especially now that unity of mankind is no longer called into question — the widespread desire that all nations, in view of this universal kinship, should daily find closer union with one another.

It is with a similar motive that efforts are being made by some, in connexion with the New Law promulgated by Christ our Lord. Assured that there exist few men who are entirely devoid of the religious sense, they seem to ground on this belief a hope that all nations, while differing indeed in religious matters, may yet without great difficulty be brought to fraternal agreement on certain points of doctrine which will form a common basis of the spiritual life. With this object congresses, meetings, and addresses are arranged, attended by a large concourse of hearers, where all without distinction, unbelievers of every kind as well as Christians, even those who unhappily have rejected Christ and denied His divine nature or mission, are invited to join in the discussion. Now, such efforts can meet with no kind of approval among Catholics. They presuppose the erroneous view that all religions are more or less good and praiseworthy, inasmuch as all give expression, under various forms, to that innate sense which leads men to God and to the obedient acknowledgement of His rule. Those who hold such a view are not only in error; they distort the true idea of religion, and thus reject it, falling gradually into naturalism and atheism. To favour this opinion, therefore, and to encourage such undertakings is tantamount to abandoning the religion revealed by God.

Nevertheless, when there is a question of fostering unity among Christians, it is easy for many to be misled by the apparent excellence of the object to be achieved. Is it not right, they ask, is it not the obvious duty of all who invoke the name of Christ to refrain from mutual reproaches and at last to be united in charity? Dare any one say that he loves Christ, and yet not strive with all his might to accomplish the desire of Him Who asked His Father that His disciples might be 'one' (John xvii. 21)? Did not Christ will that mutual charity should

---

* G.K.A. BELL, *Documents on Christian Unity*, London, 1955, pp. 189-200.

be the distinguishing characteristic of His disciples? 'By this shall all men know that you are My disciples, if you have love one for another' (John xiii. 35). If only all Christians were 'one', it is contended, then they might do so much more to drive out the pest of irreligion which with its insidious and far-reaching advance is threatening to sap the strength of the Gospel. These and similar arguments, with amplifications, are constantly on the lips of the 'pan-Christians' who, so far from being a few isolated individuals, have formed an entire class and grouped themselves into societies of extensive membership, usually under the direction of non-Catholics, who also disagree in matters of faith. The energy with which this scheme is being promoted has won for it many adherents, and even many Catholics are attracted by it, since it holds out the hope of a union apparently consonant with the wishes of Holy Mother Church, whose chief desire it is to recall her erring children and to bring them back to her bosom. In reality, however, these fair and alluring words cloak a most grave error, subversive of the foundations of the Catholic faith.

Conscious, therefore, of Our Apostolic office, which warns Us not to allow the flock of Christ to be led astray by harmful fallacies, We invoke your zeal, Venerable Brethren, to avert this evil. We feel confident that each of you, by written and spoken word, will explain clearly to the people the principles and arguments that We are about to set forth so that Catholics may know what view and what course of action they should adopt regarding schemes for the promiscuous union into one body of all who call themselves Christians.

God, the Creator of all things, made us that we might know Him and serve Him; to our service, therefore, He has a full right. He might indeed have been contented to prescribe for man's government the natural law alone, that is, the law which in creation He has written upon man's heart, and have regulated the progress of that law by His ordinary Providence. He willed, however, to make positive laws which we should obey, and progressively, from the beginnings of the human race until the coming and preaching of Jesus Christ, He Himself taught mankind the duties which a rational creature owes to his Creator. 'God, Who at sundry times and in divers manners spoke in times past to the fathers by the prophets, last of all in these days hath spoken to us by His Son' (Heb. i.I,seq.). Evidently, therefore, no religion can be true save that which rests upon the revelation of God, a revelation begun from the very first, continued under the Old Law, and brought to completion by Jesus Christ Himself under the New. Now, if God has spoken - and it is historically certain that He has in fact spoken – then it is clearly man's duty implicitly to believe His revelation and to obey His commands. That we might rightly do both, for the glory of God and for our own salvation, the only-begotten Son of God founded His Church on earth. None, we think, of those who claim to be Christians will deny that a Church, and one sole Church, was founded by Christ.

On the further question, however, as to what in the intention of its Founder was to be the precise nature of that Church, there is not the same agreement. Many of them, for example, deny that the Church of Christ was intended to be visible and manifest, at any rate in the sense that it was to be visibly the one body of the faithful, agreeing in one and the same doctrine under one teaching and governing authority. They conceive the visible Church as nothing more than a federation of the various Christian Communities, even though these may hold different and mutually exclusive doctrines. The truth is that Christ found

His Church as a perfect society, of its nature external and perceptible to the senses, which in the future should carry on the work of salvation of mankind under one head, with a living teaching authority, administering the sacraments which are the sources of heavenly grace (John iii. 5, vi. 48-59, xx. 22 seq.; cf. Matt. xviii. 18, &c.) Wherefore He compared His Church to a kingdom (Matt. xiii.), to a house (cf. Matt. xvi. 18), to a sheepfold (John x. 16), and to a flock (John xxi. 15-17). The Church thus wondrously instituted could not cease to exist with the death of its Founder and of the Apostles, the pioneers of its propagation; for its mission was to lead all men to salvation, without distinction of time or place: 'Going therefore, teach ye all nations' (Matt. xxviii. 19). Nor could the Church ever lack the effective strength necessary for the continued accomplishment of its task, since Christ Himself is perpetually present with it, according to His promise: 'Behold, I am with you all days, even to the consummation of the world' (Matt. xxviii. 20). Hence not only must the Church still exist today and continue always to exist, but it must ever be exactly the same as it was in the days of the Apostles. Otherwise we must say — which God forbid — that Christ has failed in His purpose, or that He erred when He asserted of His Church that the gates of hell should never prevail against it (Matt. xvi. 18).

And here it will be opportune to expound and to reject a certain false opinion which lies at the root of this question and of that complex movement by which non-Catholics seek to bring about the union of Christian Churches. Those who favour this view constantly quote the words of Christ, 'That they may be one ... And there shall be one fold, and one shepherd' (John xvii, 21, x. 16), in the sense that Christ thereby merely expressed a desire or a prayer which as yet has not been granted. For they hold that the unity of faith and government which is a note of the one true Church of Christ has up to the present time hardly ever existed, and does not exist today. They consider that this unity is indeed to be desired and even, by co-operation and goodwill, be actually attained, but that meanwhile it must be regarded as a mere ideal. The Church, they say, is of its nature divided into sections, composed of several churches or distinct communities which still remain separate, and although holding in common some articles of doctrine nevertheless differ concerning the remainder; that all these enjoy the same rights; and that the Church remained one and undivided at the most only from the Apostolic age until the first Oecumenical Councils. Hence, they say, controversies and long-standing differences, which today still keep asunder the members of the Christian family, must be entirely set aside, and from the residue of doctrines a common form of faith drawn up and proposed for belief, in the profession of which all may not only know but also feel themselves to be brethren. If the various Churches or communities were united in some kind of universal federation, they would then be in a position to oppose resolutely and successfully the progress of irreligion.

Such, Venerable Brethren is the common contention. There are indeed some who recognize and affirm that Protestantism has with inconsiderate zeal rejected certain articles of faith and external ceremonies which are in fact useful and attractive, and which the Roman Church still retains. But they immediately go on to say that the Roman Church, too, has erred, and corrupted the primitive religion by adding to it and proposing for belief doctrines not only alien to the Gospel but contrary to its spirit. Chief among these they count that of the primacy of jurisdiction granted to Peter and to his successors in the See of Rome. There are actually some, though few, who grant to the Roman Pontiff a primacy of honour and even a certain power or jurisdiction; this, however, they consider to arise not from the divine law but merely from the consent of the faithful. Others, again, even go so far as to desire the Pontiff himself to preside over their mixed assemblies. For the rest, while you may hear many non-Catholics loudly preaching brotherly communion in Jesus Christ, yet not one will you find to whom it ever occurs with devout submission to obey the Vicar of Jesus Christ in his capacity of teacher or ruler. Meanwhile they assert their readiness to treat with the Church of Rome, but on equal terms, as equals with an equal. But even if they could so treat, there seems little doubt that they would do so only on condition that no pact into which they might enter should compel them to retract those opinions which still keep them outside the one fold of Christ.

This being so, it is clear that the Apostolic See can by no means take part in these assemblies, nor is it in any way lawful for Catholics to give to such enterprises their encouragement or support. If they did so, they would be giving countenance to a false Christianity quite alien to the one Church of Christ. Shall we commit the iniquity of suffering the truth, the truth revealed by God, to be made a subject for compromise? For it is indeed a question of defending revealed truth. Jesus Christ sent His Apostles into the whole world to declare the faith of the Gospel to every nation, and, to save them from error, He willed that the Holy Ghost should first teach them all truth. Has this doctrine, then, disappeared, or at any time been obscured, in the Church of which God Himself is the ruler and guardian? Our Redeemer plainly said that His Gospel was intended not only for the apostolic age but for all time. Can the object of faith, then, have become in the process of time so dim and uncertain that today we must tolerate contradictory opinions? If this were so, then we should have to admit that the coming of the Holy Ghost upon the Apostles, the perpetual indwelling of the same Spirit in the Church, nay the very preaching of Jesus Christ, have centuries ago lost efficacy and value. To affirm this would be blasphemy. The only-begotten Son of God not only bade His representative to teach all nations; He also obliged all men to give credence to whatever was taught them by 'witnesses preordained by God' (Acts x. 41). Moreover, He enforced His command with this sanction: 'He that believeth and is baptized shall be saved; he that believeth not shall be condemned' (Mark xvi. 16). These two commands, the one to teach, the other to believe for salvation, must be obeyed. But they cannot even be understood unless the Church proposes an inviolate and clear teaching, and in proposing it is immune from all danger of error. It is also false to say that, although the deposit of truth does indeed exist, yet it is to be found only with such laborious effort and after such lengthy study and discussion, that a man's life is hardly long enough for its discovery and attainment. This would be equivalent to saying that the most merciful God spoke through the prophets and through His only-begotten Son merely in order that some few men, and those advanced in years, might learn what He had revealed, and not in order to inculcate a doctrine of faith and morals by which man should be guided throughout the whole of his life.

These pan-Christians who strive for the union of the Churches would appear to pursue the noblest of ideals in promoting charity among all Christians. But how should charity tend to the detriment of faith? Every one knows that John himself, the Apostle of love, who seems in his Gospel to have revealed the secrets of the Sacred Heart of Jesus, and who never ceased to impress upon the memory of his disciples the new commandment 'to love one another', nevertheless strictly forbade any intercourse with those who professed a mutilated and corrupt form of Christ's teaching: 'If any man come to you, and bring not this doctrine receive him not into the house, nor say to him, God speed you' (2 John 10).

Therefore, since the foundation of charity is faith pure and inviolate, it is chiefly by the bond of one faith that the disciples of Christ are to be united. A federation of Christians, then, is inconceivable in which each member retains his own opinions and private judgement in matter of faith, even though they differ from the opinions of all the rest. How can men with opposite convictions belong to one and the same federation of the faithful: those who accept sacred Tradition as a source of revelation and those who reject it; those who recognize as divinely constituted the hierarchy of bishops, priests, and ministers in the Church, and those who regard it as gradually introduced to suit the conditions of the time; those who adore Christ really present in the Most Holy Eucharist through that wonderful conversion of the bread and wine, transubstantiation, and those who assert that the body of Christ is there only by faith or by the signification and virtue of the sacrament; those who in the Eucharist recognize both sacrament and sacrifice, and those who say that it is nothing more than the memorial of the Lord's supper; those who think it right and useful to pray to the Saints reigning with Christ, especially to Mary the Mother of God, and to venerate their images, and those who refuse such veneration as derogatory to the honour due to Jesus Christ, 'the one mediator of God and men' (cf. I Tim. ii 5)?

How so great a variety of opinions can clear the way for the unity of the Church, We know not. That unity can arise only from one teaching authority, one law of belief, and one faith of Christians. But we do know that from such a state of affairs it is but an easy step to the neglect of religion or 'indifferentism', and to the error of the modernists, who hold that dogmatic truth is not absolute but relative, that is, that it changes according to the varying necessities of time and place and the varying tendencies of the mind; that it is not contained in an immutable tradition, but can be altered to suit the needs of human life.

Furthermore, it is never lawful to employ in connexion with articles of faith the distinction invented by some between 'fundamental' and 'non-fundamental' articles, the former to be accepted by all, the latter being left to the free acceptance of the faithful. The supernatural virtue of faith has as its formal motive the authority of God revealing, and this allows of no such distinction. All true followers of Christ, therefore, will believe the dogma of the Immaculate Conception of the Mother of God with the same faith as they believe the mystery of the august Trinity, the infallibility of the Roman Pontiff in the sense defined by the Oecumenical Vatican Council with the same faith as they believe the Incarnation of our Lord. That these truths have been solemnly sanctioned and defined by the Church at various times, some of them even quite recently, makes no difference to their certainty, nor to our obligation of believing them. Has not God revealed them all?

The teaching authority of the Church in the divine wisdom was constituted on earth in order that the revealed doctrines might remain forever intact and might be brought with ease and security to the knowledge of men. This authority is indeed daily exercised through the Roman Pontiff and the Bishops who are in communion with him; but it has the further office of defining some truth with solemn decree whenever it is opportune, and when ever this is necessary either to oppose the errors or the attacks of heretics, or again to impress the minds of the faithful with a clearer and more detailed explanation of the articles of sacred doctrine. But in the use of this extraordinary teaching authority no fresh invention is introduced, nothing new is ever added to the number of those truths which are at least implicitly contained within the deposit of Revelation divinely committed to the Church; but truths which to some perhaps may still seem obscure are rendered clear, or a truth which some may have called into question is declared to be of faith.

Thus Venerable Brethren, it is clear why this Apostolic See has never allowed its subjects to take part in the assemblies of non-Catholics. There is but one way in which the unity of Christians may be fostered, and that is by furthering the return to the one true Church of Christ of those who are separated from it; for from that one true Church they have in the past fallen away. The one Church of Christ is visible to all, and will remain, according to the will of its Author, exactly the same as He instituted it. The mystical Spouse of Christ has never in the course of centuries been contaminated, nor in the future can she ever be, as Cyprian bears witness: 'The Bride of Christ cannot become false to her Spouse; she is inviolate and pure. She knows but one dwelling, and chastely and modestly she guards the sanctity of the nuptial chamber' (*De Cath. Ecclesiae unitate*, 6). The same holy martyr marvelled that any one could believe that 'this unity of the Church built upon a divine foundation, knit together by heavenly sacraments, could ever be rent asunder by the conflict of will' (*ibid.*). For since the mystical body of Christ, like His physical body, is one (I Cor. xii. 12), compactly and fitly joined together (Eph. iv. 15), it were foolish to say that the mystical body is composed of disjointed and scattered members. Whosoever therefore is not united with the body is no member thereof, neither is he in communion with Christ its head.

Furthermore, in this one Church of Christ no man can be or remain who does not accept, recognize, and obey the authority and supremacy of Peter and his legitimate successors. Did not the ancestors of those who are now entangled in the errors of Photius and of the Reformers obey the Bishop of Rome, the chief shepherd of souls? Their children, alas! have left the home of their fathers; but that house did not therefore fall to the ground and perish for ever, for it was supported by God. Let them, then, return to their Father, Who, forgetting the insults in the past heaped upon the Apostolic See, will accord them a most loving welcome. If, as they constantly say, they long to be united with Us and Ours, why do they not hasten to enter the Church, 'the mother and mistress of all Christ's faithful'? (*Conc. Lateran*, iv, c. 5). Let them heed the words of Lactantius: 'The Catholic Church is alone in keeping the true worship. This is the fount of truth, this the house of faith, this the temple of God; if any man enter not here, or if any man go forth from it, he is a stranger to the hope of life and salvation. Let none delude himself with obstinate wrangling. For life and salvation are here concerned, and these will be lost for ever unless their interest be carefully and assiduously kept in mind' (*Divin. Inst.* Iv. 30, 11-12).

Let our separated children, therefore draw nigh to the Apostolic See, set up in the City which Peter and Paul, Princes of the Apostles, consecrated by their blood; to the See which is 'the root and womb whence issues the Church of God' (Cypr. *Ep.* 48 *ad Cornelium*, 3); and let them come, not with any intention or hope that 'the Church of the living God, the pillar and ground of the truth' (I Tim. iii. 15) will cast aside the integrity of the faith and tolerate their errors but to submit themselves to its teaching and government. Would that the happy lot, denied to so many of Our Predecessors, might at last be Ours, to embrace with fatherly affection those children whose unhappy separation from Us We now deplore. Would that God our Saviour, 'Who will have all men to be saved, and to come to the knowledge of the truth' (I Tim. ii. 4), might hear our humble prayer and vouchsafe to recall to the unity of the Church all that are gone astray. To this all-important end We implore, and We desire that others should implore, the intercession of the Blessed Virgin Mary, Mother of divine grace, Help of Christians, victorious over all heresies, that she may entreat for Us the speedy coming of that longed-for day, when all men shall hear the voice of her divine Son, and shall be 'careful to keep the unity of the Spirit in the bond of peace' (Eph. iv. 3).

You, Venerable Brethren, know how dear to Our heart is this desire, and We wish that our children also should know not only those belonging to the Catholic fold, but also those separated from Us. If these will humbly beg light from heaven, there is no doubt but that they will recognize the one true Church of Jesus Christ, and entering therein, will at last be united with Us in perfect charity. In the hope of this fulfilment, and as a pledge of our fatherly goodwill, We impart most lovingly to you Venerable Brethren, and to your clergy and people, the Apostolic Benediction.

Given at S. Peter's, Rome, on the 6th day of January, the Feast of the Epiphany of our Lord Jesus Christ, in the year 1928, the sixth of Our Pontificate.

Pius PP. XI.

BIOGRAPHICAL INDEX

ABBELOOS, Jan Baptist (1836-1906): Professor of exegesis at the Malines diocesan seminary (1868); appointed rector of the Catholic University of Louvain (1887); his conflict with D.J. Mercier concerning the establishment of the *Institut Supérieur de Philosophie* led to his resignation as rector (1898).

ACTON, John Emerich Edward Dalberg (1834-1902): First Baron Acton of Aldenham, eighth Baronet; English historian; student of N.P.S. Wiseman at Oscott; private pupil and traveling companion of J.J.I. Döllinger (1848); elected MP of the Whig party (1859); succeeded J.H. Newman as editor of *The Rambler* (1859) which was later renamed *The Home and Foreign Review* (1862) but was eventually suspended altogether (1864); an opponent of Ultramontanism, Acton rejected the *Syllabus errorum* (1864) and journeyed to Rome during the Vatican Council (1869-1870) in order to organize resistance to the definition of papal infallibility; he was the co-founder of the *English Historical Review* (1886); appointed Regius Professor of modern history at Cambridge University (1895); helped plan the first edition of *The Cambridge Modern History*, which was published after his death.

ALBERT I (1875-1934): King of the Belgians from 1909.

AMIGO, Peter Emmanuel (1864-1949): Bishop of Southwark; ordained priest (1888); consecrated bishop (1904).

AUGUSTINIS, A.M. DE (1829-1899): Italian Jesuit; ordained priest(1861); after teaching in Laval, France for several years, he was appointed professor of Sacred Scripture at the Jesuit Scholasticate in Woodstock, Maryland; assigned to the commission reviewing Jesuit theological studies (1885); appointed professor of dogma at the Gregorian University, Rome and later named rector of that university (1891-1895).

BAGOT, Richard (1782-1854): Fellow of All Souls College, Oxford (1804); appointed Bishop of Oxford (1829); later translated to the See of Bath and Wells at his own request (1845); seems to have been an opponent of the Tractarian Movement though he sometimes defended the Tractarians from attack.

BALFOUR, Arthur James (1848-1930): British statesman and philosopher; author of *A Defence of Philosophic Doubt* (1879), an apologetic work on religious faith, and *Foundations of Belief* (1895), which further developed his position; Prime Minister (1902-1905); Foreign Secretary (1916-1919).

BARBERI, Dominic (1792-1849): Italian Passionist Father; ordained priest (1818); appointed superior of the Passionist monastery at Lucca (1831) and later became the congregation's provincial for Southern Italy (1833); moved to England and established the first English Passionist monastery at Aston, Staffordshire (1842); later received J.H. Newman into the Roman Church (1845).

BATIFFOL, Pierre (1861-1929): French Church historian; appointed professor at the *École de Ste-Barbe*, Paris (1889); rector of the *Institut de Catholique de Toulouse* (1898); closely associated with a number of Modernist scholars; his series *Études d'histoire et de théologie positive* (1902) was eventually put on the Index for its unorthodox views (1911).

BEAUDUIN, Lambert (1873-1960): Belgian Liturgist, ordained priest (1879); joined the movement *Aumôniers du Travail* (1899); later entered the Benedictine monastery at Keizersberg, Louvain (1906) where he became subprior (1919); aid to Archbishop D.J. Mercier; involved in the early stages of the Liturgical Movement; appointed professor of Fundamental Theology at *Sant' Anselmo*, Rome (1921); founded the Monastery of Union, Amay-sur-Meuse (1924), which was designed for ecumenical involvement between the Roman Catholic and Eastern Orthodox Churches; later became prior of that community (1925); consultant to Archbishop Mercier at the Malines Conversations, where his opinions on reunion brought much criticism, forcing him to leave the community at Amay (1928) and eventually causing his condemnation (1931); from that time on, he devoted himself to liturgical reform; the condemnation from Rome was removed (1945) with the help of Angelo Roncalli, the then papal nuncio to France; Beauduin was later allowed to return to his community, now at Chevetogne (1951); his views on reunion were soon vindicated by Roncalli as Pope John XXIII.

BELL, George Kennedy Allan (1881-1958): Ordained priest (1908); tutor and lecturer at Christ Church, Oxford (1910-1914); secretary (1914-1929) and later biographer of Archbishop R.T. Davidson of Canterbury; appointed Dean of Canterbury (1924) and Bishop of Chichester (1929); Bell was quite active in the Ecumenical Movement; involved in the early Life and Work movement and the Stockholm Conference (1925) as well as many other activities; Chairman of the Central Committee of the World Council of Churches (1948-1954) and later the Council's honorary president (1954-1958).

BENEDICT XV (1854-1922): Giacomo P.G.B. della Chiesa; ordained priest (1878); secretary to Cardinal M. Rampolla, papal nuncio to Spain (1883); appointed Archbishop of Bologna (1907); elected pope (1914); during his pontificate, a British representative was accredited to the Holy See for the first time since the seventeenth century.

BENIGNI, Umberto (1862-1934): Italian Church historian, journalist and integralist; ordained a priest (1884); appointed secretary of the Congregation for the Propagation of the Faith (1904) and later undersecretary at the press office of the Secretariat of State (1906-1911); involved with Cardinal Merry del Val in the secret organization *Sodalitium Pianum*, which he himself founded (1909); supporter of the *Action Française*.

BENSON, Edward White (1829-1896): Educated at Trinity College, Cambridge; appointed Master of Wellington School (1859); named first Bishop of Truro (1877) and later Archbishop of Canterbury(1883); friend of W.E. Gladstone; revived the Court of the Archbishop of Canterbury in order to deal with questions concerning rubrics in *The Book of Common Prayer* and practices in the Church of England.

BESSON, Mario (1876-1945): Bishop of Fribourg (1920).

BIDWELL, Emmanuel (1872-1930): Auxilary Bishop of Westminster (1917).

BILLOT, Louis (1846-1931): Jesuit theologian; professor of Dogma; consultor to the Holy Office; created Cardinal (1911) but later forced to renounce the title due to his strong sympathy for the *Action Française* when that movement was condemned by Pope Pius XI (1927).

BISHOP, Edmund (1846-1917): English Liturgist and historian; converted to Roman Catholicism (1867) and hoped to join the Benedictine monastery at Downside but ill health kept him out; close friend to F.A. Gasquet; among his most noted writings are his works on the early history of the Roman Liturgy, many of which were later collected and published posthumously in *Liturgia Historica* (1918).

BLOXAM, John Rouse (1807-1891): Anglican ceremonialist and historian; ordained priest (1833); fellow of Magdalen College, Oxford (1836); associated with the Tractarian Movement; J.H. Newman's curate (1837-1840); considered as the originator of the ceremonial revival in the Church of England; one of the first Tractarians to establish relations with Roman Catholics.

BONNER, Edmund (1500-1569): Chaplain to Thomas Cardinal Wolsey; appointed Bishop of Hereford (1538) and later Bishop of London (1539); an uncompromising defender of traditional Catholic doctrine during the English Reformation; the last Bishop of London to be in communion with the See of Rome.

BONOMELLI, Geremia (1861-1914): Ordained priest (1855); named Bishop of Cremona (1871); deeply concerned with the pastoral and social problems of his time, the relationship between science and religion, and the Roman Question; the Lateran Treaty (1929) would reflect many of the solutions Bonomelli had proposed years earlier.

BOSSUET, Jacques-Bénigne (1627-1704): Noted French orator; Bishop of Condom (1669); tutor to the Dauphin (1670); translated to the See of Meaux (1681); author of the Four Gallican Articles (1682) presented to the *Assemblée générale du Clergé*; responsible for the condemnation of Archbishop Fénelon on the question of mysticism.

BOURNE, Francis (1861-1935): Son of an English convert; educated at Ushaw College, Durham and St Edmund's, Ware; received theological training at Saint Sulpice, Paris; ordained priest (1884); appointed rector of the house of studies at Henfield Place, Sussex (1889) and later at the diocesan seminary at Wonersh (1891); named Bishop of Southwark (1896) and later Archbishop of Westminster (1903); created Cardinal (1911).

BOURRET, Joseph Christian Ernest (1827-1896): Ordained priest (1851) and later joined the Oratorians; appointed Bishop of Rodez and Vabres (1871);

created Cardinal (1893); noted for his strong support for the French *Ralliement*.

BROWN, Thomas Joseph (1798-1880): Member of the Benedictine community at Acton Burnell (1813); ordained priest (1823); appointed professor of theology at Downside and was later elected prior of that community; consecrated bishop and appointed Apostolic Vicar of the Welsh District (1840); translated to the See of Newport and Menevia (1850); he was involved in a number of controversial discussions with English Protestants throughout his life.

BUONAIUTI, Ernesto (1881-1946): Modernist writer; ordained priest (1903); professor of philosophy at the Urbanian University, Rome and later professor of ecclesiastical history at the Apollinaris, Rome; reputed to be the author of the anonymous work *Il programma dei modernisti* (1907) which was placed on the Index (1908) and was also translated into English by G. Tyrrell; Buonaiuti was editor of the periodical *Rivista storica-critica delle scienze teologiche* (1905-1910) and the director of the review *Nova et Vetera* (1908) where his Modernist views led to his excommunication (1925); the entire body of his work was condemned on three separate occasions (1924, 1925, 1944).

BURGE, Hubert Murray (1862-1925): Fellow of University College, Oxford (1890) and later Dean of the college (1895); ordained priest (1897); appointed headmaster of Winchester College (1901); named Bishop of Southwark (1911) and later translated to the See of Oxford (1919).

CALVET, Jean (1874-1965): French critic and literary historian; ordained priest (1896); professor at the *Institut Catholique de Toulouse* (1904-1907) and the Collège Stanislas, Paris (1907-1921); later appointed professor of literature at the *Institut Catholique de Paris*; named Dean (1934) and acting rector (1942) of the *Institut* but never accepted the appointment as rector.

CECIL, Hugh Richard Heathcote Gascoyne (1869-1956): Conservative politician and devout Anglican; played an active role in the creation of the Church Assembly (1920's); unsuccessfully fought for the acceptance of the *Revised Prayer Book* in the House of Commons (1927,1928); appointed provost of Eton (1936); raised to the peerage as Baron Quickwood (1941).

CERRETTI, Bonaventura (1872-1933): Ordained priest (1895); secretary for the Congregation for External Ecclesiastical Affairs (1901); joined the Apostolic Delegation at Washington, D.C. (1906); appointed Apostolic Delegate to Australasia and consecrated bishop (1914); returning to Rome, he was named Deputy Secretary of State becoming involved in missions to France, Belgium, England and the United States; appointed papal nuncio to France (1920); created cardinal (1925).

CHOLLET, Jean Arthur (1862-1952): Ordained priest (1886); consecrated Bishop of Verdun (1910); named Archbishop of Cambrai (1913).

CLÉMENCEAU, Georges Benjamin (1841-1929): French statesman; Premier

(1906-1909, 1917-1920); noted anticlericalist who supported the complete separation of Church and State.

COFFIN, Robert Aston (1819-1885): Ordained Anglican priest (1843); converted to the Roman Church (1845) and was reordained (1847) after joining the Oratory of St. Philip Neri; later joined the Redemptorist Congregation and made his profession (1852); appointed rector of St. Mary's, Clapham (1855) and made provincial of the congregation (1865); consecrated Bishop of Southwark (1882).

DALGAIRNS, Bernard John Dobree (1818-1876): Supporter of the Oxford Movement in its early days; joined J.H. Newman at Littlemore after Newman's conversion (1845) and he himself joined the Roman Church; ordained a priest of the Oratory in London (1849); wrote a number of widely used theological and devotional works such as *The Devotion to the Sacred Heart of Jesus* (1853) and *The Holy Communion. Its Philosophy, Theology, and Practice* (1861).

DARBOY, Georges (1813-1871): Bishop of Nancy (1859) and later Archbishop of Paris (1863); due to doctrinal disagreement, Pius IX refused to elevate him to the cardinalate; during the Vatican Council (1869-1870) he was the leader of the French resistance against the proclamation of papal infallibility yet he was eventually forced to submit to the Council's decrees (1871); he was executed during the Commune Revolt that same year.

DAVIDSON, Randall Thomas (1848-1930): Son of Scottish Presbyterian parents; later converted to the Church of England (1865) and was ordained priest (1875); appointed resident chaplain to the Archbishop of Canterbury (1878); named Dean of Windsor (1883) and became a confidential advisor to Queen Victoria; after holding the Bishoprics of Rochester (1891) and Winchester (1895), he was appointed Archbishop of Canterbury (1903); following his resignation as primate (1928), he was elevated to the peerage as the Baron of Lambeth in recognition of his service to the Church and the nation.

DE LAI, Gaetano (1853-1928): Created cardinal (1907); member of the Holy Office and the Consistorial Congregation.

DE LISLE, Ambrose March Phillips (1809-1878): English Roman Catholic writer; converted from Anglicanism (1824); founder of the Association of Universal Prayer for the Conversion of England (1838) and involved in the establishment of the Association for Promoting the Unity of Christendom (1857) which included Anglican, Roman Catholic, and Eastern Orthodox members and which was eventually condemned by Rome (1864); throughout the rest of his life De Lisle continued to be active in furthering the cause of reunion between Roman Catholics and Anglicans.

DE NOAILLES, Louis Antione (1651-1729): Archbishop of Paris (1695); created cardinal (1700) and later appointed head of the Sorbonne, Paris (1710); suspected of Jansenism due to his condemnation (1695) of Pasquier Quesnel's *Réflexions morales* and his disapproval of Probablism; he opposed the bull *Unigenitus* (1713) and went so far as to formally appeal against it (1718); although he was later forced to accept the bull, he recanted privately before his death; De Noailles was a devoted pastor, ardent reformer of clerical practices and an upholder of Gallican ideals.

D'HERBIGNY, Michel (1880-1957): Ordained priest (1910); appointed professor of Scripture and Theology at the Jesuit Scholasticate in Enghien, Belgium; named director of graduate studies at the Gregorian University, Rome (1921); appointed president (1923) and later rector (1926) of the Pontifical Oriental Institute, Rome; consecrated bishop and given a mission by Pius XI to enter the Soviet Union and secretly consecrate bishops there but the mission failed and he returned to Rome, taking up his activities as special consultor to the Congregation for the Oriental Churches; he later played an important role in the foundation of the Pontifical Russian College, Rome (1929); appointed president of the Papal Commission on Russia (1930); eventually fell into disrepute with the Holy See and his title as bishop was revoked (1937).

DÖLLINGER, Johann Joseph Ignaz von (1799-1890): Bavarian Church historian; ordained priest (1822); professor at Aschaffenburg (1823-1826) and Munich (1826-1873); friend of J.H. Newman and Lord Acton; developed a notion of a German Church free from State control, which he defended in several of his writings such as *Reformation* (1845-1848) and *Luther* (1851); gradually developed a distrust for Roman influence; played a leading role in the Congress of Munich (1863) where he defended a more liberal form of Catholicism; his disagreement with Rome was furthered by the publication of Pius IX's encyclical *Quanta cura* which included the *Syllabus errorum* (1864) and the Vatican Council (1869-1870); he expressed his criticism of the Council and its definition of papal infallibility in a series of letters written under the pseudonyms Janus and Quirinus (1869-1870); excommunicated for his refusal to submit to the Council's decisions (1871); later identified himself with the Old Catholic Church; an eminent and respected scholar, *Die Papstfabeln des Mittelalters* (1863) is among the most well known of his many writings.

DUCHESNE, Louis (1843-1922): French Church historian; ordained priest (1867); appointed professor of Church History at the *Institut Catholique de Paris* (1877) but temporarily resigned (1885) due to opposition to his opinion on the history of doctrine; appointed director of the French School in Rome (1895); named a member of the French Academy (1910); among his more well known works are: *Liber Pontificalis* (1886-1892) and *L'Histoire ancienne de l'Église chrétienne* (1906-1910).

DUPANLOUP, Felix Antione Philbert (1802-1878): Ordained priest (1825); one of the foremost educationalists of France; appointed superior of the seminary of St. Nicolas-du Chardonnet (1837); named Bishop of Orléans (1849); through his efforts, rights were secured for the Church to conduct voluntary schools; at the Vatican Council (1869-1870) he was a vocal opponent of the doctrine of papal infallibility, urging members of the minority to abstain from voting on the issue; later he was forced to submit to the Council's decree (1871); he was active in French politics as a member of the National Assembly (1871) and later the Senate (1875).

Du Pin, Louis Ellies (1657-1719): French Gallican theologian with Jansenist leanings and patristic scholar; author of such controversial works as *Nouvelle bibliothèque des auteurs ecclésiastiques* (1686-1691), *Histoire des controverses et des matières ecclésiastiques* (1694-1698), *Histoire de l'Église et des auteurs ecclésiastiques du XVI siècle* (1701-1703), *Bibliothèque des auteurs ecclésiastiques du XVII et du XVIII siècle* (1708), and *Traité de la puissance ecclésiastique et temporelle* (1707); the greater part of his work was eventually placed on the Index (1757).

Errington, George (1804-1886): English theologian; ordained priest (1827); vice rector at the English College, Rome (1832), president of St. Mary's College, Oscott (1843); named Bishop of Plymouth (1851); appointed Titular Archbishop of Trebizond and coadjutor with right of succession to the See of Westminster (1855); due to growing difficulties with Archbishop N.P.S. Wiseman, Pius IX revoked his appointment to Westminster (1862); at the Vatican Council (1869-1870) he upheld a strong anti-infallibility position.

Faber, Frederick William (1814-1863): Fellow of University College, Oxford (1837); under the influence of J.H. Newman, he abandoned his Calvinist upbringing; ordained Anglican priest (1839); appointed rector of Elton (1842); several weeks after Newman's conversion, Faber also joined the Roman Church (1845); with other converts, he formed a small community in Birmingham called the Brothers of the Will of God; reordained (1847) and, together with the other members of the community, joined the Oratory of St. Philip Neri (1848); appointed head of that Oratory (1849); author of numerous hymns and devotional works.

Fawkes, Guy (1570-1606): English Protestant turned papist; involved in the so-called Gunpowder Plot to blow up the houses of Parliament and to kill the king; the plot was thwarted and he was arrested (1605) and later executed; the result of the plot was an increase in the unpopularity of Roman Catholics in England; the frustration of the plot was commemorated yearly on 5 November until 1859.

Ferrata, Domenico (1847-1914): Auditor at the papal nunciature in Paris (1879); director of the *Accademia dei Nobili Ecclesiastici* (1883); appointed undersecretary and later secretary (1889) of the Congregation for External Ecclesiastical Affairs; appointed nuncio to Brussels (1885) and consecrated bishop; sent as nuncio to Paris where he was involved in Leo XIII's policy of *Ralliement*; created cardinal (1896); successively appointed as prefect of the Congregation of Indulgences (1899), prefect of the Congregation of Rites (1900), prefect of the Congregation of Religious (1902), and prefect of the Congregation of the Discipline of the Sacraments (1908); he was also appointed as secretary of the Holy Office (1913) and Secretary of State (1914) several weeks before his death.

Fitzalan, Edmund Bernard Howard (1855-1947): First Viscount Fitzalan; educated at the Oratory School, Birmingham where he developed a strong devotion to J.H. Newman; elevated to the peerage and appointed as first Catholic viceroy of Ireland (1921) but retired a year later; a profoundly religious man, he was for years the most prominent Roman Catholic in Great Britain; elected president of the Catholic Union of Great Britain; intimate friend and confidant of Cardinal H. Vaughan.

FLEMING, David Hay (1849-1931): Historian, antiquary and critic; authority on the Scottish Reformation.

FOCH, Ferdinand (1851-1929): General, marshal of France; appointed chief of the allied armies at the end of the First World War (1918).

FOGAZZARO, Antonio (1842-1911): Italian Roman Catholic writer, poet, and philosopher; many of his writings and ideas contained the liberal characteristics of his age though he remained faithful to and active in the Roman Catholic Church; *Il Santo* (1905), his most famous novel, was eventually placed on the Index (1906) as were several of his other works but he obediently submitted; he was one of the earliest advocates of an active lay participation in the Church.

FRANCIS XAVIER (1506-1552): Apostle to the Indies and to Japan;together with St. Ignatius Loyola, he was one of the initial members of the Society of Jesus; canonized (1622).

FRERE, Walter Howard (1863-1938): Anglican High Churchman; ordained priest (1887); later joined the Community of the Resurrection, Mirfield (1892) and became its superior (1902-1913, 1916-1922); appointed Bishop of Truro (1923); active in both liturgical reform and the promotion of unity between the Anglicans and the Eastern Orthodox; resigned his See (1935) and retired to Mirfield.

FROUDE, Richard Hurrell (1803-1836): Fellow of Oriel College, Oxford; close friend of J.H. Newman and collaborator in the early stages of the Tractarian Movement; took part in the conference on Church reform held at Hadleigh Rectory (1833); the publication of his *Remains* (1838-1839) showed him to be an ascetic and to hold many traditional points of view such as clerical celibacy and devotion to the Virgin.

GASPARRI, Pietro (1852-1934): Ordained priest (1877); appointed to the newly established chair of Canon Law at the *Institut Catholique de Paris* (1890); member of the commission which investigated the validity of Anglican Orders (1896); consecrated bishop (1898); appointed secretary of the Congregation for External Ecclesiastical Affairs (1901); created cardinal (1907); appointed Secretary of State (1914); involved in the formation of the new code of Canon Law (1917); chief negotiator with B. Mussolini in concluding the Lateran Treaty (1929) which resolved the Roman Question; resigned his post as Secretary of State shortly thereafter (1930).

GASQUET, Francis Aidan (1846-1929): Historian; entered the Benedictine monastery at Downside (1866); elected prior (1878); member of the commission studying the question of Anglican Orders (1896); abbot – president of the English Benedictine Congregation (1900-1914); appointed president of the International Commission for the Revision of the Vulgate (1907); created cardinal (1914); appointed prefect of the Archives of the Holy See (1917) and later Vatican librarian (1919).

GILLE, Albert (1878-1950): Dutch born Jesuit; journalist; editor of *The Catholic Herald of India* where his criticism and advanced ideas brought him into trouble and eventually led to his dismissal (1925); sent by the Jesuits to Scotland and then to England; published *A Catholic Plea for Reunion* (1934) under a number of pseudonyms such as Father Jerome and Father Ambrose; that same year, he left the Jesuits.

GIOBERTI, Vincenzo (1801-1852): Italian politician and religious philosopher; ordained priest (1825); under the influence of G. Mazzini, he worked for the unification of Italy; eventually arrested and banished from Italy (1830); took up residence in Brussels where he outlined the platform for the Neo Guelfish party; returned to Italy (1848) to become president of the Chamber of Deputies and later a member of the cabinet of King Victor Emmanuel II (1849); the publication of his *Il Rinnovamento civile d'Italia* (1851) manifested his adoption of liberalism; he spent his last years in voluntary exile in Paris.

GLADSTONE, William Ewart (1809-1898): English statesman; had desired an ecclesiastical career but entered into politics on the wishes of his father; elected to Parliament (1832); held the positions of vice president of the Board of Trade (1841), Chancellor of the Exchequer (1852-1855, 1859-1865), leader of the Liberal party (1867), Prime Minister (1868-1874, 1880-1885, 1886, 1892-1894); noted for his strong religious convictions which were formed from a combination of High Church principles and Evangelical education; sympathetic to the Oxford Movement.

GOODIER, Alban (1869-1939): English Jesuit; ordained priest (1903); sent to quell the wartime crisis at the Jesuit University, Bombay (1915); appointed Archbishop of Bombay (1919) but later resigned the See (1926) in the face of political and religious problems; participated as an observer at the Thackeray Hotel conversations.

GORE, Charles (1853-1932): Fellow of Trinity College, Oxford (1875); appointed first principal of Pusey House, Oxford (1884); editor of *Lux Mundi*, a series of studies in the religion of Incarnation (1889); involved in the foundation of the Anglican Community of the Resurrection, Mirfield (1892); appointed Canon of Westminster (1894), Bishop of Worcester (1902), and later Bishop of Birmingham (1905); translated to the See of Oxford (1911) which he later resigned (1919); he was a scholar of note; author of many works, a number of which were apologetic concerning the Anglo-Catholic movement; he was also responsible for introducing a scientific method of exegesis and theology into that movement.

GÖRRES, Johann Joseph von (1776-1848): German Roman Catholic author; friend of J.J.I. von Döllinger and J.A. Möhler; many of his works such as *Glaube und Wissen* (1805), *Deutschland und Revolution* (1819), and *Die Triarier* (1838) were recognized as the single most influential and formative force in 19th century Roman Catholic thought and contributed to the spread of Roman Catholic ideas in modern Germany.

GOSS, Alexander (1814-1872): Educated at St Cuthbert's College, Ushaw and the English College, Rome; ordained priest (1841); appointed superior of

St. Edward's College, Everton (1842); consecrated bishop (1853) and succeeded to the See of Liverpool (1856).

GRANT, Thomas (1816-1870): Educated at St. Cuthbert's College, Ushaw and the English College, Rome; appointed rector of the English College (1844); consecrated first Bishop of Southwark (1851); attended the Vatican Council (1869-1870) where he died (1870).

GUIBERT, Jean (1857-1914): Superior of the *Séminaire des Carmes*; appointed vice rector of the *Institut Catholique de Paris* where he was also the superior of the *Institut's* seminary.

HALIFAX, Charles Lindley Wood (1839-1934): Cf. *supra* (passim).

HOPE-SCOTT, James Robert (1812-1873): Fellow of Merton College, Oxford (1833); admitted to the bar (1838); counsel for the deans and chapters against the Ecclesiastical Duties and Revenues Bill; appointed chancellor of Salisbury; promotor of the Oxford Movement and close friend of J.H. Newman; converted to the Roman Church (1850) along with H.E. Manning; his brilliance as a lawyer led to his appointment as Queen's Counsel and as standing counsel for almost every railway company in the United Kingdom.

HOWARD, Henry (1847-1917): Duke of Norfolk; educated at the Oratory School, Edgbaston; an active Roman Catholic, he maintained close relations with the Vatican throughout his life; he worked tirelessly for the development of Roman Catholic education in Ireland.

HÜGEL, Friedrich VON (1852-1925): Baron; Roman Catholic theologian and philosopher; friend of Abbé Henri Huvelin; sympathetic to liberal and Modernist tendencies in the Roman Catholic Church; founded the London Society for the Study of Religion (1905); named Gifford Lecturer at the University of Edinburgh (1924-1926); one of the chief religious influences in the cultural circles of England both within and outside of the Roman Church; though he was involved with Modernists such as G. Tyrrell and A. Loisy, he was never personally condemned by the Church.

IRELAND, John (1838-1918): Irish born American prelate; educated in France; ordained priest (1861); staunch supporter of the Union in the U.S. Civil War; appointed Bishop T.L. Grace's representative at the Vatican Council (1869-1870); appointed coadjutor with the right of succession to the See of St. Paul, Minnesota and was consecrated bishop (1875); assumed the See (1884) which was later raised to the rank of an archdiocese and Ireland became an archbishop; continually work for understanding and respect between the Church and the American democratic environment; sent on diplomatic missions to France by both the pope and the U.S. government; strong supporter of Catholic education and the Catholic labor movement.

JANSSENS, Aloïs (1887-1941): Member of the Congregation of the Immaculate Heart of Mary (Scheutists); appointed professor of dogmatic theology at the Scheut Theologicum, Louvain; helped to found the first Mariological society at Tongerloo (1931); authored many dogmatic and apologetic works which greatly contributed to a theological renewal in Belgium.

JARRETT, Bede (1881-1934): English Dominican, historian, and spiritual writer; entered the Dominican order at Woodchester (1898); first Dominican of modern times to be sent to Oxford (1904); studied theology at the Catholic University of Louvain; elected provincial of England (1916); established a Dominican house of studies at Oxford (1921) and later became prior of that house (1932).

JORDENS, Rombout (1873-1953): Norbertine canon; editor-in-chief of the *Tongerloo's Tijdschrift.*

KEATING, Joseph (1865-1939): English Jesuit; ordained priest (1899); appointed editor of *The Month* (1912).

KEBLE, John (1792-1866): Fellow (1811) and later tutor (1817) of Oriel College, Oxford; High Church clergyman; author of *The Christian Year* (1827); his sermon on National Apostasy (July 1833), which stressed the dangers of the reforming and liberal movements for the Church of England, marked the beginning of the Oxford Movement; he contributed a number of tracts for J.H. Newman's *Tracts for the Times*; after Newman's conversion to Roman Catholicism, Keble remained a firm associate of E.B. Pusey in keeping the High Church movement steadily attached to the Church of England.

KIDD, Beresford James (1864-1948): Warden of Keble College, Oxford; author of numerous works on the ancient Church and Counter Reformation periods.

KNOX, Ronald Arbuthnott (1888-1957): Author, Biblical scholar; ordained priest (1910); named fellow and chaplain of Trinity College, Oxford (1912); leader of the extreme Anglo-Catholic movement until his conversion to the Roman Church (1917); later reordained (1919); appointed chaplain to the Roman Catholic students at Oxford (1926); among his many books, there are included a number of apologetic works.

LABERTHONNIÈRE, Lucien (1860-1932): Roman Catholic Modernist theologian; ordained priest (1886); held teaching positions at the *Collège*, Juilly (1887) and the *École Massillon*, Paris (1896); appointed rector at Juilly (1900); editor of the *Annales de philosophie chrétienne* (1905-1913); associate of M. Blondel; several of his theological works were eventually placed on the Index (1906) and he was later prohibited from any further publication (1913); exercised much influence on G. Tyrrell.

LACEY, Thomas Alexander (1853-1931): Anglican theologian; ordained priest (1876); appointed Canon of Worcester (1918), an effective and original apologist for the Church of England; devoted to the cause of reunion; played an active role as adviser to the papal commission examining Anglican Orders (1896); in conjunction with E. Denny, authored *De Hierarchia Anglicana Dissertatio Apologetica* (1895), in defense of the validity of Anglican ordination.

LACORDAIRE, Henri Dominique (1802-1861): French Dominican preacher; converted to Roman Catholicism (1824); ordained priest (1827); advocate of liberalism in relations between Church and State; associated with

F.R. de Lamennais and contributor to the newspaper *L'Avenir*; disassociated himself from Lamennais and the liberal movement after its condemnation in the encyclical *Mirari vos* (1832); eventually retired to Rome and entered the Dominican order (1839); returned to France (1841) and devoted himself to the restoration of the order there; chosen as provincial (1850-1854, 1858-1861); elected to the French Academy (1860).

LA FONTAINE, Pietro (1860-1935): Appointed Bishop of Cassano all Jonio (1906); named Patriarch of Venice (1915); created cardinal (1916).

LAGRANGE, Marie Joseph (1855-1938): French biblical scholar; ordained priest (1883); founder of the *École Pratique d'Études Bibliques*, Jerusalem (1890); he was suspected of Modernism and subjected to certain disciplinary measures but he was never censured for his work; later he was praised in the encyclical *Divino afflante Spirito* (1943).

LAMENNAIS, Felicité Robert DE (1782-1854): French priest, writer, philosopher, and pioneer of liberal Catholicism; defended modern freedoms and separation of Church and State; founded the newspaper *L'Avenir* (1830), which was the voice of Roman Catholic liberalism; after an initial condemnation of the liberal program, in the papal encyclical *Mirari vos* (1832), Lamennais submitted but soon began to publish again; a new and direct condemnation in the encyclical *Singulari nos* (1834) led to his complete break with the Catholic Church; he was elected to the National Assembly (1848) but after a *coup d'état* (1851), he retired in disillusionment.

LAMY, Thomas Joseph (1827-1907): Orientalist and Biblical scholar; ordained priest (1852); appointed professor at the Catholic University of Louvain (1858); appointed consultor to the Pontifical Biblical Commission (1903).

LANG, William Cosmo Gordon (1864-1945): Scottish Presbyterian who converted to Anglicanism, studied law but later took up theology and was ordained priest (1890); appointed Dean of Divinity at Magdalen College, Oxford (1894); named Archbishop of York (1908); later translated to the See of Canterbury (1928); played an important role in the public affairs associated with the abdication of Edward VIII (1936); resigned his See (1942).

LE COURRAYER, Pierre François (1681-1776): Professor of theology and librarian at *St Geneviève*, Paris; author of *Dissertation sur la validité des ordinations des Anglais et la succession des évêques de l'Église Anglicane, avec les preuves justificatives des faits avancés* (1723) and *Défense de la dissertation* (1726); he was eventually excommunicated (1728) and later settled in England.

LEE, Fredrick George (1832-1902): Anglican priest and theological writer; active in promoting reunion with the Roman Church; involved in the founding of the Association for Promoting the Unity of Christendom (1857); converted to Roman Catholicism shortly before his death (1901); the *Directorium Anglicanum* (1865) and *A Glossary of Liturgical and Ecclesiastical Terms* (1877) are two of the better known works among his voluminous writings.

LEO XIII (1810-1903): Vincenzo Gioacchino Pecci; ordained priest; appointed nuncio to Belgium (1843); created cardinal (1853); elected pope (1878); his pontificate was characterized by a conciliatory attitude regarding civil governments, a greater openness to scholarly research, and a deep concern for the pastoral and social problems of his time.

LE ROY, Édouard (1870-1954): French Roman Catholic philosopher; appointed to the chair of philosophy at the *Collège de France* (1921); known for his development of the thought of H. Bergson which he applied not only to philosophy but also to theology as well; his work, *Dogme et critique* was put on the *Index* the year of its publication (1907).

LOISY, Alfred Firmin (1857-1940): French Biblical scholar; ordained priest (1879); inspired by his friend L. Duchesne to adopt a historical-critical approach, which he then applied to Scripture study; appointed professor of Sacred Scripture at the *Institut Catholique de Paris* (1890); dismissed as a result of his critical studies (1893); began to develop a new apologetic for Catholicism and took up a teaching position at the *École Pratique des Hautes Études* (1900); a number of his works were placed on the *Index* by Pius X; Loisy eventually made a formal submission (1904) and resigned his teaching post; his published criticism of the decree *Lamentabili* and the encyclical *Pascendi* led to his excommunication (1908); appointed professor of history of religion at the *Collège de France* (1909); continued to write prolifically on the origin of Christianity and on comparative history of religion; in his autobiographical writings *Choses passées* (1913) and *Mémoires pour servir à l'histoire religieuse de notre temps* (1930-1931), he attempted to explain his role in the Modernist movement.

MACLAGEN, William Dalrymple (1826-1910): Scottish convert to the Church of England (1843); educated at Cambridge University; ordained priest (1856); co-edited a series of essays entitled *The Church and the Age* (1870-1872) which demonstrated his moderate High Church tendencies; named Bishop of Lichfield and appointed chaplain-in-ordinary to Queen Victoria (1878); attended an ecumenical conference with the Old Catholics where he interviewed J.J.I. Döllinger (1887); translated to the Archdiocese of York (1891); together with Archbishop F. Temple, MacLagen issued a *Responsio* (1896) to the bull *Apostolicae curae* which denied the validity of Anglican orders; resigned his See due to declining health (1908).

MCNABB, Vincent (1868-1943): English Dominican theologian; ordained priest (1891); studied theology at the Catholic University of Louvain (1891-1894); while his character was somewhat enigmatic, he was well known for his writing and preaching in the area of theology, spiritual life, and especially, social concern.

MANNING, Henry Edward (1808-1892): Fellow of Merton College, Oxford (1832); ordained Anglican priest (1833); appointed Archdeacon of Chichester (1841); evolved toward the Tractarian position and after J.H. Newman's conversion (1845) was considered one of the leaders of the Oxford Movement; converted to the Roman Church (1851) and later reordained; studied at the *Accademia dei Nobili Ecclesiastici*, Rome, for two years at the request of Pius IX; appointed Provost of the Westminster Chapter (1857) and that same year, founded the Oblates of St. Charles; appointed Archbishop of Westminster (1865); staunch supporter of papal infallibility at the Vatican Council (1869-1870) and vowed to do his utmost to secure its proclamation; created cardinal (1875).

MARTINDALE, Cyril Charles (1879-1963): English Jesuit; preacher at Campion Hall; converted to Roman Catholicism (1897); joined the Jesuits and was later ordained priest (1911); promoted the intellectual development of Catholic life and the apostolic awakening of English Roman Catholicism.

MASKELL, William (1814-1890): Ecclesiastical antiquary, extreme High Church-man, ordained priest (1837); the results of the Gorham case led to his conversion to the Roman Church (1850); his works, such as *Monumenta Ritualia Ecclesiae Anglicanae* (1846), were valuable for the revival of liturgical studies in the Church of England.

MAZZELLA, Camillo (1833-1900): Italian theologian; ordained priest (1855) and later joined the Jesuits (1857); after teaching theology for several years at the University of Georgetown, and Woodstock College in the United States he was appointed to the chair of theology at the Gregorian University, Rome (1878); created cardinal (1886); later appointed prefect of both the Congregations of Studies and of Rites; involved in the papal commission, and subsequent author of the papal letter *Testem benevolentiae* (1899) which condemned the so-called Americanism; an eminent theologian, Mazzella was a strong supporter of the Neo-Thomistic revival.

MERCIER, Désiré Joseph (1851-1926): Cf. *supra* (passim).

MERRY DEL VAL, Rafael (1865-1930): Son of the secretary of the Spanish legation to London; educated at the *Accademia dei Nobili Ecclesiastici*, Rome; ordained priest (1888) and entered the papal diplomatic services; secretary to the commission which pronounced against Anglican Orders (1896); appointed Titular Archbishop of Nicaea (1900); created cardinal and named Secretary of State (1903) by Pius X; he identified himself closely with the pope's intransigent policies; appointed Secretary of the Holy Office (1914) by Benedict XV, where exercised a great deal of influence.

MONTALEMBERT, Charles René Forbes DE (1810-1870): French publicist, politi-cian, and historian; ardent religious liberal; associated with F.R. de Lamennais and contributor to the newspaper *L'Avenir*; broke with Lamennais after the condemnation of the liberal program by the encyclical *Mirari vos* (1832); later adopted a weakened form of liberalism; elected to the Chamber of Deputies (1848-1857); editor of the newspaper *Le Corres-pondent* (1855); attend the Congress of Belgian Catholics at Malines (1863) where he pleaded for "a free Church in a free State".

MYERS, Edward (1875-1956): Ordained priest (1902); appointed professor of dogmatic theology and patrology at St. Edmund's College, Ware; later named president of the college (1919); appointed canon and later auxilary bishop of Westminster.

NEWMAN, John Henry (1801-1890): English theologian; fellow (1822) and tutor (1826) of Oriel College, Oxford; vicar of St Mary's Church, Oxford (1828); one of the leaders of the Oxford Movement but later resigned due to a conflict over some of his writings; converted to Catholicism (1845) and was reordained in Rome (1846); founded the first Oratory in England (1848); named rector of the Roman Catholic University of Dublin (1851-1858); created cardinal (1879).

OAKLEY, Frederick (1802-1880): Chaplain and fellow of Balliol College, Oxford (1827); joined the Tractarian Movement under the influence of W.G. Ward; converted to the Roman Church three weeks after J.H. Newman (1845); reordained priest (1847) and appointed canon of the Archdiocese of Westminster (1852).

O'CONNELL, Daniel (1775-1847): Irish politician; champion of the rights of Irish Catholics; founder of the Catholic Association (1823) which worked for Catholic emancipation.

O'CONNELL, William (1859-1944): Ordained priest (1884); appointed rector of the North American College, Rome (1895); while in Rome, he developed cordial relations with Leo XIII, Papal Secretary of State M. Rampolla, Cardinal R. Merry Del Val, and many others in the Roman diplomatic and social circles; consecrated Bishop of Portland, Maine (1901); translated to Boston as auxiliary bishop (1906) and succeeded as ordinary a year later; created cardinal (1911).

OLDMEADOW, Ernest (1867-1949): English novelist and journalist; Wesleyan minister in Nova Scotia, Canada; converted to Roman Catholicism (1897); appointed editor of *The Tablet* (1923) by Cardinal F. Bourne, where he worked vigorously to defend the Roman Church against the Church of England in a polemical fashion; his editorship was terminated (1936) when the newspaper was sold; later authored a biography of Cardinal Bourne (1940-1944).

PARSONS, Wilfrid (1887-1958): American Jesuit, author, and journalist; ordained priest (1918); appointed professor of theology at Woodstock College, Maryland (1922); named editor of the Jesuit weekly *America* (1925).

PETRE, Maude (1863-1942): English author; involved with a number of suspected Modernists such as G. Tyrrell, who was later condemned, and F. von Hügel, who was never condemned; Petre herself was never condemned for Modernism; along with the many well known devotional works that she penned, there are a number of biographical works on Tyrrell.

PHILLPOTTS, Henry (1778-1869): Fellow of Magdalen College, Oxford (1795); named Dean of Chester (1828) and later Bishop of Exeter (1830); High Churchman sympathetic with the Oxford Movement; best known for his refusal to grant Rev. G.C. Gorham a parish due to Gorham's theological views; he continuously worked to raise the standard of public worship; championed the revival of religious orders in the Church of England.

PIUS IX (1792-1878): Giovanni Maria Mastai-Ferretti; ordained priest (1819); appointed Archbishop of Spoleto (1827) and later, Bishop of Imola

(1832); created cardinal (1849); elected pope (1846); at first appeared to be sympathetic to the liberal cause but after he was forced to flee Rome (1848), due to an uprising in favor of political reform in the Papal States, he became more and more intransigently opposed to the movement; summoned the Vatican Council (1869-1870) which proclaimed the doctrine of papal infallibility.

PIUS X (1835-1914): Guiseppe Melchiorre Sarto; ordained priest (1859); appointed Bishop of Mantua (1884); created cardinal and named Patriarch of Venice (1893); elected pope (1903); best known for his many pastoral reforms and for his conservative political and theological stances; condemned the so-called errors of Modernism in the decree *Lamentabili* (1907), the encyclical *Pascendi* (1907), and further with a mandatory oath to be taken by all priests and theologians (1910); he was later canonized (1954).

PIUS XI (1857-1939): Achille Ambrogio Damiano Ratti; ordained priest (1879); appointed prefect of the Ambrosian Library (1907); named Titular Archbishop of Lepanto and papal nuncio to Poland (1919); created cardinal and appointed Archbishop of Milan (1921); elected pope (1922); his encyclicals addressed many of the important issues of that day: *Mortalium animos* (1928) condemned Catholic involvement in the ecumenical movement, *Quadragesimo anno* (1931) dealt with social problems, and *Mit brennender Sorge* (1937) was a condemnation of the development of Nazism in Germany; he also concluded the Lateran Treaty (1929) settling the dispute between the Holy See and the Italian Government.

PIUS XII (1876-1958): Eugenio Pacelli; ordained priest (1899); entered the Vatican diplomatic corps (Secretariat of State) (1901); occupied various positions including Secretary of Congregation for Extraordinary Ecclesiastical Affairs (1914) and papal nuncio to the German Republic (1920); created cardinal and appointed Secretary of State (1930); elected as pope (1939) and took the name Pius XII.

POLE, Reginald (1500-1558): Cousin of King Henry VIII of England; opposed to Henry's break with the Roman Church and as a result, spent most of his life in voluntary exile; created cardinal (1536); appointed papal legate to the Council of Trent during its first period (1545-1547); named papal legate to England upon Mary Tudor's accession (1553) and played a major role in the reconciliation of England with the Holy See, consecrated Archbishop of Canterbury (1556), the last Roman Catholic to hold that position.

PORTAL, (Etienne) Fernand (1855-1926): Cf. *supra* (passim).

PUSEY, Edward Bouverie (1800-1882): Anglican High Church theologian; ordained priest (1828); fellow of Oriel College, Oxford (1823); studied Biblical criticism and oriental languages at Göttingen and Berlin in Germany (1825-1827); appointed professor of Hebrew and Canon at Christ Church, Oxford (1828); one of the leading personalities of the Oxford Movement and, after J.H. Newman's conversion (1945), noted for giving the Movement a more ritualistic direction; while Pusey published several tracts for the series Tracts for the Times, his most influential activity was preaching which was mostly on the practical level, stressing the offensiveness of sin and the greatness of heaven; he took an active interest in the establishment of religious life in the Church of England; he vigorously maintained the attachment of the High Church movement to the Church of England, yet he did have a vision of reunion with the Roman Church; he outlined his opinion on the possibility of reunion in his Eirenicon (1865-1870) but was severely disappointed by the results of the Vatican Council (1869-1870).

RAMPOLLA DEL TINDARO, Mariano (1843-1931): Ordained priest (1866); served on the Congregation for Extraordinary Affairs (1870); appointed chargé d'affaires at the papal nunciature at Spain (1876); after holding several curial posts in Rome, he was made papal nuncio to Spain and consecrated bishop (1882); created cardinal and named Secretary of State (1887); appointed secretary of the Holy Office and member of the Pontifical Biblical Commission during the pontificate of Pius X (1903-1914).

RAMSEY, Arthur Michael (1904-1988): Archbishop of Canterbury from 1961 till 1974.

ROBINSON, Joseph Armitage (1858-1933): New Testament and patristic scholar; fellow of Christ's College, Cambridge (1881); ordained Anglican priest (1882); appointed professor at Cambridge (1893); named Canon (1899) and later Dean (1902) of Westminster; named Dean of Wells (1911); founder of the monograph series Texts and Studies (1891) and authored many important works on ancient Church history.

ROSMINI-SERBATI, Antonio, conte di (1797-1855): Italian philosopher and liberal Catholic theologian; ordained priest (1821); founder of the *Istituto della Carità* (1828); adviser to Pius IX; his writings were placed on the Index (1849) but later removed without censure (1854); forty propositions taken from his works were finally condemned posthumously by Leo XIII (1887-1888).

RUTTEN, Martin (1841-1927): ordained priest (1867); appointed president of the *Grand Séminaire* of Liège (1879); consecrated Bishop of Liège (1902).

SENCOURT, Robert (1890-1969): English Roman Catholic layman; somewhat eccentric critic, biographer, and historian; often went by the name R. Gordon George; author of *The Genius of the Vatican* (1935) and *The Life of Newman* (1947); in the face of much English Roman Catholic criticism, he was an outspoken public supporter of the Malines Conversations.

SIBTHORP, Richard Waldo (1792-1879): Ordained priest (1815); fellow of Magdalen College, Oxford (1818); converted to Roman Catholicism (1841) and was reordained the following year only to later return to the Anglican Church (1843); readmitted to the ministry (1857) but was considered by many Anglicans to still be a Roman Catholic priest; he was permitted to celebrate Mass in Cardinal N.P.S. Wiseman's private chapel (1865).

SIMPSON, Richard (1820-1876): English author; ordained priest (1843); converted to the Roman Church (1846); adviser to the journal *The Rambler* which later became the *The Home and Foreign Review* (1850-1864) and was named co-editor (1859); Simpson maintained a liberal view of Catholicism and worked continuously to reconcile Catholic thought with modern scientific development; he was frequently in opposition to the English hierarchy which favored the Ultramontane stance.

Söderblom, Nathan (1866-1931): ordained Lutheran minister (1893); chief promotor of the Life and Work branch of the Ecumenical Movement; appointed professor at Uppsala (1901) and later Leipzig (1912); named Archbishop of Uppsala (1914); a strong proponent of reunion and a leading figure at the Stockholm Conference (1925), Söderblom was influenced by representatives of both liberal Protestantism and Catholic Modernism.

Spencer, George (1799-1866): ordained Anglican priest (1824); consecrated Bishop of Madras (1837); appointed commissary of Bishop R. Bagot of Bath and Wells but later resigned over a conflict concerning the notion of Real Presence in the Eucharist; appointed chancellor of St. Paul's Cathedral (1860) and named rector of Walton-in-the Wolds the following year.

Stamfordham, Arthur John Bigge (1844-1931) Baron Stamfordham; military officer; appointed assistant private secretary and assistant privy purse to Queen Victoria (1880) and eventually appointed private secretary to the queen (1885); later held the same position for King George V (1913) after having been raised to the peerage (1911).

Stone, Darwell (1859-1941): Anglo-Catholic theologian; ordained priest (1885); appointed vice principal (1885) and later principal (1888) of Dorchester Missionary College; appointed principal of Pusey House, Oxford (1909).

Storer, Maria Longworth (1840-1932): wife of the diplomat Bellamy Storer; friend of Cardinal B. Cerretti, papal nuncio to France; helped her husband in negotiations between the United States and the Vatican over Church lands in the Philippines which ended in failure and cost Storer his diplomatic career; converted to Roman Catholicism (1892), as her husband later would do, under the influence of Bishop J. Ireland of St. Paul.

Tait, Archibald Campbell (1811-1882): Presbyterian who converted to the Church of England; fellow of Balliol College, Oxford (1834); opponent of the Anglo-Catholic Movement while favoring a more Latitudinarian perspective; appointed Bishop of London (1856); where his Broad Church sympathies became more prominent; appointed Archbishop of Canterbury (1868).

Temple, Frederick (1821-1902): ordained priest (1847); lecturer at Balliol College, Oxford; took an interest but never became attached to the Tractarian Movement; appointed Headmaster of Rugby (1857); named Bishop of Exeter (1869); translated to the See of London (1885) where he played an important role in the Lincoln Judgement (1890); appointed Archbishop of Canterbury (1897); involved with the Lambeth Conference of that same year and the Lambeth Opinions (1899-1900); in his later years, he increasingly came into conflict with the High Church party.

TYRRELL, George (1861-1909): Anglican High Church theologian; converted to the Roman Church (1879) and joined the Jesuits (1880); ordained priest (1891); taught moral theology at the Jesuit college at Stonyhurst; friend of F. von Hügel; expelled from the Jesuits due to the publication of some unorthodox writings; his public protest of Pius X's encyclical Pascendi (1907) led to his excommunication as a Modernist.

ULLATHORNE, William Bernard (1806-1889): Entered the Benedictine monastery at Downside (1824); ordained priest (1831); appointed Vicar General of Australia (1832) where he did much to organize the Roman Church; returned to England (1840) and given charge of the Benedictine mission at Coventry; appointed Vicar Apostolic for the Western District (1846) and later transfered to the Central District (1848); took an active part in the negotiations for the restoration of the hierarchy (1850) upon which he was named Bishop of Birmingham (till 1888); took part in the Vatican Council (1869-1870) where he held a moderate Ultramontane position.

VAN HOONACKER, Albin (1857-1933): Biblical exegete; one of the Roman Catholic pioneers of scientific Scripture study in Belgium; appointed professor of Old Testament at the Catholic University of Louvain (1889-1927); named consultor to the Biblical Commission (1901); later accused of Modernism but never formally condemned.

VAN ROEY, Joseph-Ernest (1874-1961): Ordained priest (1897); received both the degrees of Doctor and Magister of Theology (1903); appointed Vicar General to Cardinal D.J. Mercier (1907); named Archbishop of Malines-Brussels (1926); created cardinal (1927).

VAUGHAN, Bernard John (1847-1922): Brother of Archbishop H. Vaughan of Westminster; joined the Jesuits (1866); ordained priest (1880); internationally known for his preaching.

VAUGHAN, Herbert Alfred (1832-1903): Ordained priest (1854); appointed vice president of St. Edmund's Seminary, Ware (1855) where he began to champion the Ultramontane cause; joined the Oblates of St. Charles (1857); founded St. Joseph's Missionary Society, Mill Hill (1866); bought the periodicals The Tablet (1868), of which he acted as editor for three years, and The Dublin Review (1878) to promote the Ultramontane cause; appointed Bishop of Salford (1872) and later Archbishop of Westminster (1892); created cardinal (1893); obtained permission from Roman authorities for Roman Catholics to attend the ancient English universities; officially involved in the discussions on the validity of Anglican Orders.

VAUGHAN, Roger William (1834-1883): Brother of Archbishop H. Vaughan of Westminster; entered the Benedictine monastery at Downside (1854); ordained priest (1859); appointed Archbishop of Sydney, Australia (1877).

WAKE, William (1657-1737): Chaplain to the English ambassador to Paris (1682-1685) where he became acquainted with French Gallicanism; later appointed Dean of Exeter (1703) and Bishop of Lincoln (1705); named Archbishop of Canterbury (1716); author of Principle of the Christian Religion (1700) and The State of the Church and Clergy of England (1703).

WALKER, Leslie Ignatius (1877-1958): English convert to Roman Catholicism (1897); joined the Jesuits (1899); ordained priest (1911); attached to Campion Hall, Oxford (1919) and appointed lecturer of Medieval philosophy at the university; author of numerous articles on Church unity.

WARD, Wilfrid (1856-1916): Biographer and Roman Catholic critic; son of W.G. Ward; wrote biographies of his father (1889,1893), N.P.S. Wiseman (1897), and J.H. Newman (1912); sympathetic to the Modernist Movement.

WARD, William George (1812-1882): Theologian and philosopher; fellow of Balliol College, Oxford (1834); follower of J.H. Newman; pushed the Tractarian principles to their furthest extremes; published *The Ideal of a Christian Church* (1844) which praised the Roman Church; converted to Roman Catholicism (1845) and later supported the Ultramontane party condemning all sorts of liberalism.

WATTSON, Paul James Francis (1863-1940): Ordained Episcopalian priest (1886); founder of the Society of the Atonement at Graymoor, New York (1898) with objective of working for Church unity; along these lines, inaugurated the Church Unity Octave (18 till 25 January); later the entire community was corporately received into the Roman Church (1909) and Wattson was reordained (1910).

WAUGH, Evelyn Arthur St. John (1903-1966): English author.

WESTON, Frank (1871-1924): Member of the Anglican Universities' Mission to Central Africa (1898); appointed principal of St. Andrew's Training College, Kiungani (1901); appointed Bishop of Zanzibar (1908); leading inspiration behind the Lambeth Appeal (1920); named president of the Second Anglo-Catholic Congress (1923).

WILBERFORCE, Robert Isaac (1802-1857): Son of the famous philanthropist W. Wilberforce; fellow of Oriel College, Oxford (1826); close associate of J.H. Newman and R.H. Froude; most theologically knowledgeable of the Tractarians; entered into extended theological correspondence with H.E. Manning; converted to Roman Catholicism (1854).

WISEMAN, Nicholas Patrick Stephen (1802-1865): Professor of oriental languages at the *Sapienza*, Rome; rector of the English College, Rome (1828); appointed coadjutor to the Vicar Apostolic of the London District; at the restoration of the English hierarchy (1850), he was named Cardinal Archbishop of Westminster.

WOOD, Edward Frederick Lindley (1881-1959): Baron Irwin (1925) and First Earl of Halifax (1944); son of Charles Lindley Wood, Lord Halifax; appointed Viceroy of India (1926-1931), named Chancellor of Oxford University (1933); Foreign Secretary (1938-1940); British ambassador to the United States (1941-1946); noted High Church Anglican; author of *The Life of John Keble* (1909).

WOODLOCK, Francis (1871-1940): English Jesuit and anti-Modernist; ordained priest (1903); professor at the Jesuit College, Stonyhurst; author of a number of apologetic works on Roman Catholicism.

WORDSWORTH, John (1843-1911): Son of C. Wordsworth, Bishop of Lincoln; fellow of Brasenose College, Oxford (1867); professor of the interpretation of Holy Scripture (1883); appointed Bishop of Salisbury (1885); adviser to Archbishop E.W. Benson of Canterbury; devoted to the cause of reunion, especially with the Swedish and Old Catholic Churches; wrote two treatises on the validity of Anglican Orders: *De successione episcoporum in ecclesia anglicana* (1890) and *De validitate ordinum anglicanorum* (1894) as well as the *Responsio* (1897) which he sent to the Archbishops of Canterbury and York in reply to Leo XIII's encyclical *Apostolicae curae* (1896).

BIBLIOGRAPHY

I

UNPUBLISHED SOURCES FROM ARCHIVES

ABBREVIATIONS

AAM   Archives Archdiocese of Malines
AAW   Archives Archdiocese of Westminster
AEPSJ   Archives English Province of the Society of Jesus
ALPL   Archives Lambeth Palace Library
BIY   Borthwick Institute York

The following archives were consulted and found to contain documents important for the subject of this study:

I. THE BORTHWICK INSTITUTE OF HISTORICAL RESEARCH, YORK, ENGLAND [BIY]

Here were found the Malines papers of Lord Halifax. The documents which have been especially important for our study are:

Box One

N° 12	05.11.21	Jarrett to Halifax
N° 35	29.11.21	Halifax to Portal
N° 39	01.12.21	Portal to Halifax
N° 44	12.12.21	Robinson to Halifax
N° 52	19.12.21	Portal to Halifax
N° 54	22.12.21	Halifax to Portal
N° 60	06.03.22	Portal to Halifax
N° 61	17.03.22	Martindale to Halifax
N° 65	11.04.22	d'Herbigny to Bell
N° 67	26.04.22	Interview of G.K.A. Bell with L. Walker
N° 72	14.06.22	Portal to Halifax
N° 73	11.06.22	Mercier to Portal
N° 87	05.08.22	Stone to Halifax
N° 93	16.09.22	Halifax to Portal
N° 95	20.09.22	Mercier to Halifax
N° 97	22.09.22	Halifax to Mercier
N° 98	24.09.22	Bourne to Halifax
N° 99	24.09.22	McNabb to Halifax
N° 102	29.09.22	Mercier to Halifax
N° 112	09.10.22	Pullan to Halifax
N° 114	12.10.22	Halifax to Mercier (draft)
N° 125	20.11.22	Portal to Halifax

N° 126	23.11.22	Portal to Halifax
N° 127	27.11.22	Portal to Halifax
N° 128	28.11.22	Mercier to Halifax
N° 131	02.12.22	Portal to Halifax

Box Two

N° 7	09.01.23	Bell to Halifax
N° 8	10.01.23	Portal to Halifax
N° 21	16.01.23	Portal to Halifax
N° 60	10.02.23	Halifax to Portal
N° 94	02.03.23	Halifax Mercier
N° 100	08.03.23	Portal to Halifax
N° 115	20.03.23	Halifax to Portal
N° 122	22.03.23	Halifax to Robinson
N° 124	23.03.23	Portal to Halifax
N° 127	24.03.23	Davidson to Mercier
N° 131	26.03.23	Halifax to Frere
N° 157	11.04.23	Davidson to Halifax
N° 164	16.04.23	Lang to Halifax
N° 166	—	Memorandum of Davidson and Lang
N° 167	19.04.23	Halifax to Portal
N° 170	21.04.23	Portal to Halifax
N° 176	27.04.23	McNabb to Halifax
N° 198	28.05.23	Portal to Halifax
N° 200	05.06.23	McNabb to Halifax

Box Three

N° 9	02.07.23	Halifax to Mercier
N° 11	07.07.23	Davidson to Halifax
N° 28	27.07.23	Davidson to Halifax
N° 41	10.08.23	Halifax to Portal
N° 44	18.08.23	Halifax to Frere
N° 45	19.08.23	Memorandum of Davidson
N° 46	19.08.23	Halifax to Robinson
N° 66	10.09.23	Mercier to Halifax
N° 67	10.09.23	Halifax to Mercier
N° 71	13.09.23	Kidd to Cecil
N° 74	18.09.23	Woodlock to Halifax
N° 76	20.09.23	Gore to Halifax
N° 77	20.09.23	Woodlock to Halifax
N° 79	21.09.23	Woodlock to Halifax
N° 80	22.09.23	Halifax to Woodlock
N° 81	23.09.23	McNabb to Halifax
N° 83	23.09.23	Mercier to Halifax
N° 86	24.09.23	Jarrett to Halifax
N° 88	24.09.23	Woodlock to Halifax
N° 95	26.09.23	Portal to Halifax
N° 97	27.09.23	Halifax to Gore

N° 101	30.09.23	Woodlock to Halifax
N° 105	03.10.23	Halifax to Portal
N° 106	04.10.23	Woodlock to Halifax
N° 110	09.10.23	Halifax to Portal
N° 135	03.11.23	Gasparri to Halifax
N° 142	13.11.23	Halifax to Portal
N° 144	15.11.23	Portal to Halifax
N° 150	22.11.23	Portal to Halifax
N° 159	11.12.23	Portal to Halifax

Box Four

N° 5	04.01.24	Halifax to Portal
N° 6	05.01.24	Portal to Halifax
N° 7	05.01.24	Halifax to Portal
N° 17	25.01.24	Halifax to Portal
N° 18	25.01.24	Portal to Halifax
N° 28	07.02.24	Mercier to Halifax
N° 41	15.02.24	Portal to Halifax
N° 45	25.02.24	Portal to Halifax
N° 82	13.04.24	Portal to Halifax
N° 88	24.04.24	Halifax to Portal
N° 93	25.04.24	(Approximate date) Account of Lord Halifax's visit to Malines and his interviews with Davidson and Bourne after his return.
N° 99	06.05.24	Halifax to Davidson
N° 130	15.06.24	Halifax to Portal

Box Five

N° 5	09.07.24	Halifax to Editor of the Times
N° 61	05.11.24	Portal to Halifax
N° 77	—	List of people seen by Halifax in Paris
N° 111	25.12.24	Gordon George to Halifax

Box Six

N° 6	06.01.25	Gordon George to Halifax
N° 9	11.01.25	Gordon George to Davidson
N° 11	17.01.25	Gordon George to Halifax
N° 12	20.12.25	Woodlock to Halifax
N° 14	22.01.25	Nickerson to Frere
N° 15	22.01.25	Halifax to Portal
N° 18	29.01.25	Davidson to Halifax
N° 19	30.01.25	Nickerson to Halifax
N° 31	25.02.25	Gordon George to Halifax
N° 32	26.02.25	Halifax to Portal
N° 33	26.02.25	Frere to Halifax
N° 39	30.03.25	Nickerson to Halifax
N° 41	06.04.25	Nickerson to Halifax
N° 49	18.04.25	Kidd to Halifax

N° 87	01.06.25	Portal to Halifax
N° 90	07.06.25	Halifax to Portal
N° 100	27.06.25	Kidd to Halifax

Box Seven

N° 5	06.07.25	Hill to Halifax
N° 9	10.07.25	Woodlock to Halifax
N° 14	21.07.25	Woodlock to Halifax
N° 17	27.07.25	Portal to Halifax
N° 18	28.07.25	Halifax to Woodlock
N° 24	01.08.25	Halifax to Woodlock
N° 33	09.08.25	Gordon George to Halifax
N° 34	10.08.25	Halifax to Davidson
N° 46	25.08.25	Gordon George to Halifax
N° 49	28.08.25	Kidd to Halifax
N° 56	07.09.25	Beauduin to Halifax
N° 60	13.09.25	Portal to Halifax
N° 61	18.09.25	Nickerson to Halifax
N° 72	01.10.25	Portal to Halifax
N° 82	10.10.25	Woodlock to Halifax
N° 92	19.10.25	Storer to Halifax
N° 102	23.10.25	Halifax to Gasparri
N° 103	25.10.25	Mercier to Davidson
N° 106	26.10.25	Mercier to Woodlock
N° 107	26.10.25	Mercier to Halifax
N° 115	30.10.25	Dessain to Halifax
N° 119	02.11.25	Portal to Halifax
N° 121	03.11.25	Mercier to Halifax
N° 140	26.11.25	Davidson to Halifax
N° 151	05.12.25	Portal to Halifax
N° 160	21.12.25	Mercier to Halifax
N° 163	22.12.25	Woodlock to Halifax

Box Eight

N° 16	18.01.26	Halifax to Portal
N° 18	18.01.26	Halifax to Portal
N° 21	22.01.26	Portal to Halifax
N° 22	23.01.26	Portal to Halifax
N° 23	24.01.26	Bourne to Halifax
N° 24	24.01.26	Halifax to Portal
N° 25	—	Notes in Halifax's hand as to what Mercier said to him during Halifax's last visit to Mercier.
N° 28	25.01.26	Portal to Halifax
N° 29	25.01.26	Halifax to Portal
N° 31	26.01.26	Halifax to Portal
N° 70	19.03.26	Portal to Halifax
N° 78	25.03.26	Portal to Halifax
N° 99	16.04.26	Kidd to Halifax

N° 101	24.04.26	Kidd to Halifax
N° 102	24.04.26	Van Roey to Halifax
N° 103	24.04.26	Davidson to Halifax
N° 108	07.05.26	Halifax to Frere
N° 109	07.05.26	Fitzalan to Halifax
N° 114	13.05.26	Davidson to Kidd
N° 116	19.05.26	Batiffol to Halifax
N° 118	??.05.26	Portal to Halifax
N° 121	26.05.26	Portal to Halifax

Box Nine

N° 15	20.05.27	Boyreau to Halifax
N° 17	31.05.27	Gore to Halifax
N° 21	05.06.27	Kidd to Halifax
N° 26	10.06.27	Hemmer to Halifax
N° 37	25.06.27	Halifax to Davidson
N° 40	26.06.27	Gordon George to Halifax
N° 46	28.06.27	Gordon George to Halifax
N° 47	29.06.27	Gordon George to Halifax
N° 49	30.06.27	Batiffol to Halifax
N° 54	02.07.27	Kidd to Halifax
N° 58	08.07.27	Gordon George to Halifax
N° 70	05.08.27	Halifax to Kidd
N° 80	13.08.27	Gordon George to Halifax
N° 88	24.08.27	Beauduin to Halifax
N° 103	03.09.27	Gordon George to Halifax
N° 109	18.09.27	Halifax to Hemmer
N° 116	23.09.27	Telegram:Halifax to Frere
N° 124	09.10.27	Gordon George to Halifax
N° 129	15.10.27	Cerretti to Halifax
N° 130	15.10.27	Dessain to Halifax
N° 133	18.10.27	Gordon George to Halifax
N° 141	24.10.27	Lang to Halifax
N° 143	19.11.27	Halifax to Davidson
N° 144	19.11.27	Halifax to Kidd
N° 150	25.11.27	Storer to Painter
N° 151	26.11.27	Cerretti to Painter
N° 155	22.12.27	Davidson to Halifax

The assistance of Dr. David Smith has been appreciated.

II. ARCHDIOCESE OF WESTMINSTER, LONDON, ENGLAND [AAW]

Here were found Cardinal Bourne's papers. Classification of these documents was irregular.

1907	17.10.07	Merry del Val to Bourne
	07.12.07	Bourne to Merry del Val

1922	24.09.22	Draft letter: Bourne to Halifax
	28.11.22	Mercier to Halifax
1923	31.07.23	Gasparri to Bourne
1924	02.02.24	Draft letter: Bourne to Moyes
	04.02.24	Dean to Bourne
	06.02.24	Bourne at Rome to Editor of *The Tablet*
	14.07.24	Halifax's secretary to Editor of *The Tablet*
	22.07.24	Halifax's secretary to E. Oldmeadow
1925	26.10.25	Mercier to Woodlock
	08.11.25	Mercier to Bourne
	17.11.25	Draft letter: Bourne to Mercier
	07.12.25	Mercier to Bourne
	—— 25	Memoranda about Malines
	14.12.25	At Rome, Caccia to Bourne. On reverse Bourne's handwritten outline of matters to be discussed with Pius XI.
1926	25.01.26	Halifax to Bourne
	31.01.26	Halifax to Bourne
	08.04.26	d'Andria to Bourne,
	30.04.26	Fitzalan to Bourne
	02.05.26	Fitzalan to Bourne
	06.05.26	Bourne to Fitzalan
1927	24.10.27	Draft letter: E. Oldmeadow to Editor of *The Times*
1928	20.01.28	Merry del Val to Bourne
	29.10.28	Lockhart to Oldmeadow
	30.10.28	Oldmeadow to Philip Allan and Co.
	02.12.28	Couturier to Oldmeadow
	14.12.28	Oldmeadow to Philip Allan and Co.
1929	04.01.29	Oldmeadow to Lockhart
1930	08.01.30	Merry del Val to Sir Stuart. This copy given to Bourne by Oldmeadow.
	07.02.30	Merry del Val to Bourne
1931	14.01.31	d'Herbigny to Bourne
	27.01.31	Bourne to d'Herbigny
	18.06.31	Memorandum: Marchant about Thackeray Hotel Conference
	19.06.31	Marchant to Archbishop of Canterbury
	01.07.31	Marchant to Bourne
	24.10.31	Marchant to Archbishop of Canterbury
	28.10.31	Goodier to Bourne

The assistance of Miss Elisabeth Poyser has been appreciated.

III. Archdiocese of Malines, Malines, Belgium [AAM]

Here were found the Malines Conversations papers of Cardinal Mercier and the unclassified papers of Cardinal Van Roey. These — along with the Halifax papers at York — are essential documents for understanding the before, during, and after of the Malines Conversations. Prof. R. Aubert has already called attention to many of these Malines documents in a variety of publications which are cited in our text as well as in our bibliography of published sources.

Specific documents which have been especially helpful for this dissertation are,

From Cardinal Mercier's Malines Conversations Papers:

1921: Section II

| N° 1 | 24.01.21 | Portal to Mercier |

1922: Section A I

| N° 10 | 12.10.22 | Halifax to Mercier |

1922: Section B I

	21.12.20	Mercier to Benedict XV
	11.03.22	d'Herbigny to Mercier
N° 1	11.04.22	Gasparri to Mercier
N° 1A	09.04.22	d'Herbigny to Mercier
N° 2A	not dated	Memo: d'Herbigny for Gasparri
N° 3	15.05.22	d'Herbigny to Mercier
N° 3D	30.03.22	Bell to d'Herbigny
N° 3I	not dated	Walker's outline
N° 4	19.05.22	Mercier to d'Herbigny
N° 5	31.05.22	Gasparri to Mercier
N° 6	13.06.22	Walker to Mercier
N° 7	14.11.22	Mercier to Pius XI
N° 8	25.11.22	Gasparri to Mercier

1922: Section B II

N° 2	27.03.22	Portal to Mercier
N° 6	01.12.22	Portal to Mercier
N° 8	13.12.22	Portal to Mercier

1922: Section B III

| N° 1 | 30.11.22 | Mercier to Bourne |
| N° 2 | 04.12.22 | Bourne to Mercier |

1923: Section A I

| N° 17 | 04.03.23 | Mercier to Halifax |

1923: Section A II

N° 8	24.03.24	Davidson to Mercier
N° 9	11.04.23	Mercier to Davidson
N° 10	13.04.23	Davidson to Mercier
N° 11	15.05.23	Davidson to Mercier
N° 17	15.12.23	Mercier to Davidson (telegram)

1923: Section A III

N° 7	10.11.23	Gore to Mercier
N° 8	12.11.23	Kidd to Mercier

1923: Section B I

N° 3	01.03.23	Mercier to Pius XI
N° 5	30.03.23	Gasparri to Mercier
N° 6	01.04.23	Mercier to Pius XI
N° 8	30.12.23	Gasparri to Mercier

1924: Section A III

N° 12	27.07.24	Mercier to Bell

1924: Section B I

N° 1	06.01.24	Mercier to Gasparri
N° 3	30.01.24	Mercier to Pius XI

1924: Section B II

N° 1	04.01.24	Portal to Mercier
N° 2	08.01.24	Portal to Mercier

1924: Section B III

N° 2	18.02.24	McNabb to Mercier
N° 4	22.03.24	Mercier to McNabb
N° 6	24.04.24	Mercier to McNabb

1924: Section Pastoral II

N° 24	12.02.24	Barton Brown to Mercier

1925: Section A I

N° 7	28.07.25	Halifax to Mercier

From Unclassified Papers of Cardinal Van Roey

	29.04.28	Storer to Van Roey
	08.05.28	Storer to Van Roey
	14.05.28	Storer to Van Roey
	04.02.30	Carton de Wiart to Van Roey

09.02.30	Hemmer to Van Roey
21.02.30	Van Roey's press release
22.02.30	Kidd to Times
23.02.30	Kidd to Van Roey
26.05.30	Bivort de la Saudee to Van Roey
04.06.30	Hemmer to Van Roey
03.11.30	Pribilla to Van Roey
05.02.34	Halflants to Van Roey

The assistance of Prof. C. Van de Wiel has been appreciated.

IV. DOWNSIDE ABBEY, BATH, ENGLAND

Here were found, among Gasquet's papers, a few letters between Merry del
Val and Vaughan and between Merry del Val and Gasquet — all touching on
the nineteenth century Anglican Orders issue. The following documents provided
background especially on the attitude and role of Merry del Val.
All are from Section 942:

1895	21.07.95	Merry del Val to Vaughan
	24.07.95	Merry del Val to Vaughan
	29.07.95	Merry del Val to Vaughan
	29.07.95	Merry del Val to Gasquet
	20.08.95	Merry del Val to Gasquet
	15.12.95	Merry del Val to Gasquet
1896	06.01.96	Merry del Val to Gasquet
	12.01.96	Merry del Val to Gasquet
	06.02.96	Merry del Val to Gasquet
1897	06.02.97	Merry del Val to Gasquet
	26.03.97	Merry del Val to Gasquet
	21.12.97	Merry del Val to Gasquet
1898	03.06.98	Merry del Val to Gasquet
	30.11.98	Merry del Val to Gasquet

The assistance of Dom Daniel Rees has been appreciated.

V. ENGLISH PROVINCE OF THE SOCIETY OF JESUS, LONDON, ENGLAND [AEPSJ]

Here were found the Francis Woodlock papers.
Especially important for our study was his correspondence with Merry del Val.
All documents are from classification BH/6:

1925	03.07.25	Merry del Val to Woodlock
	28.07.25	Merry del Val to Woodlock
1926	07.04.26	Gasparri to Woodlock

1927	31.03.27	Merry del Val to Woodlock
1928	15.01.28	Merry del Val to Woodlock
	24.01.28	Merry del Val to Woodlock
	26.01.28	Gasquet to Woodlock
	16.06.28	Merry del Val to Woodlock
	22.06.28	Merry del Val to Woodlock
1930	26.01.30	Merry del Val to Woodlock
	16.01.30	Merry del Val to Woodlock

The assistance of the Rev. Francis Edwards, S.J., has been appreciated.

VI. LAMBETH PALACE LIBRARY, LONDON, ENGLAND [ALPL]

Here were found the papers of Archbishop Davidson, some of Archbishop Lang's papers, and some of Armitage Robinson's papers. The papers which have been helpful for our study are listed below. Classification was irregular. They are here listed according to person and years:

Davidson Papers
1920 and 1921

13.08.20	Davidson to Bourne
03.05.21	Davidson to Mercier
06.05.21	Bourne to Davidson
21.05.21	Mercier to Davidson
27.10.21	Memorandum of Davidson's meeting with Boudier

1923 and 1924

18.04.23	Memorandum by the Archbishops of Canterbury and York
11.04.23	Mercier to Davidson
31.12.23	McNabb to Davidson
12.05.24	Storer to Halifax

1925 and 1927

03.06.25	Newspaper clipping, La Nation Belge
03.06.25	Grahame to Stamfordham
05.06.25	Stamfordham to Davidson
06.06.25	Davidson to Stamfordham
22.11.27	Davidson's Memorandum
06.12.27	Bourne to Davidson

Lang Papers
1922 and 1923

26.04.22	Memorandum - Bell to Davidson
19.12.23	Davidson to Lang

The assistance of Mr. E.G.W. Bill has been appreciated.

VII. Aloïs Janssens Papers, Scheut Community, Leuven, Belgium

Here were found A. Janssens' notes and correspondence with Lord Halifax as well as several unclassified documents from Mrs. Bellamy Storer. All of these documents provide helpful background and reinforce facts and impressions gained in other archives. The most important documents, Janssens' correspondence with Lord Halifax and his notes about his friendship with Lord Halifax, have already been published by D. Verhelst and are cited in our text and in our and bibliography of published sources.

The assistance of Prof. D. Verhelst has been appreciated.

VIII. Other Archives Consulted

The following archives were consulted but were found to contain no materials available to scholars which could help with this project:

Archdiocese of Southwark, England
Archivio Segreto Vaticano, Rome, Italy
Beauduin Archives, Chevetogne, Belgium
Catholic Record Society, London, England
Collège Notre Dame de la Paix, Namur, Belgium
Georgetown University Jesuitica, Washington, D.C., U.S.A.
Propaganda Fide, Rome, Italy
Secretariat for Christian Unity, Rome, Italy
Sint Jan Berchmanscollege, Brussels, Belgium
Stonyhurst College, Blackburn, England
The Month, London, England
The Tablet, London, England
Ushaw College, Durham, England
Venerable English College, Rome, Italy

II

PUBLISHED SOURCES

Acta Apostolicae Sedis, Annus XIV, Vol. XIV, Rome, 1922, pp. 696-697.

Actes de S.S. Pie XI, Paris, 1927.

J. ALTHOLZ (ed.), *Correspondence of Lord Acton and Richard Simpson*, London, 1952.

J.L. ALTHOLZ, *The Liberal Catholic Movement in England*, London, 1962.

Anglican-Roman Catholic International Commission. The Final Report, London, 1982.

R. AUBERT, *Aux origines de la réaction antimoderniste. Deux documents inédits*, in *Ephemerides Theologicae Lovanienses* 37 (1961) 557-578.

R. AUBERT, *Cardinal Mercier, Cardinal Bourne, and the Malines Conversations*, in *One in Christ* 4 (1968) 372-379.

R. AUBERT, *Cardinal Mercier. A Churchman Ahead of his Time*, s.l., s.d.

R. AUBERT, *Le Cardinal Mercier dans le monde et l'Église de son temps*, in *Unité des Chrétiens* 23 (1976) p. 4.

R. AUBERT, *Les Conversations de Malines. Le Cardinal Mercier et le Saint-Siège*, in *Bulletin de l'Académie Royale de Belgique*, Classe des Lettres, 5th series, vol. 53 (1967) 87-159.

R. AUBERT, *Le Saint-Siège et l'union des Églises, textes choisis et introduits*, Bruxelles, 1947.

R. AUBERT, *Problèmes de l'unité chrétienne*, Paris, 1952.

R. AUBERT, P.E. CRUNCIAN, J.T. ELLIS, F.B. PIKE, J. BRULS, J., HAJJAR, *The Christian Centuries*, vol. V: *The Church in a Secularized Society*, New York and London, 1978.

J.C.H. AVELING, D.M. LOADES, H.R. MCADOO, *Rome and the Anglicans*, edited with a postcript by Wolfgang Haase, Berlin and New York, 1982.

B. BARLOW, *The Conversations at Malines*, in *Louvain Studies* 4 (Spring 1972) 51-72.

L.F. BARMANN, *Baron Friedrich von Hügel and the Modernist Crisis in England*, Cambridge, 1972.

E. BEAUDUIN, *Le Cardinal Mercier*, Tournai, 1966.

L. BEAUDUIN, *L'Église anglicane unie non absorbée*, Malines, 1977.

G.A. BECK (ed.), *The English Catholics 1850-1950*, London, 1950.

G.K.A. BELL, *Christian Unity: The Anglican Position*, London, 1948.

G.K.A. BELL, *Documents on Christian Unity* (A selection from the second series 1920-1930), London, New York, Toronto, 1955.

G.K.A. BELL, *Randall Davidson Archbishop of Canterbury*, London, New York, Toronto, 1952.

G.K.A. BELL, *The Church and Humanity* (1939-1946), London, New York, Toronto, 1946.

G.K.A. BELL (ed.), *The Stockholm Conference 1925*, London, 1926.

A.C. BENSON, *The Life of Edward White Benson*, 2 vols., London, 1899.

E.G.W. BILL (ed.), *Anglican Initiatives in Christian Unity*, London, 1967.

Bishop of Zanzibar, *To Members of the Anglo-Catholic Congress*, in *The Church Times*, June 29, 1923.

A. BOLTON, *A Catholic Memorial of Lord Halifax and Cardinal Mercier*, London, 1935.

R. BOUDENS (ed.), *Alfred Plummer Conversations with Dr. Döllinger 1870-1889* (BETL, 67), Leuven, 1985.

R. BOUDENS, *George Tyrrell and Cardinal Mercier. A Contribution to the History of Modernism*, in *Église et Théologie* 1 (1970) 313-351.

R. BOUDENS, *Kardinaal Mercier en de Vlaamse Beweging*, Leuven, 1975.

R. BOUDENS, *Le Saint-Siège et la crise de l'Institut Supérieur de philosophie à Louvain 1895-1900*, in *Archivum Historiae Pontificiae* 8 (1970) 301-322.

R. BOUDENS, *Lord Halifax: An Impression*, in *Ephemerides Theologicae Lovanienses* 50 (1984) 449-452.

R. BOUDENS, *Tyrrell's Beati Excommunicati*, in *Bijdragen* 34 (1973) 293-305.

F. BOURNE, *Catholic Emancipation 1829-1929*, London, 1929.

F. BOURNE, *The Union of Christendom*, in *The Tablet* 143 (March 8, 1924) 309-310.

F. BOURNE, *York: The Thirteenth Centenary of King Edward's Baptism*, in *The Tablet* 149 (April 23, 1927) 555-557.

L. BOUYER, *Newman: sa vie, sa spiritualité*, Paris, 1958.

H.R.T. BRANDRETH, *Dr. Lee of Lambeth*, London, 1951.

P. BRENDON, *Richard Hurrell Froude and the Oxford Movement*, London, 1974.

B.R. BRINKMAN, *Tâche pour un cinquantenaire*, in *Unité des Chrétiens* 23 (1976) 26-28.

B.C. BUTLER, *United Not Absorbed*, in *The Tablet* 224 (January 31, 1970) 220-221.

C. BUTLER, *The Life and Times of Bishop Ullathorne 1806-1889*, 2 vols., London, 1926.

M.C. BUEHRLE, *Rafael Cardinal Merry del Val*, London, 1957.

The Call to Reunion, in *The Tablet* 140 (December 2, 1922) 720-721.

Cardinal Merry del Val, in *The Tablet* 145 (May 9, 1925) 625-626.

Catholics and Lord Halifax, in *The Tablet* 151 (April 7, 1928) 466.

W.R. CARSON, *Reunion Essays*, London, 1903.

O. CHADWICK, *The Victorian Church*, 2 vols., London, 1970.

M. CHILD, *The Shadow of Peter*, London, 1915.

R.W. CHURCH, *The Oxford Movement: Twelve Years*, London, 1891.

The Commemoration of the Malines Conversations 1926-1966, in *Collectanea Mechliniensia* 52 (1967/1) 3-78.

Conference of Bishops of the Anglican Communion (Lambeth Palace July 5 to August 7, 1920), *Encyclical Letter*, London, 1920.

The Conferences at Malines, in *The Tablet* 143 (January 5, 1924) 4-6.

Converts Aid Society Annual Meeting, in *The Tablet* 146 (July 4, 1925) 13-14.

J. COPPENS, *Een groot theoloog. Pater Aloïs Janssens, C.I.C.M.*, in *Boekengids* 23 (1945) 1-3.

J. COPPENS, *Une lettre inédite de Lord Halifax*, in *Union et désunion des chrétiens* (*Recherches Œcuméniques*), Bruges-Paris, 1963, 139-143.

J. COVENTRY, *Anglican Orders*, in *The Tablet* 236 (December 25, 1982), 1286-1288.

J. COX, *The English Churches in a Secular Society*, Lambeth 1870-1930, New York and Oxford, 1982.

C. CREWS, *English Catholic Modernism: Maude Petre's Way of Faith*, London, 1984.

C.F. CREWS, *The Role of Miss Maude Petre in the Modernist Movement*, New York, 1972.

F. CRISPOLTI, *Zes Pausen die ik kende*, Heemstede, 1941.

P.A. CROW, *The Ecumenical Movement in Bibliographical Outline*, New York, 1965.

F.J. CWIEKOWSKI, *The English Bishops and the First Vatican Council*, Louvain, 1971.

G. DAL-GAL, *Il Cardinal R. Merry del Val*, Roma, 1953.

V. DALPIAZ, *Cardinal Merry del Val*, London, 1937.

E. DAUDUIN, *Le Cardinal Mercier et le P. Portal*, in *Unité des Chrétiens* 23 (1976) 12-14.

R.T. DAVIDSON, *The Character and Call of the Church of England*, London, 1912.

R.T. DAVIDSON (ed.), *The Five Lambeth Conferences*, London, 1920.

H. DAVIES, *Worship and Theology in England*, in *The Ecumenical Century 1900-1965*, Princeton, 1965.

C. DAWSON, *The Spirit of the Oxford Movement*, New York, 1933.

J. DE BIVORT DE LA SAUDÉE, *Anglicans et catholiques. Le problème de l'union anglo-romaine (1833-1933)*, Paris, 1948.

J. DE BIVORT DE LA SAUDÉE, *Documents sur le problème de l'union anglo-romaine (1921-1927). Anglicans et catholiques*, Paris, 1949.

E.A. DE MENDIETA, *Rome and Canterbury*, London, 1962.

J. DENIS, *Pie XI*, Bruxelles, 1939.

F. DESMET (ed.), *Le Cardinal Mercier*, Bruxelles, 1927.

J. DESSAIN, *Le Cardinal Mercier tel que ma famille et moi l'avons connu*, in *Unité des Chrétiens* 23 (1976) 20-21.

J. DESSEAUX, *Mercier appartient à toutes les Églises*, in *Unité des Chrétiens* 23 (1976) 1-2.

J. DUGGAN, *Steps Toward Reunion*, London, 1897.

P. DUPREY, *Développement actuel des relations entre l'Église catholique et la Communion anglicane*, in *Unité des Chrétiens* 23 (1976) 29-30.

D. EDWARDS, *Christian England*, vol. 3: *From the 18th Century to the First World War*, London, 1984.

D.L. EDWARDS, *Leaders of the Church of England 1828-1944*, Oxford, 1971.

L.E., *Religion in the Victorian Era*, London, 1936; second edition, 1953.

G. FABER, *Oxford Apostles*, London, 1954.

Farm Street Lectures, in *The Tablet* 146 (September 5, 1925) 305.

E.R. FEARWEATHER (ed.), *The Oxford Movement*, Oxford, 1964.

W.K. FERGUSON and G. BRUUN, *A Survey of European Civilization*, Part Two. *Since 1660*, Third Edition, Boston, 1962.

R.P. FLINDALL, *The Church of England 1815-1948. A Documentary History*, London, 1972.

F.A. FORBES, *Rafael Cardinal Merry del Val*, London, New York, Toronto, 1932.

M. FOSSEYEUX, *Le Cardinal Noailles et l'administration du diocèse de Paris (1695-1729)*, in *Revue Historique* 114 (1913) 261-284.

B. FOTHERGILL, *Nicholas Wiseman*, London, 1963.

J. FOWLER, *Richard Waldo Sibthorp*, London, 1880.

W.H. FRERE, *Recollections of Malines*, London, 1935.

J.A. GADE, *The Life of Cardinal Mercier*, New York, London, 1934.

F.A. GASQUET, *Lord Acton and his Circle*, London, 1906.

J. GOOD, *The Church of England and the Ecumenical Movement*, London, 1961.

G. GORDO, R.E., *The Church in France in its Relation to Christian Unity*, in *Theology* 13 (1926) 21-30.

G. GOYAU, *Le Cardinal Mercier*, Paris, 1930.

G. GOYAU, *Papauté et chrétienté*, Paris, 1922.

A. GRATIEUX, *L'amitié au service de l'union: Lord Halifax et l'Abbé Portal*, Paris, 1950.

A. GRATIEUX and J. GUITTON, *Trois serviteurs de l'unité chrétienne*, Paris 1937.

R. GRAY, *Cardinal Manning: A Biography*, London, 1985.

R. GREENACRE, *Lord Halifax*, Oxford, 1983.

G. GREENE, *Letters from Baron von Hügel to a Niece*, London, 1928.

J. GUITTON, *Dialogue avec les précurseurs*, in *Journal Œcumenique 1922-1962*, Paris, 1962.

J. GUITTON, *Souvenirs concernant Lord Halifax*, in *La vie intellectuelle* (May 31, 1937) 9-49.

R. HALE, *Canterbury and Rome: Sister Churches. A Roman Catholic Monk Reflects upon Reunion in Diversity*, London, 1982.

E.E.Y. HALES, *Pio Nono*, London, 1954.

P. HALFLANTS, *Autour des conversations de Malines*, three articles in *La Libre Belgique*, February 26, 1934; February 28, 1934; March 2, 1934.

Viscount HALIFAX, *A Call to Reunion Arising out of Discussions with Cardinal Mercier*, London, Milwaukee, 1922.

Viscount HALIFAX, *Catholic Reunion Together with an Account of the Last Days of Cardinal Mercier and Some Appreciations*, London, Milwaukee, 1926.

Viscount HALIFAX, *English Church Union Presidential Address, Royal Albert Hall, June 25, 1931*, London, 1931.

Viscount HALIFAX, *Further Considerations on Behalf of Reunion*, London, Milwaukee, 1923.

HALIFAX, *Leo XIII and Anglican Orders*, London, 1912.

Viscount HALIFAX (ed.), *The Conversations at Malines 1921-1925. Report presented to the Archbishop of Canterbury by the Anglican participants*, London, 1928.

Viscount HALIFAX (ed.), *The Conversations at Malines 1921-1925: Original Documents*, London, 1930.

Viscount HALIFAX, *The Good Estate of the Church*, London, New York, Toronto, 1930.

Viscount HALIFAX, *Reunion and the Roman Papacy*, London, Milwaukee, 1925.

A.B. HASLER, *How the Pope Became Infallible*, New York, 1981.

A. HASTINGS (ed.), *Bishops and Writers*, Wheathamstead-Hertfordshire, 1977.

F. HAYWARD, *Un pape méconnu Benoît XV*, Tournai, Paris, 1955.

C. HEALY, *Maude Petre: Her Life and Significance*, in *Recusant History* 15 (1979) 23-42.

P. HEBBLETHWAITE, *John XXIII Pope of the Council*, London, 1985.

H. HEMMER, *Fernand Portal Apostle of Unity*, London, 1961.

H. HEMMER, *Monsieur Portal prêtre de la mission*, Paris, 1947.

H.H. HENSON, *The Church of England*, Cambridge, 1939.

G. HIMMELFARB, *Lord Acton: A Study in Conscience and Politics*, Chicago, 1952.

W.R. HOGG, *Ecumenical Foundations*, New York, 1952.

J.D. HOLMES, *Archbishops of Westminster and the Reunion Movement During the 19th Century*, in *One in Christ* 8 (1972) 55-68.

J.D. HOLMES, *Cardinal Merry del Val — An Uncompromising Ultramontane: Gleanings from his Correspondence with England*, in *The Catholic Historical Review* 60 (1974) 55-64.

J.D. HOLMES, *The Papacy in the Modern World 1914-1978*, New York, 1981.

J.D. HOLMES, *The Triumph of the Holy See — A Short History of the Papacy in the Nineteenth Century*, London, 1978.

J.D. HOLMES, *More Roman than Rome*, London, 1978.

J.D. HOLMES and B.W. BICKERS, *A Short History of the Catholic Church*, New York, 1984.

J.J. HUGHES, *Absolutely Null and Utterly Void*, Washington, D.C., 1968.

P. HUGHES, *Pope Pius the Eleventh*, London, 1937.

A.W. HUTTON, *Cardinal Manning*, London, 1892.

A. JANSSENS, *Anglicanism*, London, 1934.

A. JANSSENS, *Anglo-Catholicism and Catholic Unity*, in *Ephemerides Theologicae Lovanienses* 1 (1924) 66-70.

A. JANSSENS, *De Beweging van Oxford*, Brugge, 1930.

A. JANSSENS, *De wedergeboorte van het Katholicisme in Engeland*, Sint-Niklaas, 1934.

E. JAY (ed.), *The Evangelical and Oxford Movements*, Cambridge, 1983.

H. JEDIN, K. REPGEN and J. DOLAN (eds.), *History of the Church*, vol. 10: *The Church in the Modern Age*, London, 1981.

Fr. JEROME (Albert Gille), *A Catholic Plea for Reunion*, London, 1934.

J.P. JURICH, *The Ecumenical Relations of Victor De Buck, S.J., with Anglo-Catholic Leaders on the Eve of Vatican I*, licentiate mémoire, Université Catholique de Louvain, 1970.

J. KEATING, *A Last Word on Malines*, in *The Month* 149 (August 1925) 163.

J. KEATING, *Clearing the Air*, in *The Month* 143 (February 1924) 97-105.

J. KEATING, *Malines and Corporate Reunion*, in *The Month* 144 (March 1924) 260-262.

J. KEATING, *Once More Malines*, in *The Month* 155 (February 1925) 158-161.

J. KEMPENEERS, *Le Cardinal van Roey en son temps 1874-1961* (BETL, 30), Bruxelles, 1971.

R. KOTHEN, *Catholiques et Anglicains. Vingt ans après les Conversations de Malines*, Lille, 1946.

T.A. LACEY, *A Roman Diary and Other Documents Relating to the Papal Inquiry into English Ordinations MDCCCXCVI*, London, 1910.

R. LADOUS, *L'Abbé Portal et la compagne anglo-romaine 1890-1912*, Lyon, 1973.

R.J. LAHEY, *Cardinal Bourne and the Malines Conversations*, in *Bishops and Writers*, by A. Hastings (ed.), London, 1976, pp. 81-86.

R.J. LAHEY, *The Origins and Approval of the Malines Conversations*, in *Church History* 43 (1974) 366-384.

G. LEASE, *Merry del Val and Tyrrell: A Modernist Struggle*, in *Downside Review* 347 (1984) 133-156.

J.F. LESCRAUWAET, *Compendium van het œcumenisme*, Roermond, 1962.

J.F. LESCRAUWAET, *Critical Bibliography of Ecumenical Literature*, Nijmegen, 1965.

S. LESLIE, *Cardinal Gasquet: A Memoir*, London, 1953.

S. LESLIE, *Henry Edward Manning*, London, 1921.

S. LESLIE (ed.), *Letters of Herbert Cardinal Vaughan to Lady Herbert of Lea 1867 to 1903*, London, 1942.

H.P. LIDDON, *Life of Edward Bouverie Pusey*, 4 vols., London, 1894-1898.

J.G. LOCKHART, *Cosmo Gordon Lang*, London, 1949.

J.G. LOCKHART, *Charles Lindley Viscount Halifax*, 2 vol., London, 1935-1936.

Lord Halifax, in special issue of *The Antidote* 8 (February 1926).

Lord Halifax and Father Woodlock, in *The Month* 146 (September 1925) 256-260.

Lord Halifax's "Call to Reunion", in *The Tablet* 140 (November 11, 1922) 624-625.

J.H. LUPTON, *Archbishop Wake and the Project of Union*, London, 1896.

P.G. MACY, *An Ecumenical Bibliography*, New York, 1946.

J. MACQUARRIE, *What Still Separates Us From the Catholic Church? An Anglican Reply*, in *Concilium* 4, N° 6 (1970) 45-53.

T. MALONEY, *Whitehall, Westminster, and the Vatican*, London, 1985.

H.E. MANNING, *The Workings of the Holy Spirit in the Church of England*, London, 1864.

B. MARTIN, *John Henry Newman His Life and Work*, London, 1982.

C.C. MARTINDALE, *Bernard Vaughan*, London, 1924.

C.C. MARTINDALE, *The Faith of the Roman Church*, London, 1950.

C.C. MARTINDALE, *The Life of Monsignor Robert Hugh Brown Benson*, 2 vols., London, 1917.

D. MATHEW, *Catholicism in England. Portrait of a Minority: Its Culture and Tradition*, London, 1936 and 1948.

D. MATHEW, *Lord Acton and His Times*, London, 1968.

V.A. MCCLELLAND, *English Roman Catholics and Higher Education 1830-1903*, Oxford, 1973.

A. MCCORMACK, *Cardinal Vaughan*, London, 1966.

D. MCELRATH, *The Syllabus of Pius IX Some Reactions in England*, Louvain, 1964.

D.J. MERCIER, *Les Conversations de Malines*, in *Œuvres Pastorales* 7 (1924) 288-305.

Merry del Val Death Notice, in *The Tablet* 155 (March 1, 1930) 262.

R. MERRY DEL VAL, *Memories of Pope Pius X*, London, 1939.

R.D. MIDDLETON, *Newman and Bloxam*, Westport, 1947, reprinted 1971.

C. MOELLER, *Dom Lambert Beauduin, un homme d'Église*, in *Unité des Chrétiens* 23 (1976) 22-23.

A. MOORE, *Edmund Bishop as a Commentator on Modernism*, in *The Downside Review* 343 (April 1983) 90-107.

J. MORRIS, *Catholic England in Modern Times*, London, 1892.

J. MOYES, *An Anglican "Call to Action"*, in *The Tablet* 145 (May 9, 1925) 617-619.

J. MOYES, *What Does Lord Halifax Mean?*, in *The Tablet* 146 (July 18, 1925) 74-75.

L.D. MURPHY, *Bishop Gore Once More*, in *The Month* 141 (February 1923) 137-146.

J.H. NEWMAN, *Apologia Pro Vita Sua* (1865), London, 1902

J.H. NEWMAN, *The Present Position of Catholics in England*, London, 1903.

News and Notes, in *The Tablet* 143 (May 10, 1924) 621.

B. NEVRU, *Mgr Duchesne et son mémoire sur les ordinations anglicanes (1895 ou 1896)*, in *Journal of Theological Studies* 29 (October 1978) 443-482.

E. NORMAN, *Church and Society in England 1770-1970*, Oxford, 1976.

E. NORMAN, *Roman Catholicism in England from the Elizabethan Settlement to the Second Vatican Council*, Oxford, New York, 1985.

E. NORMAN, *The English Catholic Church in the Nineteenth Century*, Oxford, 1984.

G.F. NUTTALL and O. CHADWICK (eds.), *From Uniformity to Unity 1662-1962*, London, 1962.

M.R. O'CONNEL, *Oxford Conspiration*, New York, 1953.

E. OLDMEADOW, *A Layman on Malines*, in *The Tablet* 144 (November 22, 1924) 660.

E. OLDMEADOW, *Continuity Continued*, in *The Tablet* 149 (April 30, 1927) 573.

E. OLDMEADOW, *Francis Cardinal Bourne*. Vol. I, London, 1940; Vol. II, London, 1944.

E. OLDMEADOW, *More About Malines*, in *The Tablet* 143 (February 9, 1924) 168-169.

B. O'REILLY, *Life of Leo XIII*, London, 1887.

Our Common Christianity, in *The Tablet* 143 (March 1, 1924) 294.

W. PARSONS, *Canterbury and Rome*, in *America* (April 5, 1924) 587-588.

L. PAUL, *A Church by Daylight*, London, 1973.

B. PAWLEY and M. PAWLEY, *Rome and Canterbury through Four Centuries. A Study of the Relations between the Church of Rome and the Anglican Churches 1530-1981*, London, Oxford, 1981.

W. PETERS, *The Life of Benedict XV*, Milwaukee, 1959.

M.D. PETRE, *Autobiography of G. Tyrrell*, London, 1912.

A. PHILLIPPS, *On the Future Unity of Christendom*, London, 1857.

C.S. PHILLIPS, *Walter Howard Frere, Bishop of Truro: A Memoir*, London, 1948.

W.S. PLAVSIC, *Le Cardinal Van Roey*, Bruxelles, 1974.

F. PORTAL, *Le rôle de l'amitié dans l'union des églises*, in *La revue catholique des idées et des faits* 5 (December 11, 1925) 5-8.

E. POULAT, *Catholicisme, démocratie et socialisme*, Paris, 1977.

E. POULAT, *Intégrisme et catholicisme intégral*, Paris, 1969.

E. PRECLIN, *L'union des églises gallicane et anglicane*, Paris, 1928.

G.L. PRESTIGE, *The Life of Charles Gore*, London, Toronto, 1935.

M. PRIBILLA, *Canterbury und Rom*, in *Stimmen der Zeit* 120 (November 1930) 94-110.

E.S. PURCELL, *Life of Cardinal Manning*, 2 vols., London, 1896.

E.S. PURCELL, *Life and Letters of Ambrose Phillips de Lisle*, London, 1900.

E.B. PUSEY, *Eirenicon*, London, 1865.

S.A. QUITSLUND, *Beauduin. A Prophet Vindicated*, New York, Paramus, Toronto, 1973.

S. QUITSLUND, *"United Not Absorbed" Does It Still Make Sense*, in *Journal of Ecumenical Studies* 8 (1971) 255-285.

M. RAMSEY, *Charles Gore and the Anglican Theology*, London, 1948.

A.M. RAMSEY, *From Gore to Temple*, London, 1961.

Report of the Anglo-Catholic Congress, London, 1923.

Report of the Anglo-Catholic Congress, London, 1927.

Report of the Second Anglo-Catholic Priests' Convention, Oxford, 1932.

A. RHODES, *The Vatican in the Age of the Dictators 1922-1945*, London, 1973.

R. ROUSE and S.C. NEILL, *A History of the Ecumenical Movement 1517-1948*, London, 1967; Philadelphia 1968.

O. ROUSSEAU, *Le sens œcuménique des Conversations de Malines*, in *Irenikon* 44 (1971) 341-348.

O. ROUSSEAU, *Les Conversations de Malines*, in *Unité des Chrétiens* 23 (1976) 7-14.

H. ST. JOHN, *Essays in Christian Unity*, Westminster, 1954.

H. ST. JOHN, *Le problème anglo-catholique*, in *La vie intellectuelle* (May 31, 1937) 51-62.

H. ST. JOHN, *The Anglo-catholic Problem*, in *Blackfriars* 10 (1929) 1176-1183.

W.J. SCHOENL, *The Intellectual Crisis in English Catholicism. Liberal Catholics, Modernists and the Vatican in the Late Nineteenth and Early Twentieth Centuries*, New York, London, 1982.

T.M. SCHOOF, *A Survey of Catholic Theology 1800-1970*, Glen Rock, New York, Amsterdam, Toronto, London, 1970.

J. SCHYRGENS, *La destinée de Lord Halifax*, in *Vingtième Siècle*, February 2, 1934.

W.B. SELBIE, J.S. LIDGETT, P.C. SIMPSON, *The Lambeth Joint Report on Church Unity*, London, 1925.

A. SENAUD, *Christian Unity: A Bibliography*, Geneva, 1937.

A. SIMON, *Le Cardinal Mercier*, Bruxelles, 1960.

J.G. SIMPSON (ed.), *The Lambeth Joint Report on Church Unity*, London, 1925.

J.C. SNEAD-COX, *Life of Cardinal Vaughan*, 2 vols., London, 1910.

A Speech by Lord Halifax with Comments by Father Woodlock, in *The Month* 146 (August 1925) 157-167.

G.S. SPINKS, E.L. ALLEN and J. PARKES, *Religion in Britain since 1900*, London, 1952.

A.M.G. STEPHENSON, *Anglicanism and the Lambeth Conferences*, London, 1978.

R.L. STEWART, *A Century of Anglo-Catholicism*, London and Toronto, 1929.

R.L. STEWART, *Les Catholiques et le dialogue œcuménique en Angleterre*, in *Unité des Chrétiens* 23 (1976) 24-25.

L.J. SUENENS, *Présence du Cardinal Mercier*, in *Unité des Chrétiens* 23 (1976) p. 3.

B. SUNDKLER, *Nathan Söderblom, His Life and Work*, London, 1968.

E.F. SUTCLIFFE, *The Fathers and the Historicity of Paradise*, in *The Month* 153 (April 1929) 331-339.

N. SYKES, *William Wake, Archbishop of Canterbury*, Cambridge, 1957.

G. TAVARD, *Two Centuries of Ecumenism: The Search for Unity*, New York, 1962.

W. TEELING, *Pope Pius XI and World Affairs*, New York, 1937.

G. THILS, *Histoire doctrinale du mouvement œcuménique* (BETL, 8), Louvain, 1955; ²1963.

P. THUREAU-DANGIN, *Le Cardinal Vaughan*, Paris, 1911.

G. M. TRACY, *Le catholicisme britannique*, Paris, 1956.

G. TYRRELL, *Medievalism. A Reply to Cardinal Mercier*, London, 1908.

W.H. VAN DE POL, *Anglicanism in Ecumenical Perspective*, Pittsburg, 1965.

H. VAUGHAN, *Leo XIII and the Reunion of Christendom. Inaugural address delivered at the Catholic Conference at Hanley, September 28, 1896*, London, 1896.

D. VERHELST, *Lord Halifax and the Scheut Father Aloïs Janssens*, in *Ephemerides Theologicae Lovanienses* 43 (1967) 222-258.

A.R. VIDLER, *A Variety of Catholic Modernists*, Cambridge, 1970.

A.R. VIDLER, *Essays in Liberality*, London, 1957.

A.R. VIDLER, *The Church in an Age of Revolution. 1789 to the Present Day*, Harmondsworth, New York, 1961; reprinted, 1981.

A.R. VIDLER, *The Modernist Movement in the Roman Church*, Cambridge, 1934.

L. WALKER, *Anglia Quaerens Fidem*, in *Gregorianum* 3 (1922) 219-238; 337-354.

B. WARD, *The Sequel to Catholic Emancipation*, 2 vols., London, 1915.

M. WARD, *Father Maturin, A Memoir*, London, 1920.

M. WARD, *The Wilfrid Wards and the Transition*, London, 1934.

W. WARD, *The Life and Times of Cardinal Wiseman*, 2 vols., London, 1900.

E.I. WATKIN, *Roman Catholicism in England from the Reformation to 1950*, London, 1957, reprinted 1958.

M.E. WILLIAMS, *The Venerable English College Rome*, London, 1979.

J. WILLIBRANDS, *Diversity without Separation*, in *The Tablet* 224 (January 24, 1970) 92.

E.M. WILMOT-BUXTON, *A Catholic History of Great Britain*, London, 1921.

F. WOODLOCK, *At an Anglican Reunion Lecture*, in *The Tablet* 143 (March 8, 1924) 306-308.

F. WOODLOCK, *Modernism and the Christian Church*, London, 1925.

F. WOODLOCK, *Modernism and a United Christendom*, in *The Tablet* (January 24, 1925).

F. WOODLOCK, *The Malines Conversations Report*, in *The Month* 155 (March 1930) 238-246.

F. WOODLOCK, *The Malines Conversations*, in *The Tablet* 146 (October 17, 1925) 484-485.

F. WOODLOCK, *The Upshot of Malines*, in *The Month* 145 (February 1928) 158-163.

D. WOODRUFF (ed.), *Essays on Church and State*, London, 1952.

LIST OF NAMES

All names mentioned in the text (pp. 11-192) are listed here. References to the Biographical Index (pp. 233-253) are in heavy print.

278 LIST OF NAMES

VAUGHAN, B.J. 39, **251**
VAUGHAN, H.A. 12, 39-49, 52, 71, 125, 172, 184, 191, **251**
VAUGHAN, R.W. 39, **251**
VIDLER, A. 19

WAKE, W. 15-18, 75, 152, **251**
WALKER, L. 76-77, 81-88, 93, 135, 169, **252**
WARD, W. 53, 82, **252**
WARD, W.G. 21, 22 (n.), 30, 33, 34, 35, **252**

WAUGH, E. 52, **252**
WESTON, F. 103-104, **252**
WHEELER, G. 52
WILBERFORCE, R.I. 21, **252**
WISEMAN, N.P. 15, 20, 23, 27-30, 31 (n.), 33, 35, 37, 39-40, **252**
WOOD, E. 129, 162, **252**
WOODLOCK, F. 13, 82, 105-109, 119-120, 128, 135, 136, 143, 145-149, 151-157, 161, 165-166, 170-171, 179-181, 184, 187, 189, 191, **252**
WORDSWORTH, J. 42, **253**

BIBLIOTHECA EPHEMERIDUM THEOLOGICARUM LOVANIENSIUM

LEUVEN UNIVERSITY PRESS / UITGEVERIJ PEETERS LEUVEN

SERIES I

* = Out of print

*1. *Miscellanea dogmatica in honorem Eximii Domini J. Bittremieux*, 1947.

*2-3. *Miscellanea moralia in honorem Eximii Domini A. Janssen*, 1948.

*4. G. PHILIPS, *La grâce des justes de l'Ancien Testament*, 1948.

*5. G. PHILIPS, *De ratione instituendi tractatum de gratia nostrae sanctificationis*, 1953.

6-7. *Recueil Lucien Cerfaux*, 1954. 504 et 577 p. FB 1000 par tome. Cf. *infra*, nᵒˢ 18 et 71.

8. G. THILS, *Histoire doctrinale du mouvement œcuménique*, 1955. Nouvelle édition, 1963. 338 p. FB 135.

*9. J. COPPENS et al., *Études sur l'Immaculée Conception*, 1955.

*10. J.A. O'DONOHOE, *Tridentine Seminary Legislation. Its Sources and its Formation*, 1957.

*11. G. THILS, *Orientations de la théologie*, 1958.

*12-13. J. COPPENS, A. DESCAMPS, É. MASSAUX (éd.), *Sacra Pagina. Miscellanea Biblica Congressus Internationalis Catholici de Re Biblica*, 1959.

*14. *Adrien VI, le premier Pape de la contre-réforme*, 1959.

*15. F. CLAEYS BOUUAERT, *Les déclarations et serments imposés par la loi civile aux membres du clergé belge sous le Directoire (1795-1801)*, 1960.

*16. G. THILS, *La « Théologie Œcuménique ». Notion-Formes-Démarches*, 1960.

17. G. THILS, *Primauté pontificale et prérogatives épiscopales. « Potestas ordinaria » au Concile du Vatican*, 1961. 103 p. FB 50.

*18. *Recueil Lucien Cerfaux*, t. III, 1962. Cf. *infra*, n° 71.

*19. *Foi et réflexion philosophique. Mélanges F. Grégoire*, 1961.

*20. *Mélanges G. Ryckmans*, 1963.

21. G. THILS, *L'infaillibilité du peuple chrétien « in credendo »*, 1963. 67 p. FB 50.

*22. J. FÉRIN & L. JANSSENS, *Progestogènes et morale conjugale*, 1963.

*23. *Collectanea Moralia in honorem Eximii Domini A. Janssen*, 1964.

24. H. CAZELLES (éd.), *De Mari à Qumrân. L'Ancien Testament. Son milieu. Ses Écrits. Ses relectures juives* (Hommage J. Coppens, I), 1969. 158*-370 p. FB 900.

25. I. DE LA POTTERIE (éd.). *De Jésus aux évangiles. Tradition et rédaction dans les évangiles synoptiques* (Hommage J. Coppens, II), 1967. 272 p. FB 700.

26. G. THILS & R.E. BROWN (éd.), *Exégèse et théologie* (Hommage J. Coppens, III), 1968. 328 p. FB 700.

27. J. COPPENS (éd.), *Ecclesia a Spiritu sancto edocta. Hommage à Mgr G. Philips*, 1970. 640 p. FB 1000.

28. J. Coppens (éd.), *Sacerdoce et célibat. Études historiques et théologiques*, 1971. 740 p. FB 700.
29. M. Didier (éd.), *L'évangile selon Matthieu. Rédaction et théologie*, 1971. 432 p. FB 1000.
*30. J. Kempeneers, *Le Cardinal van Roey en son temps*, 1971.

Series II

31. F. Neirynck, *Duality in Mark. Contributions to the Study of the Markan Redaction*, 1972. Revised Edition with Supplementary Notes, 1988. 252 p. FB 1200.
32. F. Neirynck (éd.), *L'évangile de Luc. Problèmes littéraires et théologiques*, 1973. Nouvelle édition augmentée, 1989.
33. C. Brekelmans (éd.), *Questions disputées d'Ancien Testament. Méthode et théologie*, 1974. Nouvelle édition augmentée, 1989. FB 1200.
34. M. Sabbe (éd.), *L'évangile selon Marc. Tradition et rédaction*, 1974. Nouvelle édition augmentée, 1988. 601 p. FB 2400.
35. B. Willaert (éd.), *Philosophie de la religion – Godsdienstfilosofie. Miscellanea Albert Dondeyne*, 1974. Nouvelle édition, 1987. 458 p. FB 1600.
36. G. Philips, *L'union personnelle avec le Dieu vivant. Essai sur l'origine et le sens de la grâce créée*, 1974. Édition révisée, 1989. 299 p. FB 1000.
37. F. Neirynck, in collaboration with T. Hansen and F. Van Segbroeck, *The Minor Agreements of Matthew and Luke against Mark with a Cumulative List*, 1974. 330 p. FB 900.
38. J. Coppens, *Le Messianisme et sa relève prophétique. Les anticipations vétérotestamentaires. Leur accomplissement en Jésus*, 1974. Édition révisée, 1989. xiii-265 p. FB 1000.
39. D. Senior, *The Passion Narrative according to Matthew. A Redactional Study*, 1975. New impression, 1982. 440 p. FB 1000.
40. J. Dupont (éd.), *Jésus aux origines de la christologie*, 1975. Nouvelle édition augmentée, 1989.458 p. FB 1500.
41. J. Coppens (éd.), *La notion biblique de Dieu*, 1976. Réimpression, 1985. 519 p. FB 1600.
42. J. Lindemans & H. Demeester (éd.), *Liber Amicorum Monseigneur W. Onclin*, 1976. 396 p. FB 1000.
43. R.E. Hoeckman (éd.), *Pluralisme et œcuménisme en recherches théologiques. Mélanges offerts au R.P. Dockx, O.P.*, 1976. 316 p. FB 1000.
44. M. de Jonge (éd.), *L'Évangile de Jean. Sources, rédaction, théologie*, 1977. Réimpression, 1987. 416 p. FB 1500.
45. E.J.M. van Eijl (éd.), *Facultas S. Theologiae Lovaniensis 1432-1797. Bijdragen tot haar geschiedenis. Contributions to its History. Contributions à son histoire*, 1977. 570 p. FB 1700.
46. M. Delcor (éd.), *Qumrân. Sa piété, sa théologie et son milieu*, 1978. 432 p. FB 1700.
47. M. Caudron (éd.), *Faith and Society. Foi et Société. Geloof en maatschappij. Acta Congressus Internationalis Theologici Lovaniensis 1976*, 1978. 304 p. FB 1150.
48. J. Kremer (éd.), *Les Actes des Apôtres. Traditions, rédaction, théologie*, 1979. 590 p. FB 1700.

49. F. Neirynck, avec la collaboration de J. Delobel, T. Snoy, G. Van Belle, F. Van Segbroeck, *Jean et les Synoptiques. Examen critique de l'exégèse de M.-É. Boismard*, 1979. xii-428 p. FB 1400.

50. J. Coppens, *La relève apocalyptique du messianisme royal. I. La royauté – Le règne – Le royaume de Dieu. Cadre de la relève apocalyptique*, 1979. 325 p. FB 1000.

51. M. Gilbert (éd.), *La Sagesse de l'Ancien Testament*, 1979. 420 p. FB 1700.

52. B. Dehandschutter, *Martyrium Polycarpi. Een literair-kritische studie*, 1979. 296 p. FB 1000.

53. J. Lambrecht (éd.), *L'Apocalypse johannique et l'Apocalyptique dans le Nouveau Testament*, 1980. 458 p. FB 1400.

54. P.-M. Bogaert (éd.), *Le Livre de Jérémie. Le prophète et son milieu. Les oracles et leur transmission*, 1981. 408 p. FB 1500.

55. J. Coppens, *La relève apocalyptique du messianisme royal. III. Le Fils de l'homme néotestamentaire*, 1981. xiv-192 p. FB 800.

56. J. van Bavel & M. Schrama (éd.), *Jansénius et le Jansénisme dans les Pays-Bas. Mélanges Lucien Ceyssens*, 1982. 247 p. FB 1000.

57. J.H. Walgrave, *Selected Writings – Thematische geschriften. Thomas Aquinas, J.H. Newman, Theologia Fundamentalis*. Edited by G. De Schrijver & J.J. Kelly, 1982. xliii-425 p. FB 1400.

58. F. Neirynck & F. Van Segbroeck, avec la collaboration de E. Manning, *Ephemerides Theologicae Lovanienses 1924-1981. Tables générales. (Bibliotheca Ephemeridum Theologicarum Lovaniensium 1947-1981)*, 1982. 400 p. FB 1600.

59. J. Delobel (éd.), *Logia. Les paroles de Jésus – The Sayings of Jesus. Mémorial Joseph Coppens*, 1982. 647 p. FB 2000.

60. F. Neirynck, *Evangelica. Gospel Studies – Études d'évangile. Collected Essays*. Edited by F. Van Segbroeck, 1982. xix-1036 p. FB 2000.

61. J. Coppens, *La relève apocalyptique du messianisme royal. II. Le Fils d'homme vétéro- et intertestamentaire*. Édition posthume par J. Lust, 1983. xvii-272 p. FB 1000.

62. J.J. Kelly, *Baron Friedrich von Hügel's Philosophy of Religion*, 1983. 232 p. FB 1500.

63. G. De Schrijver, *Le merveilleux accord de l'homme et de Dieu. Étude de l'analogie de l'être chez Hans Urs von Balthasar*, 1983. 344 p. FB 1500.

64. J. Grootaers & J.A. Selling, *The 1980 Synod of Bishops: «On the Role of the Family». An Exposition of the Event and an Analysis of Its Texts*. Preface by Prof. emeritus L. Janssens, 1983. 375 p. FB 1500.

65. F. Neirynck & F. Van Segbroeck, *New Testament Vocabulary. A Companion Volume to the Concordance*, 1984. xvi-494 p. FB 2000.

66. R.F. Collins, *Studies on the First Letter to the Thessalonians*, 1984. xi-415 p. FB 1500.

67. A. Plummer, *Conversations with Dr. Döllinger 1870-1890*. Edited with Introduction and Notes by R. Boudens, with the collaboration of L. Kenis, 1985. liv-360 p. FB 1800.

68. N. Lohfink (éd.), *Das Deuteronomium. Entstehung, Gestalt und Botschaft / Deuteronomy. Origin, Form and Message*, 1985. xi-382 p. FB 2000.

69. P.F. FRANSEN, *Hermeneutics of the Councils and Other Studies*. Collected by H.E. MERTENS & F. DE GRAEVE, 1985. 543 p. FB 1800.

70. J. DUPONT, *Études sur les Évangiles synoptiques*. Présentées par F. NEIRYNCK, 1985. 2 tomes, XXI-IX-1210 p. FB 2800.

71. *Recueil Lucien Cerfaux*, t. III, 1962. Nouvelle édition revue et complétée, 1985. LXXX-458 p. FB 1600.

72. J. GROOTAERS, *Primauté et collégialité. Le dossier de Gérard Philips sur la Nota Explicativa Praevia (Lumen gentium, Chap. III)*. Présenté avec introduction historique, annotations et annexes. Préface de G. THILS, 1986. 222 p. FB 1000.

73. A. VANHOYE (éd.), *L'apôtre Paul. Personnalité, style et conception du ministère*, 1986. XIII-470 p. FB 2600.

74. J. LUST (éd.), *Ezekiel and His Book. Textual and Literary Criticism and their Interrelation*, 1986. X-387 p. FB 2700.

75. É. MASSAUX, *Influence de l'Évangile de saint Matthieu sur la littérature chrétienne avant saint Irénée*. Réimpression anastatique présentée par F. NEIRYNCK. Supplément: *Bibliographie 1950-1985*, par B. DEHANDSCHUTTER, 1986. XXVII-850 p. FB 2500.

76. L. CEYSSENS & J.A.G. TANS, *Autour de l'Unigenitus. Recherches sur la genèse de la Constitution*, 1987. XXVI-845 p. FB 2500.

77. A. DESCAMPS, *Jésus et l'Église. Études d'exégèse et de théologie*. Préface de Mgr A. HOUSSIAU, 1987. XLV-641 p. FB 2500.

78. J. DUPLACY, *Études de critique textuelle du Nouveau Testament*. Présentées par J. DELOBEL, 1987. XXVII-431 p. FB 1800.

79. E.J.M. VAN EIJL (éd.), *L'image de C. Jansénius jusqu'à la fin du XVIIIᵉ siècle*, 1987. 258 p. FB 1250.

80. E. BRITO, *La Création selon Schelling. Universum*, 1987. XXXV-646 p. FB 2980.

81. J. VERMEYLEN (ed.), *The Book of Isaiah – Le Livre d'Isaïe. Les oracles et leurs relectures. Unité et complexité de l'ouvrage*, 1989. X-472 p. FB 2700.

82. G. VAN BELLE, *Johannine Bibliography 1966-1985. A Cumulative Bibliography on the Fourth Gospel*, 1988. XVII-563 p. FB 2700.

83. J.A. SELLING (ed.), *Personalist Morals. Essays in Honor of Professor Louis Janssens*, 1988. VIII-344 p. FB 1200.

84. M.-É. BOISMARD, *Moïse ou Jésus. Essai de christologie johannique*, 1988. XVI-241 p. FB 1000.

85. J.A. DICK, *The Malines Conversations Revisited*, 1989. 278 p. FB 1500.

86. J.-M. SEVRIN (ed.), *The New Testament in Early Christianity – La réception des écrits néotestamentaires dans le christianisme primitif*, 1989. FB 2500.

87. R.F. COLLINS (ed.), *The Thessalonian Correspondence*, 1989 (forthcoming).